16 Volumes

Vol 1-15, 17

only of 22

In print 295⁰⁰ each

(i.e. 472-)

THEOLOGICAL INVESTIGATIONS

VOLUME I

GOD, CHRIST, MARY AND GRACE

by

KARL RAHNER

Translated with an Introduction by
CORNELIUS ERNST, O.P.

LONDON
DARTON, LONGMAN & TODD
NEW YORK
THE SEABURY PRESS

1974
DARTON, LONGMAN & TODD LTD
85 Gloucester Road, London, S.W.7
ISBN 0 232 48098 2

A Crossroad Book
THE SEABURY PRESS
815 Second Avenue, New York, N.Y. 10017
Library of Congress Catalog Card No.: 61-8189

A Translation of
SCHRIFTEN ZUR THEOLOGIE, I
published by Verlagsanstalt Benziger & Co. AG., Einsiedeln–Zürich–Köln in 1954

Reproduced and printed by photolithography and bound in
Great Britain at The Pitman Press, Bath
Nihil obstat: Fr. Marcus Brocklehurst, S.T.L. Fr. Aelredus
Squire, S.T.L., Imprimii potest: Fr. Henricus St John, O.P.,
Prior Provincialis. Nihil obstat: Carolus Davis, S.T.L., censor
deputatus. Imprimatur: E. Morrogh Bernard, Vic. Gen.
Westmonasterii, die 13a Junii, 1960.

CONTENTS

ABBREVIATIONS

AAS	*Acta Apostolicae Sedis*
CIC	*Codex Iuris Canonici*
Denz	Denzinger-Rahner, *Enchiridion Symbolorum* (1953)
DAFC	*Dictionnaire Apologétique de la Foi Catholique*
DTC	*Dictionnaire de Théologie Catholique*
NRT	*Nouvelle Revue Théologique*
RSPT	*Revue des Sciences Philosophiques et Théologiques*
RSR	*Recherches de Science Religieuse*
RT	*Revue Thomiste*
TQ	*Theologische Quartalschrift*
TS	*Theological Studies* (U.S.A.)
TWNT	*Theologisches Wörterbuch zum Neuen Testament*
ZKT	*Zeitschrift für Katholische Theologie*

Note.—The author very rarely quotes Scripture directly in German, and when he does so appears to make his own translations. In the present translation, accordingly, the author's renderings are retained, though of course the standard English versions have been consulted.

INTRODUCTION

THE author of the studies presented here in translation is perhaps the most influential theologian in German-speaking Catholicism today. Some indication of his authority in the world of theology is the fact that he is the present editor of Denzinger's *Enchiridion Symbolorum*, and co-editor of the new *Lexikon für Theologie und Kirche* now in course of publication. The editorship of standard works of reference such as these is a guarantee that Fr Rahner possesses one of the essential qualifications of a theologian: a detailed and thorough acquaintance with the sources of theology in the teaching of the Church as this has been propounded throughout her history, not only in the first centuries of her existence but by her living voice today. For Fr Rahner is profoundly aware of that fundamental teaching laid down by Pius XII in the Encyclical *Humani Generis*, that God has given his Church, together with the sources of Revelation in Scripture and Tradition, a living *magisterium* for the authentic interpretation of the deposit of faith (cf. Denz 3014).

As the reader will see in these studies, the Catholic theologian's sense of the living utterance of the Church here and now need not be merely a recognition that he has always an external court of appeal to which he must submit his private speculations, as though his faith and his endeavours to deepen and articulate it were fundamentally a private affair though of course subject to some external restraint. Far more than this, the Catholic theologian must be deeply aware, as Fr Rahner is, that his faith is the faith of the Church, that his life of faith, as this is manifested in his theological activity, is a participation in the life and faith of the Church, so that his 'private' and personal life is a manifestation of the Spirit in the open and the 'public' Church. And this is Fr Rahner's second qualification as a theologian. For while he is a professional theologian in the strongest sense of the word, acquainted with the sources and with the writings of other theologians past and present, and normally engaged in the teaching of theology, he is also a man of the Church, no mere academic figure for whom theology is just one specialized study among others, but a theologian who precisely as a theologian recognizes that his specialized study demands a special obedience in faith and love to the living and authoritative voice of the Church here and now, since his own special task is to receive that teaching as fully and precisely as possible and transmit it and proclaim it to the world and the Church in the world here and now. His very status as 'private theologian', not immediately associated with the authoritative teaching Church in the successors of the Apostles, is a status in the public Church, his personal task of investigation and articulation a task only to be fulfilled in the hierarchical community of the Church.

Consequently the theologian's work will only be of value if it is an independently personal contribution to that historical process by which the community of the Church realizes herself in the world and the world in herself. The theologian's fidelity to the teaching Church can never be the purely passive acceptance, the mechanical registration, of a *corpus* of doctrine which is definitively dead because it is definitively closed in the past and has nothing to look forward to in the future. Certainly we hold that the Church received her final form and content with the death of the last Apostle; but that form was a living form, the form of a reality living with a more than biological life, whose unity and continuity are guaranteed by the assistance of the Spirit of Christ. The life of the Church is at least the life of an historical community, nourished by the Spirit: that is to say, it is an organized life which realizes itself through a process of generation in time, it is in continual 'happening'. And the happening is both personal and directed. It is personal, because like any human historical happening it takes place in and is affected by the personal life of spiritual beings and their institutions. It is directed, because it is conducted consciously or unconsciously under the guidance of the Spirit who leads all things into the truth of Christ as this will be realized in a here and now at the Second Coming: the living voice of the *magisterium* is a manifestation of that living guidance. The theologian's life must be independently personal because it would otherwise cease to be human; but it is independently personal *within* the historical life of the community of the Church. Historical happening is not an unfortunate accident with which the Church must put up as best she may: it is the very mode of the Church's existence in the human beings who are brought into her historical community by the Spirit of the Christ who was and is her founder and head. Fr Rahner's 'originality' as a theologian is the creativeness of a thinker whose very remarkable resources as a human person have found expression in the historical growth of the Church. Human creativeness is at the very least the 'material' of the Church's history, however often it may unfortunately have been the case that it has set up tensions within her community at any given time which, by the impatience and pride of the creative spirits or the uncomprehending intransigence of the individuals who exercised her authority, or both, have never been resolved and have resulted in heresy and schism.

The Church's historical happening, we have said, is a realization of herself in the world and the world in herself. Her happening is not just a strand in the complex web of human history: it is rather, we may say, the figure in the carpet, reminding ourselves again that *we* are the carpet, that we by our active historical lives constitute the texture of history. We may conveniently regard Fr Rahner's theological work from these two points of view, as contributing to the Church's realization of herself in the world, and as contributing to the realization of the world in the Church.

The realization of the Church in the world is the continuous process by which she re-presents to the world the saving event of Christ's Death and Resurrection by tradition and sacrament. The Event was an historical event in the dimension of all created being; and it is the task and the mission of the Church to bring home to the world the Event both in its meaning and in its effectual cosmic consequences. From the earliest times of the Church, even in the inspired documents of the New Testament, we may see that the mission of communicating to the world the meaning of the Event has involved reflexion upon that meaning, primarily a searching of the Scriptures. Theology is still reflexion upon the meaning of the Event; still primarily a searching of the Scriptures, it is also a searching of the historical life of the Church as it has brought that meaning to light in various manifestation. The theologian's chief task is to explore that meaning in and for itself; his professionalism consists in a 'mastery of the sources', which is the continuous endeavour to make those sources the springs of his own life of faith, and so to display them in an ordered whole that each feeds the other and contributes to the intelligibility, at once complex and simple, of the whole. The first study in these two volumes, and the sketch for a new treatment of dogmatic theology which follows it, show how deeply Fr Rahner has meditated on the synthetic scope of a theology which would be adequate to our need today for an intelligible grasp of the meaning of the Event. The particular studies which follow range so widely that Fr J. Hamer seems to be right in suggesting that Fr Rahner has deliberately taken up one by one all or most of the problems which arise for the Catholic in the modern world.[1] But while it is true that in most cases the questions have already been asked, the 'problematic' determined in advance, so that the theologian's business would seem to be no more than a choice of one or other of the available answers, no one can fail to observe in Fr Rahner's studies at least an awareness of the possibility of asking *different* questions, questions which have not been asked before. He has indeed more than once asked, and offered an answer to, new questions, often surprisingly new questions.

It is this openness to the pressure of new questions and the capacity to formulate them which constitutes Fr Rahner's contribution to what has here been called the realization of the world in the Church. In a providential economy whose character is shaped by the Incarnation, historical happening must take the form of a *conversatio*, a traffic between Church and world. If divine providence is to be regarded as being at work not only in the past but also now and for the future, then secular history, the history of what is not Church, must also somehow have its relevance in the total course of human history in the divine dispensation. The relevance need not always take the form of an indigence, a deviation into the emptiness of error and sin; it can also have the form of a 'partial plenitude', an achievement whose whole meaning can only be discovered when it is assumed into the sacred history of the Church. But whichever form this relevance takes, it is part of the theologian's task to discern and to disclose it; and this he can only do if he is open to the world to the full extent of his powers, allowing always for his own weakness, and conscious often of the need for prudence in so exposing himself—not every theologian can undergo and satisfy every one of the world's needs, not every theologian can provide in himself an arena for the total triumph of the victorious truth of Christ. It seems to me that Fr Rahner's greatest

---

[1] 'Bulletin de théologie dogmatique', RSPT XLI (1957), p. 552.

virtue as a theologian is that he has been able to undergo and bring to luminous manifestation in the Church so many and such profound needs of the world which is not the Church, to contribute so largely to the realization of the world in the Church. No reader of the studies here translated can fail to admire the astonishing generosity of mind and heart which Fr Rahner brings to his activity as a theologian.

And yet it is here, unfortunately, that the English reader is likely to find Fr Rahner most difficult.[1] It is true enough that in a large sense the spiritual needs of the world today are the same everywhere, and in a still larger sense that they are the same as the needs of the world yesterday; but it must be confessed that the English-speaking world has not been especially concerned to admit the existence of these needs, and that American and still more English Catholicism has largely tended to ignore them. It is difficult to regard the English cultural scene, either inside or outside the Church, without a sense of dissatisfaction often amounting to an exasperated despair.[2] But this is not the place in which to examine the blinkered complacency of so much English philosophy and letters, or the curiously freakish eccentricity of the few attempts which have been made to disturb it; after all, any such examination would also have to recognize the genuine sanity and civilized good manners which is so attractive a feature of English culture, and the almost total lack of these virtues (so it would seem) in continental culture. The relevant fact is that English, and to a lesser extent American, culture has become exceedingly remote from continental culture; and this presents considerable problems in attempting to make available to English readers the work of a theologian who is acutely sensitive to the issues which engage so profoundly the existence of European man.

The key word here is perhaps 'existential'; it is at least a word which the reader of these studies will meet fairly frequently. Although the word itself does not occur in the following extremely penetrating

---

[1] While apologizing for the personal reference, I feel bound to point out here that, in spite of my name, I have never been to Germany, and my German ancestry is extremely remote, whatever atavistic tendencies the reader may detect.

[2] The trivialization of Wittgenstein by English philosophers is a case in point. What Wittgenstein himself felt about this may be seen from some of the remarks quoted by N. Malcolm, in *Ludwig Wittgenstein. A Memoir* (1958).

delineation of a tendency common to both philosophy and theology on the Continent today, the approach described by the writer may fairly be called for the moment 'existentialist'. In a footnote to the discussion of a passage from Heidegger's *Was heisst Denken?*, the writer remarks:

> In this text there comes to the fore in a very striking way an essential aspect of the present-day picture of man. Man's future is no longer conceived of in terms of what he is, from his eternal nature; but what man is is rather conceived of in terms of the future to which he is directed. Transcendence is no longer conceived of in terms of being, but being in terms of transcendence. We find this kind of thinking in Heidegger, Jaspers, Sartre and their followers, and in Merleau-Ponty. . . . A point of contact, so it seems to us, is to be found here between modern philosophy and modern theology. The latter, it would seem, conceives of man in terms of his future as this is revealed in Christ; it sees more and more in Christ the revelation of what we really are.[1]

How many English readers, it may be wondered, will respond sympathetically to this passage? And yet there can be no doubt that it does represent, both in itself and in what it describes, the dominant movement of continental thought; perhaps the fact that it is a Dutch writer we have quoted will help to bring this home: similar discussions may be found in Spanish publications. When, a few years ago, 'Existentialism' became briefly fashionable as a topic of conversation at Oxford sherry parties or in Bloomsbury pubs, it had all the limited interest of a freakish intruder upon the urbane insularity of English culture. Potted introductions to 'Existentialism' poured into print, and caused hardly a ripple on the broad, smooth surface of English sensibility. No single writer of any importance gave any serious attention to what was there offered; and perhaps the most significant episode in this little blind-alley of history was the delivery and publication of Marcel's Gifford lectures on *The Mystery of Being*. It is not without interest that the translation of Marcel's *Metaphysical Journal* which followed some time after is now being remaindered in bookshops up and down the country. Protestant interest in Bultmann's work on the New

[1] R. C. Kwant, 'De Historie en het Absolute', *Tijdschrift voor Philosophie* XVII (1955), p. 256.

Testament and 'demythologization' has led to some attention being given to Heidegger, chiefly in Scotland.[1] But on the whole it is fair to say that for the great majority of English readers, 'Existentialism' is associated with the exotic and the queer, a continental 'new look'. Catholic readers suffer from the further handicap of being dimly aware that 'Existentialism' has somehow been officially condemned, though they are not very clear about what exactly has been condemned or in what terms. It can categorically be stated that this condemnation has no application whatsoever in the present case.[2] It would not even be true to say that Fr Rahner is an 'Existentialist' theologian: it would be far less true to call him an 'Existentialist' theologian than it would be to call St Thomas an 'Aristotelian' theologian. It would in fact be an odd sort of theologian who simply took over a philosophy ready-made and somehow applied it to revealed sources. Philosophy for the theologian can never be simply a technique of demonstration but also a process of discovery, a critique.

What has been said so far in this discussion of Existentialism in England has been intended to bring into the open the problem of presenting to an English audience the contributions of a continental theologian to the Church's mission of realizing the world in herself. Fr Rahner's openness to the world involves a good deal more than a sympathy for Existentialism; but since the English reader is likely to

[1] The S.C.M. Press has published a thoroughly honest study of Bultmann and Heidegger, *An Existentialist Theology*, by John Macquarrie (1955); a translation by Dr Olive Wyon of a more specialized study of demythologization, *The Christian Message and Myth* (1958), by Fr L. Malevez, S.J.; and a translation of Heidegger's first major work, *Sein und Zeit*, is announced, some thirty years after its first publication in Germany. The remarkable series of translations of Kierkegaard should also be mentioned here. Other publications could be listed, but this is hardly the place in which to provide a bibliography of Existentialist writing in English.

[2] The relevant documents of the *magisterium* are: (1) the condemnation of the *opera omnia* of Sartre, AAS XL (1948), p. 571, and *Clergy Review* XXXI (1949), pp. 59–60; (2) the Encyclical *Humani Generis* (cf. Denz 3006, 3023); (3) the *allocutio* to the *Fédération Mondiale des Jeunesses Féminines Catholiques* concerning *Situationsethik*, AAS XLIV (1952), p. 413, and *Clergy Review* XXXVII (1952), p. 619. For a comprehensive discussion of what is involved in the references to Existentialism made by *Humani Generis*, see A. Dondeyne, 'Les Problèmes philosophiques soulevés dans l'Encyclique "Humani Generis"', *Revue Philosophique de Louvain* XLIX (1951), pp. 5–56, 141–88, 293–356.

find some of his language puzzling, it seems worthwhile to draw attention to its sources and also—though this is even more difficult—to provide a context in which that language has some depth of meaning. It would obviously be impossible to present here, even if I were competent to do so, a survey of the whole field of Existentialist writing; and in any case a survey of this kind would remain external to the real movement of thought out of which the language developed. On the other hand it might be profitable to suggest the kind of question which has been put and variously answered on the Continent during the last thirty years, in the hope that it will provide an exercise in communication, contribute to a community of spirit, between English and continental theologians.

Since this exercise is not to be a piece of history, some historical remarks should be made beforehand. Firstly, our English word 'Existentialism' should properly be applied only to the French movement associated with Sartre in particular: since 'Existentialism' first reached England from France it has unfortunately been usual to speak of all the writers who concern themselves with 'existence' as 'Existentialists'; the German term for the movement is *Existenzphilosophie*, the philosophy of existence.[1] However, it is often convenient to use a single word rather than a phrase, and I have made no attempt to be consistent in this matter. Secondly, within the German movement there have been and are marked divergences of approach and emphasis. It is Heidegger's approach that we shall primarily have in mind, since it seems clear that Fr Rahner has found most to interest him in this particular tendency of the movement. But thirdly, Heidegger's own work falls into two fairly distinct phases, roughly before and after 1940. To the first phase belong the major work *Sein und Zeit* and a very remarkable book on Kant; to the second phase a number of smaller pieces, chiefly lectures and essays.[2] It is, I think, fair to say

---

[1] A brief but authoritative history of the German movement may be found in O. F. Bollnow's introduction to his select bibliography *Deutsche Existenzphilosophie*, fascicule 23 of the *Bibliographische Einführungen in das Studium der Philosophie*, Berne, 1953. Fascicule 9, by R. Jolivet, deals with the French movement.

[2] An excellent study of this later phase will be found in A. Dondeyne, 'La Différence ontologique chez M. Heidegger', *Revue Philosophique de Louvain*, LVI (1958), pp. 35–62, 251–93. See also A. de Waelhens, *Phénoménologie et Vérité* (Paris, 1953).

that Fr Rahner's writings reflect an engagement with the earlier rather than with the later phase of Heidegger's development. The first edition of Fr Rahner's book *Geist in Welt*, a study of St Thomas's metaphysics of knowledge, dates from 1939; and he explains in the Preface to the second edition (Munich 1957) that the original work was in fact completed in 1936. It is in this work that Fr Rahner made explicit a philosophical position within the Thomist tradition which was a response to the whole movement of German thought from Kant to Heidegger by way of Hegel; and the philosophical density of his theological studies (notably the essay on Christology in this volume) is not to be fully appreciated without reference to this extremely difficult and yet rewarding statement of position.[1]

We must all of us at some time or other, in some situation or other, have asked ourselves the question, 'What does it all mean?' We should not ordinarily expect an immediate answer when we ask this question: it is not the same question as 'What does it mean?', which we might ask in some limited context, e.g. a passage in a foreign language. When we ask 'What does it all mean?' we reject, by using the

---

[1] This is not to say that I can wholly accept it. In fact, I am prepared to say that, as far as I can understand it, the foundation laid down by Fr Rahner is wholly unacceptable, however interesting the developments upon this foundation may be. What I take to be the foundation runs as follows: 'Erkennen ist Beisichsein des Seins, und dieses Beisichsein ist das *Sein* des Seienden', 'knowledge is the being-present-to-itself of Being, and this being-present-to-itself is the *Being* of any entity' (p. 82). I have translated 'any entity', because this is in fact what Fr Rahner maintains, with the utmost seriousness and cogency. Put in colourful terms, this amounts to saying that every entity (every material entity too) is a more or less deficient angel. My main objection to this approach is that what is said *cannot* be said if the Thomist thesis which the book is supposed to be maintaining is true, namely that our metaphysical knowledge derives from our experience of the world, or, putting it in Fr Rahner's (and Heidegger's) terms, that our 'ontological' knowledge derives from our 'ontic' knowledge. It is not without significance that Fr Rahner *apologizes* in one place (p. 87) for appealing to experience for the existence of entities which are not themselves capable of knowing. I very much doubt whether the convertibility of Being and intelligibility can be made the subject of *thematic* treatment, whether it can ever be more than a disclosure within an act of discovery, remaining always then a horizon of our understanding: the light of this disclosure is what enables us to use the language of *participation*. However, it is really improper to comment so briefly on a major philosophical work, especially since I cannot pretend to have wholly assimilated it.

word 'all', the ordinary limitation of the context; we are generalizing the question. In fact the situation in which we put ourselves the generalized question is frequently one of loss or injury or sin: a death, a disloyalty—the characteristically 'tragic' situations, exploited in a familiar way by Shakespeare. More rarely, we might ask the question after experiencing some great joy or happiness; but only *after* the experience, for the experience of joy is itself the answer to a question, the satisfaction of the need to ask the question.

But are these situations in any way metaphysically privileged, or have we here merely a sort of exclamation, a cry of pain, the registration of a private 'experience'? It will only be possible to adopt this psychological solution, and so to answer the question by explaining it away, if we assume that, for a human being, to be in a situation is as obvious as for a dog to be in a kennel or a pea in a pod. For scholastic philosophy 'the soul' is only in place *per accidens*; but unless we are careful to recreate the philosophical meaning of 'soul', this statement may simply leave us with an image of something not-body 'located' in the body but only vaguely located there. It is important to renew this notion of soul by regarding it as the principle which makes possible and actual the kind of being-in-a-situation which is proper to human beings, i.e. we must start from human being-in-a-situation and work back to the 'soul', and not *vice versa*. We 'inhabit' the earth, we dwell 'in' cities by creating organs and tools of inhabitation which we share in community with others. We only behave humanly in situations because we have made situations possible by being human; our actual behaviour in a situation is a particularization of the human possibility of being-in-a-situation. The fundamental actualization of our human existence, we may say, is being-in-a-situation. Thus while the human body, just like any other body, is really located in space and time, it is also true that the actualization of a human body which can be located in a spatio-temporal system of reference is the actualization of a system of reference which includes spatio-temporal axes of reference as a special part. This larger and indefinitely extensible system of reference is the possibility of situation, of 'world', which is to say civilization, art, morality, religion, science. It may once have been possible to identify this human 'world' with the cosmos; but we can now see that this identification was properly a mythical reconciliation of inner and outer, we no longer live under the vault of heaven but in an historical culture. The fundamental actualization of human existence

is the generation of meaning. 'O' as printed is a shape; it is also a
nought or a letter of the alphabet, and it could be neither of the latter
without being the former. But we do not ordinarily, nor need we,
advert to the shape when we use the sign: we do not advert to the
given world when, by actively inhabiting it, we use it as the sign of a
human world. *Anima est magis continens quam contenta.*

The move from situation to the possibility of situation is characteristic of Heidegger's philosophy. We are *in fact* in situations, situations
which do not merely succeed each other but involve each other and
develop one out of the other, forming a biography, a more or less
significant, more or less coherent growth not simply 'up and down'
(Aristotle saw that 'up and down' were biological orientations), but
in a dimension of human 'existence' in which meaning is generated,
co-ordinated, condensed or dispersed, renewed and authenticated or
conventionalized and trivialized. But to inquire into the *possibility* of
this 'existence' is to raise the 'transcendental' question, in Kant's
sense[1]: this is the *existenzial* as opposed to the *existenziell* question[2];
and the inquiry which attempts explicitly to discuss this *existenzial* or
transcendental question of the possibility of human existence as a
generation of meaning is 'fundamental ontology'.

The word 'ontology' should remind us that by philosophizing in
this way we are continually concerned with one single question, the
question of the meaning of Being, *die Frage nach dem Sinn von Sein*,
as Heidegger has never ceased to insist, although with rather different
emphasis in his first and second phases. We cannot disclose, make
apparent, the *existenzial* basis which makes our *existenziell* existence
possible except by exhibiting or expounding (phenomenologically)
the concealed orientations latent in this existence, but it is this actual
being manifesting itself as already orientated which is the subject of
our exposition. The exposition discloses what Heidegger calls
'Existenzialien', Fr Rahner (more in accordance with German in-
flexion) 'Existentialien', *existentials*, which are these latent orientations

---

[1] Cf. K. Rahner, 'Introduction au concept de philosophie existenziale
chez Heidegger', RSR XXX (1940), pp. 152–71. This is perhaps the place
to point out that there are two Rahners, Karl and Hugo, both members of
the Society of Jesus, both Professors (of Dogmatic Theology and Church
History respectively) at Innsbruck, both of whom have written on Origen.

[2] I have only distinguished these two words in the translation when it
seemed specially important to do so.

of human existence, corresponding to the 'categories' of traditional ontology. They are not particularized phenomena of human
existence but the *a priori* conditions in order that human existence
should exhibit particularized phenomena; and again they are not *a
priori* conditions in the sense of ultimate propositional formulations
but the modalities of the ontological structure of human existence
itself. Thus when Fr Rahner speaks of a 'supernatural existential',
what he has in mind is a modality of human existence as this is concretely realized in an economy within which by God's free decision
this existence is ordained to supernatural beatitude—a modality prior,
that is, to its particularization as either grace or damnation. It should
be clear that an 'existential' is an ontological and not a moral determination. There are indeed privileged situations in the *existenziell*
order in which the questionability of our human existence is obscurely
revealed; but the *existenzial* point is the possibility of asking the
question at all, 'What does it *all* mean?' How is it that I am in a
situation at all? Why is there Being at all and not rather nothing?
What is the intrinsic, not extrinsic, meaning of Being?

Being-in-a-situation is an event, the happening (*Geschehen*) of a
revelation, and it is the unfolding of this revelation which constitutes
history (*Geschichte*). The revelation of the truth of Being, the event
and the happening of truth, has been the particular theme of the later
Heidegger. It has been very well said that while in his earlier writings
Heidegger started from human existence (*Dasein*) in order to reach
the truth of Being, in his later writings he starts from Being in order
to reach an interpretation of man in which man is called to be the
guardian and the 'shepherd' of the truth of Being.[1] But in both earlier
and later writings the truth of Being is presented as revelation, disclosure: an event and a happening, the inexhaustible fertility of which
constitutes human historicity as the manifestation of that secret communion with and in Being which is latent in being-in-a-situation,
being *there* (*Da-sein*). Being *in* for human existence is essentially being
out, ek-sistence into history. In this sense it is 'project' towards a
horizon, the transcendental limit of a total situation whose circum-
scribing finitude is foreshadowed in the light of the revelation. Once
human inwardness in no longer sustained by the myth of a hierarchical

---

[1] Walter Biemel, *Le Concept de monde chez Heidegger* (Louvain–Paris
1950), p. 86.

cosmos of the spheres beyond which is God, its ultimate revelation tends to be one of self-enclosed finitude; but there is no reason why we should not learn to seek God as the source of that marriage of man and earth which is consummated in the Event of truth, and which can serve as the sacramental sign of the revelation of the divine Truth itself. Our encounter with a Man can be the revelation of God; our inhabitation of the earth can be and is a sacred history. We are not merely the spectators of a cosmic play, with God behind the scenes as stage-manager and producer; we are the actors and God is our author.[1]

I am keenly aware of the inadequacies of this attempt to put the philosophical question which engages the concern of philosophers on the Continent today. And I am aware too that in spite of its inadequacy it is still quite out of proportion to the proper part played by philosophical concerns in Fr Rahner's studies. My excuse must once again be that the style of these concerns is what English readers are going to find most disconcerting in the studies, and that an introduction to Fr Rahner's work must give it special attention. The philosophy of existence is important for Fr Rahner, as it should be for us, because it has given explicit formulation to that sense of his own being as deeply questionable which is characteristic of man in the modern world; and it is to this man in this world that the old appeal to be converted and to turn to the living God must be addressed.[2]

It will be appreciated that the translation of these studies has been a matter of the utmost difficulty. Fr Rahner naturally assumes a familiarity with scholastic and modern theology, Biblical and speculative, Protestant and Catholic theology, as well as with the philosophy

[1] Sooner or later someone is going to write a book called *Wittgenstein and Heidegger*. It would be a book very well worth writing, its main theme being the way in which these two very different philosophers have overcome the division (which is an existential as well as a 'philosophical' one) between inner and outer.

[2] It has been suggested by Fr John F. Sweeney, S.J., in a review of the German edition of this work ('Some Recent Developments in Dogmatic Theology', TS XVII (1956), pp. 375–80) that the anthropological preoccupations of the modern world do not favour new developments in theology, and there is some truth in this observation. And yet anthropological preoccupations are surely at least as relevant to an Incarnational economy as cosmological ones, but no one would wish to deny the importance of Aristotelian cosmology in scholastic theology.

of existence.[1] The German language still enjoys, in scientific usage anyway, the fluidity which made Elizabethan and Jacobean prose and drama possible, and Fr Rahner exploits its resources to the full. For instance, it is always possible, at least in technical literature, to domesticate a Latin word by the simple process of giving it a German termination, thus practically doubling one's vocabulary. By a process of 'agglutination' pretty well any complex of thought can be presented as a single concept, so that each writer tends to develop his private vocabulary. While this latter process certainly increases and intensifies the expressiveness, the 'pregnancy',[2] of the writing, it does not always promote clarity. Fr J. M. Oesterreicher, now an American citizen though an Austrian by origin, once gave me an instructive example of this from his own experience, which I hope he will forgive me for repeating. While still thinking and speaking in German he evolved a statement, *die Juden sind ein Menschheitsvolk* (literally, 'The Jews are a humanity people') which seemed to him to sum up pregnantly all he wanted to say. Looking back on that statement now, he claims that he is unable to say which of three possible English meanings he intended it to have. The translation of these studies has frequently involved selective interpretation. Again, Fr Rahner delights in the relatively highly differentiated accidence of German which allows the construction of long periodic sentences: one of his sentences in these studies runs to twenty-five lines of print. It has constantly been necessary to rethink and recast a great part of what he has written. I have in general assumed a serious reading public willing to put up with awkwardness and 'heaviness' for the sake of what Fr Rahner has to offer. The 'Scheme for a new Treatise of Dogmatic Theology' was only included after much anxious reflexion, because this formidable list of apocalyptic titles and headings proved quite intractable to the process of 'solution' which can generally be adopted in translating a continuous passage. The final decision to include it, as well as to

[1] For instance, the notion of 'Heilsgeschichte', normally translated here by 'saving history', since it refers not merely to the historical record of salvation but to the actual *happening* of salvation, its manifest incarnation in event.

[2] For a simple example, without 'agglutination', of 'pregnancy' we may take *das Wort*, which I have frequently translated 'the Word' even when no reference is being made to the Second Person of the Trinity. Eighteenth-century English was much more lavish with capital letters than we are.

persevere with a number of the studies,[1] was only taken in virtue of a principle which I think Mr T. S. Eliot once stated about 'difficulty' in poetry, and which applies to Mr Eliot's own poetry too: that 'difficulty' can be tolerated (and will eventually not be felt as such) if a first reading gives sufficient guarantee of the real worth of what is being said. I am myself sufficiently convinced of the worth of these studies to recommend them to at least a first reading by English readers, in spite of their often extreme difficulty. In fact I should like to acknowledge here my profound debt to Fr Rahner; I could never provide an adequate account of the influence these studies have had on me, and my hope is that they will prove equally rewarding to English readers.[2] I must not, however, necessarily be taken to agree with everything Fr Rahner says.

Partly owing to the difficulties of translation, and partly owing to circumstances beyond my control, the publication of this translation has been painfully delayed. I should like publicly to apologize to the English and German publishers, and to Fr Rahner himself, for this delay.

CORNELIUS ERNST, O.P.

[1] The Dutch translation of these studies, *Theologische Verkenningstochten* (Haarlem 1958), omits all the longer, more difficult, pieces. In the present version, only one or two very small omissions have been made, to which attention is drawn in each case. A few notes have been added, including references to later writings by Fr Rahner where these are known to me.

[2] It has also given me particular pleasure as a Dominican to be instrumental in making so eminent a member of the Society of Jesus better known in England.

PREFACE

THE number of specialist journals of theology is gradually becoming incalculable. The result is that essays which 'appear' in them tend rather to be hidden than to be published. Naturally it is not the business of the author to judge whether the obscurity into which these essays fall is a just fate or a regrettable misfortune. But if he has the right to make anything appear at all, he cannot be reproached for trying to publish his work in some other form which will make it more probable that someone will read it. And so we have attempted here to disinter a few essays from periodicals, leaving out work concerned purely with the history of dogma.[1]

The essays on the theology of the spiritual life will appear in a separate volume.

---

[1] E.g. 'Die geistliche Lehre des Evagrius Pontikus', ZAM VIII (1932), pp. 21–38; 'Le Début d'une doctrine des cinq sens spirituels chez Origène', RAM XIII (1932), pp. 113–45; 'La Doctrine des sens spirituels au moyen âge', RAM XIV (1933), pp. 263–99; 'Der Begriff der ecstasis bei Bonaventura', ZAM IX (1934), pp. 1–19, 'Cœur de Jésus chez Origène', RAM XIV (1934), pp. 171–4; 'Sünde als Gnadenverlust in der frühkirchlichen Literatur', ZKT LX (1936), pp. 471–510; 'Die protestantische Christologie der Gegenwart', Theologie der Zeit I (1936), pp. 189–202, 'Ein messalianisches Fragment über die Taufe', ZKT LXI (1937), pp. 258–71; 'De termino aliquo in Theologia Clementis Alexandrini', Gregorianum XVIII (1937), pp. 426–31; 'Augustinus und der Semipelagianismus', ZKT LXII (1938), pp. 171–96; 'Die Sündenvergebung nach der Taufe in der regula fidei des Irenäus', ZKT LXX (1949), pp. 450–5; 'La Doctrine d'Origène sur la Pénitence', RSR XXXVII (1950), pp. 47–97, 252–86, 422–56; 'Zur Theologie der Busse bei Tertullian', Festschrift für Karl Adam (Düsseldorf 1952), pp. 139–67; 'Busslehre und Busspraxis in der Didascalia Apostolorum', ZKT LXXII (1950), pp. 257–81; 'Die Busslehre des heiligen Cyprian von Carthago', ZKT LXXIV (1952), pp. 257–76, 381–438.

(Many of the studies here translated have been enlarged and revised. Fr Rahner gives in the text a chronological list, which I do not reproduce, of the places of first publication.—Tr.)

The presumptuous intention of this modest collection of theological studies will be achieved if they help just a little (before they are finally forgotten) to confirm young theologians in the conviction that Catholic theology has no reason to rest on its laurels, fine though those may be; that on the contrary it can and must advance, and in such a way that it remains true to its own laws and its tradition.

Innsbruck,   KARL RAHNER, S.J.
  July 1954

I

THE PROSPECTS FOR DOGMATIC THEOLOGY

UNFULFILLED programmes, pronouncements about 'how it should be done' (when nothing has in fact been done) are cheap enough. They arouse the suspicion that their author is one of those people who always know better. But on the other hand no human being has ever got anything done without some sort of plan in mind. Programmes are unavoidable. If it is beginning to seem impossible today for a single theologian to write a complete treatise of dogmatic theology—something more than a textbook or, speaking generally, a convenient summary of received opinions—then even an unfulfilled programme for a treatise may perhaps be more than just a pretension to superior knowledge, in that it can open and support discussion of the question: How should a group of theologians attempt to work out together a treatise of Catholic theology for today?

A brief and open-minded survey of Catholic theological writing in our time brings us to some surprising conclusions. Such conclusions are inevitably onesided and schematic, and will, happily, be unjust in particular cases. It can always be said to the critic who offers them: *medice, cura teipsum*. But is it really true that a man who lives in a glass house may never throw stones? He might very well be prepared to put up with the breaking of his own windows for the sake of the thing. In a word: if we review the productions of Catholic theology over the last twenty or thirty years—speaking schematically, of course, and with some injustice in particular cases and to particular individuals —we may divide them into three groups[1]: textbooks, historical

---

[1] We ignore of course the literature of 'haute vulgarisation', theological journalism and theological freebootery (which is naturally also to be found), and still more the often necessary and sometimes superfluous writings in which the mass of the faithful needs to have the daily bread of its religious instruction new baked, new every day, even if it looks just the same today as it did yesterday. We have in mind here only those theological productions which are usually characterized as 'scientific'. Admittedly, the distinction between

studies of Christian dogma, and theological studies of special or marginal topics.

The textbooks are—textbooks. Whoever has tried his hand at it will be well aware that it is no easy matter to write a properly planned textbook or even part of one. A whole series of well-arranged textbooks is available in Latin and in modern languages. It follows from the nature of Catholic understanding of the faith, and from its concern with theologians who are beginning the basic study of the Church's teaching, that it should not be the ambition of these Catholic textbooks to seek 'originality' at any price. But is it blasphemous to condemn them (that there are exceptions is not denied) for a quite startling kind of 'unoriginality'? They may have been filled out in many respects over the last twenty or thirty years: some improvement on the historical side, references to literature (seldom assimilated, admittedly) and so on. But let us bear this in mind: no one can deny that in the last two centuries cultural and spiritual transformations have taken place which, to say the very least, are comparable in depth and extent and power to mould men's lives, with those which took place between the time of Augustine and that of the golden age of scholasticism. If we hold that theology is an endeavour of the spirit and a science which has to be of service to its own time, just as it has, or should have, grown out of its own time; and if we hold this because it has to serve salvation and not mere theoretical curiosity (granting always that pure understanding as such is itself a part of salvation) and salvation is always the salvation of individual men here and now; if we hold in faith that divine revelation is a source of such treasures of truth that it can never be exhausted (Denz 3014): then we should have expected to find at least as pronounced a difference between a theological compendium of today and one of, say, 1750, as between the *Summa Theologica* of St Thomas and the writings of Augustine.

What are the facts? We might just as well look up the average *tractatus* of Billuart or the Wirceburgenses as a modern treatise. Where it is properly dogmatic theology—that is to say, neither history

---

science and popularization is especially problematic in theology; for here 'science' rests on the faith of the 'people'. And perhaps it has almost always been the case that 'armchair [sitzende]' scientific theology (to make use of an expression, itself problematic, of H. U. von Balthasar's) has learnt more from 'praying' (and preaching) non-scientific theology than the reverse. But that is not our concern here.

of dogma or its pitiful crumbs, nor *haute vulgarisation*—such a modern theological treatise in no way differs from its predecessors of 200 years ago.[1] Let no one say that of course it could not be different from its predecessors in view of the immutability of the *depositum fidei*. That is simply not true. We need only try to form an idea of the historically contingent character of the uniform canon which has regulated the choice of topics and treatises in a theological textbook for over two hundred years, in order to see that such an assertion concerning the unavoidable immutability of our textbooks is false.[2] How much is missing from our modern manuals which was dealt with at length in the textbook composed by St Thomas (it is called the *Summa Theologica*)! Where is it laid down that the seven sacraments should be dealt with one after the other and should demand approximately a third of the contents of a textbook? Let us observe how much space is allotted to the tractate *De Resurrectione Christi* or, more generally, the *De Mysteriis Vitae Christi*, and let us ask ourselves whether this allotment of space, in itself betraying something of the deeper attitudes and perspectives of the writers' minds, is just the obvious one. We should ask ourselves why for instance in the treatise *De Paenitentia* the personal, existential side of the sacramental action usually receives explicit and extended treatment (*De Virtute Paenitentiae*), while in every other sacrament, with a pathetic sense of its obviousness, the treatment of this aspect is supposed to be superfluous, or at most disposed of in a couple of footnotes. Or again, let us imagine a Biblical theology, of a kind which we hardly possess yet but of which we can form a rough idea, and ask ourselves what themes and proportions we

[1] Omitting here the consideration of *theologia fundamentalis*.

[2] The vicious circle of a Denzinger Theology is beginning to threaten us here. However 'objective' Denzinger may be as to actual texts chosen and collected there, it is equally subjective as to their choice and collection. It is obviously affected by the canon which regulates the questions and theses of current seminary theology: what it has collected and selected is what is needed in the way of authoritative doctrinal pronouncements in just this context. May not much else be found in Denzinger's sources (Papal letters, bullaria, etc.) if only this other material were thought to be as important as this or that question on which Denzinger does in fact supply explanatory material? Now that Denzinger with its selection (and its *Index Systematicus*) is in existence, the theologian feels almost instinctively that it is the canonical norm for what questions are to be treated of in dogmatic theology; for other questions, no evidence may be adduced from Denzinger. The vicious circle is complete.

might not unreasonably suppose it would give rise to in the field of systematic theology as well. There is a very large number of treatises on dogmatic and moral theology (or is it all of them?) in which practically nothing is said on the Pauline theme of Law and Freedom.[1] Is it simply obvious that this is right? We may test the average textbook's views of history: between Adam (*De Deo Creante et Elevante*; *De Peccato Originali*) and Christ we find—nothing. Surely there is room for a theology of saving history in general, treating of both the Old Covenant and of the way of salvation outside the history of Israel (the latter in its own right). Similar examples to illustrate the general approach to problems in the average textbook may easily be produced, in regard to its themes alone.

No one will be able to deny that in fact the history of dogma and Biblical theology have hardly acted as a ferment in the treatment of questions of dogmatic theology itself.

From yet another point of view it can be shown, quite formally, that we cannot make the immutability of dogma the excuse for the uniformity and stagnation of our textbooks. When a scientific discipline loses its power to forge concepts it becomes 'sterile' (to use a word from *Humani Generis*).[2] Technical concepts are necessary if a science is to develop, because accumulated experience can only become fruitful for the achievement of a new, exact and various understanding when what has been acquired is made available for further employment by resolution into a determinate concept. Hypostasis, the supernatural, *opus operatum*, transubstantiation, contrition, attrition, *habitus*, *gratia sanctificans*, *gratia gratis data* and many others are concepts of this kind, which have emerged as the condensed results of theological work which has often gone on for centuries, and so could and still can

---

[1] I have not been able to find an entry for 'Sermon on the Mount' in Noldin's *Index Systematicus*. In the Encyclical of Leo XIII on Freedom (*Libertas praestantissimum*) not a word is to be found on the freedom which has become ours by the gift of Christ's redemptive grace. The Encyclical speaks, in terms of philosophy and the Natural Law, only about the freedom which we just always have. Are observations of this kind, which could be multiplied at will, simply to be explained by every author's own personal choice of his theme?

[2] 'Experiundo novimus', according to *Humani Generis* (Denz 3014). Thus the sterility of theology may very well be not just an abstract possibility, but something already experienced as a fact. We cannot naively suppose that something of the sort could only happen in the 'bad old days'.

each form a point of departure and a conceptual tool for further theological reflexion. They are as it were symbols and trophies of theological achievements of past centuries. In the field of dogmatic theology proper, are there to be found theological *termini technici*, accepted as classical and familiar to every theologian, which have been added during the last few centuries to the available stock of means of theological clarification? *Corredemptio-corredemptrix* perhaps; but there is still a great deal of controversy about this concept.

Is this state of affairs inevitable? We cannot say that all those concepts which we require for our properly theological equipment—or which we would require if we possessed them—have already been developed. Of course this assertion can hardly be demonstrated to self-complacent theologians. But the point here is that anyone who does not hold the (strictly blasphemous) view that theology has pretty well exhausted divine revelation and translated it all into theological intelligibility, must find it strange and disturbing that there is so little active formation of concepts in theology today.

One small example of this may be given. It is admitted that there is an objective distinction between venial and grave sin, not only as regards the 'matter' of the act, but also from the side of the subject, that is, as regards the degree of existential depth, the centrality or superficiality, with which the personal core of the subject is engaged. The same distinction must then be applicable to the morally *good* act, from the very nature of the case, and in such a way that the ethical quality of these good acts, so various in kind, is only 'analogically' to be comprehended in the same concept of the morally good act. Now there is not a single word in theology for this distinction and for what it should distinguish. If there were an appropriate *terminus technicus* we could ask, among other things, in another theological field: Does *every* morally good act (in the supernatural order) increase grace, or only (how are we to put it?) the 'grave' act? Or again, where may we find the theologically and ontologically exact conceptual and terminological equipment with which to determine *positively* the relation of the angels to the rest of creation, including the material world? (If we qualify them merely as 'pure' spirits, the greater part of what Scripture tells us about their relation to the world remains unexpressed, just a blur in our minds today.)

It must not be supposed that this theological 'progress' as regards themes, the setting and solving of questions, the formation of concepts

and so on, could be merely a matter of more or less worthless 'refine-
ments'—apart from a few special fields like Mariology. So long as a
new formulation of the question is not worked out (the question itself
generally doesn't exist!) and an answer achieved, it always looks as
though everything is really quite clear and that all that remains to be
discussed is one or two controversies of the schools, fundamentally
trivial from the religious point of view. But when we have trained our
vision by the study of the history of dogma (or more accurately here,
the history of theology), we may recognize that theology does not
always advance to ever better and clearer solutions but that its history
is always at the same time one of false approximations to a 'mean'
(which is to say often mediocre) path. We may recognize too that,
through 'exhaustion', it is the history of what are often merely verbal
solutions, in which questions are forgetfully allowed to escape by
being overlooked in favour of a convenient clarity and comprehen-
siveness, *ad usum delphini*. Anyone who pursues the study of theology,
moved by the spirit of his time and an eager religious life and a desire
to make a real proclamation to his own time, will experience soon
enough the impact of new questions, questions which only obtain
their clarification and solution by careful and disciplined theological
investigation.[1] But because properly-conducted studies in the history
of dogma and of theology (of which we have still to speak) have had
in fact no far-reaching effect on dogmatic theology; and because
religious life and theology seldom form a truly living unity (excepting
again individual theologians and limited special questions like Mariology); and finally because the impulses of our time only reach theology
in a weakened and as it were disinfected form—that is why our textbooks of dogmatic theology look the same today as they did two
hundred years ago.

When we attempt to evaluate this situation, we must not suppose
that the difference we are looking for need and can consist of a merely

---

[1] By way of a small example of this, I may refer to my little book *Die
vielen Messen und das eine Opfer* (Freiburg 1951). Cf. B. Neuheuser, 'Die
vielen Messen', *Catholica* IX (1953), pp. 151–3, and the essay by F. Vanden-
broucke, 'La Concélébration, acte liturgique communautaire', *La Maison-
Dieu* XXXV (1953), pp. 48 s. (See also K. Rahner, 'Die vielen Messen als
die vielen Opfer Christi', ZKT LXXVII (1955), pp. 94–101, and H. F.
Davis, 'The Pope and Private Masses', *Clergy Review* XLII (1957), pp.
2–14.—Tr.)

literary, verbal or rhetorical adaptation of an old theology to our time, in new 'applications', 'outlooks' or corollaries in the practical order. It is much more a matter here of a dogmatic theology, a genuinely scientific one (in the sense that it listens with exactness and seriousness, and reflects with exactness on what it hears), whose concern it is to be adequate to reality; for then it can allow itself to try to be adequate to its time—a preoccupation full of danger and generally quite unprofitable. For if it is in fact more intimately adequate to reality (than it has been), it spontaneously becomes adequate to its time: it makes the time its own and need not worry about suiting itself to the time, always after the event. From the practical point of view the most serious misunderstanding defended or at least encouraged by the so-called 'kerygmatic theology' was the growth of the belief upon which this theology was based, that speculative theology could remain as it is now, provided that 'by its side' a kerygmatic theology were built up. Essentially, this would consist in saying 'the same' as what had achieved systematic expression in scholastic theology, but only in a slightly different way, 'kerygmatically', together with a few practical modifications. But in fact the strictest theology, that most passionately devoted to reality alone and ever on the alert for new questions, the most scientific theology, is itself in the long run the most kerygmatic. The fact that our textbooks are so little alive, serve proclamation and witness so little, is not due to their superabundance of scholastic and scientific theology but because they offer too little of it, precisely because as relics of the past they are unable even to preserve the past in its purity. For the past can only be preserved in its purity by someone who accepts responsibility for the future, who preserves in so far as he overcomes.

The studies in the history of dogma, forming the second of the groups into which we divided current work in scientific theology, cannot make good this deficiency of the textbooks; not only because dogmatic theology and the history of dogma are not the same thing, but also for a reason almost more important: the greater part of these works has its eye exclusively on the past. They derive from the past no impulse for the future of dogmatic theology. They confine themselves to showing how what prevails today came into being; starting from today they simply go backwards. It is only rarely that one of these works comes upon an old crossing of the ways, past which the theologians of the time had gone their way unnoticing and perhaps even fatefully, and finds there a route which we today can follow into a territory not yet explored. Of course there is bound to be a number of works of an historical kind which were originally undertaken out of a simple historical interest in past facts and processes; as far as these are concerned, we must for the moment leave undecided the question whether it might not be possible at some time—either in conjunction with other studies or in a larger context—to derive from them further results of greater significance for theology than the mere backward-looking acquaintance with their own past. Perhaps it may be possible to keep our gaze turned forwards while we glance to the rear and find in the past an ingredient of a future not yet attained. Anyone who demands quick theological returns from individual historical works (and this is specially true of the beginner, who tends to be much too impatient in looking for what can be 'got out of' historical studies) exposes historical investigation in theology to the dangers of triviality and superficiality, and encourages a dilettantism which would reap before it has sown. But however important a truth this may be, it must still be asked whether current Catholic writing in the field of the history of dogma has not been too sterile for theology proper. On the one hand it has not approached the past with a real question, one which is still open to the test of the facts. On the other it has not interrogated the past closely enough to hear it with all the overtones with which it once resounded, overtones which at that time were not perhaps the explicit formulations of a scientific theology, but rather the echoes of preaching, faith and Christian life. Yet utterances of this kind could very well be more important for us today than many other truths or *theologoumena* which exhibit a more immediately comprehensible history. If they are to have any value for dogmatic theology, histories of dogma must not propose merely to chronicle in a summary way what was said about this or that in times past. The historian of such a course of the spirit must look at reality itself with the very eyes of the theologian of the past, listening to what he says: not chronicle past theology but practise the study of theology in company with it. It is true of course that such a method runs a greater danger of misinterpreting the sources by reading modern problems into them than the mere report. But in the last resort it is by this method alone that we can get at the thoughts and not just the words of our source-texts. Success in an attempt of this kind is not demonstrated by the fact that someone has examined the body of texts available, has arranged them and imposed a quite exterior structure upon them, and then, from the judgment seat of modern theology, has uttered a summary pronouncement upon the fact and extent of the intelligence of the author concerned as compared with ours. This lecture-room method puts everything on the same level; it cannot elicit the hidden energies of an old theology, it fails to discover what has remained implicit and what is consequently most active there, the secret presuppositions. It is insensitive to the opposition or the gap which may sometimes be present between what is said and what is meant, between the perhaps over-facile solution of a particular problem and the fundamental principle; possessing the parts, it lacks the spirit which informs the whole. Thus it fails to discover precisely that in the theology of the past which might be of value for theology today. Consider for example Hermann Lange's treatise *De Gratia*. This work is the best-informed scholastic manual on the theology of grace. Lange really knew the 'results' of historical investigation in this field, in so far as they were readily available.[1] But if we ask ourselves what significance these 'results' had for the properly *theological* content of his book we are bound to answer with all due respect (the judgment is a summary one of course): none at all. The fault is not Lange's but that of the historical works of which we have been speaking, their lack of dogmatic fruitfulness. Similar remarks could be made about our best scholastic manual *De Paenitentia*, by P. Galtier. Galtier is one of the best-informed scholars on the history of penance and has done some of the best research in this field. But if we leave out of his treatise the historical notes and the apologetic for the Church's teaching against misinterpretations of the history of penance, we are left with a dogmatic treatise which is the split image of any treatise written over the last two centuries. Is this Galtier's fault as a dogmatic theologian? By no means: it is the fault of the historical works themselves. That this need not necessarily be the case may be seen from Poschmann's research into the history of indulgences, to choose intentionally a quite unpretentious example.[2] What is it that makes the properly historical in studies like those of de Lubac or de la Taille so stimulating and to the point? Surely it is the art of reading

[1] Up to the date at which his book appeared of course. Is it too much to hope that after the work of Bouillard, de Lubac, Auer, Landgraf and Alfaro, there will be some changes over a great part of this field?

[2] See vol. II of these studies, 'Remarks on the Theology of Indulgences'.

texts in such a way that they become not just votes cast in favour of or against our current positions (positions taken up long ago), but say something to us which we in our time have not considered at all or not closely enough, about reality itself. This is not to say that we should study the history of theology in order to justify our own private innovations, although this sort of culpable silliness is by no means unknown; but that we should enter into association with a thinker of the past, not only to become acquainted with his views but in the last resort to learn something about reality. It is because historical theology is too much lecture-room disquisition and too little συνθεολογεῖν that we generally learn from it only about that part of the past which is in any case already preserved in modern theology, but not about that part which shapes our future in our past. It is no wonder then that the great work of historical theology, one which deserves our constant praise as regards our positive gains from it, has so far been able to exert so little pressure to overcome the deficiencies of the textbooks.

The third group which we distinguished above has for its theme special and marginal questions of dogmatic theology. That is to say, there are many works, especially in the field of Mariology, the only objection to which is that they are not supported by a sufficiently large number of other works dealing with more central questions. It is thus that we gain the impression (quite unjustly, perhaps, as regards individual theologians) that these works are being made use of as a 'convenient alibi', 'as a means of evading issues which, although they cannot be ignored when the architectural laws of revealed truth are taken into account, yet would demand a more resolute and variously cultivated spirit' than the subject which is in fact chosen for treatment. The doctrines of the Trinity, of the God-Man, of Redemption, of the Passion and Resurrection, of Predestination and the Last Things, simply bristle with formulations which no one examines but towards which everyone makes a reverential bow. This deference is a mistake. The thought of earlier generations, even if it has had results in the form of conciliar definitions, is not a sort of couch for the thought of later generations. Definitions are much less an end than a beginning. A *Hic Rhodus*. An opening. No real achievement is ever lost to the Church. But theologians are never spared the task of prompt renewal. Anything which is merely conserved, or which is merely handed down without a fresh, personal exertion beginning at the very sources of Revelation, rots as the manna did. And the longer living Tradition is interrupted by mere mechanical handing down, the more difficult it may become to restore contact again.[1] All honour to the countless number of Mariological works being written today; and let there be no doubt that the greater part of them, at least, is sustained by that Marian movement in the Church today which is a gift of her Spirit. But how many themes, just as important in themselves, remain unexamined! Over how many questions does there reign the grave-yard calm of weariness and boredom! There persisted into the late Middle Ages sharp differences of Trinitarian teaching within the limits of orthodoxy. Today 99 per cent of those who have followed a regular course of theological studies will have to admit that they are quite ignorant of these differences and that they were told hardly anything of them during their studies. Where are *theological* works to be found on the mysteries of Christ's life? A thick volume in French and Spanish on the Ascension, for instance, pays no attention to matters other than textual criticism and the apologetic defence of the Ascension as an historical event. In spite of its enormous size the *Dictionnaire de Théologie Catholique* has simply forgotten to have an article about it at all. An even more notable deficiency in current theology is the lack of any fundamental consideration of the mysteries of Christ's life in general. In modern dogmatic theology the only moments in the life of Jesus to which attention is still given are the Incarnation itself, the foundation of the Church, Christ's teaching, the Last Supper and the death of Christ. In addition the Resurrection is considered in Apologetics from the point of view of *theologia fundamentalis*. Everything else to do with the mysteries of Christ's life is no longer to be found in dogmatic theology but only in the literature of edification. Where may we find an up-to-date work on the doctrine of transubstantiation and the worldview of modern physics?[2] The Encyclical *Humani Generis* has not given a warning against the dangers of false attempts in this matter just so that nothing at all should be done about it. We

---

[1] H. U. von Balthasar, 'Was soll Theologie? Ihr Ort und ihre Gestalt im Leben der Kirche', *Wort und Wahrheit* VIII (1953), pp. 325–32. (Citation from p. 330.)

[2] The new edition of Filograssi's treatise on the Eucharist says nothing at all on this point. When shall we ever have a scholastic treatise on the Eucharist which at last abandons the usual superficial division according to which first the Real Presence and then the sacrifice of the Mass is treated of, as though this division arose from the very nature of the case?

may consult any bibliography we like, and yet be horrified by the thinness or the entire lack of properly dogmatic investigation into the theology of death. Poets and philosophers reflect on it; but in our theology all we find is a few chilly remarks on death as a penal consequence of original sin. And that is pretty well all. What is said about it in Eschatology is at most a tenth of what we could learn from revealed sources, if we really read them with all our mind and heart. What thinness and lack of interest in Eschatology itself! Why can we find no work, at least no exact, thorough and patient work, on the rules of interpretation of eschatological utterances in the revealed sources? The eschatological reality itself and the mode of its manifestation inevitably act as co-determinants of the *genus litterarium* of such utterances. And yet all we find on the question as to what is content and what form in such utterances is *ad hoc* improvisation. Who has ever written a theology of the concept of time and of our understanding of it?[1] Until as late as the eighteenth century there was at least some speculation about Heaven and its local character. Today we say that Heaven is a place and that no one knows where it is. Simple, but a little too convenient. Surely there is more to be said than that. In the field of eschatology a great deal more could be done from the point of view of history of dogma alone. How poor we still are in the 'theology of history'! A formal theology of the history of the Church after Christ is entirely lacking. The Introductions to Church history are astonishingly thin. Are there for example genuine theological criteria of an intrinsic kind for assigning the history of the Church into periods? How far is Church history a theological science? What is its subject and its formal object, distinguishing it from the Christian part of the general history of religion (even if the latter is treated of by a Catholic, for whom the Christian doctrine and conviction of the divine foundation of the Church furnish a negative norm for his consequent researches into the history of religion)? All these are offered as a few random examples of the fact that special studies on the history of dogma and dogmatic theology are clearly influenced by an unacknowledged selective principle by no means obvious in itself, and that in consequence a vast number of topics in

[1] The work by F. Beemelmans, *Zeit und Ewigkeit nach Thomas von Aquin* (Münster 1914), although it belongs to Bäumker's *Beiträge* series, is startlingly naive, a typical example of the 'chronicle', instead of the reflective renewal of someone else's thought, and for that reason quite profitless.

dogmatic theology receive no treatment at all. It is not at all easy to see what this curious principle of selection might be: a diffidence before difficult questions, perhaps; the false idea that in certain fields dogmatic theology has entered upon the final phase of its development; the paralysing impression made by the massive immobility of certain controversies of the schools, apparently stranded for good; the shrinkage of collaboration between theologians[1]; the false but widespread feeling that there is no longer any way of going beyond 'differences of opinion' when discussing new questions. The result of this last misapprehension is a despondent belief that it would be gratuitous to commit oneself too 'enthusiastically' to just one point of view which must always remain controversial; and so people prefer to express their 'point of view' in works of edification, where it will not be challenged but will be accepted in a spirit of pious faith.[2]

One common feature emerges to view from a consideration of these three divisions of theological literature: dogmatic theology today is very orthodox.[3] But it is not very vividly alive. To have established this point is to offer no sort of reproach about its being 'long-winded', 'flat', 'dry' or 'boringly pedantic', or that it isn't stylistically elegant, or that it doesn't 'edify' everyone at first go. Scientific work in dogmatic theology can dispense with all these qualities provided it does just one thing: that it devotes itself to the reality in question with that passionate sympathy which this unique reality can demand more

---

[1] For example, it is worth pointing out that even in the field of theology, although it has fortunately not caught up with the others yet, reviewers have adopted the modern practice of a more or less uncommitted 'notice' of new publications, and have given up any concern to come to terms with a writer by a close and reasoned examination of his thought.

[2] This may be just one reason why more originality and vitality of thought is often to be found in such writings than in the so-called 'specialist' literature.

[3] That such orthodoxy can also be a danger is shown in K. Rahner, *Gefahren im heutigen Katholizismus* (Einsiedeln 1950). (Also in *Wort und Wahrheit* IV (1949), pp. 881–91.) Once the danger of explicit and theoretically formulated heresy appearing *within* the Church and seeking to spread *within* it has been largely excluded by a very high degree of reflective precision concerning the formal principles of faith and theology, then heresy can appear in just two forms: as 'cryptogamic' heresy, merely lived out existentially and avoiding self-expression in a theoretical reflexive form, and as dead orthodoxy, which may be true to the letter simply because it is fundamentally uninterested in the whole business.

than any other, and without which it does not become truly accessible. Then what we find too little of today would be bound to emerge spontaneously : theological treatises which are not just mechanically repetitive textbooks (adorned with bibliographical data and historical notes); studies in the history of dogma which look backwards so as to go beyond the current position; specialized theological studies which have the courage to make investigations in the many dogmatic fields over which there prevails today more or less the stillness of a building site abandoned while building was still in progress. The three desiderata for the three divisions of theological literature are interconnected. They may be reduced to a single requirement: more dogmatic theology in the handbooks, more dogmatic theology in the historical studies, more dogmatic theology in the special studies over the whole range of dogmatic theology and not just in limited fields. The tentative sketch, following this essay, of a more inclusive treatise of the whole of dogmatic theology is offered as a small contribution to the task described in this critique. Perhaps it may have some significance even if a treatise constructed exactly on its model never comes into being. All this sketch is intended to do (however much laborious reflexion it has involved[1]) is just to show in its own way what we tried to see just now from a different standpoint, namely the abundance of undeveloped themes which awaits the dogmatic theologian.

Only a fully elaborated synthesis could, if at all, establish and justify its plan of construction. Consequently we shall not attempt here to explain and justify this sketch. We shall only make a few preliminary remarks and some brief notes on a few points without any intention of offering a complete commentary.

Every Catholic theology must be a theology of both essence and existence, or putting it simply, it must both look for necessary and intrinsic structures and connexions and it must report what in fact, without metaphysical or logical necessity, took place in saving history. The second requirement needs no explanation. But the first retains its truth in spite of every kind of modern Existentialism. For theology is thinking; and it is quite impossible to think irreducibly atomized facts.

[1] It should be mentioned here that the first draft of this sketch goes back to reflexions upon which the author was engaged together with Hans Urs von Balthasar many years ago. It is no longer possible to distinguish what in it, whether good or bad, is due to him and what to me. I am alone responsible for the published version.

For even what is freely posited has its nature and structure, its connexions, homologies and analogies. Thus in the very midst of the report that this or that took place, it has always to be said what intrinsically it was that took place. And this *what* is never absolutely incommensurate with other things. There are structures which persist even in the most surprising novel event. Otherwise it would be meaningless to speak of a single saving history taking its course according to a comprehensive and eternally abiding divine plan, although one which only slowly discloses itself to us. It is impossible, at every point in the report of the history of salvation, to deal with such common characters of an 'essential' kind in an entirely new way. Here too it becomes a matter of seeing and saying the common precisely as such. And so it is necessary to practise an *abstract* theology of essence, granted always that authentic knowledge of such things is only had when it is read off the facts of saving history. Consequently when we find in dogmatic treatises of a traditional sort what is apparently a 'methodologically impure' mixture of theology of essence (i.e. statements about how things always and everywhere went on and will go on in the history of salvation—those statements, precisely, about what is necessarily the case) and of saving history itself ('narrative', 'Biblical history'), this is no defect but a necessity arising from the very nature of the reality studied by theology. But there is a real inadequacy if no reflexive account is given of these fundamental relationships; and this inadequacy is to be observed in pretty well all dogmatic treatises. The consequence of this is that either the theology of essence or the theology of existence is abbreviated without due inspection. Many fundamental themes remain undeveloped because they are merely 'narrated': so, for instance, Revelation and Time.[1] On the other hand many events are not narrated because concern is directed exclusively to the universally significant in the history of salvation. We have already pointed out above that for the average dogmatic treatise nothing really took place between Adam and Christ which might not very well be left to Bible stories for children. A tractate *De Gratia* is so timeless and anhistorical that everything in it gives the appearance

---

[1] For instance, where are we to find in our treatises a fundamental, compact and closely worked-out dissertation on the questions why, how and in what measure God has spoken to the fathers at various times and in various ways, why nevertheless this does not go on now since the coming of the Son, what follows from this, and so on?

of being universally applicable at any time, even when some brief reference is made to the fact that the just of pre-Christian times possessed the grace of Christ.[1]

This inevitable co-operation and interpenetration of the theologies of essence and existence (theological ontology and historical report) must be realized and appreciated for a better understanding of the way in which the following sketch has set out and distributed its themes.

It is no longer practicable to abandon the division into dogmatic and moral theology which was still unknown to the Middle Ages— fortunately for them, we might feel. The consequences of this division, which may be avoidable but are in fact generally not avoided, are well known. Dogmatic theology tends to become an esoteric doctrine, the significance of which for the achievement of the Christian life is barely adverted to. Moral theology is always in danger of becoming a peculiar mixture of philosophical ethics, natural law, a positivism based on canon law, and casuistry; in such a mixture the *theology* (both positive and speculative) in 'moral theology' is only a distant memory. We have only to look at the usual plan of such a treatise of moral theology in this light, or to examine the Bible for some indication of the contents and mode of treatment proper to a moral theology, in order to realize that the average treatise could do with a little more theology.[2] But that is not our business here. Yet dogmatic theology cannot abdicate its task of declaring the fullness of dogmatic truth to moral theology itself; for this task is no one else's. Moreover dogmatic theology is the older and more venerable discipline; it has the privilege of the first word. If moral theology sets itself up as a theological discipline in its own right, it must come to terms with this right of primogeniture of dogmatic theology, and must itself examine the adequacy of the reasons it

---

[1] This is quite correct. But is the difference between the ways in which grace is given sufficiently described by saying that before Christ the grace of Christ was not given so 'abundantly'? From the point of view of Biblical theology, is this not on the one hand to say too little, if we think of Abraham, Father of the faithful, in Heb 11, etc., and on the other hand too much, if we look at Jn 7:39 and other texts like it? Why is it not possible to have the beatific vision as Christ's grace before Christ, in the same way as it is possible to have Christ's grace before Christ? Where is the question, Grace and Time (History), in the tractate *De Gratia*?

[2] For instance, how much importance is given in current moral theology to Scriptural themes such as the Pauline conception of freedom, the imitation of Christ, charismata, the Beatitudes, being crucified with Christ and so on?

alleges for its own separate existence. In fact dogmatic theology has to this very day regarded as its own many themes which we find also in treatises of moral theology, or which perhaps we should even be tempted to suppose would be found there alone. If there is discussion, and lengthy discussion, of such subjects as 'de virtute Paenitentiae', 'de virtutibus theologicis' or 'de Fide' in a dogmatic treatise, the fundamental claims of dogmatic theology in this direction are clear. But if these claims are *justified*, then to this fundamental right there corresponds a fundamental duty, which may not be evaded by cheap talk about 'practical division of labour' or 'avoiding duplication of labour'. That is to say, then: it is the business of dogmatic theology itself comprehensively and with uniform thoroughness to establish the authentic foundations of the Christian Can, Ought and May: to answer the question, 'What must I do that I may enter into eternal life?' All dogmatic theology can say is that moral theology should concern itself with what, once this answer is presupposed, remains to be done. Suppose there is a science which tries as closely as possible to listen to and understand and, whatever its situation might be, to appropriate what God has said; suppose too that this understanding and appropriating science of Listening is called dogmatic theology; now God's utterance contains *both* the one indissolubly actual Truth (always and in every case—not just facts plus circumambient 'ideals') *and* the Love to be actualized (always and in every case): then it follows that dogmatic theology cannot be made into something morally neutral. But then we must ask with some bewilderment why current dogmatic treatises treat of this or that notably moral topic (quite correctly) and (quite problematically) abandon others to moral theology, where they are treated of in a manner notably—moralistic. If this state of affairs is considered, there will be no difficulty in seeing the justification for inserting a number of themes into this sketch for a dogmatic treatise.

The status of *theologia fundamentalis* as an independent discipline alongside of or prior to dogmatic theology can, or perhaps better *must*, be granted and recognized. Moreover if a dogmatic theology grasps its own nature as something supported by the faith which comprehends and judges all things but is judged by no other court and is beyond the comprehension of reason (in the sense of a superior tribunal), then it is clear that dogmatic theology must develop out of itself and within itself a theology of *theologia fundamentalis*. It must, that is to say, declare as a part of its own proper discourse, the existence, mode and meaning of a rational demonstration of the faith from without and with a view to those without, as possible and necessary. Dogmatic theology does not execute this demonstration; but it autonomously determines the possibility, the sense and the limits of such a demonstration. We call this task of dogmatic theology *fundamental theology*, which is not to be confused with what is currently known as *theologia fundamentalis*. Such a fundamental theology has to consider in like manner both the subjective and the objective aspects of this possibility of a *theologia fundamentalis*.

Where (as is the case in dogmatic theology) a unified and yet incomprehensibly manifold reality has to be expounded, the primary axiom of which is the infinite Incomprehensibility of God, the overlapping of individual themes is unavoidable; and it is impossible to lay down a single logically compelling scheme which is simply the best. There is no need to be frightened of such overlapping: it does no harm for the whole to return in every part. Extremely plain and lucid schemata in dogmatic theology are only purchased in exchange for an impoverishment of points of view. On the other hand it may very well contribute to the elucidation of the plenitude of reality contained in a truth and reality of faith if 'the same thing' is treated of in different places, as though it had apparently been divided up. For instance, one does not really do justice to the central place of the Mass as Sacrifice of the Church and in the Church, to treat of the Eucharist as one of the seven sacraments and take the occasion to speak of it as being a sacrifice too (if possible after it has already been discussed as a sacrament). Thus it can very well be maintained that the general theory of the sacraments should form part of the dogmatic theology of the *Church*,[1] and that the individual sacraments should be treated of according to their appropriate places in the Christian life. Enough of introductory remarks. Some attempt will be made to clarify particular points in the notes.

[1] If this is not done, no genuine principle is available for determining the essential structure common to the sacraments. Consequently the *De Sacramentis in genere* can be regarded only from the point of view of the individual sacraments, and infant baptism becomes in fact the unique model of a sacrament as such. The result of this is that all the sacraments are monotonously discussed according to one and the same pattern, the existential side of the sacrament (with the striking exception of Penance) is given no clear place 'by rights', and the essential differences between the individual sacraments (cf. Denz 848, a text which is hardly ever explored theologically) are obscured.

2

A SCHEME FOR A TREATISE OF DOGMATIC THEOLOGY

---

[1] So far as this is possible in advance (although what is involved is a permanent feature of all we know concretely by faith about God and the world), the point here is to determine the formal nature of that fundamental relationship between God and the world which may serve as standard for the whole of theology in its treatment of particular questions: God as the ever greater God, who is never contained within a formula derived from the world ('Deus semper maior'; cf. Denz 432). To this ever greater God the world is always open, without being able of itself to capture him in this openness; the world, as what has been created by God's free love, and which in spite of its radical finitude and contingency, is no mere negative quantity before God and over against him (so that here a protective wall is to be set up against that danger which always threatens pure ontology, of conceiving finite beings as mere 'limitation' of a pure Being—a view with which a really eternal validity of the world before God is no longer compatible); the basic Christian law that nearness to God and distance from him increase in direct (and not in inverse) proportion, that the means by which God shows forth his divinity among us is the very fact that we are and become.

[2] Following on from A, the point here is to develop the *theological* concept of divine transcendence, which is not simply identical with that of a philosophical doctrine of God. To this there would have to be added a close examination of the concept of a revelation of God which need not be identical

4. God's speech and deed: *verbum efficax*.
5. The 'personal' relationship between God and man arising from God's Call. Revelation as formal prototype of God's supernatural love of grace, in which he discloses himself.

II. Revelation in the world: Revelation as belonging to the world.

1. The Revelation of the Absolute in the finite, conditioned and temporal.
   Revelation in space and time.
   The Activity of Salvation and space-time.
2. The Historicity of Revelation.
   Saving history.
   'Tradition'.
3. Revelation as essential and as existential.
4. The social character of Revelation, 'Church'.
5. The symbolic order.
   a. Sign, word, image, concept, myth, symbol. The nature, possibility and limits of revelation by word. Revelation and mysticism.
      Revelation and gnosis.
   b. Miracle (as 'sign' of the sign).
   c. The sacramental character of God's Word in general.
6. Provisional and definitive Revelation (the history of Revelation). The formal distinction between Old and New Covenants. Definitive Revelation: Revelation as an eschatological value; the two aions.
7. Revelation as *Mysterium*.

III. Revelation in the Bearer of Revelation.

1. The idea of the Prophet.
2. The idea of the Mediator.
3. The idea of enduring Revelation: Church.

---

with the (creation of the) world but which is uttered by God to the world: the examination, that is, of the concept of a revelation which is not the world but takes place in the world, and takes place through the Word. The Word would have to be exhibited as a reality the place of which in the self-disclosure of the transcendent God can be taken by absolutely nothing belonging to the intramundane realm of the created or the creatable.

IV. Revelation in the apprehending subject.

   1. The *power* to hear Revelation: man's constitution as a power to apprehend Revelation.

     a. The power of hearing as nature.[1]

     b. The power of hearing as effect of grace.

   2. Hearing.

     a. Hearing as apprehension of inner and outer Word (corresponding to God's speech and deed in Revelation). Appropriation of the tidings: Faith.

     b. The formal relationship between nature and grace, reason and faith (the meaning and limits of Apologetics).

     c. The historical, social and symbolic order, in the ever new and changing subject who apprehends (development of dogma).

     d. The freedom to hear or not to hear, and the possibility of rebellion: the supernatural in itself as a cross of nature.

   3. Stages of hearing. Faith—gnosis.

C. *The Idea of a Redemptive Revelation*

Transposition of the formal Revelation relationship to a new mode, the order of sin and redemption.

I. Redemptive Revelation as proceeding from God.

   1. Modification of the 'content' of Revelation.

     a. The Revelation of Wrath and Judgment, and hence of man's situation as one lost.

     b. The Revelation of atoning grace.

   2. Modification of the mode in which Revelation is manifested.

     a. Revelation as 'Law'; as 'scandal'; as 'Judgment'.

     b. Revelation as kenosis and extinction: *theologia crucis.*

II. The form of the Mediator as Redeemer.

III. The hearer of Revelation as a sinner in need of redemption.

   1. Sinfulness as unwillingness to hear Revelation.

   2. The transformation of the sinner into a hearer: the grace of faith as submission and obedience.

---

[1] Cf. K. Rahner, *Hörer des Wortes* (Munich 1941). ('Hören' means both *to hear* and *to listen to.*–Tr.)

3. The qualification of the historical, social and symbolic orders, and of the two aions.

D. *The Idea of Theology as Science*

I. 'Theology'; Revelation, Proclamation, Faith and Theology.

II. Theology as grace.

III. Theology as rational system.

IV. Theology and revealed 'sources' (Scripture—Tradition).

V. Theology and the magisterium.

VI. Theologia viatoris—theologia peccatoris—theologia crucis *in rational theology.*

VII. Theology and theologies.
  The typology of theologies.
  The theological meaning of the history of theology.

VIII. Dogmatic theology in the narrower sense as a discipline within theology.

Part Two: Fundamental Theology

(Revelation *within* a concrete civilization, already in existence)
The Differentiation of Roman Catholic Christianity from other forms of religion

A. *Phenomenology of religion in general*

Nature, existence, justification.

Theology—Philosophy of religion—History of religion—Phenomenology of religion—Psychology of religion.

B. *'Religion' and the individual's approach to it*
Principles by which the true religion may be distinguished

The general question of truth in matters of religion.
The possibility of a decision.
The obligation of a decision, of profession, etc.
Existential criteria of decision.

C. *Phenomenology of non-Christian religions*

I. Phenomenology of religious forms.

II. The Meaning of religious forms and of the history of religions from the point of view of the theology of history.
The Theology of the history of religions.

III. Christianity as the total religion.

D. *Phenomenology of Christianity*

I. Human religion from below and Christianity as a religion instituted by revelation.
The claim to absoluteness.
Syncretism and complexio oppositorum.

II. Christ the Founder (legatus divinus *as a concept of Apologetics*).

III. The Church. Notes of the true Church in the world.

E. *Phenomenology of Christian heresies*

I. The philosophical and theological theory of heresy.
  1. The possibility of error.
  2. Heresy in the Church.
      a. As yet undifferentiated: tendencies of schools. Faith and gnosis, etc.
      b. In the precise sense: secret heresy.
  3. Heresy as splitting off from the Church.
      Heresy and truth in faith.
      Heresy and unity in love.

II. Heresies as opinions and as churches, in the light of the theology of history.

F. *Phenomenology of Roman Catholic Christianity*

G. *The theory of the individual's approach to the true religion*

I. The possibility and limits of such a theory (in the graced mode of existence proper to faith).

II. Interior grace and external criteria in the recognition of the duty of faith.

III. Naive and scientific proofs. The meaning of scientific apologetics for the individual believer or pagan.

DIVISION TWO: SPECIAL DOGMATIC THEOLOGY

Part One: Man (and his world) as a nature with a supernatural finality [1]

A. *Creatureliness as such* [2]

I. Createdness (Creation and conservation).

II. The freedom of God's creative act.

III. The temporal mode of created being.

IV. The finitude of created being. The finite creature as a positive quantity.

V. God's transcendence and omnipotence as regards all created being.

VI. The formal doctrine of the ends of creation and of created being.

VII. The unity and interconnectedness of all created being. [3]

B. *Man as a unity (of 'nature' and 'supernature')*

I. The single concrete end; supernaturality as the ultimate form *of man in the concrete.*

　　1. The concrete end and the obligation it imposes.

　　2. The supernaturality of this end.

[1] It is impossible to speak here either of man alone, or with such generality of created being in general that man is not the end in view. It is the single reality of all created being that is meant, but in such a way that we have to see it from the point of view of humanity; and this precisely in the sense that this reality is prior to the order of sin and redemption, and furthermore persists in that order (though admittedly transposed into a different key).

[2] 'Creatureliness' is not here a characterization of Nature in so far as this is distinguished from Grace and the supernatural finality of all created being; it is a fundamental property of all reality other than God, prior to the distinction between Nature and Grace: indeed it achieves its fullest realization in the order of supernatural grace, because 'creatureliness' is not a merely negative expression.

[3] It is not just the unity of the material cosmos, of humanity, etc., that is meant here, but a unity to which the angels belong too. It would be really worthwhile to attempt to state in properly ontological terms how far the angels, in spite of their 'pure' intellectuality, belong to the world by their very nature, contrary to certain neo-Platonic tendencies in theology.

II. 'Nature' as 'remainder' and genuine, but still formal, 'possibility'.[1]

The diversity and interconnectedness of statements about these two aspects of 'nature'.

C. *'Nature'*

I. The possibility of a theology of nature

1. In terms of an immediate revelation of 'natural' truths.
2. In terms of a 'preservation' and 'interpretation' by revelation and the magisterium of truths known naturally. The possibility of a 'neutral' theological anthropology.

II. Nature: Man.

1. The inner dimensions of man.
   a. Man as person.
      (i) The immediacy to God of man as person (individualism; creationism).
      (ii) Intellectuality and freedom.
      (iii) Logic and ethics.
   b. Man as 'nature' (a bodily, spatio-temporal person).
      (i) Spiritual personality as belonging to nature.
      (ii) The theology of the corporeality of the human person.
      (iii) The theology of the duality of the sexes.
      (iv) The theology of the states and events of human life.
      Birth.
      Age.
      Eating and drinking.
      Work.
      Seeing, hearing, etc. Speech, silence, laughter, tears.
      The arts (music, dance, etc.)
      The basic achievements of the intellectual life.
      Civilization.
      Death (as a natural phenomenon).
      The natural 'other-world'.[2]

---

[1] See pp. 297–317, below.

[2] We are thinking here of a theology of man's ontological condition, in so far as he loses his bodily place in the world of space and time when he dies, and yet belongs to the world; he is not simply withdrawn from the world and its conditions, but continues to belong to it in reciprocal action and reaction, all this without prejudice to the question whether his final

2. The outer dimensions: the world.
   a. The human realm.
      (i) The theology of marriage and of the family.
      (ii) The theology of race and of the state, and of the plurality of races.
      (iii) The theology of humanity.
         The unity of the human race (Adam as a natural reality).
         The purposive unity of human history: the formal theology of history.
   b. The realm below man: the theology of Nature.
      (i) The theology of physics and biology: the overt manifestations of Nature.
      (ii) Nature as symbol.
      (iii) Magic and taboo (Nature and the spirit world).
         Spiritualism, etc., sorcery.
   c. The realm above man.
      (i) The existence and nature of the angelic world.
      (ii) The angelic world and the human world (as a natural unity).
3. Nature: Man and God.
   a. God as knowable from the world and man.
   b. The theology of the ('natural') Creator-God.
      (i) The formal doctrine of God (his 'necessary' attributes).
      (ii) The material-existential doctrine of God: his free countenance to the world.
         Wrath; love; the alternation of the two; his general purpose of salvation, etc.
   c. God and man.
      (i) God over man: his omnipotence; providence; predestination.
      (ii) Man under God: religion.
         Freedom and God's omnipotence.

---

condition as an individual person is blessedness or damnation. This would also be the place to clarify such questions as the ontological presuppositions for the possibility of Purgatory, of the 'poena sensus', and the significance of general eschatology for the individual in spite of the individual judgment.

D. *The Supernatural dimension of human reality*

I. The God of the order of supernatural life and revelation.

1. The three Persons of the Godhead as an economy.
   Three different modes of relatedness of the graced man to God.
   a. Spirit.
   b. Son.
   c. Father.
2. The three Persons in God as immanently constituting the absoluteness of the supernatural world.
   a. The three Persons:
      (i) Father.
      (ii) Son.
      (iii) Spirit.
   b. The formal doctrine of the Trinity.

II. Participation in the Trinitarian life of God.

1. Supernatural sanctification (*de gratia habituali*)
   a. *Gratia increata:* participation in God.
   b. Created habitual grace.
   c. Grace as original state.
      (i) The grace of the angels and the grace of Paradise.
      (ii) The *dona praeternaturalia* as consequences of the grace of Paradise.
          'Paradise.'
      (iii) The supernatural unity in Adam of the human race, in itself and with the angels.
2. The active accomplishment of supernatural sanctification.
   a. The life of the human spirit and supernatural grace in general: The necessity, nature and formal object of 'actual' grace; how far we may be aware of it.
   b. Logic and supernatural grace: faith.
   c. Ethics and supernatural grace:
      Hope and Love.
      The supernatural moral virtues.
   d. Growth in grace (merit), stages in the development of moral life.

    c. The basic specifications of the spiritual life: *vita activa* and *vita contemplativa*.

    d. God's supralapsarian economy of Grace.

III. The Mediator: the God-man.[1]

  1. The theology of the God-man.

    a. The God-man. *Unio hypostatica; communicatio idiomatum*, etc.

    b. The consequences of the hypostatic union for Christ's human nature.

    c. Christ's 'offices'.

    d. The general significance of the hypostatic union in its onto-logical-metaphysical and ethical aspects.

  2. The participation of humanity in the Mediator.

    a. Mary's divine Motherhood. Mary as the representative of humanity.

    The fundamental principle of Mariology.[2]

    b. The supernatural unity of humanity in Christ (the mystical Body of Christ in its universality).

[1] No difficulty will be found in granting that our scheme for inserting the doctrine of the Trinity into a theology of the sanctification of man need do no injury to the intrinsic value of the former topic, if it is remembered that the interior life of the Blessed Trinity is revealed to us just because and in so far as our redemption and sanctification have been revealed to us. It will readily be admitted that it is only by drawing into close connexion the doctrines of grace and the Trinity that the empty formalism of the average modern teaching on the Trinity can be overcome. More problematic (it must be admitted) is the suggested treatment of Christology under the head of theological anthropology. But it must be remembered that Christology is taken up again from the point of view of the Redemption. Christology more easily avoids the appearance, otherwise not easily avoidable, of the mythological and the miraculous, when the Incarnation of the Logos (granting its uniqueness and gratuitousness, and its imprevisibility from this world) is seen as the supreme realization of that fundamental relationship which prevails between God and the spiritual creation in general. In this context Christ's Person and Office are more clearly seen in their unity. And finally a viewpoint 'quoad nos', of an anthropological kind, need not conceal the structures of reality 'in se', of a different kind; rather it can release them more fully than a treatment which proceeds from the first in the most objectivistic way possible. See pp. 149–200, below.

[2] Cf. K. Rahner, 'Le Principe fondamentale de la théologie mariale', RSR XLII (1954), pp. 481–522.—Tr.

c. The unity of all creation in Christ.
    (i) Christ and the world below man.
    (ii) Christ and the angels.

Part Two: Fall and Redemption

A. *Sin*

I. The nature of Sin.

II. The fall of the angels.

  1. In itself.
    a. The fact. Its nature.
    b. Eternal reprobation.
  2. The cosmic and anthropological consequences of the fall of the angels: *potestas diaboli*; the demonization of Nature (idolatry).

III. Original culpability.

  1. The Fall.
  2. Original Sin. The kingdom of sin. Sin and death.

IV. The sins of men.

  1. The possibility and the fact of personal sins.
  2. The state of sin.
  3. Social sins other than the sin of the human race.

B. *God and Sin*

I. The Wrath of God.

II. Reprobation and hell.

III. Sin as something positive before (and through) God alone ('felix culpa').

IV. God's saving purpose after the Fall.

  1. His general saving purpose.
  2. His differential saving purpose.
    (Sufficient and efficacious grace after the Fall, predestination.)

C. *The Redeemer*

I. The theology of the history of humanity up to the time of the Redeemer.

1. Primitive revelation and the revealed content of the world religions.
2. From Adam to Abraham. The 'natural law'; paganism.
3. The theology of the nature and history of the Old Covenant. Salvation under the Law.
4. The fullness of time.

II. The Incarnation as redemption ('physical' redemption).

1. As establishing the reconciling Mediator.
2. As *assumptio carnis peccati*, the acceptance in principle of death and the consecration of humanity.

III. The theology of the human life of Our Lord.

1. The general theology of the life of Jesus.
   a. The events of Jesus' life as 'model'.
   b. The events of Jesus' life as 'mysteries'.
2. The theology of individual events in the life of Jesus.

IV. The theology of the Cross.

1. The Cross as Jesus' reality in his own eyes: the Way of kenosis and of glory (Christ's merit for himself).
2. The Cross as vicarious sacrifice and expiation for humanity (the Cross as merit for others).
3. The descent into hell.

V. The theology of the glorified Lord.

D. *The Church of Christ*

I. Christ and the Church.

1. The Church and Christ as incarnate Logos.
   The Church and consecrated humanity.
   Christ as the Head who dispenses grace (*gratia capitis*; the sanctifying function of Christ's humanity).
2. The Church and Christ as *legatus divinus*.
   The Church as Christ's foundation.
   The Church as Christ's authority (speaking).
   The Church as Christ's obedience (hearing).

3. The relation between the two.
4. The extent of the Church's realm.

II. *The basic structure of the Church: the total sacrament of Christ. The effectual visibility of her life, her truth and her grace.*

III. *The sacramentality of the Church in her essential offices (the shape of the Church).*

1. The presence of Christ's truth.
   a. Tradition: as conservation of truth;
      as ever new effective presence of Revelation;
      as history and development of Revelation.
   b. The teaching office as authoritative articulation of Tradition (bearers, sources, report, extent of the teaching office, infallibility, limits, etc.).
   c. The Scriptures.
      (i) as Word of God; inspiration.[1]
      (ii) as the Book of the Church (the Scriptures in the Church and over the Church).
      (iii) as ever new truth (typical, spiritual sense, etc.).
2. The presence of Christ's will: jurisdiction and law.
   a. The existence of divine law in the Church, and the bearers of this law.
   b. *Ius humanum* in the Church's law.
   c. The formal character peculiar to the New Testament law of the Church as opposed to secular and Old Testament law.
3. The presence of Christ's grace in the Church.
   a. The Church as total sacrament.
      Membership of the Church as 'res et sacramentum' of grace and salvation.
   b. The Mass as central *mysterium* of the Church, in which she realizes herself totally towards God, Christ and her members.
      (i) The Mass as Christ's effective presence in the Church.
      (ii) The Mass as sacrifice.
      (iii) The Mass as realization of the Church.
   c. The articulation of the *mysterium* of the Church in individual sacraments (*de sacramentis in genere*).

[1] Cf. K. Rahner, 'Über die Schriftinspiration', ZKT LXXVIII (1956), pp. 137–68.—Tr.

Their mode of efficacy (*opus operatum*).
Ministers of the sacraments.
Opus operatum and *opus operantis*.
The sacraments and Christ.
The sacraments and the Church. 'Character sacramentalis'.
The sacraments as signs of Him that cometh.
   d. The sanctification of the whole sphere of the profane through the Church.

IV. The inner shape of the Church.

1. The relation between 'exterior ' and 'interior' hierarchy.
2. Christ as Head ('firstborn among many brethren') of the interior Church.
3. Mary as perfection of the Church.
   a. The Immaculate Conception; freedom from sin.
   b. Co-patient and co-agent in our Redemption.
   c. Assumed into heaven.
   d. Mediatrix of all graces.
4. The Biblical fathers of the Church:
   Patriarchs and prophets (the 'sages' of old).
   The Baptist.
   The Apostles, Joseph.
5. States of life in the Church in general.
6. Gnostics and charismatics.
7. The saints and the veneration of saints.
8. The extra-sacramental life of grace as a life of the Church ('spiritual reception' of the Sacraments).

V. The Church of sinners[1]*: the erring Church.*
                                the sinful Church.

VI. Historical theology of the Church.

1. The ontology and gnoseology needed for a theological consideration of the history of the Church.
   Sources: prophecy, experience. Subject, etc.
2. The formal theology of history.

[1] Cf. K. Rahner, *Die Kirche der Sünder* (Freiburg 1948); Flemish translation *Kerk der Zondaren* (ingeleid door F. Fransen, Antwerp 1952). In this Flemish edition a more precise account is given of what is meant, and with what restrictions, by the phrase 'erring Church'.

a. The possibility of *theologically* assigning the Church's history into periods.
b. Historical forces in the history of the Church.
c. The eschatological achievement of the Church's history.
d. The 'growth' and 'development' of the Church (extensively and intensively).
e. The 'decrease' of the Church (intensively and extensively).
f. Concepts such as 'Renaissance', 'Reformations', 'Persecution'.
3. The material theology of the Church's history.
a. The Church *ex Iudaeis*. The annulment and persistence of the Old Covenant.
b. The Church of the Gentiles.
c. The Church in the Roman Empire.
d. The World Church.
e. The Church of the last days, Antichrist, etc.
f. The 'Church' of eternity.
   (i) The Church and the definitive establishment of the kingdom of God.
   (ii) The suffering and the triumphant Church.

E. *The Theological Anthropology of the Redeemed*

. *The general nature of Christian morality.*
1. The basic norm (*norma honestatis supernaturalis* [*hominis lapsi et reparati*]).
2. Law and freedom.
3. Conscience and guidance by the Holy Spirit.

I. Dying with Christ.
1. The interior process of justification.
   The precise character of penitential conversion (and consequently of life after it) in contrast to the 'ideal' virtues of 'pure' supernature.
   a. The faith (of 'unbelievers' and 'sinners').
   b. Metanoia; dying.
   c. Love.
   d. The graciousness and gratuitousness of 'vocation'.
2. Baptism as the sacramental visibility of this process.

3. Life dying (mortified, hidden) with Christ as form of the Christian life (*vita contemplativa* as a Christian category).
   a. As a form of life common to all Christians.
      The nature of *Christian* asceticism[1] (the Sermon on the Mount, following in the footsteps of the Crucified, etc.).
   b. As monasticism: the representation of Christian life in monnsticism; the evangelical counsels.
   c. As mysticism considered as a form of asceticism.[2]
   d. As martyrdom as a quasi-sacramental visibility of the Christian form of life.
   e. Christian 'asceticism' in the face of the great secular complexes (State, civilization, etc.).

III. Living out of Christ (vita activa; *divine life as manifest in human life*).

Mission into the world by the Spirit who becomes manifest in Christians.
1. The general mission.
   a. Apostolate (witness, etc.) as a basic Christian attitude.
   b. Confirmation as the sacramental visibility of mission.
   c. Martyrdom as witness which overcomes the world.
2. Individual vocation.
   a. Charisms in general; professions; choice of a profession.
   b. The free charisms.
   c. Marriage. The widow.
   d. Ordination and the priesthood.

---

[1] Cf. e.g. K. Rahner, 'Passion und Aszese', *Geist und Leben* XXII (1949), pp. 15–36; 'Zur Theologie der evangelischen Räte', *Orientierung* XVII (1953), pp. 252–5 (see also vol. III of these studies).

[2] This would be the place to inquire into the nature of mysticism, in so far as it is not just a psychological phenomenon but something specifically Christian. If asceticism is conceived not as a moral drill, but as participation in our Lord's Passion and Death (and as their practice), it follows as a further consequence that mysticism is a renunciatory asceticism in faith practised by the spiritual person: not an anticipation of the beatific vision but an entry into the Passion of the Lord (through 'passive purification of the spirit', through the 'night' of the senses and of the spirit). Thus it follows that mysticism is to be conceived in terms of asceticism and not vice versa, assuming that something generally Christian is understood by both concepts.

3. The ultimate relation between *vita activa* and *vita contemplativa*.
4. The idea of Christian perfection.

V. The central sacrament of the Christian life: the Eucharist as the sacramental connexion between II and III.

  1. Continuing participation in Christ's death.
  2. Life in the Church.
  3. *Communio mundi*; the transformation of the world.
  4. 'Spiritual' communion.
  5. 'Eucharistic piety'.

V. The Christian's struggle with sin.

  1. The Christian's sinfulness.
    a. Concupiscence.
    b. Temptation by the world and the devil.
    c. 'Venial' sin.
  2. The consciousness of sin.
  3. The possibility of the loss of grace.
    a. The grave sins of the Christian.
    b. Unbelief.
  4. The possibility of the repeated remission of sins.
  5. The struggle with sin.
    a. The personal acts of the Christian (penance, contrition, attrition, etc., metanoia as an habitual attitude, prayer for perseverance).
    b. The necessity of remedial grace for the justified.
    c. The sacramentality of ecclesiastical penance.
    d. Indulgences.
  6. Concern for salvation in general.
    a. Hope and trust.
    b. The hiddenness of salvation.
    c. The grace of perseverance.

VI. The theology of death.[1]
  1. The supernatural dimensions of death.

    a. The supernatural character of death in general in the present dispensation.

---

[1] Death must first of all be seen as something which takes place in this Christian world here and now, as a part of the Christian life. However much

   b. Death as punishment. First and second death and their
      relationship.
   c. Death as dying with Christ and redemption.
   d. Death as supernatural consummation and as supernatural
      separation from this world.
2. The sacramentality of dying: extreme unction.
3. Individual death as the beginning of the Last Things, as judgment.
   a. The possibility of eternal reprobation.
   b. Hell as private destiny.[1]
   c. The definitive character of union with God.

F. *Eschatology*

*I. The theological gnoseology of eschatological statements considered in
their possibility and their limits.*[2]

II. The Eschata.
   1. The new Aion as a whole.
      a. The transformation of time.
      b. The transformation of matter.
      c. The consummation of the spirit.
      d. The consummation of the new aion.
   2. The relation between individual eschatology and collective
      eschatology.

---

it may be the end of the whole of life, it is also an inner reality *within* the
whole; so that our whole life through we are dying into our death. Death
must not be left out of account by immediately looking forward to what
properly comes *after* it. For some reflexions on the whole theme of Christian
death, see K. Rahner, 'Zur Theologie des Todes', *Synopsis*, no. 3 (Hamburg
1949), pp. 87–112. (See also by the same author 'Zur Theologie des Todes',
ZKT LXXIX (1957), pp. 1–44. Also printed separately.—Tr.)

[1] 'Private' in a twofold sense, as applying to the destiny of the individual,
and as applying to the destiny of this individual, condemned to a loveless
isolation by his own fault. 'Individual' eschatology is intentionally introduced here, before Eschatology, so as to make it clear in this way too that
Eschatology is fundamentally 'general' eschatology and thus that something
essential remains to be said over and above 'special' eschatology.

[2] It would be necessary here to discuss the question whether these limits
are the same for 'Heaven' and for 'Hell', or whether (what would be more
correct) we are bound in certain respects to deny this. This would then have
to be kept in mind when in what follows the two final states are treated of
in succession as though they were on the same level.

3. The relation between the present and the future aion.
4. The individual elements of Eschatology.
   a. The Return of Christ.
   b. The Resurrection of the body.
   c. The general Judgment.
   d. Hell as the collective destiny of the 'Corpus diaboli'.
   e. Heaven as the eternal kingdom of God the Father.

3

THE DEVELOPMENT OF DOGMA

Many of the Church's doctrines are characterized by the fact that they have not always been present in the Church and in her consciousness in faith in an expressly apprehensible form. The bodily Assumption of our Lady into Heaven is an example of this which touches us especially closely today. This doctrine has not always been in existence as an explicit statement; at any rate we today cannot grasp it or point to it as something in the past with a persistent identity; it seems not to have been proposed to the faith of every age with the clarity, the precision, the definiteness and the binding character which it has today. That is to say it has—in a certain sense— 'developed', it has, in a sense still to be determined, 'come to be' within the course of Christian history, for when the Gospel was first preached this doctrine was not to be found in its present form.

But if we are to gain a true understanding of this doctrine (and all those others which are characterized by such a 'development'), we are forced to make some fundamental reflexions on the meaning, the possibility and the limits of such a 'development of dogma' in general.[1] Of course this is a heavy undertaking, because whatever the

---

[1] We cannot do more here than offer a few summary indications. Without writing a whole book on the subject it is clearly out of the question to consider the history of the doctrine of development, or to take up positions with regard to the particular theories defended by theologians today. Consequently we cite only a selection of the relevant literature (omitting purely historical studies), above all the more important works or those which treat the subject with special reference to the new dogma. General works: J. H. Newman, *An Essay on the Development of Christian Doctrine*, 1845 and (notably revised by Newman) 1878; J. B. Franzelin, *De divina Traditione et Scriptura*[4], Rome 1896; J. Bainvel, 'Histoire d'un dogme', *Etudes* CI (1904), pp. 612–32; Ch. Pesch, *Glaube, Dogmen und historische Tatsachen* (*Theologische Zeitfragen* IV), Freiburg 1908; A. Gardeil, *Le Donné Revélé et la théologie*[2], Paris 1910; A. Rademacher, *Der Entwicklungsgedanke in Religion und Dogma*, Cologne 1914; M. Tuyaerts, *L'Evolution du dogme*,

Lyons 1919; R. M. Schultes, *Introductio in historiam dogmatum*, Paris 192. (with a valuable bibliography, pp. 149–52); F. Marin-Sola, *L'Evolutio homogène du dogme catholique* I and II², Fribourg 1924; H. Dieckmann, *D. Ecclesia* II, Freiburg 1925; L. de Grandmaison, *Le Dogme chrétien*, Pari 1928; H. Pinard, art. 'Dogme', DAFC I, 1122–84; E. Dublanchy, art 'Dogme', DTC IV, 1574–650; L. Charlier, *Essai sur le problème théologiqu* Thuilles 1938 (on the Index); Fidel García Martínez, 'A proposito de l₂ Llamada "fe ecclesiastica": ¿Debe ser admitida en teologia?', *Miscelane(Comillas* VI (Santander 1946), pp. 9–45; J. Hocedez, *Histoire de la théologi au XIXe siècle* III, Brussels 1947, pp. 161–72; H. de Lubac, 'Le Problèm(du développement du dogme', RSR XXXV (1948), pp. 130–60; E. Seite rich, 'Das kirchliche Verständnis der Dogmenentwicklung', *Oberrhein Pastoralblatt* (1952), pp. 225–31, 255–63; E. Dhanis, 'Révélation explicit(et implicite', *Gregorianum* XXXIV (1953), pp. 187–237 (further reference p. 226 s.). See also *Lo sviluppo del dogma secondo la dottrina cattolica. Rela ʒioni lette nella seconda settimana teologica 24–28 settembre 1951*, Rome 1953 We cannot here go into the studies by Flick, Spiazzi, Rambaldi, Bea, Balic Filograssi, Dhanis and Boyer assembled there, as this essay was already complete when they appeared.

Works with special reference to the dogma of the Assumption (th(general question is often only touched on here): L. Carli, 'La definibilit; dommatica dell'Assunzione di Maria', *Marianum* VIII (1945), pp. 59–77 C. Balic, *De definibilitate Assumptionis B.V.M. in coelum*, Rome 194 (=*Antonianum* XXI (1946), pp. 3–67); E. Sauras, 'Definibilidad de l; Asunción de la Santissima Virgen', *Estudios Marianos* VI (1947), pp. 23– 44; C. Colombo, 'La definibilità dommatica dell'Assunzione di Maria SS nella teologia recente', *La Scuola Cattolica* LXXV (1947), pp. 265–81 LXXVI (1948), pp. 1–16; J. Ternus, *Der gegenwärtige Stand der Assumpta frage*, Regensburg 1948; G. M. Paris, 'De definibilitate dogmatica assump tionis corporeae B.M.V. in coelum', *Divus Thomas* (Plac) LI (1948), pp 354–5; G. Philips, 'Autour de la définibilité d'un dogme', *Marianum >* (1948), pp. 81–111; R. Garrigou-Lagrange, 'L'Assomption est-elle formelle ment révélée de façon implicite?', *Doctor Communis* (*Acta Pont. Acad. Rom S. Thomae*) I (1948), pp. 28–63; C. Dillenschneider, 'L'Assomption cor porelle de Marie', *Etudes Mariales* VI (1948), pp. 13–55 (further reference given); J. Filograssi, 'Traditio divino-apostolica et Assumptio B.M.V.' *Gregorianum* XXX (1949), pp. 481–9; C. Balic, 'De Assumptione B.V Mariae quatenus in deposito fidei continetur', *Antonianum* XXIV (1949) pp. 153–82; C. Koser, 'Cualificación teológica de la Asunción', *Actas de Congresso Asuncionistico Franciscano de America Latina* (Buenos Aires 1949) pp. 329–53; H. Rondet, 'La Définibilité de l'Assomption. Questions d(methode', *Etudes Mariales* VI (1949), pp. 59–95; J. Filograssi, 'Theologi; catholica et Assumptio B.M.V.', *Gregorianum* XXXI (1950), pp. 323–60 J. F. Bonnefoy, 'L'Assomption de la T. S. Vierge est-elle définissable comm(révélée "formaliter implicite"?', *Marianum* XII (1950), pp. 194–226; J Filograssi, 'Constitutio Apostolica "Munificentissimus Deus" de Assump tione B.M.V.', *Gregorianum* XXXI (1950), pp. 483–525; B. Capelle general meaning, possibility and limits of a development of dogma may be, they cannot be deduced with the necessary exactness and precision from general theological considerations alone but must be arrived at inductively from the actual facts of such a development. In itself this is not remarkable: we discover the possible from the real. We discover the laws of development of a living thing—and of something spiritually alive too, regarded as a process of spiritual unfolding—from its actual development. But in our case this has its special difficulties; for the living spirit with which we are concerned here appears in its authentic form in a solitary instance: the unique historical fortune of the Gospel of Christ under the direction of that Spirit which leads us into all truth, from the time of Christ himself to the moment when by his return faith will be transformed into the vision of God, face to face. We have here a homogeneous process of which there is just one instance. Certainly it has its laws, with which it emerged from the very beginning; it takes place according to laws promulgated at the very beginning, by which it remains bound for ever and ever and which are in force throughout the whole course of a history that has been guaranteed by the Spirit. Moreover laws certainly exist which may be observed in a section of this total process, and which can then be applied to other (later) phases and partial developments. The *perfected* law of dogmatic development however may only be laid down when the whole unique process has reached its term. And because it is a genuinely historical process, under the impulse of the Spirit of God, who never makes himself accessible without remainder to laws which can be grasped by human minds, it is never just the working out of a formula and an all-embracing law.

'Théologie de l'Assomption d'après la bulle "Munificentissimus Deus"', NRT LXXXII (1950), pp. 1009–27; M. Labourdette and M.-J. Nicolas, 'La définition de l'Assomption', RT L (1950); C. Colombo, 'La Constituzione dommatica "Munificentissimus Deus" e la Teologia', *La Scuola Cattolica* LXXIX (1951); J. Ternus, 'Theologische Erwägungen zur Bulle "Munificentissimus Deus"', *Scholastik* XXVI (1951), pp. 11–35; A. Kolping, 'Zur theologischen Erkenntnismethode anlässlich der Definition der leiblichen Aufnahme Mariens in den Himmel', *Divus Thomas* (Fribourg) XXIX (1951), pp. 81–105. Further literature in: *Marianum* XII (1950) Supplementum, nn. 396–434 (pp. 37–9); C. Balic, *Testimonia de Assumptione B.V.M.* Pars Altera. Rome 1950, pp. 442–5; E. Dhanis, *loc. cit.*, pp. 226 s.

It is manifestly erroneous *a priori* to attempt to construct an adequate formula of this kind, and by this means to master the single sense of this process and combat possible 'deviations' as false developments. The historical course of the development of dogma is itself the process in which its own mystery is progressively unveiled. It is in the very act of developing, and not in any prior reflexion, that the living reality of the Church's consciousness in faith comes progressively into a fuller possession of itself. Let us suppose that in the development of the doctrine of the Assumption, for example, forms and properties of the development of dogma become apparent which cannot be demonstrated with the same clarity in other phases and sectors of this development; these properties may even clearly be of a kind which do not harmonize with the accounts of development given in the ordinary theological treatment (not of course in the authoritative pronouncements of the Church). Yet this would not indicate any false development here, a 'rank growth' in the development of doctrine; at most it would be a sign that the scheme proposed in the average treatment requires to be improved, qualified or enlarged.

An anxious theologian may enquire, 'How are we to get anywhere, if no adequate laws of this development can be formulated? Are we not leaving the field open to the rankest proliferations of pseudo-theological speculation and callow visionary enthusiasm?' The answer is that this danger, one which is involved in all human experience, is not going to be realized for three reasons. In the first place there are of course certain laws of dogmatic development which, because they are known *a priori* (we shall discuss this later), may be applied to 'developments' in an obvious way—though certainly with prudence —in order to determine whether they are genuine developments of the faith of the Church or on the other hand contain the danger of a wrong turning. Such laws do exist, even if they can be applied only in the Church and in the last resort only *by* the Church herself; for applications made by individual Christians and theologians are never more than appeals to the Church herself, who consequently has to be recognized as the court of last appeal. Secondly, just as with all living things, every advance achieved in this world of the finite, of shadows and images, always has something final about it and inevitably marks a restriction of future possibilities. The fuller and clearer truth becomes, the more strict it becomes, and more thoroughly excludes possibilities of future error. Looked at from this point of view, progress in the development of dogmas must in a certain respect become progressively slower, which is not to say that it must come to a standstill. Thirdly, and this is the decisive point, the danger of the human factor simply remains a danger, and no precautionary measures exist which can exclude it unambiguously at the very start. Any attempt to protect oneself by human sharpsightedness against such a danger, so that it is simply not *possible* for anything to 'slip through', is itself radically false. It is the promise of the Spirit and that alone which prevents the final realization of an ever-present danger.

After these preliminary remarks we have now to consider a few essential features of a Catholic doctrinal development. From what has been said it will be clear why it is impossible to propose an interpretation *merely* in terms of a universally applicable formula or indeed one which is authoritatively taught by the Church. The general theory of the development of dogma is still in a rudimentary stage, because the history from which it must in large part be derived is not nearly sufficiently investigated for the purpose. All the same a few principles may be set down.

In the first place it is obvious that a revealed truth remains what it is, remains precisely 'true', i.e. it corresponds to reality and is always binding. What the Church has once taken possession of as a portion of the Revelation which has fallen to her share, as the object of her unconditional faith, is from then on her permanently valid possession. No doctrinal development could be merely the reflexion of a general history of humanity, a history of civilizations containing nothing but the objectivization of the everchanging sentiments, opinions and attitudes of a continual succession of historical epochs. Such an historical relativism is simply false, metaphysically and still more theologically. Yet all human statements, even those in which faith expresses God's saving truths, are finite. By this we mean that they never declare the *whole* of a reality. In the last resort every reality, even the most limited, is connected with and related to every other reality. The most wretched little physical process isolated in a carefully contrived experiment can only be described adequately if the investigator possesses the one comprehensive and exhaustive formula for the whole cosmos. But he does not possess such a formula; he could have it if and only if he could place himself in his own physical reality at a point which lay absolutely outside the cosmos—which is impossible. This is even more true of spiritual and divine realities. The statements which we make about them, relying on the Word of God which itself became 'flesh' in human words, can never express them once and for all in an entirely adequate form. But they are not for this reason false. They are an 'adaequatio intellectus et rei', in so far as they state absolutely nothing which is false. Anyone who wants to call them 'half false' because they do not state everything about the whole truth of the matter in question, would eventually abolish the distinction between truth and falsehood. On the other hand, anyone who proposes to regard these propositions of faith, because they are wholly true, as in themselves *adequate* to the matter in question, i.e. as exhaustive statements, would be falsely elevating human truth to God's simple and exhaustive knowledge of himself and of all that takes its origin from him. Just because they are true, an infinite qualitative difference separates them, in spite of their finitude, from false propositions, however hard it may (even often) be in individual cases accurately to determine in the concrete where the boundary lies between an inadequate and a false statement. But because our statements about the infinite divine realities are finite and hence in this sense inadequate—that is, while actually corresponding to reality, yet not simply congruent with it—so every formula in which the faith is expressed can in principle be surpassed while still retaining its truth. That is to say, in principle at least it can be replaced by another which states the same thing, and what is more states it not only without excluding more extensive, more delicately nuanced prospects, but positively opening them up: prospects on to facts, realities, truths, which had not been seen explicitly in the earlier formulation and which make it possible to see the same reality from a new point of view, in a fresh perspective.

Now this evolution within the same truth is not, at any rate not necessarily, the play of empty curiosity; it can have an essential significance for man and his salvation. The human mind is not like a photographic plate, which without preference or alteration simply registers anything which falls upon it at a particular isolated moment. Rather, in order simply to understand what he sees or hears, a human being must react, take up a stand, bring the new experience into connexion with what he already knows or has been affected by or dealt with, the whole historical sum of his experience. He must find a place for his own reality, his own life and conduct in the order of divine truth, and direct his life accordingly; and this is a matter of faith and love and observance, in worship, in the ordinances and the activity of the Church, and in his day-to-day life in the world. And so he can never abstract from what he is, from his ever new, changing historical reality. For it is not just his unchangeable metaphysical 'entity' which he has to insert into the economy of God's Message, but his concrete, historical 'contingent' reality, his 'existence' with all it includes: his talents, his particular, limited and evolving endowments; the spirit of his time, the possibilities of his epoch; his concepts, which, granting all the fixity of metaphysical truth, are none the less historically conditioned; the particular task, always changing and always sharply defined, which is set him by his inescapable situation in the world—and this situation again must never be thought of as just the result of a secular historical development, but is itself the result of Christ's government of his Church, as he gradually leads her, sometimes by new ways, through a changing reality to his own single Truth. If a human being does all this—and he must do it, because he always has his eye (metaphysically and theologically) on the Absolute, though always from a finite historical viewpoint—no change takes place in the divine reality, nor do the true propositions concerning this reality become false; but there is a certain change in the perspective in which he sees the reality through these propositions: he expresses this reality differently, he can state something new about it which he had not explicitly noticed before. The decisive feature of such a change is not 'progress' in the sense of acquiring a sort of plus-quantity of knowledge (as though the Church were somehow to become 'cleverer'), but (in principle, at least) the change, the new look, of the same reality and truth, appropriate to just this age of the Church: it is change in, not of, identity. By this again is not meant that the change is necessarily an entire abandonment of the earlier view or perspective; this would be a conception of change as we see it in the material and not in the spiritual realm. The mind of humanity, and even more the Church, has a 'memory'. They change while they preserve, they become new without losing anything of the old. We today have our own philosophy, while we still philosophize with Plato and his abiding truth. And still more we have our theology, which bears the undeniable stamp of our time, while we continue to learn anew from Scripture, the Fathers, the Scholastics. If we fail either to preserve or to change, we should betray the truth, either by falling into error or by failing to make the truth our own in a really existential way.

Now it may at first sight seem that this formulation of the concept of a change within a single abiding truth is concerned just with what could be called 'theology' as opposed to revealed faith. We should then be dealing merely with the human understanding of revelation which as it were circles continually round this fixed point of Scripture and perhaps a few fixed data of (early) Tradition too: at once removed from it and gravitating towards it. Thus we should be dealing all the time with *theology*, with something which could never become the authentic and plenary revealed Word which grasps Revelation itself. Such a relation between Revelation on the one hand, and human understanding (always conditioned by time and situation, and striving to reach perfection) on the other, does undoubtedly exist. In relation to Revelation there is such a thing as theology, the human word which seeks to express and understand the Revealed; so that one can have no certain guarantee from Revelation itself that the attempt has been successful. But there is question not only of a theology which evolves and revolves round the fixed point of a revealed utterance which has been pronounced once and for all. There exists not only a development of theology but also a development of dogma, not only a history of theology but also (after Christ, if only in the same Christ) a history of faith; and this for two reasons. Firstly the Church understands her doctrinal decisions not just as 'theology' but as the Word of faith—not indeed as newly revealed but as the Word which utters Revelation itself truly and with binding force. Secondly this doctrinal Word can be understood within broad limits and at the same time not as a merely external, verbal modification of the original revealed propositions. On the contrary it is very often impossible to say that the new doctrinal utterance is simply the old one 'differently expressed', so that the individual Christian cannot invariably limit its doctrinal content *a priori* to what he himself could recognize as 'identical' with the corresponding declaration made previously. For example, the declarations of Nicaea and Florence on the mystery of the Blessed Trinity, which are intended to be propositions of faith and not merely theological explorations, have a fixed meaning. This meaning is proposed as an object of faith, even if I myself as an individual Christian and a private theologian do not succeed in demonstrating off my own bat i.e. by the methods of philological exegesis, that these declarations say 'just the same as', 'only in other words', what I have been able to extract from Scripture and early Tradition 'by a critical study of the

sources'. There can of course be no question of a contradiction between the two sets of propositions, and such a contradiction could
never be demonstrated historically. We shall return later to the
question as to how the difference (varying in magnitude, presumably,
according to the matter under consideration) between an earlier and a
later pronouncement of the magisterium may more exactly be understood *objectively*. For the moment it is sufficient to establish the fact that
quoad nos, at least, i.e. for the individual and his private theology, such a
difference can and in many cases does exist: that is, that at least in this
one sense *quoad nos* a development of dogma does in fact exist, as shown
in the actual practice of the Church when she proclaims a doctrine.

It is also relatively easy to see that a development of this kind must
necessarily exist. God's revealing Word is directed through the medium
of the historical process at the *total* history of humanity (speaking
generally).[1] For this reason the historically conditioned mode in
which Revelation is appropriated at any time need not lie absolutely
outside this Revelation itself. For the real understanding of what is
revealed and its existential appropriation by men is wholly dependent
on the transformation of the propositions of faith, as they were
originally heard, into propositions which relate what is heard to the
historical situation of the men who hear; it is only then that they
become propositions of faith, emerging into the real, historically
conditioned world of men as decision and living deed. If these translating propositions are just theology and nothing more, 'private
interpretations' of the original propositions; if there were no guarantee
that the proposition heard has been correctly understood: then on the
one hand the proclamation of faith itself could only be a monotonous
repetition, with a purely material accuracy, of the same propositions of
Scripture (and perhaps of a limited early Tradition as well); and on
the other what we have understood of it, in the situation which is
precisely ours, would be subjective theology—an appropriation of
the faith, which is itself faith, would not come to pass.

What has so far been said is only intended to indicate briefly the
fact[2] of a dogmatic development, and offer a first approximation to

[1] It is not possible to say any more here about how we should determine
more exactly the ontological and theological conditions which make it
possible for a statement arrived at at a definite point in history to be directed
at all men at all periods of that history.

[2] And so stands still more in need of *a posteriori* proof from history itself.

an understanding of its nature. In order to grasp its nature more clearly, we shall take as our starting-point a proposition which belongs to the basic pronouncements of the magisterium on faith, and which apparently points in a direction contrary to that indicated by the proposition that a development of dogma is both possible and has actually taken place.

It is a doctrine of the Church, though not in the strict sense a defined one, that Revelation 'was closed with the death of the (last) Apostle(s)' (Denz 2020 s.). What does this proposition mean? It would be false to interpret it as meaning more or less that when the last Apostle died there was left a fixed summary of strictly drafted propositions like a legal code with its clearly defined paragraphs, a sort of definitive catechism, which, while itself remaining fixed, was going to be for ever expounded, explained and commented upon. An idea like this would do justice neither to the mode of being proper to intellectual knowledge nor to the fullness of life of divine faith and its content. When we try to discover the profound reasons for the completeness of Revelation, we begin to see how we should approach the interpretation of this proposition. To start with, Revelation is not the communication of a definite number of propositions, a numerical sum, to which additions may conceivably be made at will or which can suddenly and arbitrarily be limited, but an historical dialogue between God and man in which something *happens*, and in which the communication is related to the continuous 'happening' and enterprise of God. This dialogue moves to a quite definite term, in which first the *happening* and *consequently* the communication comes to its never to be surpassed climax and so to its conclusion. Revelation is a saving Happening, and only then and in relation to this a communication of 'truths'. This continuous Happening of saving history has now reached its never to be surpassed climax in Jesus Christ: God himself has definitively given himself to the world. Christianity is not a phase or epoch of a history of world civilizations which could be displaced by another phase, another secular 'Aion'. If formerly, before Christ, something took place in history, it was and is invariably conditioned, provisional, something with its own limited range and endurance and thus leading to death and emptiness: one aion after another. The present always dies in the future. Each age goes by in successive rise and fall, infinitely far from the true Eternity which abides beyond: each carries its own death within it, from the moment of its birth:

civilizations, nations, states, or intellectual, political, economic systems. *Before* Christ even God's enterprise in revealing himself to the world was 'open': times and orders of salvation were created and displaced each other, and it was still not apparent how God was going at last to respond to the human answer, usually negative, to his own initiating act: whether the ultimate utterance of his creative Word would be the word of wrath or of love. But 'now' the definitive reality is established, one which can no longer become obsolete or be displaced: the indissoluble, irrevocable presence of God in the world as salvation, love and forgiveness, as communication to the world of the most intimate depths of the divine Reality itself and of its Trinitarian life: Christ. *Now* there is nothing more to come: no new age, no other aion, no fresh plan of salvation, but only the unveiling of what is already 'here' as God's presence at the end of a human time stretched out to breaking-point: the Last and eternally the latest, newest day. It is because the definitive Reality which resolves history proper is already here that Revelation is 'closed'. Closed, because open to the concealed presence of divine plenitude in Christ. Nothing new remains to be said, not as though there were not still much to say, but because everything has been said, everything given in the Son of Love, in whom God and the world have become one, for ever without confusion, but for ever undivided. That Revelation has been closed is a positive and not a negative statement, a pure *Amen*, a conclusion which includes everything and excludes nothing of the divine plenitude, conclusion as fulfilled presence of an all-embracing plenitude.

It is further to be observed that the 'closed' Revelation with which we are concerned here is a Revelation made to the believing Church, in possession of the revealed Reality itself. A sure knowledge of this reality of divine salvation can only be gained through the divine tidings and through the faith which comes from hearing and speaks in human concepts and human propositions. Any attempts to transcend this divine message—in some 'religious experience' or emotive state, some experimental contact eliminating the faith which hears—so as to grasp this reality immediately and without reference to the message, is delusive and impossible, and must inevitably lead to a modernistic rationalization of Christianity. Our religion, in so far as it moves within the sphere of our intellectual and moral 'consciousness', is inseparably dependent upon the announcing Word. But in the aion of Christ it is not just of the remote future that this Word brings us tidings, a mere anticipatory shadow of a reality still to come, but it utters what is present. The believing Church possesses what she believes: Christ, his Spirit, the earnest of eternal life and its vital powers. She cannot leave the Word behind in order to grasp this reality. But no more does she possess a word about the thing instead of the thing itself. Consequently her hearing of the Word and her reflexion upon the Word heard are not *merely* a logical activity, an attempt gradually to squeeze out all the logical virtualities and consequences of the Word heard as though it were a numerical sum of propositions; they are a reflexion on the propositions heard in living contact with the thing itself. This reflective consideration practised by the Church, which takes place in us as a 'theological' comprehension, unfolding and clarification of the Church's faith, results in 'new' propositions of faith and not just theology, takes place simultaneously in the word and in the thing itself: each in the other, neither without the other. Or putting it differently, the light of faith and the assistance of the Spirit which are at work in this reflexion and progressive self-achievement do not mean just a sort of supervision given by a teacher. The teacher's concern is to see that his pupil does not go astray in his calculations and deductions, so that what the pupil learns (if he proceeds correctly) is due only to his own insight and logical acumen and the virtualities of his own premises. It is much more in the actual result that the light of the Spirit and of faith exert their influence: the hidden but present and posited Reality takes part in its own understanding. The 'unction' teaches. We find a reflected image there of what we have seen with our own eyes of the living Word of Truth, what we have looked upon and touched with our hands (1 Jn 1:1). Consequently we need not be able to isolate this light and its operation reflexively, as against other impulses by which we grow and advance in the knowledge of faith. Even in the natural order reflexion upon our mental processes never quite exhausts what are in fact the grounds and motives at work in our intellectual growth or our behaviour: we always understand more by a direct and simple view of things than reflexion and the detailed analysis of this intellectual vision can produce for inspection, our behaviour is always more variously motivated than prior or subsequent reflexion upon it can make explicit. The common man, still more, in his direct apprehension of the objects of everyday life, has not reflexive or theoretical awareness of the nature of his intellectual powers or of formal logic, while he does in fact make use of both. How much more true this is of knowledge in faith, and how much more it is a question of principle here! The light of faith, the impulse of the Spirit, do not permit of being isolated for inspection by a reflexive process in which attention is turned back upon itself and withdrawn from the object of faith. They are the brightness which illuminates the object of faith, the horizon within which it is contained, the mysterious sympathy with which it is understood, and not properly the object directly regarded, not a sun which we can immediately contemplate. But they are present and take part in the apprehension and unfolding of the object of faith; they form the co-operating subjectivity (God's and caused by God) with which the Word is for the first time understood in the act of hearing and understood ever new. Knowledge in faith takes place in the power of the Spirit of God, while at the same time that Spirit is the concrete reality believed: Spirit of the Father and of the Son, Spirit of the Crucified and Ascended, Spirit of the Church and earnest of eternal life, Spirit of justification, holiness and freedom from sin and death. It follows that the object of faith is not something merely passive, indifferently set over against a subjective attitude to it, but simultaneously the principle by which it is itself grasped as object. This statement of course only acquires its full significance on the assumption that the actual support given to faith under the grace of the Holy Spirit is not a merely ontological modality of the act of faith beyond conscious apprehension, but also has a specific effect in consciousness (which is not necessarily to say that it is reflexively distinguishable). This effect makes it possible to apprehend the objects of faith given through the hearing of the external announcement, under a 'light', a subjective *a priori* under grace (the formal object), which is not available to someone without grace. As is well known, this assumption is a controversial topic in Catholic theology. Nevertheless the Thomist view, which does make this assumption, seems to us to be true on Biblical and theological grounds, and we have consequently the right to make this assumption ourselves without being able further to justify it here. But if we do proceed on this assumption, we cannot allow that the unfolding of the Church's consciousness in faith is supported merely by an insight of a conceptual and logical kind and an 'assistentia per se negativa' (i.e. a protection against final error in this work of human, logical understanding) given by the Holy Spirit. It must be insisted upon that between firstly a new revelation, delivering materially new elements, and secondly an *assistentia per se negativa* which contributes nothing to the treasury of faith as it unfolds but only prevents erroneous decisions and *consequently* offers an external guarantee of the validity of decisions in matters of faith, a third possibility is open: and that is a development and unfolding of the original treasures of faith under a positive influence of the light of faith bestowed upon the Church.

If from this point of view we ask what tasks and limits are imposed upon the logical activity which can and does take place upon the original propositions of faith as such (i.e. in so far as the act of grasping them can be distinguished in any way from the possession of the concealed object of faith itself as an apprehended datum, in and through these propositions with the help of the Spirit as light), we come to the following conclusion: the faith of the Church is ever reflected anew in the propositions of faith. It discovers what is implicitly contained in them, the logical and real implications which result from individual propositions or the combination of several. These 'consequences' can be binding even from a purely logical point of view; but they need not necessarily be so. There is also the possibility, in the abstract, of relations between propositions, of consequences from them, which, considered from a purely logical point of view, may be 'proximate', etc., but just by themselves can produce no conclusion which is absolutely binding logically. It may occur that a more particular or more exact statement appears to fit in harmoniously with a more general, less determined combination of statements or ideas; in this way each throws light on and supports the other, without its being possible to see that the more particular statement can be inferred with logical stringency from the more general one as its only possible consequence. In this case we have the so-called 'theological *convenientia*' 'probable' arguments from Scripture or Tradition, and the like. But it would be false to suppose that in such a case any sure knowledge in faith is in principle automatically excluded. For such a supposition proceeds from the explicit or tacit assumption that progress in theological understanding in the order of faith relies uniquely upon human operations of a logical kind. This is not so. A *sure* knowledge is acquired in the form of knowledge in *faith* proper to the *Church* as such (if she steps in) not just through the merely logical explication[1]

---

[1] *Explikation.* It seemed proper to translate this technical term by 'explication', and *explizieren* by 'explicate', both of which terms are permitted by the Oxford Dictionary.—Tr.

of propositions as such but through the luminous power of the Spirit in contact with the *res* itself. This power makes use of logical processes but its influence does not cease there, because it possesses the very *res* in question as a present principle of knowledge of it and not just propositions about a (remote) reality, always remembering that the former cannot be had without a basic minimum of the latter. It is quite possible for there to be doctrinal progress on the ground of 'arguments of convenience', 'proofs' depending on similarity.[1] Naturally the individual theologian as such cannot say when an assured progress has in fact been achieved by means of (and 'in spite of') such arguments, for it is only the (conditional) force of the logical argument as such which can become apparent to his reflexive understanding. This decision belongs rather to the faith of the Church, who finds herself in actual fact in secure[2] possession of definite knowledge in faith by means of and in spite of such mere considerations of 'convenience'; and *in consequence* sees that her development in understanding has taken place in the power and the light of the Spirit.

For our purposes we can ignore the question whether such an 'argument of convenience', which provisionally at least is 'purely' such *quoad nos*, is in given circumstances, objectively considered, really *only* such and *in consequence* appears to us as such; or whether *in itself* there *must* always in any case be concealed in an argument of this kind, if assured knowledge in faith is acquired by it, what is in fact a logically stringent argument, which merely *quoad nos* has not yet reached such a degree of objectivity by accurate reflexive analysis as to be evidently so to us. A theologian who proposes to explain the development of dogma as strictly as possible in terms of the logical explication of propositions is bound to regard the second hypothesis as

---

[1] A more prudent formula may be preferred: 'It is not demonstrably impossible *a priori* ...'. Whether *in fact* doctrinal progress has been made in this way, and when it has done so, are questions to be answered *a posteriori* from the examination of individual cases in the history of doctrine. Once again we should have to distinguish two possibilities: *either* this progress took place just in consequence of what at first sight was a mere argument of 'convenience', which turned out to be quite stringent when larger contexts of theological relevance were brought to bear on it; *or* so long as we remain in the field of theological argument we have nothing but an 'argument of convenience'.

[2] Of course 'secure' does not mean here 'logically compelling', but 'firm', 'undoubted', 'undisturbed'.

the only permissible one.[1] In the natural order there undoubtedl¡
occur many cases in which we know something with complete cer
tainty in an unreflexive, 'global' way, where on the one hand th¡
reflexive proof in fact offered for it could still be found very loose an¡
inadequate (as 'merely probable'); and on the other hand a mor¡
stringent proof, the possibility of which must be accepted in principle
is all the same going to be produced or has already been produced t¡
the satisfaction of some more penetrating thinker. All that concerns u¡
here is simply the idea, which even a theologian of this persuasion wi¹
have to admit, that it is not possible to assert that a sure knowledge i¡
faith cannot be had, where what is had *hic et nunc quoad nos* is 'merely
a theological 'argument of convenience'. An assertion of this kin¡
would in fact be a piece of theological naturalism, which would reduc¡
to the level of merely human processes of thought that specific an¡
peculiar kind of knowledge in faith which belongs to the Church as
whole, in virtue of the Spirit's abiding presence in her as the ver¡
object of faith. What is primary and more comprehensive in thi¡
knowledge in faith would be surrendered to the inferior and secondar¡
to 'scientific theology', which does indeed form an ingredient c
knowledge in faith but certainly does not adequately represent it¡
nature.

Conversely it follows from what has been said that it is superfluou¡
and injurious to the honesty which is one of the virtues of theolog¡
to attempt at all costs to produce a logically stringent argument of
reflexive kind from the sources of faith for every doctrine of faith t
which there is firm testimony in the magisterium of the Church. Th¡
theologian should try to find such an argument and not try to lighte¡
or simplify the disciplined labour of historical investigation and ratioı¡
al speculation proper to his science with the explanation that it doesn¹
matter very much because he always practises his theology in depeı¡
dence on the faith of the Church. Such a view would be false an¡
reprehensible. But even where he is unable to find an argument whic¹

[1] Only he has then to be able to show that he can do justice in terms c
this postulate to the legitimate development of dogma which has in fac
taken place. But he has no right suddenly to relax his conditions for logica
stringency when he is considering the 'stringent' deduction from origina
Revelation of propositions *already* defined, if he is never prepared to rela
them when it is a question of the theological deduction of propositions *no*
yet defined. Let us forgo examples involving the use of a double standard.

is honestly justified by the facts, he should avoid giving the appearance of supposing that his own mind and his own theological reflexions are simply the point at which the Holy Spirit of the Church has achieved its fullest manifestation.

In any case the attempt is superfluous in view of the undeniable fact that in many cases the Church's sure conviction in faith has temporally preceded such logical deductions (perfectly possible ones, in certain circumstances). Even in the concrete logic of everyday discovery the consequence, the conclusion, must very often be arrived at and brought to light by quite other means than those of logical deduction, so that one can generally look for possible premises or more general concepts in which this conclusion may have been contained implicitly. If we transfer this to the field of theological knowledge, we may ask: Why should a (individual or collective) consciousness not arrive by a concrete logic of discovery at a theological proposition, which (when it is a question of the Church's consciousness in faith) is apprehended as true and certain in this direct, global and concrete knowledge belonging to the supernatural *life* of faith, even before the theologian's reflective work of deductive intelligence has produced a reflexive 'proof'? In the theological field too, where the knowledge of Revelation becomes progressively more profound, there exists a 'concrete experience', a cognition which integrates a thousand and one merely 'instinctive' observations, and which only with great difficulty, if at all, permits of being exhibited in a chain of syllogistic formulae. For this extremely 'rational' knowledge of an unreflexive kind is richer than in its reflexive articulation and logical exposition, which is always subsequent to it (though within certain limits necessary). Any living thing of a certain degree of complexity needs a skeleton but is more than this skeleton, which itself lives by the life of the whole. So too it may be impossible for every theologian strictly to demonstrate *hic et nunc* that more explicit knowledge in faith is contained in less explicit (earlier) knowledge; but this is at any rate no criterion by which we may judge of whether in fact the later knowledge is contained in the earlier or not.

If we go on to ask how this 'being-contained' of new formulations of dogmatic propositions in an earlier form of consciousness in faith is to be understood *objectively* (now some such 'being-contained' must be allowed if Revelation is held to have 'closed' with the Apostles), then we come up once more against a very large number of dark and difficult problems, on which Catholic theologians have long failed to reach agreement. It must be pointed out once more that such a lack of clarity and unanimity is not surprising, and cannot serve as an argument against a genuine development of dogma. Spiritual processes continue to function with complete adequacy even though a satisfactory theory of their subjective and objective presuppositions has not yet been offered.

To clarify the point at issue once again. We have so far tried to show that a development of dogma does *in fact* exist and exist necessarily. Further we have learned to see that it takes place in vital contact with that *res* which is the 'closed' plenitude of revealed reality, in a contact which does indeed include as an intrinsic factor an objective givenness of the *res* in propositions and the possibility of their logical expansion, but is not simply exhausted therein. The 'motive' force which is at work in the development of dogma and guarantees its correctness is not simply to be identified with formal logic. If there does in fact exist a movement from the earlier to the later knowledge in virtue of this force, then we must yet again and more precisely put the question how the earlier and the later knowledge are related to each other. There is of course no doubt that the objective realities grasped in both the knowledge which acts as foundation and that which is founded upon it, are really connected *in themselves*, the only presupposition being that the knowledge which has emerged is a genuine dogmatic truth. But this mere connexion of the (known) *realities* in themselves is not in question: rather it is the connexion of the actual states of knowledge.[1] This connexion must be present. Not only because Revelation was 'closed' with the death of the Apostles, a fact that implies both the abiding plenitude and perfection of the Reality which is the object of faith, and in some sense the continual presence of the plenitude of faith in this reality as well. But also because if there were present only a connexion in the known object itself but not in earlier and later knowledge of it in faith, then there would have to be either a new revelation for the later proposition or an apprehension of the object independent of the earlier divine

[1] This distinction is not easy to make conveniently in English. In St Thomas's terms, we distinguish between the *res intellecta*, the independent reality in fact known, and the *intellectum*, the meaning or content immediately apprehended by the mind in the act of knowing, and through which the *res* is known.—Tr.

pronouncements about this object; now both these views are unacceptable.

The theologians have attempted to explain this necessary connexion
in terms of the explication of an implicit cognition in an explicit one.
So far all are agreed. Something is really 'explained' in this way, for
attention is directed by these concepts to a phenomenon which may be
actually observed in the advance of knowledge in faith as well as
elsewhere. There does actually exist such a thing as 'explication' of a
cognition, the fullness of whose content is thereby displayed in an
explicit and articulated way. We have the clearest example of this sort
of propositional connexion in formal logic and pure mathematics, the
propositions of which are related to each other as implicit to explicit.
Moreover it cannot be denied that explications which seem to correspond exactly to those of formal logic may be found in theology too.
Even if there are other, essentially different ways in which spiritual
activity can achieve explicitness (as we shall see), yet the process of
explication (speaking quite generally) does exist. And so this process
would seem to be quite a suitable way of representing, at least in general
terms, the connexion between two states of knowledge in faith, one
of which arises from the other by a development of dogma.

But this catch-word 'explication' does not offer much 'explanation'
of what we want, the way in which this connexion holds. For the
precise nature of this explicative connexion, just that with which we
are concerned, remains obscure.

We may begin with a brief account of the direction in which the
average explanation offered by the theologians moves, and of the
controversies which have their origin in this common starting-point.
The point of departure of the explanation is tacitly and with a sense of
self-evidence taken to be the proposition. The only question is how a
proposition, which, it is assumed, is a fixed quantity, can be explicated.
It follows that the explication of the proposition must take place by
means of formal logic. Explication is the analytic exposition of the
content of the proposition or of the logical consequences of several
propositions with the help of the principle of contradiction. The
model which is expressly or tacitly employed as an example in this
view is the procedure of logic or mathematics.

When the explication is that of a *single* proposition contained in
original Revelation, and when this explication only states more
expressly ('in other words', in a different conceptual language, etc.)

'the same thing' as the original proposition (of course with the guarantee of the magisterium that the new proposition correctly renders the sense of the old), there can be no doubt that the new proposition too states what God has revealed, that it is believed with divine faith as materially *God* himself,[1] that it is 'dogma' and not just theology. But it may seriously be doubted whether the actual course of the development of dogma may be adequately interpreted in this way, by an explication of what is 'formally implicit' in a proposition. We shall discuss this in a moment.

Alongside this explication of what is formally implicit in a *single* proposition, however hard it may be to make sharp distinctions in individual cases, there exists a different form of explication of propositions: the explication of what is 'virtually' implicit in a proposition with the help of another proposition. Let us suppose that the following proposition is valid: All men born more than two hundred years ago are now dead. If I do not know that there was a Socrates who was born more than two hundred years ago, I cannot know that the general proposition includes Socrates as a particular case, not only in the real state of affairs under consideration but in the proposition as such. But if I do know the second proposition, the first contains something 'virtually' implicit: Socrates is dead, an implication which could never have been explicated by a mere analysis of the first proposition just in itself. Operations of this kind (of course more complex usually) do undoubtedly exist in the theological field. Without them it would be impossible to think of theology as a body of intelligibly connected ideas at all. In order to simplify our problem we leave out of account the case (which does undoubtedly occur too) when in a properly deductive procedure of this kind not only the formal technique (logic) but also part of the propositions and their intelligible content have their source not in original Revelation but in our natural knowledge; we shall consider only those cases in which the whole intelligible material of such a deductive explication, of the movement from the purely *virtually* implicit to the explicit, is provided by Revelation itself. Cases of this kind do certainly exist. And there is no doubt that they have their part in 'theological' development (as we wish to point out in advance, because the immediate question is whether a genuine development of dogma can be explained in this way).

---

[1] 'Credere Deum', as opposed to 'credere Deo' or 'in Deum'.—Tr.

We can now go on to ask whether new knowledge derived in this properly deductive way as a *conclusion* from *several* previously given propositions, can still be said to be 'revealed by God', and so can properly be believed, in the proper sense of 'divine faith', 'on the authority of God'; or whether it is a merely human knowledge, not properly believed with divine faith, but at most to be accepted with 'ecclesiastical faith' on the authority of the *Church* (really infallible in this case too, with the necessary qualifications). The theologians are divided on this question. One group, the majority today, hold that these inferred propositions are purely human ones, the correctness of which can of course be guaranteed by the Church. The others believed that this kind of explication of what is contained merely 'virtually' in the immediate propositions of Revelation can and must still really be called 'Revelation', and as such can be proclaimed by the Church as the object of divine faith in the strict sense. The second view would seem more correct.

We have already noted that in a concrete instance distinguishing between formally and virtually implicit and their explication can be very difficult, for the reason that the explication of even what is formally implicit can and often must, for the sake of clarity, take the form of a syllogistic operation. But it then becomes difficult in the concrete case to decide whether we have an instance of one or the other kind of explication. It is consequently always open to the theologians holding the first opinion, even where there has been a long chain of deductive reasoning, to explain that objectively after all we are dealing with the explication of something formally implicit and no more. So far it is not easy to dispose of this opinion. But if the concepts are allowed to keep their plain, original simple meaning, we are bound to say that an explication of what is formally implicit in a revealed proposition is present only when the new proposition really states the *same thing* as the old one in other words, has the same content as the old one, however useful and necessary it may be for various reasons to formulate the new proposition. Putting it differently: an explicit proposition has been contained in another proposition as something formally implicit only when it results from the latter in consequence of a *hermeneutic* and exegetical operation, not involving (as a necessary feature) the use of a properly deductive procedure. Where pure analysis of the meaning and significance of a proposition according to linguistic and grammatical rules does not by itself produce the new proposition, there can be no question of something formally implicit. For instance, instead of the proposition: One and the same Logos is God and man, we can say: The 'person' of the Logos has both a human and a divine 'nature'. If theological or metaphysical theories (very important ones perhaps, but in need of justification on other grounds) are not attached to the concepts 'person' and 'nature', we may conceive of the second proposition as the bare explication of what is formally implicit in the first. Explications of this kind do undoubtedly exist, the only question here being whether it is particularly illuminating to distinguish between 'explicit' and 'implicit', when in both cases we are meant to be dealing with something stated really 'formally', i.e. something which the initial proposition *itself* really states, for this belongs to the concept of the 'formally stated', if these words are allowed to have their natural sense.

But it is still very doubtful whether all the cases in which a development of dogma in the proper sense, one guaranteed by the Church, does undoubtedly take place, can be interpreted according to this schema. If we try to use it in order to explain such doctrines as those of Transubstantiation, Sacramental Character, the validity of heretical Baptism and so on, which have not always been found in an explicit form and yet belong to the Church's treasury of faith today, it is clear that we can only do so by arbitrary and violent measures. Granted that there does *in fact* exist a development of dogma which goes beyond the explication of what is formally implicit, then it precisely *can* exist. And so there *must* exist (if we are going to take as our basis the logical explication of *propositions*) at least an explication of what is virtually implicit, the result of which may yet be claimed as the Revelation of God himself and consequently may be believed on the testimony of God himself.

Nor is it particularly hard, in the case of *God's* utterances, to answer the question *why* a proposition of this kind, the result of an explication of what is virtually implicit, can be conceived of as stated by *God*, and hence credible on his personal authority. A human speaker can never survey all the necessary consequences which in fact follow from his statements. In this kind of speech, then, we cannot be sure whether these consequences too could be intended as a communication of the speaker's own mind. The inner drive towards the infinite openness of truth which is inherent even in human concepts and propositions, is beyond the scope of the human speaker's knowledge, and therefore ceases to be fully the expression of his own subjectivity. *We* always begin by talking 'above our heads'. The whole of what we 'really' state is not an expression of what *we* ourselves want to state. But when *God* speaks the case is different: he is necessarily conscious of the actual vitality and dynamism of his immediate communication, and aware of all its virtues and consequences. Moreover he has from the very beginning the intention and the will to bring about its explication and to guide it in his own Spirit. It is God himself then who states even what is only disclosed *as* stated in the historical life of what was (immediately) stated. And so even what is merely virtually implicit in his speech is his Word. Virtual explication, looked at from the point of view of *God* as speaker, is simply explication and nothing more, even if it requires real deduction by *us*, looked at from our point of view as hearers. What *we* 'deduce' in this way, God has not indeed *stated* 'formally' in the initial propositions from which our deduction proceeds (i.e. he has not expressed it in the immediate meaning of the propositions), but he has really 'com-municated'[1] it, so that entire faith can be given to it as *his* knowledge. It cannot be objected that on this hypothesis, in view of the absolutely unlimited virtualities of what has been revealed immediately, absolutely every-thing, that is, every conceivable true proposition, will in the last resort have to be regarded as revealed. For in the first place it is not true of every proposition of 'natural knowledge' that its referential content possesses that objective connexion with the original, immediate pro-positions of Revelation which is needed to support the claim that the proposition was communicated by God himself. Secondly the lack of the guarantee which must (usually) be given by the Church's con-sciousness in faith (her magisterium) will make it impossible to recog-nize the 'consequence' of one proposition from the other with enough certainty to permit of faith in the first proposition as something revealed by God. Thirdly, in the theory just outlined, it is only possible to regard as something 'stated' by God to man what God knows man will himself in fact evolve from what was stated immedi-ately, under the impulse and in the light of the divine Spirit. But

[1] *mit-geteilt.* By inserting this hyphen Fr Rahner wishes to suggest the *inclusive* character of the divine utterance. Later he will show that this character is present to some degree even in human speech; and by an un-translatable emphasis suggests the *com*munion of the hearer with the speaker in the *com*munication.—Tr.

what has in fact evolved or is in course of evolution is limited and finite.

A further objection, taken this time from inspired Scripture, might be offered to the distinction which has been made between something stated formally and something over and above this but really communicated; an objection, then, to the possibility of claiming the virtually revealed too as something which can be assented to with divine faith and authoritatively defined. In Scripture, it might be said, the inspired human author is not only a messenger delivering a message (for it is quite conceivable that a messenger should not comprehend the full bearing of the message, the range of the communication); he is also really an author, so that only that sense of the propositions is inspired which the *human* author, constructing his own propositions, intended and expressed. And so it is impossible to assert that in Scripture (which is nevertheless the most important starting-point of our deductions) more has been communicated by God than has been stated formally. For our purposes we need not concern ourselves here with the question whether this objection concerning inspiration as such really proceeds from a correct appreciation of the relation between human and divine authors.[1] But even apart from this it does not prove what it sets out to prove. It may (in just this context) be safely granted that nothing more is *inspired* than what the *human* author as such intended to state and write down. Yet it follows from this that more can be communicated, even if God, as *literary author* of Scripture and no more, should not be able to communicate more than what he and the human author have stated formally (i.e. written down). We have only to consider the fact that what is now found written in Scripture was also in historical fact, indeed primarily, the object of the Apostles' oral preaching. As preachers of this kind ('prophets'), i.e. as original, non-literary bearers of that revealed content which was also deposited eventually in inspired Scripture, they are however essentially messengers and transmitters, not authors of their message; they pass on their message not as their own but simply as God's, so that what they communicate is in itself perfectly capable of being in excess of what they themselves have explicitly appropriated of it.[2]

[1] Cf. K. Rahner, 'Über die Schriftinspiration', ZKT LXXVIII (1956), pp. 137–68.—Tr.

[2] Fr Rahner's point is that even on this limited view of literary inspiration, more can be communicated by the written word than the human

Summing up what we have seen so far, we may say that the connexion between the original propositions and those reached in consequence of dogmatic development can consist in the connexion between something formally or virtually implicit in a proposition and the explication of this by logical procedures with the support and in the light of the divine Spirit, leaving it open as to whether or not this connexion must be logically compelling in every case 'quoad nos'.

But this does not bring us to the end of our discussion. So far we have with the majority of theologians tacitly assumed that the starting-point of a dogmatic explication is *always* a *proposition* in the proper sense. But that this should always be the case may by no means be assumed.

In the first place it cannot be doubted that there exists in the natural order a kind of knowledge, which, while it is itself not articulated in 'propositions', is the starting-point of an intellectual process which develops into propositions. Let us suppose that a young man has the genuine and vital experience of a great love, an experience which transforms his whole being. This love may have *presuppositions* (of a metaphysical, psychological and physiological kind) which are simply unknown to him. His love *itself* is his 'experience'; he is conscious of it, lives through it with the entire fullness and depth of a real love. He 'knows' much more about it than he can 'state'. The clumsy stammerings of his love-letters are paltry and miserable compared to this knowledge. It may even be possible that the attempt to tell himself and others what he experiences and 'knows' may lead to quite false statements. If he were to come across a 'metaphysics' of love, he might perhaps understand absolutely nothing of what was said there about love and even his love, although he might know much more about it than the dried-up metaphysician who has written the book. If he is intelligent, and has at his disposal an adequately differentiated stock of ideas, he could perhaps make the attempt, slowly and gropingly, approaching the subject in a thousand different ways, to state what he knows about his love, what he is already aware of in the consciousness

---

author may have grasped, because the literary authorship may consist merely in making a record of a *message*, something which need not be fully understood by the messenger.

It should perhaps be noted at this point that Fr Rahner is leading up to his distinction between 'something formally stated' (*ein formell Gesagtes*) and 'something formally communicated' (*ein formell Mitgeteiltes*).—Tr.

of simply possessing the reality (more simply but more fully aware), so as finally to 'know' (in reflexive propositions). In such a case it is not (merely) a matter of the logical development and inference of new propositions from earlier ones, but of the formulation for the first time of propositions about a knowledge already possessed, in an infinite search which only approaches its goal asymptotically. This process too is an explication. Here too there is a connexion *in re* between an earlier knowledge and later explicit propositions. But the starting-point and the procedure are not those of the logical explication of propositions, which we first took as model for the development of dogma.

This case, which we are going to make use of in the field of dogma as a natural analogue for an explication other than that of the logical explication of propositions, must however be examined from a different angle. The lover knows of his love: this knowledge of himself forms an essential element in the very love itself. The knowledge is infinitely richer, simpler and denser than any body of propositions about the love could be. Yet this knowledge never lacks a certain measure of reflexive articulateness: the lover confesses his love at least to himself, 'states' at least to himself something about his love. And so it is not a matter of indifference to the love itself whether or not the lover continues to reflect upon it; this self-reflexion is not the subsequent description of a reality which remains in no way altered by the description. In this progressive self-achievement, in which love comprehends itself more and more, in which it goes on to state something 'about' itself and comprehends its own nature more clearly, the love itself becomes ordered; it has an increasing understanding of what must properly be the foundation of its own activity, mirrors its own nature with increasing clarity, approaches as its goal, with an increasingly clear awareness, what it always has been. Reflexion upon oneself (when it is accurate) in propositions (i.e. in *pensées* which the lover produces about his love) is thus a part of the progressive realization of love itself; it is not just a parallel phenomenon, without importance for the thing itself. The progress of love is a living growth out of the original (the originally conscious) love *and* out of just what that love has itself become through a reflexive experience of itself. It lives at every moment from its original source *and* from that reflexive experience which has immediately preceded any given moment. Original, non-propositional, unreflexive yet conscious possession of a reality on the one hand, and reflexive (propositional), articulated consciousness of this original consciousness on the other—these are not competing opposites but reciprocally interacting factors of a single experience necessarily unfolding in historical succession. Root and shoot are not the same thing; but each lives by *the other*. Reflexive consciousness always has its roots in a prior conscious entering into possession of the reality itself. But just this original consciousness possesses itself later in a new way, such that its life is now the accomplishment of that personal act of reflexive apprehension by which it has enriched itself. Reflexive consciousness would inevitably wither if its life were not rooted in the simpler basic consciousness, or if it were to reproduce this in every particular. The simple basic consciousness would become blind if, because it is richer and fuller, it refused to allow itself to grow out into a reflexive consciousness involving 'pensées' and 'propositions'.

The question now arises whether in the development of dogma there is to be found an interrelationship of types of explication, (analogically) similar to that which has just been indicated by way of example in the natural order. We believe that it is possible to reply in the affirmative.[1]

In the first place it may be supposed that the *Apostles* themselves had a global experience of this kind, lying behind propositions and forming an inexhaustible source for the articulation and explication of the faith in propositions. Christ, as the living link between God and the world, whom they have seen with their eyes and touched with their hands, is the objective content of an experience which is more elemental and concentrated, simpler and yet richer than the individual propositions coined in an attempt to express this experience—an attempt which can in principle never be finally successful. The vivid experience of Christ's relationship to sin, for example, his death, his attitude to Peter and a thousand other experiences of the kind, which the Apostles lived through in an unreflexive and global way, *precede*

---

[1] In order to exclude the possibility of misunderstanding at the very start, let us draw attention to the following point. In the sphere of faith this global, still (in itself) non-propositional and unreflexive basic consciousness is manifestly an intelligence received from the historical revelation of God in Christ. It does not arise, any more than a dogma explicitly formulated in propositions, from some *a priori* religious consciousness or subconsciousness, itself the only source of an explication in dogmatic propositions.

the doctrinal propositions (at least in many cases, though also *only* in many, not in all cases!) and form a part of the original Revelation, the explication of which, already begun by the Apostles, is not of the same character as the logical explication of propositions. Even in the many cases where our Lord's *spoken* word as such is the necessary starting-point of the Apostles' faith because the actual content of Revelation is available in no other way, these words are heard in the context of a vivid experience of daily life in his company. And so, even in these cases, the concrete experience is an essential presupposition for the true and ever-deepening understanding of the words spoken and heard. These sayings are not in themselves explicit enough; rather they require the complete experience, which in turn becomes continually more explicit and reflexively intelligible as the content of these sayings is unfolded. An explication of this kind, then, is not just a matter of deduction from propositions: it takes a proposition which is offered as a conceptual expression of experience, measures it by the original experience and finds it correct by this standard. Nevertheless this experience depends for its realization upon its actually stating what it knows. The initial degree of self-reflexion in the experience may be slight but it cannot be entirely lacking. Every explication which has been successfully established in propositional form illuminates the original experience, allows it to grow to its proper stature, and becomes an intrinsic factor in the abiding life of this experience itself. Every theological proposition—in St Paul's Epistles, for example—is uttered out of the entirety of this living conscious contact with the incarnate God. *Quoad nos* the 'theology' of the Apostles is original Revelation, because it is guaranteed by the infallibility of prophetic mission and Apostolic inspiration as the new Word intended for us by God. Yet in a certain sense it is also, for the bearers of Revelation themselves, their 'theology', in relation to a more primitive communication made to them before, i.e. it is an explication and an inference from the most primitive data of Revelation.[1] In their case at any rate we have the right to speak of a development of dogma which takes place not just through the logical explication of propositions but through living self-explication within a mind's possession of a given

---

[1] If the Apostles use 'arguments' in their letters, they do so not merely from a pedagogic concern for their readers; rather they give us in this way an insight into the manner in which their own knowledge in faith unfolds, their own 'development of dogma' and 'theology'.

reality. The objective connexion between the new proposition and the old knowledge is not merely that between something logically explicit and something logically implicit in two propositions; it is rather a connexion between what becomes partially explicit in a proposition and the unreflexive, total spiritual possession of the entire *res*, so that the explicit proposition is at the same time more and less than its implicit source. More, because as reflexively formulated it elucidates the original, spiritually simple possession of the reality and in this way enriches it. Less, because it never does more than express reflexively and remotely a part of what was spiritually possessed before. This alone is sufficient to make it clear how one may conceive of the *full* consciousness in faith possessed by the Apostles and the primitive Christian community, and yet avoid anachronisms. It is true that men did not 'know' much then, if we understand by 'knowledge' a form of knowledge which is set up with the help of a reflexive, highly articulated conceptual system. There could have been for the most part so little acquaintance with a system of this kind that we may safely assume that it quite certainly would not have been immediately intelligible at the time, because concepts like this only emerge at a definite point in time and require a definite period of pedagogic activity to become intelligible. Yet at the same time all was known, because men had laid living hold upon the total reality of God's saving Act and now lived in it spiritually. Let us remember that in actual fact (if not in essential principle) greater reflexive articulateness of a spiritual possession is nearly always purchased at the cost of a partial loss in unhampered communication ('naive' in the good sense) with the reality given in faith (and which is still possessed in its entirety). Then we shall see that our more complex and highly differentiated consciousness in faith and the theology which corresponds to it need not fancy themselves 'superior' to the simple faith of Apostolic times! God allots to every age its mode of consciousness in faith. Any romantic desire of our own to return to the simplicity and unreflexive density and fullness of the Apostolic consciousness in faith would only result in an historical atavism. We must possess this fullness in a different way.

It may be urged that in the Apostles we have an exceptional case which can contribute nothing to the explanation of the connexion between old knowledge and new formulation, because the Apostles could only pass on their completed reflexive explication in propositional form and not their original living experience; so that in every age after them only a logical connexion between implicit and explicit in propositions could support the possibility of further development of dogma. But this objection has no force. It is not only propositions about their experience that the Apostles bequeath, but their Spirit, the Holy Spirit of God, the very reality, then, of what they have experienced in Christ. Their own experience is preserved and present together with their Word. Spirit and Word together form the permanent active potentiality of an experience which is in principle the same as that of the Apostles even if, because it is supported on the Apostolic Word handed down in Tradition, it is an experience, resting on that of the Apostles and prolonging *theirs*, which has historical roots and can never continue to live if it is cut off from connexion with the Apostles through Word, Sacrament and the handing down of authority. But just this 'successio apostolica', in a full and comprehensive sense, hands on to the post-Apostolic Church, and precisely with respect to knowledge in faith, not simply a body of propositions but living experience: the Holy Spirit, the Lord, who is ever present in the Church; the keen flair and instinct of faith, the acute sensibility which is a gift of the Spirit, ever alert for the true and the false in the sphere of faith, for what as formulated proposition is or is not homogeneous with the undispersed vitality of truth possessed in innocence. To this extent there exists here too, in post-Apostolic development of dogma, the connexion between what is implicit as a living possession of the whole truth in an unreflexive but conscious way, and what is always only partially explicit in propositions. It is only an explication of this kind that provides both the required bond with earlier explications, already propositional in form, and also the simultaneous passage to a new explication from the original experience through the tradition already formulated; and provides them with greater power and cogency than in the Apostolic age.

If we are properly to appreciate what has been said, we must first make a critical examination of an inadequate way of regarding propositions, all the more active for being tacit. An ordinary statement of everyday life, like those which appear among the propositions of faith too, is tacitly represented under the schema of propositions belonging to mathematics, geometry or formal logic. The latter have in fact—approximately speaking—a fixed content; it is possible—approximately—to *state* unambiguously and exhaustively in a few words (no only to know in an unreflexive and global way) what their concepts mean and what is said with them. Their content, as ascertainable in the form of definitions, is (more or less) identical with what is communicated in them (the object seen through them). It is possible to establish that they state or communicate *this* and *that*, so much and no more. Anything over and above this which it may be possible eventually to infer from them in the way of further knowledge is precisely—newly inferred, precisely then something else. It is possible completely and exhaustively to understand the manifest sense of the initial proposition or propositions and reflexively to exhibit their content without knowing anything about the consequences inferred from them. But this is *not* the case with a normal human proposition. It does indeed have a determinate sense which can be clearly distinguished from the sense of another or contrary proposition. But any attempt reflexively to declare its content comes up against an intrinsic and irreducible marginal indistinctness of this content: its reflexive interpretation does not allow us to state adequately and *exhaustively* all that is concomitantly stated and known in it and all that is not; it is easy to establish unambiguously the minimum but not the maximum of what may in fact be its intelligible content. The proposition is always a kind of window through which a view may be gained of the thing itself, and implies in its full sense (as Com-munication) this view of the thing through the proposition (in its 'stated' sense).[1] A proposition of this kind is in the nature of a window that has been opened to give a view of the thing; not of a package with sharply defined contents. For example, if I say, 'N.N. is my mother,' what has been communicated by this? What have I thought of here and *communicated*? The minimum is clear: what would make the proposition false if it did not exist: such-and-such a well-known biological relation. But do we mean by this that the proposition has nothing more to communicate, that when I spoke, I thought of nothing more and had nothing more to state? When I make a statement like this, there can and almost must be an abundance of other things in mind at the same time, globally and implicitly no doubt, but very really (as we have already said). But all this, in excess of the given minimum of propositional content, can concomitantly be heard by the hearer of the proposition: the specifically human character

---

[1] In communication, what the proposition 'states' serves as a frame for a view of the thing'.—Tr.

of the motherhood, the relation between mother and son lasting long after the events of generation and birth, and all the other circum stances involved. The hearer too, just like the speaker, looks in and through the proposition with the speaker at the thing itself, and see what he sees in the things *as* the communication made to one who i taking part as hearer. He rightly hears in the proposition not just it more or less definable minimum content, but concomitantly all tha further content of the speaker's unreflexive awareness not yet proposi tionally objectified; and he hears it *as* something known to th speaker. This state of affairs must not be mistaken for one in whic further truths, themselves precisely *not* spoken or communicated, ar *inferred* from the propositional content spoken and heard, on the basi of its objective nature and specific cogency. Of course this is some times the case, but it need not invariably be so. It would invariably b so only if the proposition spoken and heard were in the nature of package with clearly definable contents capable of exhaustive enumera tion. But if this is not the case for the speaker, whose speech take place in and with a knowledge, not yet articulated propositionally, c the thing discussed; and if *this* kind of speech, *together with* its 'trair of what is not yet propositionally articulate, is intelligible to th hearer[1]: then it is quite possible for the hearer to hear this knowledg of the thing too *as* the speaker's communicated knowledge, somethin had in common with the speaker about the thing, although not yet pro positionally objectified. Or putting it the other way round, it is qui possible for the speaker to pass this knowledge on in proposition It will then very often be the case that what seems to be somethin merely virtually implicit, from the purely logical point of view, will l in fact something formally communicated[2]; it is not merely deducib

---

[1] That this intelligibility is a *fact* cannot be doubted; but we cannot ar need not proceed here to a further analysis of the presuppositions concernir intellectual knowledge on which it is based.

[2] It should now become possible to offer some clarification of the term used by theologians in a controversy which has lasted up to our own time One school (especially from the time of Suarez onwards) appeals to tl conception of the 'formally implicit' to explain how on the one hand develo ment of dogma is possible and on the other how what has been made expli is still God's utterance. By the use of this conception they intend to circur vent the difficult question of how something which is properly speakir inferred by a specifically syllogistic procedure (the virtually implicit) c still be regarded as stated by God himself. The other school interprets t

as new knowledge (not stated) from some other (stated) knowledge, but even regarded as something in the mind which is propositionally *not* articulated, it is in fact communicated and so understood; and this is true even if it is only made propositionally objective by the hearer and this operation is exhibited (not, properly speaking, performed) in deductive form. Suppose someone says, 'I, A, sincerely love B'; it is quite possible that this statement should be made with the *fidelity* of the love in mind, and should consequently also be heard precisely as A's express communication of his love's fidelity. Now if C says, 'A

---

formally implicit as a more or less self-contradictory conception, because on their view what is formally stated in a proposition must be capable of being ascertained from the very concepts employed, with the help of grammars and dictionaries, by hermeneutical and exegetical methods. Now in practice 'explication' of this alleged formally implicit always takes place by means of what is often highly complex argumentation. In reality, then, this formally implicit is something virtually implicit, so that it will finally have to be granted that this too can become dogma.

In accordance with what we have just said in the text, the following distinction may be proposed. It is possible for something to be stated formally (the above-mentioned necessary minimum sense of a proposition); and for something to be formally *communicated* (the total meaning of the utterance, in fact communicated and intended in the speaker's utterance, but neither by speaker nor by hearer always articulated reflexively and propositionally, or even capable of immediate articulation). Strictly speaking then, what is formally stated cannot be implicit, but what is formally *communicated* certainly can. Thus even when something is deduced, it may nevertheless have been something formally communicated—against the second view; and where something is made explicit, it need not have been something formally stated (implicitly)—against the first view. This distinction between what is formally stated and what is formally communicated is materially that recognized by E. Dhanis ('Révélation explicite et implicite', *Gregorianum* XXXIV (1953), pp. 187–237, especially pp. 219, 221 s.), who distinguishes what is 'formellement signifié' from what is 'formellement ttesté'. The latter may itself be signified in various ways: it may be signified explicitly or implicitly, and if implicitly signified, either immediately (sc. capable of analytic explication) or mediately (sc. by demonstration or even merely as *suasio* or *convenientia*). Consequently Dhanis allows for something formally attested which is yet signified only mediately and persuasively. Nevertheless he does not discuss in any detail the *noetic* connexion which *as such* must obtain between this mode of signification and its formal attestation. It is not merely a matter of its being known in fact (this again is possible with various degrees of certainty), shall we say in the 'dépôt pris concrètement' (cf. pp. 227 s.).

has affirmed his sincere love; *atqui* sincere love is faithful: then A is
faithful,' it is only in appearance that C's knowledge of A's fidelity
(derived from A's first statement) seems to belong to C alone, as a
piece of reflexive, propositional explication; it is quite possible that in
fact his propositional knowledge is a real ('formal') communication
from A, even when it is not stated *as* a proposition.

Now it is not clear why this sort of communication should not be
found in the sphere of Revelation: in fact, it must exist there too
Revelation too works with human concepts and propositions. Yet i
follows then that we cannot ignore the irreducible distinction between
what is explicitly stated on the one hand, and what is co-present in
mind and com-municated on the other.[1] Its importance is felt, and
legitimately so, where propositions and concepts are used to com
municate knowledge of a reality to which we could not have access in
our present state without verbal information: in Revelation. When
for example, someone says, 'Christ "died" for us', everyone under
stands what is meant by dying or death in this statement. But what i
meant by 'death' in this statement is not (or more prudently: need no
be) just a physiological exit. The whole human experience of deat
can be really *stated* (i.e. com-municated) and heard (not just deduced
in this word, an experience which neither speaker nor hearer has eve
translated adequately and objectively into propositions ('definitions
of death). If the hearer should ever arrive at a reflexive propositiona
analysis of what the word 'death' has always meant to him, it is the
perfectly *possible* (though not in *every* case necessary) that what ha
been analysed in this way and minted into propositional coin, ma
still be conceived of precisely *as* communicated by the speaker. An
this can still be so even when 'historically' we may grant that th
speaker himself has never used a propositionally objective form t
clarify his communication 'like this', or indeed if we grant that in h
particular situation he *could* never have done so. If we believe a speake

---

[1] For every propositional explanation (definition) of the concepts
another proposition employs concepts in its turn; and these again can b
explained propositionally. A process *ad infinitum* would begin. For it wou
be quite false to suppose that by a finite number of members this chain
explanations would reach an absolutely simple concept, in which the prop
sitionally expressible would exhaust the object known non-propositional
without remainder. What an infinitely large number of things can be sa
about the 'ultimate' and the 'absolutely simple', about an entity as such

when he says something, then it is still this very speaker whom we
believe when what he says has been explicated in propositions, because this is just what he has (or could have) known and *communicated*
(though not propositionally).

This leaves room for an explication of a more complex kind (as to
its *express*, propositional development) than any we have so far considered. It need not always be the case that from a proposition A,
taken in its most immediate sense, a proposition B is deduced as
formally, or above all, as virtually, contained in A. It might happen
that in this explication the proposition B, taken strictly, should follow
from what is *com-municated* in A or what is 'formally' contained in
his com-munication. If the explication is to take place and to be set
forth with all possible propositional and logical explicitness, the
course of the explication in this case must run as follows. The immediately intelligible and express statements of Revelation in its manifold
variety (propositional series A) are heard and questioned with a view
to discovering what is compresent to mind and com-municated by
them, that is, their background and the principle which comprehends
the whole of this variety and gives it unity. This basic idea compresent
to mind and con-signified (*mit-gesagte*) is extracted by making use of
the individual propositions to give a view of the *res* on which they are
based; in this way the basic idea is formulated expressly in propositions (proposition B). It is only from this intermediate proposition B
that the desired terminal proposition is deduced, i.e. recognized as
con-signified. If what has so far been said is correct, it immediately
becomes clear that the procedure described does not (or need not in
every case) move outside the sphere of what is properly speaking
revealed. This schema according to which an explication of Revelation
might proceed has been so briefly outlined that it may at first sight
give the impression of something peculiar and artificially constructed.
Yet a closer examination would show that in fact it is very often
employed instinctively. Biblical theology always works like this: it
invariably gives form to a multiplicity of concrete individual expressions in Scripture on the basis of a unifying conception, as it emerges
from a consideration of various themes. For example, when an
inquiry is made into the New Testament conception of God or the
way in which it understands Time, or again into St Paul's idea of
pneuma, the same thing is always being done, from a methodological
point of view: what is being sought is always the basic conception

con-signified in all the individual statements, the fundamental idea
behind them, the leitmotiv, call it what you will. Now if, on the basis
of this inquiry, an answer is given to a further special question, such
as the incompatibility of this or that philosophical or metaphysical
proposition with a 'fundamental conception' discovered in Scripture
then we have the whole procedure outlined in our formal schema.

Nothing of what we have been saying is intended to postulate or
recommend a new method of expounding dogma in theology. Theo
logy as the practice of reflexive and scientific understanding will
continue to work with its usual methods: strict attention to what has
been said in original Revelation; concern for the exact sense of what
has been heard, making use of all the methods at the disposal of a
liberal and humane discipline (philology, history, logic, etc.); com
parison and correlation of the propositions so heard and understood
('analogia fidei'); inquiry into the logical consequences resulting
from these correlations (deductions), and so on. Theology as such can
neither introduce the immediate guidance of the Holy Spirit as
source or as a logical principle for its methods, nor can it proposition
ally articulate and explicate what is formally communicated (implicitly
if you will) otherwise than by logical operations. But what it is per
missible to conclude (more clearly, perhaps, than before) with regard
to these usual and unchanging theological methods is this: however
complex and protracted the methodical conduct of this sort of theo
logical investigation may be, it need not necessarily lead to a result
outside the sphere of what has been really stated and communicated
formally by God (as though its discovery must necessarily be a piece
of merely human wit). And this is so precisely because (from God's
point of view) the God who speaks surveys in himself from the very
beginning all the virtualities of his speech, and by his own Spirit in
the Church inspires, guides and watches over their very actualization
and because from the point of view of men and their properly human
words and propositions, even in human speech more is actually com
municated formally than can formally be stated. So, for example, we
can give ourselves up to theological discussion of the Assumption
with a kind of unhampered confidence,[1] and yet the result, considered

---

[1] Following the practice in this matter and elsewhere of all the classic
theologians of the Middle Ages, who with every right quite calmly took
that the results of accurate theological reflexion formed part of the content
of faith Cf., e.g., St Thomas, Ia.32.4 c: 'indirecte vero ad *fidem* pertinet

bjectively, need not necessarily be just 'theology'. It is for the agisterium of the Church, which has the advantage of the isolated eologian in being able to make use of a higher criterion, to decide any concrete case where the boundary lies between dogma and ere theologoumenon,[1] between certainly correct and merely prob-le explication. The Church possesses an organ of perception by hich she can tell whether something which, from our point of view, merges as a result of theological activity, is in fact objectively some-ing more than the result of human speculation; whether it is still od's Word, though now expressed propositionally, in a new form, a new articulation and explication. At any rate it need not neces-rily be the case that what to us seems to be the fruit of theologically mplex exegesis and speculation should in actual fact lack the character f Revelation, even if in a given case this character is only guaranteed y the verdict of the magisterium.

Thus where we have an explication of faith in which it is possible demonstrate historically that theological reflexion has co-operated vhether this be in a properly scientific way or merely prescientifically, r there is no essential difference between the two inasmuch as both ork with the same instruments), the magisterium, assisted by the pirit, has a double function. Firstly it can in certain circumstances uarantee the correctness of this theological activity even where (in rinciple or up to now *de facto*) the activity, just as such, has led to no rict consequence but only to a *convenientia*. (We have at least left this ossibility open.) Moreover it guarantees not only that the conse-uence is correct, but also that it is still God's Word.

In this process of exploring dogma we have restricted the theo-gian to the use of those means which are made available to him by

---

, ex quibus negatis *consequitur* aliquid contrarium fidei.' According to . M. Schultes, it was the general teaching from the fourteenth to the fteenth century 'ad *fidem* pertinere non tantum ea quae expresse S. Scriptura el Traditione habentur, sed simul, quae inde bona et necessaria consequentia educuntur' (*Introductio in historiam dogmatum*, Paris 1922, pp. 115 s.).

In the last resort between a theologoumenon logically *certain* in itself ud something in the strict sense revealed (explicitly or implicitly) by God. Vhether *every* strict deduction from the propositions of faith must be aimed as formally implicit Revelation, is a question which we leave open. he only purpose of our discussion is to show that one has no right to say at every deduction *eo ipso* can no longer be regarded as revealed. But it oes seem to us that our discussion has at least shown this.

his exegetical and rational methods, so far as they enter *objectively* in
his actual demonstrative procedures, that is, in so far as he may nc
as theologian, rely upon any sort of intuition or illumination of fai
or the like, in his actual demonstration. But that does not mean that
the long run he could come to any real result if he thought of workir
with the data of original Revelation rather as though he were mere
an historian or a philosopher of religion. Rather it is as a member
the Church and in the light of faith that he must work, in real posse
sion of the object of faith and in real contact with it through grac
As such these presuppositions play no immediate part in the demo
stration itself, but in the long run it would be impossible witho
them to see the objective force of a piece of theological argumentatic
and give it its proper weight. In the long run the correctness of o
arguments and deductions from the propositions of faith can on
proceed from the heart of a faith known by being lived, that fai
which still possesses all in undivided unity and totality. But *th*
original faith can only be explicated when we attend to the bindir
formulations in which it has never failed to express itself, and nece
sarily in objective propositional form. Neither is wholly possib
without the other. For it was only to the Church as a whole that tl
promise was made that she should possess the original faith entire ar
unclouded. She alone, and not every isolated individual, has the orga
which, without fear of error, can bring this reflexion to completic
with universally binding authority. In the last resort this is why it
only in the Church that there is a secure guarantee of a permane
connexion between the original faith (in part global and implicit)
contact with the reality itself by grace and the light of faith, and tl
'new' explication by theological means. The individual recognizes tl
faith as binding and certain only in so far as he grasps it in the Chur
and with her.[1] In no case however may one side of the connexion l
played off against the other. Living, growing, as it were instinctiv
awareness in faith must not suppose that it can do without sob
theology, on the ground that it is more clairvoyant than theolog
prudently and meticulously carrying out its historical and ration

---

[1] This does not necessarily and invariably mean that the individual the
logian is only able to recognize as revealed by God (*fides divina*) what
explicitly taught as such by the ordinary or extraordinary magisterium
the Church (*fides catholica*). But even where this is not the case, he hea
God's Word as such *in* the Church.

tasks. On the other hand, theology, in its work of rational, conceptual deduction and historical investigation, must not suppose that in the Church's awareness in faith there can only be present as a real object of faith what it has already clearly demonstrated to be present by the use of its own proper theological instruments. It is only when the Church, after consideration of some 'new' proposition, knows herself to be in definitive possession of the truth, and declares this explicitly and with binding force for the awareness in faith of her individual members, that the just balance of the two aspects in any given case is finally guaranteed.

4

THEOS IN THE NEW TESTAMENT[1]

I. Preliminary Remarks

A FEW preliminary remarks concerning matter and method will be in order before we begin the discussion of our theme, the conception of God in the New Testament.

1. *Method*. In view of the extent and complexity of the subject, it is evident that we can only offer an inadequate and provisional treatment of it in a short lecture. It need only be recalled that the relevant article in Kittel's *Wörterbuch zum Neuen Testament*[2] runs to sixty large, closely printed pages. Clearly a detailed exegetical discussion of individual passages is practically impossible. All that the lecture can offer is a general survey of the question; and thus it will unavoidably assume at least the external character of a study in the philosophy of religion and in speculative theology.

2. *Matter*. A preliminary observation of more far-reaching consequence has to be made here. If the Biblical theology we are practising

---

[1] This essay was originally delivered as a lecture to a small theological study circle in Vienna, and was intended merely to prepare the way for further discussion. Consequently no attempt was made in the lecture to supply references or the usual apparatus. External circumstances made revision impossible. However, even in its present form, the essay may perhaps stimulate attempts to provide a better foundation in Biblical theology for our usual dogmatic treatises *De Deo Uno*, which are in most cases just philosophy with a few trimmings of Scripture.

[2] G. Kittel, TWNT III, pp. 65–123. Anyone who is acquainted with this article, by Kleinknecht, Quell, Stauffer and Kuhn, will not need individual references to see how much this essay owes to it.

is to be Biblical *theology* and not simply the historical study of Biblical religion, we are justified as regards both matter and method in considering what fundamental lines of approach are laid down for us, as men who read the Scriptures in the Church with a faith instructed by the Church, by the whole of our prior knowledge of theology. This general theological *a priori* for our investigation into the teaching of Scripture need not prejudice the historical accuracy of what we are going to claim as Scriptural teaching. On the contrary: even the most recent Biblical theology, as it is practised by Eichrodt or Stauffer or Kittel, for instance, invariably shows itself on closer inspection to be dominated by *a priori* theological concepts, formulations of the question and so on. Precisely because this *a priori* is not explicitly identified and reflexively formulated in advance, it involves a greater danger of 'eisegesis' and misinterpretation of the texts than when the general theological presuppositions from which we proceed to an examination of Scripture are honestly and plainly stated beforehand.

With regard to our question, then, we must try to discover in what way, according to the teachings of the Church, the *Christian* conception of God is bound to stand out in relief against pagan and philosophical conceptions. If we speak of a pagan conception, we have in mind for all practical purposes the conception of God in Greek and Roman antiquity; if we speak of a philosophical conception, by this is meant both non-Christian philosophy actually in existence (and so again for practical purposes Greek and Roman philosophy) as well as an 'ideal' philosophy. A review of Greek and Roman antiquity, not taking into account the religions of the rest of paganism, is sufficient for our purposes, because (apart from the practical impossibility of further extending our field of vision) the variety and range of Greek and Roman religion allow it to serve as typical for pagan religion in general, and because it is in fact the religious context into which the Christian message of God first entered.

What we shall investigate, then, is the way in which the conception of God in paganism and philosophy may in advance be expected to coincide with and depart from the Christian conception of God in the faith of the Church.

In order to answer this question we must first go a little further back. According to the Church's teaching, the *world* in which we live is in fact *supernatural*, that is, a world which as a whole is ordered to

he personal, Trinitarian God beyond the world. It is ordered as a
whole to a supernatural end: originally graced as a whole, then fallen
as a whole (for truly 'all creation groans for redemption'), yet a
world ever under the binding call of the God of supernatural life, shot
through by the rays of primitive Revelation and even before Christ
stirred by grace, at last redeemed as a whole in Christ. The whole of
Nature, then, has always been embedded in a supernatural context.
And so too the whole development of religion and all philosophy are
included under a theological *a priori*. In spite of their newness, Christ
and his Revelation are not the first in time to bring the supernatural
into the world, although all that is supernatural depends on him; but
Christ and his Revelation can indeed bring to light again the supernatural character of God's activity and of the world which stands
before him, rescuing it from the oblivion in which it had been lost;
and this oblivion itself might be due to forgetfulness and inadvertence
arising from original sin, and thus 'theological'. It is Revelation, then,
which can first tell us precisely what is natural and what supernatural
in non-Christian religion and thought, what is simply lack of knowledge in the non-Christian world and what *voluntary* ignorance, and
also what is supernatural knowledge or presentiment there (derived
from primitive Revelation or the inner dynamism of grace). So it is
Revelation which first throws light on the half or even completely
concealed supernatural, theological factor in pre-Christian and non-
Christian religion and philosophy, which cannot be regarded as some
sort of purely natural religion or purely natural speculation, nor again
as religion and philosophy which have become corrupted in some
purely natural way. It follows from these considerations that the
Christian faith must not and cannot owe anything to non-Christian
religion and speculation; clearly its content and its formulations can
appear nowhere else, either in principle or in fact. If similarities can be
traced, they are purely *a posteriori* in character, matters of fact. Putting
it the other way round, we may say that wherever some element or
formulation of Christian faith is pointed out to us outside Christianity,
even if the two are clearly shown to be connected empirically, there
need be no embarrassment or disquiet in accepting such an identification, provided that it is really there and is not achieved by a levelling-
down of what is specifically Christian, in the fashion widely current
today among historians of religion. All that such a fact would prove is
that the living God who revealed himself in Jesus Christ is at work

with his light and grace even outside the zone of saving history in the narrower, theological sense.

Let us now apply these general considerations of principle to the *knowledge* of *God*.

We know from the teaching of the Church that the one God as *principium et finis* of the world can be known with intrinsic certainty 'by the light of *natural reason*' from the objective world. All that is immediately given in this declaration is that such knowledge is possible for human nature. We say 'for human nature'; that is, concretely, this possibility of knowing God (concerning the content and extent of which more will be said in a moment) is something which belongs to the constitution of man even in independence of Revelation and the vocation which raises him by grace to a participation in the life of God in Trinity. It is a possibility, then, which man still has even when he has as a sinner lost the possibility of participating in God's personal life; one which consequently is still operative where and in so far as man's philosophy and religion lie under the law of sin; and so one which must in some form or other necessarily be met with in the non-Christian world of man's religion and philosophy, simply because he is man. The phrase 'rational knowledge from the world' demarcates this way of reaching God, firstly, from a personal divine revelation to man (both as inner illumination by grace and as exterior historical revelation). Further, this knowledge is distinguished from an immediate experience of God (whether present in fact or not), as this is understood in every form of ontologism, no matter whether it is mystical or rational in tendency. Thirdly, the phrase guards against a conception of experience of God which would make it something purely irrational, emotive, not available to critical examination and incapable of mediation by rational concepts and statements. Moreover, only a *possibility* of this kind of knowledge of God is in question. A whole series of problems arises here. Does this possibility ever become a reality, and if so to what extent? How does this realization come about? Is it due in fact to human nature alone, or are there in fact causes at work such as primitive Revelation and the supernatural grace which falls to every man's share? How far does this realization depend not merely on rational and logical factors but also on a moral decision, on which again both the inherited and the personal sin of man have their influence as well as healing supernatural grace? For the concrete acquisition of this knowledge of God in a concrete man, how far is growth in awareness of values always a presupposition, how far are sociological preconditions required like language, tradition, education, training of the religious sense? All these are questions on which no decision is made in the Vatican Council's definition. Taken by itself, all that is said in this definition about the content of the rational knowledge of God is that God can be known as cause and end of the world. Nothing is finally decided about the question as to whether God can be known as Creator of the world, in the strict theological sense of the word 'creation'. What in concrete terms forms the content of this possible natural knowledge of God, appears perhaps most simply when we try to determine the *theological sense* of this pronouncement about a possibility of human nature; for it becomes immediately apparent that Revelation could have absolutely no interest in determining a possibility of human nature, since it always has to deal with the concrete man, the man, then, who is always within the supernatural order. The theological sense of this decision (which in the last resort must always be related to a theological situation and not a purely natural one, in which, just in itself as a fact purely of this world, Revelation would have no interest) is clearly this: that in this conception of human nature alone is it possible for man to be a potentially receptive subject of theology and of Revelation. It is only if man stands before God always and of necessity and on every presupposition, even, then, as sinner, as turned away from God and deprived of the free gift of divine life—'by nature', then—that he is that being who has to come to terms with Revelation, who has the power to perceive Revelation, for whom the failure to perceive Revelation involves not merely deficiency but guilt. Precisely in order to be able to experience God's personal self-disclosure as *grace*, that is, to be able to apprehend it as neither obvious nor immanent (just a part of the divine constitution), man must be a subject who in the very nature of things has to come to terms with God's disclosure or withholding of himself. Only if it is in the nature of things that he has something to do with God can he freely and spontaneously experience God's self-disclosure as it is actually promulgated in Revelation: in other words, precisely so that Revelation might be grace, it is necessary at least in principle that man should have something to do with God from a locus which is not already grace.[1]

[1] Cf. K. Rahner, *Hörer des Wortes* (Munich 1941). It must of course be noted that this necessary 'natural' openness of man to God is, in the

We are now in a position to state more precisely what the content of this natural knowledge of God must be. It makes no difference to us here whether the notes which we shall enumerate are held to belong to the natural conception of God in virtue of an authoritative definition, or are merely derived by us from the definition. We say: any knowledge of God's transcendence and his existence as *personal* belongs to the content of the natural conception of God. It is true that man is that being who has to give ear to a possible Revelation in history and in speech; and if he is to experience this personal self-disclosure by God not just as God's free act but also as free grace to him, man, as already constituted in being (and this is the Biblical, Christian conception of Revelation), then he must from the very beginning ('by nature') be that being who has to reckon with God's speech or silence, God's bestowal or refusal of himself. It is only if this kind of bivalent relatedness to God belongs to man's very essence that he is on the one hand a potentially receptive subject of Revelation, only then that his constitution is such that even while remaining conscious of his obligation he can culpably reject Revelation (for he would not otherwise remain capable of receiving the Word); and on the other hand it is only then that he can experience Revelation, in case it is promulgated, as free grace (for in the nature of things he has also to reckon with God's silence). In other words, even naturally speaking man must stand before God conceived of as a free Person transcending the world.

We may ask what consequences follow from all this with regard to the question as to what conception of God we may expect to find in advance *outside* the genuine historical Revelation, and hence with regard to the question how far the revealed conception of God is bound to stand out in relief against the non-Christian one. In a certain way all the influences we have found actually at work in man's religious life and enumerated when we began these reflexions, will play a part in the non-Christian conception of God: natural man's knowledge of God ascending from below through the world, the deterioration due to original sin, grace and primitive Revelation.

---

historically realized scheme of things, always necessarily 'overlaid' (even when man is not in a state of justifying grace) by a supernatural 'existential' ordering the spiritual person to the God of eternal life. See below pp. 297–317.

Consequently all three factors will be seen most clearly at work at that point in the conception of God which is formally decisive for the Christian conception, namely, in God's free, personal existence transcending the world as *Lord* of Nature and History. Granted that even in man's fallen state his nature and divine grace are still continually active, it will never be possible that the consciousness of a God, unique, transcendent, free and freely treating with man in history, should disappear. But if man lives in a fallen state, and if in the last resort sin is the will not to allow God to be God and the attempt to shut the world in upon itself, then every non-Christian religion, in so far as it is and must be qualified theologically as sin, is bound to give God's infinity the meaning of an infinity of powers and forces active in the world, will be in fact a polytheism. Each one of these religions, in a metaphysical and religious pursuit of unity which is quite justified in itself, will try to comprehend the multiplicity of deified powers and forces of the world in a unity; and so inevitably each will turn into a form of pantheism. Each will be guilty of forgetting God as Person and as free to enter into historical communication with the world by his revealing Word; and in the last resort each will become devotion to the world instead of obedience to the unique and living God. All these elements (in varying measure, of course) will be met with in every non-Christian religion. It becomes basically impossible, then, to interpret any one of them in terms of an absolutely clear-cut formula, by means of which it should be distinguished merely negatively from the Christian conception of God. Which of the elements present in it actually decides the issue before God for the *individual* man and his concrete, existential achievements, is in the last resort not for us to judge.

Inversely, we may note three corresponding features of the *Christian* conception of God. In the first place, it will confirm that knowledge of the unique, transcendent, personal God which is always stirring into life, whether naturally or supernaturally, even outside the history of Revelation; and, precisely from the viewpoint of Revelation, it will free what is naturally true in non-Christian religion and philosophy from the encumbrance of sin, allowing what is supernatural in these truths to appear *as* such, and restraining the attempt to claim it as part of man's innate, inadmissible nobility. Secondly, the Christian conception will always express God's passionate protest against every kind of polytheistic or pantheistic deification of the world caused by original sin and everywhere at work, even today. Thirdly, it will alone be able to say unambiguously and definitively just how the personal, transcendent God desires *in actual fact* to stand to the world in his sovereign freedom: namely, as the God who actually discloses his inmost self to man out of grace, so compelling man in a unique, climactic situation to an absolute gravity, either bliss or damnation; as the God who gives his definitive sanction to the world in the Incarnation of his Son and so precisely summons it to share in his triune life.

3. We must now proceed to a further preliminary discussion of the material for this study. What we have so far said has been concerned with the features which distinguish the non-Christian from the Christian conception of God, still taking the history of Revelation as a unified whole. The preparatory remarks which follow are concerned with distinctions in the conception of God *within the history of Revelation itself.* In other words, the question here is whether the conception of God in Revelation itself permits of differentiation and change, and in what way it does so. In the concrete terms of our theme, this is the question whether a more or less fundamental difference between the conceptions of God in the Old and in the New Testament is to be expected in advance, and what kind of difference this may be.

For this purpose we must start somewhat further back. Revelation (by which we mean not just God's speech but also and above all his active dealings with men) does have a real *history.* Precisely because God, who is already known by man's natural reason from the world, is a free person transcending the world, the knowledge which is man's by nature must release this personal God. It cannot work out the concrete manner in which God wishes to enter into relations with man, to deal with him, by calculations starting from below, from man; it cannot, in the last resort, establish a clearly defined, concrete religion. In the last resort all it can settle with respect to religion remains enclosed within the brackets of God's free sovereignty and the knowledge of this sovereignty, at the disposal of which man must put himself by obedience in true *religio,* and in which God either denies himself to man or bestows himself in free grace. And on this either-or rests the final decision as to the concrete shape taken by a truly and existentially significant religion. Now this question cannot be answered by men, in terms of a metaphysical outline of God's essence, but only by God himself, by his own free decision as event. But a decision of this kind is essentially historical, and historical in a twofold sense: firstly in the sense of a *divine* historicity (if we may be allowed the expression), by which all that is meant is simply that God's decision is personal and free, a moment in a dialogue with men already constituted in being. In so far as God's actually evinced speech to men always meets a human being for whose nature and existence God's Revelation can never become a self-evident constituent, and hence may never be interpreted in accordance with some physical law as a factor in the immanent development of human nature, it is clear that Revelation is always a free event, free even when and indeed in so far as man is presupposed as something given. It is not just because man himself is an act of God's freedom that God's Word and his saving Act are free; this metaphysical freedom is not to be confused with God's freedom within the world already in being. His Word and Act are free in the further sense that they are freely directed to men already in existence, and so are essentially Event and History, not Thing, metaphysical Idea or Norm. What happens in saving history is not the natural outcome of some unchanging ideal law, but the free, incalculable, ever new Event of God's activity. In this sense God's speech and action would take the form of an historical and temporal dialogue even if it were uniformly to accompany the whole duration of human history and physical process. But in actual fact God's decision is historical in a second sense—in *human* historicity: there does in fact exist a real history of Revelation. That is to say, God has certainly not established one and the same thing once and for all, but what he has said and done was said and done at quite definite points in space and time, so that even considered in extension saving history and world history do not coincide.

In spite of its character as event, its variety and multiplicity, God's historical activity in the world has as a whole an inner connexion, an inner teleology, so that any act in this saving history only becomes comprehensible and meaningful as an element in the whole. Comprehensible and meaningful, of course, not in the sense that we could on our own construct the whole from a part by some sort of physical or biological extrapolation, see it as possessing a conceptual necessity; but it is meaningful and unified just in that sense in which the manifold, changing behaviour of a free spiritual person is a *single* significant unity.

We have now to distinguish more sharply in Revelation and saving history between the saving *process* itself (e.g. Paradise, the rejection of man, the Incarnation, the Church, Judgment) and the *Word* which necessarily accompanies it, and through which every saving process first exists for us as a saving action performed among us by God in the area of our spiritually perceptive personality. God's central and definitive saving act, one precisely for that reason different from all the others, is the single inner unity of Incarnation, Cross and Resurrection, in which he definitively and radically communicated himself to the world and in which he really came to us. In this sense all the earlier saving acts are intrinsically directed to Christ as their end, and every revealed Word which enters into composition with them and accompanies them thus has intrinsic reference to the definitive and unsurpassable Revelation of God in Christ. And so Augustine's statement is really true, that the New Testament is already present concealed in the Old. In accordance with what we have said this presence is of course *prophetic*, that is, the Word of the Old Testament already possesses in actual fact an inner orientation to God's definitive Word in and through Christ. It really is the first Word of a uniform, inwardly coherent dialogue, the final Word of which is Christ. But of necessity this first Word is spoken by God in such a way that within the historical dialogue of salvation man too retains freedom of speech and action, scope for genuine venture and decision. It must then be the case (returning to our question and its concrete terms) that the Word of the Old Testament, in so far as it already contains the tidings of the New, is necessarily obscure. This Word is primarily an utterance concerning God's saving Act in the time of the Old Covenant, and contains a prophetic anticipation of the saving reality of the New inasmuch as the reality of God's saving acts in the history of the Old Covenant possesses inner teleological reference to the New. It follows as a matter of intrinsic necessity that the Word of the Old Testament is in a characteristic way at once historical with respect to contemporary events and prophetic with respect to the future. It says enough about what has just happened to allow the hearer to come to a decision with regard to the future by abandoning himself in faith to the work of salvation then taking place; and what it says is so little and so obscure that his decision is still not really committed in advance. God always retains sovereign control over the course of this historical dialogue: what he had already laid down as its definitive sense from its very first Word, is disclosed to someone who can directly perceive its last Word in a quite different and specifically higher way than it is disclosed to someone who only perceived the first Word. The Old Testament unfolds only in the New; and yet the inner nature of the Old Testament Word is such that anyone who abandons himself to its hidden dynamism and allows himself to be carried beyond the limits of his personal interpretation and the letter of the text, will mysteriously and secretly partake of the benediction really contained in the New. In principle, then, we can never interpret the Old Testament except in terms of our existential situation in the plan of salvation, in terms, then, of the New Testament. If we try to take up an objective, neutral position and ask what the Old Testament meant for a man under the Old Covenant, in precisely his situation and for him alone, it is in principle almost impossible to avoid the danger of seeing too much or too little in the text: we should either make the continuity of Old and New into an already manifest presence of the New in the Old or harden the Old into a stiff, self-contained block.

What relation should we expect to find, then, between the idea of God in the Old Testament and that in the New, in accordance with these general considerations? We may say that the New Testament idea of God cannot take its place alongside the Old Testament as something simply new, as it were by a *generatio aequivoca*; it must already be active in the Old Testament, concealed in prophecies which must by their very nature be obscure. The New Testament idea of God must be the unveiling and the fulfilment of the Old Testament idea, the Word which for the first time declares the final and unambiguous meaning of what God has said about himself in the Old Testament by his speech and action, and on the basis of which we must interpret all its statements if we are to understand them properly in their significance for ourselves. This unity and sameness of the idea of God in the New and in the Old Testaments must not be misinterpreted by falsely reducing similar statements to the static necessity proper to a metaphysical idea of God. In the last resort, God is the Same in the Old Testament and in the New, not because he is in possession of a necessary, immutable essence, but because the whole of saving history is a progressive revelation of the way in which the free God who is active in history has wished to enter into relationship with his world.

II. The Greek and Old Testament Conceptions of God

1. The Greek Conception of God

If we begin by speaking of the Greek conception of God, this is because we must have some acquaintance with the concrete world in which the Christian Gospel appeared. It is only in this way that we can understand why the conversion from idols to God in order to serve the true and living God (1 Thess 1:9), why 'monotheism', that is, does not mean a self-evident metaphysical assumption for Christianity, but belongs to the very heart of its message. The following remarks about the Greek conception of God are restricted to conditions in the Greek, Roman, Oriental *oikoumene* of the time; they are not offered as a description of the whole long development of the Greek conception of God. And even these indications can only be summary in character, without any attempt to explore the historical material.

a. By θεός the Greeks did not mean the unity of a definite personality in the monotheistic sense, but rather the unity of the religious world, clearly felt as *one* in spite of its multiplicity of forms. The Greek conception of God is essentially polytheistic, not indeed in the sense of many isolated gods but as an ordered totality of gods, such as appears in Homer's divine polity, for instance, where the gods are ranged in order, one above the other. This view naturally promoted the use of the term θεός and achieved its most generously conceived form in the person of Zeus, the πατὴρ ἀνδρῶν τε θεῶν τε, the monarchic θεῶν ὕπατος καὶ ἄριστος, the ultimate exponent of divine dominion. This view of a pluralistic cosmos of gods was maintained to the end, in spite of the most strenuous attempts to establish unity in a philosophical conception of God from which all traces of anthropomorphism had long since disappeared. The Stoa still rejected monotheism as a diminution of God. According to Plotinus, God's greatness is proved by the multiplicity of gods, because the divine must not be compressed into a point but must be unfolded in all its multiplicity, over the whole range of its own self-unfolding. The forms of the Greek gods are nothing but the basic forms of cosmic reality, whether these are conceived of mythically (as in Homer) or in terms of an ultimate homogeneous ἀρχή (as in Ionian physics) or as the ἰδέα of the philosophers. This reality is multiform, and approaches men with the most various demands, demands which exist in free and unruffled opposition in the divine world above but which often intersect each other in man's heart with tragic results. Hence the plural θεοί and polytheism. Wherever something profoundly actual, some massive, pregnant reality emerges majestically in the world, the Greek can only say: just this—not, shall we say, the 'wholly Other'—is God. Gods, then, are powers, which as Order, Form and Meaning penetrate the whole world with their influence, and continually restore the chaotic to coherence. The world's unfolding as Order, its realization as Form and Whole, its potent intelligibility—this is God; but the gods have not created the world *ex nihilo*. The historical development of the Greek conception of God invariably turns on the question of how this aspect of the Absolute in the world is precisely to be understood. The development of the Greek idea of God is the history of the forms in which the divine has expressed itself in Being. According as the world itself is metaphysically unified—and only so far—the conception of God too becomes henotheistic: it does not for that reason become any less cosmological. Θεός continues to be a predicate, and the subject of this predicate is the cosmos.

b. In spite of this dominant polytheism and pantheism which is found throughout Greek thought even in its most sublime forms, a genuinely monotheistic note, a shadowy, unrealized knowledge of a truly personal, transcendent God, should not be overlooked. We must allow for this at least in the sense that under all the formulas, the rites and the religious practices which entered into the concrete activities of the individual man as he sought salvation and reflected on things under the touch of grace, man could enter into a truly personal relationship with a living God. It is always possible that primitive Revelation and rational, monotheistic reflexion may have contributed to the forms of Zeus and Jupiter. Something of true monotheism was really alive—it makes no difference what the ultimate motive was—wherever men simply prayed to God and so in some way or other a personal, urgent, unqualified *Thou* was uttered; wherever men asked to be told the will of the gods, or where, as in the philosophy of Plato or Aristotle, an attempt was made to discover an absolute and supreme *One*, transcending the Many; or when it happened, as in the case of the Presocratics Xenophanes and Heracleitus, that the polytheism of the

Homeric pantheon was explicitly combated. In some such way the world became open and men attentive to what lay beyond: although this openness of the world to the living One transcending all might suddenly close in again, as soon as men tried to say who this ultimate One was to whom they prayed in real need; and the mysterious depths of the world as suddenly become again, no longer the unknown God, but the divine 'It' of νόμος, δίκη, Mind, Idea, beyond which εἱμαρμένη still maintained its incomprehensible and inscrutable sway.

2. The Conception of God in the Old Testament

a. A preliminary remark about method has to be made here, even if it is an obvious one. If we are going to discuss the Old Testament conception of God, we are not going to inquire what conception of God prevailed in historical fact among the individuals who composed the People of the Covenant, granting that this conception was of course reflected in the Old Testament literature. Our inquiry is directed to finding out what portrait of God is offered in the Old Testament as true and binding. And here too we must forgo any attempt to describe the historical development of the conception.

b. The religion of the Old Testament is commonly spoken of as *monotheism*. This basic characterization is quite just, provided that we understand what we mean by 'monotheism' when we apply the term to Old Testament religion. Monotheism must not be understood here as a metaphysical denomination of a static kind, to be applied with equal justice to Deism. In the last resort, the monotheism of the Old Testament is not based on the rational considerations of a man who is seeking for the ultimate unity of the world and can only find it in a transcendent Source of all things; rather it is based on the experience of Yahweh's saving deeds in the midst of this world and in the history of his People. The heart of Old Testament monotheism is found in the fact that Yahweh, i.e. the definite Person with a proper name who actually intervenes in the history of a people and of all men by his own free will, has seized hold of this definite people, without regard to their natural qualities, has chosen it and made it his own People by entering into a covenant with it; and as the jealous God has forbidden it to venerate all other numinous powers so that he might establish his uniqueness as the only God with whom his People can be concerned. Old Testament monotheism involves a conscious recognition of this fact: it knows that this Person Yahweh, freely active in history, can alone legitimately claim the title El-Elohim; that all other Elohim are not such in reality, are Nothings; that this Yahweh is the absolute sovereign Lord of the World and of Nature (so that every kind of worship of Baal, as a cult of the powers of Nature and fertility, is a service of idols and nonsensical); that this Yahweh is wholly Spirit and Person, on whose free 'creation' absolutely everything depends. The further working out of this conscious recognition could safely be left to the historic development of this basic idea of Old Testament monotheism; it forms in fact the greater part of what is revealed in Old Testament history. This history does not of course advance by a merely human reflexion upon the basic datum we have described, but rather through an experience of the unceasing novelty of Yahweh's personal action (so that really it is not a history of theology, but a history of Revelation and Salvation, of God's own speech and action in the world). A cosmological metaphysics ascends to a first cause of the world, to an intellectual first cause, and thence to a first cause transcending the world, and thus (in principle, at least) proceeds until it has in fact achieved some understanding of God as Person (in purely formal terms, of course); in this way it terminates in the ultimate question as to whether and how this personal God might not only continue to cause the world but also—appearing alongside the world, as it were—might wish to deal with it. The development of the Old Testament conception of God proceeds in exactly the reverse order: first comes the experience of God as a free Person active in the world, a Person generous and abundant, who reveals himself in his proper name, who calls and chooses; and it is only from this historical experience of who Yahweh is that it becomes progressively clearer *what* he is—not just *a* God, not just *a* powerful Lord in the history of perhaps this people alone, but *the* Lord of the history of all peoples and so Lord of Nature too: the transcendent, spiritual Cause and Source of all reality, lifted up above every earthly limitation. This Lord (because of the original starting-point of his People's knowledge of him) is not dissolved in the empty indistinctness of an impalpable metaphysical concept but remains in his absolute transcendence of all earthly things concretely and unambiguously *He*, just as He wished in his sovereign freedom to show himself, in the course of the unique history of his covenant with this People. A brief formulation of what we have learnt would run as follows: the basic form of Old Testament monotheism is not, 'One God exists' (there is a single primary cause of the world); but 'Yahweh is the unique God'. We shall content ourselves for the moment with this brief sketch of what is decisive for Old Testament thought about God, and return to the Old Testament as occasion offers in the course of our discussion of the New Testament conception.

PART TWO: THEOS IN THE NEW TESTAMENT

I. The Point of Departure

1. The *unquestioning assurance* which characterized consciousness of God.

The first thing that strikes us when we try to find out how the men of the New Testament thought about God is the unquestioning assurance which characterized their consciousness of him. It never occurred to these men to raise the question of his existence as such. The New Testament knew nothing of all those characteristic features of our consciousness of God today: an anxious sense that questioning must come first, a sense that it is first necessary slowly and reflectively to lay a firm foundation before any sort of intimation, developed feeling or recognition of God can be admitted; a feeling that God never fails to withdraw himself from the grip of man's questions; a fear that after all God may be nothing but a monstrous projection of man's subjective needs and yearnings; a suffering in religious doubt. For the New Testament God is in the first place simply there. He is there: in spite of all his incomprehensibility and sublimity, all the fear and trembling and the overwhelming joy which this divine Reality may have in store for men, nevertheless as simply the most evident fact of all, the fact in no need of proof or explanation, he is really there. For the men of the New Testament the question is not whether the reality of the world which they can see and touch might perhaps point beyond itself to the infinite darkness of a wholly Other; all they are concerned with is how this God, who has always been given and self-evident, actually behaves, so that man might for the first time learn how things really stand with himself and the world. It is not the immediate reality of the world and its visible magnitude which serve as a kind of permanent base from which, subsequently as it were, God is going to come within reach, but just the reverse: it is only under

God that men find their own reality and the reality of the world really clear and comprehensible. This unquestioning assurance of God's existence does not arise from any properly metaphysical considerations, nor is it troubled or put off balance by the awareness that this kind of genuine knowledge of God is absent in the rest of the New Testament world.

Firstly, then, this unquestioning assurance does not really arise from *metaphysical reflexion*. Proofs for the existence of God are never produced. There is never any guidance on how man might by himself develop a consciousness of God, nowhere an appeal to a need for God with the intention of eliciting a conscious conviction of his existence. The New Testament is indeed aware of a self-consistent possibility of knowing God from the world. The one and only true God, his δύναμις and θειότης (this abstract metaphysical term occurs only twice in the New Testament), his σοφία and the δικαίωμα τοῦ θεοῦ, God's sanction of the natural moral law as a divine ordination (1 Cor 1:21; Rom 1:32; 2:14), can be known through what is made (ποιήματα, Rom 1:20) always and everywhere, hence in independence of God's historical action in the world (ἀπὸ κτίσεως κόσμου, Rom 1:21); and they can be known with such certainty that the refusal to acknowledge God by revering him or giving thanks (Rom 1:21) involves moral guilt, which provokes the wrath of God (Rom 1:18). For St Paul, something knowable exists in God, which while remaining objective, presents itself openly (φανερόν) for man's recognition (Rom 1:19). According to St Paul again, the character of the world as created must always have been apparent to man (Rom 1:20). There is always the possibility for the world of a σοφία which can come to know God from the σοφία θεοῦ objectivized in the world (1 Cor 1:21). In spite of its certainty this possible knowledge of God, which is moreover always somehow present in actual fact (φανερόν ἐστιν ἐν αὐτοῖς, Rom 1:19; γνόντες τὸν θεόν, Rom 1:21), always essentially involves man's moral and religious decision. Although God is never far from men (Ac 17:27), their situation is such that they must seek him (ζητεῖν); so that in consequence of his character of the knowledge of God as *decision*, it is uncertain (εἰ ἄρα γε) whether they will in fact touch him and find him (Ac 17:27).

But for the actual consciousness of the men of the New Testament his metaphysical possibility is *not* the *existential* support and cause of their consciousness of God. The metaphysical knowledge of God is never discussed at length. It is never invoked by the men of the New Testament as far as their own experience of God is concerned; reference is only made to it so as to show how ignorance of God is comprehensible as moral depravity, to convict someone who does not know God of sin. Even where this metaphysical possibility is briefly touched on in the context of an apologetic for monotheism (Ac 17:22 s.) the final motive of conversion to the living God is not the metaphysical argument but the historical activity of God himself revealing himself in the foolishness of the Cross (1 Cor 1:18 s.) and the Resurrection (Ac 17:31). These are facts which are brought home to men not in the form of a truth in itself basically reasonable and available at all times for inspection, by helpful guidance and instruction, but by preaching and proclamation, by an announcement which exacts not intelligent comprehension but obedient acknowledgment (εὐαγγελίζεσθαι, Ac 14:15; ἀπαγγέλλειν, Ac 17:30; κηρύσσειν, 1 Cor 1:21.23).

In the second place, the unquestioning assurance of God's self-evident reality is not disturbed by the awareness of an ignorance of God in the pagan world round about. The New Testament knows of χρόνους τῆς ἀγνοίας (Ac 17:30), an ἄγνοια (Eph 4:18; Ac 17:23, ἀγνοεῖν), an ignorance of God (Gal 4:8, οὐκ εἰδέναι; 1 Thess 4:5; 2 Thess 1:8), a failure to apprehend God (1 Cor 1:21), ἄθεοι ἐν τῷ κόσμῳ (Eph 2:12). For the New Testament this failure to apprehend God is always a moral fault and also its punishment. It knows of no ignorance or doubt about God which is morally neutral, any religious problematic which remains purely theoretical[1]; wherever God is not known, it is a matter of a ματαιότης τοῦ νοός (Eph 4:17; Rom 1:21), a πώρωσις τῆς καρδίας (Eph 4:18), a darkening of man's foolish heart (Rom 1:21) and his understanding (Eph 4:18), a μωρία (Rom 1:22). St Paul deals with this ignorance of the true God, involving moral guilt, in the concrete form of idolatry (Rom

---

[1] When a particular δεισιδαιμονία is attributed to the Athenians (Ac 17:22), it is an extensive and manifold religious activity which is meant—St Paul intentionally keeps the word as neutral as possible (TWNT II, p. 21). But it seems clear from St Paul's general view that the word is certainly not supposed to recognize the existence of a piety which while it is false theoretically, is morally praiseworthy, as though human guilt did not enter essentially into the form of this piety.

:23; Ac 14:15; 17:29; 1 Cor 8:1–7; 12:2; 1 Thess 1:9).[1] And in the
ast resort St Paul sees idolatry as the worship of demonic powers
1 Cor 10:20.21; cf. Apoc 9:20). The New Testament knows quite
vell, in an almost rationalistic way, that the pagan gods[2] are 'nothing'
Ac 19:26; 1 Cor 8:4; 10:19, Gal 4:8); but the polytheistic pagan
ults do in fact come into contact with a numinous reality, the demons.
or St Paul there really are powers and forces in the world which may
vith a certain right be called θεοί and κύριοι (1 Cor 8:5). He
naintains that a specific and essential connexion must hold between
piritual powers and Nature, even if he does not explicitly state what
is (Eph 6:12, κοσμοκράτορες; Col 2:18, θρησκεία τῶν ἀγγέλων;
f. the notion of στοιχεῖα τοῦ κόσμου, Gal 4:3.9; Col 2:8.20);
ɔ that for him, to treat the world as an absolute (ἐλάτρευσαν τῇ
τίσει παρὰ τὸν κτίσαντα, Rom 1:25) is really equivalent to wor-
nipping the spiritual powers who have turned away from God, and
vho as at once στοιχεῖα τοῦ κόσμου and spirits hostile to God, hold
way in and over the visible world.

We have seen that this failure to know God consists in culpably
naking an absolute of the multiple reality of a world become demonic,
nd so becomes objectively a cult of the demons who form the meta-
hysical background of this world-power. For St Paul the failure is
ius a *refusal* to know God (Rom 1:18 s.), and the refusal is intrinsi-
illy and necessarily coexistent with actually knowing something
ɔout God all the time (καὶ καθὼς οὐκ ἐδοκίμασαν τὸν θεὸν
χειν ἐν ἐπιγνώσει: they would not admit that they had know-
·dge of God, Rom 1:28; cf. Rom 1:19.21.32; 2:14). This is not the
lace to discuss this remarkable coexistence in man of a continual
nowledge of God and a deliberate ignorance of him, and how we are
ɔ interpret it in logical and psychological detail; how it may be
ecessary to distinguish various layers in man's existential con-
iousness; how reference might be made to the phenomena of bad
ɔnscience, repression, self-deception, masked conscience; to meta-
hysical conceptions like the *scintilla animae* and synderesis. Yet this
hole complex makes it clear why the men of the New Testament did
ɔt feel that their unquestioning assurance of God's self-evident
·ality was affected by the atheistic polytheism which surrounded

---

[1] On polytheism in *Acts*, see TWNT III, p. 100.
[2] εἴδωλον: TWNT II, p. 375.

them. In it they saw guilt and the operation of demonic power, precisely in order to combat which they were sent in the strength of the true God who went with them. They were convinced that their Word did not encounter men to whom something till then simply unknown had to be brought home for the first time by careful instruction, but rather that it encountered men who had already had some kind of knowledge of God, even if they would not admit its truth, even if this truth was heavily overlaid in their minds by a settled ignorance—settled only in appearance. They brought tidings of the living God who had freely acted in history and so had disclosed himself to man as something infinitely beyond the capacities of the visible world; and at the same time their tidings laid bare a knowledge of God buried under original and personal sin—a kind of theological psychoanalysis, as it were. Thus the revealed Word and natural knowledge of God mutually condition each other. The revealed Word presupposes men who really know something of God in spite of being lying and lost through sinfully idolizing the world; and on the other hand this concealed knowledge of God only becomes really conscious of itself when it breaks through men's hardness of heart and is released by the Word of the God who reveals himself as utterly beyond the world.

2. The *inner reason* for the unquestioning assurance of God's reality.

The basic reason for this unquestioning assurance which characterizes men's consciousness of God in the New Testament is the simple and massive fact that God had *revealed himself*, that by his action he himself had intervened in these men's history and so had given testimony to his own actuality. Above all else the men of the New Testament are convinced that God had revealed himself in the Old Testament history of the People of the Covenant. For 'God at sundry times and in divers manners spoke to the fathers by the prophets' (Heb 1:1). Their God is the God of the fathers (Ac 3:13; 5:30; 7:45; 13:17 s.; 22:14; 24:14), the God of Abraham, Isaac and Jacob (Mt 22:32 par.; Lk 1:72 s.; 2:32; Ac 3:13), who showed himself to Abraham (Ac 7:2), who by the Covenant had made the People his People (Mt 2:6; Lk 1:72; 2:32; Ac 3:25; 13:17; Rom 9:4; 11:2; Gal 3:17; Heb 8:9; 9:15) and himself Israel's God (Lk 1:68). The men of the New Testament see this God at work throughout the history of this, their People (Stephen's speech, Ac 7:2–53; St Paul's preaching at Antioch, Ac 13:16–41). They know God by seeing his action in the saving history peculiar to Israel. So too the prophetic monotheism of the Old Testament is for them the foundation of their knowledge of God. But their knowledge of God is not derived just from his self-disclosure in the past history of their People; they experience the living reality of God in his new activity in their own history. God reveals himself anew to them too. God has spoken to them in his own Son *now* (Heb 1:2), now made known his saving grace (Tit 2:11; 3:4; 2 Tim 1:10), through the Son of God, through whom they have come to faith in God (1 Pet 1:21). The Son has declared God to them, whom no one has seen (Jn 1:18); they have seen the Son of God with their own eyes, have heard him and touched him with their hands (1 Jn 1:1). God's glory shines for them in the face of Christ (2 Cor 4:6; Jn 12:45). For the men of the New Testament and just *their* situation in the plan of salvation, an indissoluble bond connects their experience in faith of the reality of Christ and their knowledge in faith of God. Hence the large number of expressions in which Christ and God are associated: eternal life is the knowledge of the only true God and of him whom he has sent (Jn 17:3); the turning away from idols to the service of the true and living God and waiting for his Son are as it were the basic formula of Christianity in 1 Thess 1:9–10. What St John preaches is κοινωνία with the Father and his Son (1 Jn 1:3). Salvation is fulfilled in the ἐπίγνωσις τοῦ θεοῦ καὶ Ἰησοῦ τοῦ κυρίου ἡμῶν (2 Pet 1:2). And these two realities do not stand unrelatedly side by side, nor are they connected merely objectively; they are now so inseparably connected even in the experience of the believer that whoever abandons one does away with the other too: 'Whosoever denieth the Son, the same hath not the Father' (1 Jn 2:23; cf. Jn 5:23; 14:6–14). The New Testament does indeed allow for a true and enduring knowledge of God even without the possession in faith of his Son. But in that crisis in which the man whom Christ has encountered has to make a decision, this kind of true knowledge of God, such as the Jews perhaps have (cf. Rom 2:17 s.), ceases to be the only knowledge which matters to the New Testament: that knowledge which brings man into real relationship with the living God as Saviour. And in this sense those who do not have the Son do not in fact 'know' God at all, not as though it were only as Father of the Son precisely that they do not know him. So the Lord can say: 'If I glorify myself, my glory is nothing. It is my Father that glorifies me. You call him your God, and yet you know him not. But I know him' (Jn 8:54–5). Because they do not acknowledge and love the Son come from the Father (ἐκ τοῦ θεοῦ) and sent by him (Jn 8:42), they no longer acknowledge the God whose sons they are convinced they are in virtue of the Old Covenant. But the men of the New Testament, the witnesses of the whole reality of Christ (Ac 2:22.32; 3:15; 10:39; 13:31), have had the living, tangible experience of Christ, his reality, his miracles and his Resurrection, with overwhelming clarity. They have encountered God there. They know him from his living, powerful action among them in Christ. The primary thing for them is not a carefully constructed philosophical conception of God, but God's own concrete self-disclosure to them in Christ.

II. The Content of the New Testament Conception of God

1. The Uniqueness of God

a. The central *significance* of the New Testament doctrine of God's uniqueness.

When Jesus was asked which was the first of all the commandments and answered that it was the commandment of love—and this is the heart of the Pauline and Johannine message too (Rom 13:10; 1 Cor 8:3; ch. 13; Col. 3:14; 1 Jn 3:11)—he himself in this critical context (Mk 12:29) cited the Shema: ἄκουε, ᾽Ισραήλ, κύριος ὁ θεὸς ἡμῶν κύριος εἷς ἐστιν. The Scribe can only confirm Jesus' profession of the faith of his People, once more in the words of the Old Testament (Deut 6:4; 4:35): εἷς ἐστιν καὶ οὐκ ἔστιν ἄλλος πλὴν αὐτοῦ (Mk 12:32). This confession of the *one* God runs through the entire New Testament. In Jesus' own words, eternal life is that they should know the only true God (Jn 17:3) and be mindful of the glory which is from this *one* God alone (Jn 5:44); οὐδεὶς θεὸς εἰ μὴ εἷς (1 Cor 8:4). Thus testimony to the uniqueness of the sole God is constantly recurring: εἷς ὁ θεός (Rom 3:30; 1 Cor 8:6; Gal 3:20; Eph 4:6; 1 Tim 2:5; Jas 2:19), μόνος θεός (Rom 16:27; 1 Tim 1:17; 6:15; Jude 25; Apoc 15:4). Now this monotheism is not just a fragment of tradition taken over from the Old Testament, although it is in fact usually expressed in the old traditional

ormulas. It is bound up with the basic Christian confession; and
when Christ wanted to state as briefly as possible what that eternal
fe was which he offered men, he spoke of the knowledge of the one
true God (Jn 17:3). When St Paul, in the earliest portion of the New
Testament, sums up what has come about in the Thessalonians who
ave become Christians, once again the first item to be mentioned is
onversion to the living and true God in opposition to the many
alse gods (1 Thess 1:9). And from God's uniqueness St Paul derives
upport for two of his central themes: the calling of the Gentiles to the
ame rights in the New Israel (Rom 3:28–30; 10:12, 1 Tim 2:4–5),
nd the unity of the multiple workings of the Spirit among Christians
a the one Body of Christ (1 Cor 12:6 ; Eph 4:6). Again the notion
ϵὐαγγέλιον τοῦ θεοῦ seems in many places (Rom 15:16; 1 Thess
: 2.8.9) in view of the context, to have the sense, 'Gospel of the one
ue God'. Confession of faith in the one true God is one of the
ssential elements in the Gospel of Christ.

The *meaning* of the monotheism of the New Testament.
The central significance of New Testament monotheism becomes
ill clearer when we try to discover what is meant by this teaching.
his confession is not concerned with a mere metaphysical matter of
ourse, merely the primary cause of every sort of reality, necessarily
onceived of as an ultimate unity. This one God is indeed spoken of
the primary cause of all things: ἐξ οὗ τὰ πάντα (1 Cor 8:6), he is
ατὴρ πάντων, ὁ ἐπὶ πάντων καὶ διὰ πάντων καὶ ἐν πᾶσιν
Eph 4:6), ὁ ἐνεργῶν τὰ παντα ἐν πᾶσιν (1 Cor 12:6); it is he who
ves to all life and breath and all things (Ac 17:25), 'in whom we
ve and move and are' (Ac 17:28), so that 'he is not far from every
ne of us' (Ac 17:27); and because of this ontological relationship to
e world, it is possible in principle, according to St Paul, for this one
od to be known from the world in his θειότης (Rom 1:20). We
ave already noted that this metaphysical knowledge of God is a
uried knowledge, only brought to some understanding of itself by
tual contact with God's revelation in action; but even apart from
is fact the confession of the εἷς θεός of its very nature goes beyond
nowledge of a unified First Cause and End of the world. Here too we
ve an instance of what has been called 'prophetic' monotheism.
In the first place, it is not simply a matter of establishing the unique-
ss of this one God in a neutral way; rather he is confessed in faith:

ἀλλ' ἡμῖν εἷς θεός (1 Cor 8:6), although (and because) there are
θεοὶ πολλοὶ καὶ κύριοι πολλοί in the world (1 Cor 8:5) although
(and because) behind the polytheism in the face of which monotheistic confession is made, there stand real demonic powers and
not just error and misconception. As in the Old Testament, the
one God of whom confession is made is not primarily the end-term
of autonomous human knowledge, but the living, acting God who
makes himself known by his own action. And so the formula for New
Testament monotheism does not run, There exists one God, somewhat in the sense of the Enlightenment, We all believe in one God
but on the contrary, He who has actively manifested himself in Christ
and in the pneumatic reality of salvation which has come into being
with Christ, that is the unique God. And here too it is distinguished
from Old Testament monotheism: the *Father* of our Lord *Jesus*
Christ is the unique God, and just this is the denial of Judaism.
Because the one God (ὁ θεός) whom the men of the New Testament
confess is the living Person who was at work in the saving history of
the Old Testament and definitively revealed himself in his Son, the men
of the New Testament like to go on using the old expressions 'God
of the fathers' (Ac 3:13; 5:30; 22:14), 'God of Israel' (Mt 15:31;
Lk 1:68; Ac 13:17; 2 Cor 6:16; Heb 11:16), 'God of Abraham,
Isaac and Jacob' (Mk 12:26; Lk 20:37; Ac 3:13; 7:32; Mt 22:32)
and speak in the manner of the Old Testament about 'our' God (Mt
12:29; Lk 1:78; Ac 2:39; 3:22; 1 Cor 6:11; 1 Thess 2:2; 3:9;
2 Thess 1:11–12; 1 Tim 1:1; Heb 12:29; 2 Pet 1:1; Apoc 4:11; 5:10;
7:3; 12:10; 19:1.5) or quite personally of 'my' God (Lk 1:47; Rom
1:8: 2 Cor 12:21; Phil 1:3; 4:19; Phm 4; Apoc 3:12—4 times); on
the other hand they speak also of the God and Father of our Lord
Jesus Christ (Rom 15:6; 2 Cor 1:3; 11:31; Eph 1:3) or again more
briefly of the God of our Lord Jesus Christ (Eph 1:17). This concrete
God is the unique God intended when monotheism is professed.
Anyone who confesses the One God and does not thereby intend to
confess in this God the God of the fathers and of our Lord Jesus
Christ, certainly does not mean the God of whom the primitive
Church made confession: ἀλλ' ἡμῖν εἷς θεός (1 Cor 8:6).

Secondly, the uniqueness of the divine nature in the world and in
history is *not* supposed to be something established in a merely *static*
way. God's uniqueness has first to become operative in the world and
in history. God must first *become* for man the unique God. For men

confess the unique God does not imply merely the confession of a
ct but the acceptance of a task; for this God who acts in history
tends precisely by this means to extend his βασιλεία, the acknow-
dgment of his unique divinity, so it is truly only by a slow process
hat he becomes the unique God (ἔσομαι αὐτῶν θεός, 2 Cor 6:16;
. Heb 8:10; Apoc 21:7), until at the end of time he will really be
θεὸς [τὰ] πάντα ἐν πᾶσιν (1 Cor 15:28). In consequence it is
recisely in the commandment of all-embracing and exclusive love for
is one God that monotheism finds its achievement. 'For in this
one can it become apparent whether the one God is really God, and
deed the unique God, for those who confess him. They must have
o idols by the side of God, neither Mammon (Mt 6:24) nor the belly
hil 3:19), neither statues (1 Cor 10:21; 12:2; 2 Cor 6:16) nor
rces of the cosmos (Gal 4:8 s.), neither local rulers (Ac 4:19; 5:29)
r the Emperor in Rome (Mk 12:17)', nor again the angels (Col
:18). 'What matters is to serve God and give him what is his, to
ten to him and rely on him alone; what matters is to remain faithful
God in face of the gravest threats, to the point of death by martyr-
m': a continually new ἐπιστρέψαι πρὸς τὸν θεὸν ἀπὸ τῶν εἰδώλων
υλεύειν θεῷ ζῶντι καὶ ἀληθινῷ (1 Thess 1:9)—'in this Jesus and
imitive Christianity see the real meaning of εἷς θεός. As a profes-
on of faith monotheism may have been a matter of course to the
en of the New Testament; in the actual conduct of their lives it was
ways a new task.'[1]

From what has been said it becomes a little clearer perhaps—this
an old problem of the Schools—how there can be a πίστις ὅτι εἷς
τιν ὁ θεός (cf. Jas 2:19). When the New Testament refers to the
nviction that one God exists, it does indeed often make use of
utral concepts which do not necessarily imply a decision of a moral
d religious kind but can in fact also signify, at least in themselves,
neutral theoretical knowledge (γιγνώσκειν θεόν, Rom 1:21;
Cor 1:21; Gal 4:9. ἐπιγιγνώσκειν, Rom 1:28.32; Eph 1:17.
έναι τὸν θεόν, Gal 4:8; 1 Thess 4:5; 2 Thess 1:8; Tit 1:16).
t on the other hand the New Testament characterizes this (or at
st a) knowledge of God as πιστεύειν ὅτι εἷς ἐστιν ὁ θεός
as 2:19), as πίστις ἐπὶ θεόν (Heb 6:1), as πίστις ἡ πρὸς τὸν θεόν
Thess 1:8), as πιστεῦσαι τῷ θεῷ ὅτι ἔστιν (Heb 11:6). We

[1] TWNT III, p. 102.

have already discussed the relation between the natural knowledg
of God and the knowledge of God from Revelation in the New Testa
ment. The question which concerns us here is whether, on the basi
of what has been said about the content of New Testament mono
theism, it is possible to explain at least in part how the first article o
the Creed as such can be an object of faith—which St Thomas Aquinas
for instance, denied (Ia.2.2 ad 1; IIa-IIae.1.5). There is nothing wron
in saying that anyone who has recognized that an ultimate cause o
the world exists, cannot at the same time believe this in faith. In th
sense St Thomas is perfectly correct when he says: 'Impossible es
quod ab eodem idem sit scitum et creditum' (*loc. cit.*). But this sort o
faith is not in question at all in monotheistic faith, as we have seer
We do not believe by faith in a unified, ultimate cause of the worl
which as such is known and not believed in; but we believe by fait
in a Person living and active in history, of whose existence we ca
become aware because of his activity, before it is known as the abso
lute Being which is the foundation of everything: we believe wh
this Person says, namely that he and he alone is the absolute God.
is possible to *believe* that Yahweh, that the Father of our Lord Jesu
Christ (both understood as proper names in the strict sense) is th
unique God, because logically it is not yet necessary nor is it possib
that, before the content of this self-disclosure is known, the Perso
who reveals these things should be known in that respect precisely
which he reveals himself by actually speaking.

2. God as Person

A further consequence of the inner reason for the unquestionir
assurance of the New Testament consciousness of God is that for th
men of the New Testament God's personal being is a living realit
Their knowledge of God is not the result of their own theoretic
study of the world but of their experience of God's living activi
among them. 'The countless examples of living prayer in the Ne
Testament are so many testimonies to the personal God in who
primitive Christianity believed; and they indicate at the same time
what sense the concept of God's personality must be understood her
the God of the New Testament is a God whom men may address
Thou, in a way in which only a personal being can be addressed

Thou.[1] We shall see in more detail what was involved in thinking of God as a Person by attempting to set out the individual elements in this conception of a personal God.

God is He who Acts; He who is Free; He who Acts in an Historical Dialogue with men; and He who in the true sense tells us about his 'attributes'—which would otherwise remain hidden—only through this activity. Here we have four points of view in terms of which we propose to characterize the New Testament conception of personality; it goes without saying that these four aspects continually merge into one another.

2. God as He who *Acts*.

In metaphysical knowledge of God from the world, where God is apprehended in the sense of the Vatican definition as 'principium et finis' of all reality, God is also in a certain sense one who acts, he who sets up all reality. We may leave out of account here the fact that because of original sin the unity of the one transcendent God is concealed by man's subjection to a plurality of cosmic powers which he makes into idols, the στοιχεῖα τοῦ κόσμου. But even setting this aside, God's activity is in a certain sense concealed in 'natural' theology by the mere fact that for the metaphysician absolutely *everything* is an objectivization of God's activity. In this way God's activity remains absolutely transcendent: it has no Here and Now *within* the world such that in this Here and Now it might be grasped and experienced in distinction from all that it is not. Because *everything* is God's action, this action fades as it were into the anonymity of the Always and Everywhere, as far as human knowledge is concerned, for human knowledge remains essentially dependent on recognizing something by bringing it into relief against other things of a different kind. Now what characterizes the experience of God in the New Testament (as of course it did in the Old Testament too) is that it knows of a definite and distinct activity of God *within* the world: it knows of God's saving activity in history, an activity which, as God's new, free initiative, neither instituted jointly with the world nor already contained in it, possesses a quite definite Here and Now in the world and in human history, distinct from all other being and becoming. The New Testament does indeed also know with complete assurance

[1] TWNT III, p. 111 s.

that *everything* is, moves and lives in him (Ac 17:27–9), God as τὸ θεῖον; it sees the πατὴρ πάντων (Eph 4:6) at work everywhere, in Nature too; it sees how he makes the sun rise and the rain fall, clothes the lilies of the field and feeds the birds of heaven, as the God of the fruitful seasons, sating men's hearts with food and gladness (Ac 14:17); it sees him at work too in the history of humanity as a whole, the spreading abroad of the races of men as the historical epochs succeed each other, the coming and going of peoples (Ac 17:26).

But close observation shows that the New Testament completely lacks any expression of numinous feeling for the cosmos, excited by the world, its greatness and glory. And this is quite apart from the fact that the New Testament, when it speaks of the glory of the lilies, also remembers that they wither and are cast into the oven, and is generally aware that the whole of creation has been caught up in man's sinfulness and is thus remote from God, groaning for the revelation of its own glory (Rom 8:22). Thus on the one hand the New Testament is capable of seeing God powerfully at work in the whole of reality and history, and on the other God never becomes for it the mysterious glimmer of an Absolute immanent in the world, the world is never deified but remains always the creature of the Lord beyond all world who shapes it freely by his Word. And this is because the New Testament has experienced God's activity *within* the world, and for that reason can never be in any uncertainty about that activity of his either, from which the total reality of the cosmos derives. For the New Testament, God's self-revelation in the world is never a quality which adheres uniformly to every reality in the world. In his sovereign freedom he has chosen a people for himself to the exclusion of all others and made it his People (Ac 13:17 s.); this People alone possessed the Covenant and the giving of the Law and the Promise (Rom 9:4; σωτηρία ἐκ τῶν Ἰουδαίων, Jn 4:22); he has sent his Son (Rom 8:3; Gal 4:4), so that upon this unique historical event depend man's entire salvation and the transfiguration of the whole world (Ac 4:12; Eph 2:18). The New Testament is strongly conscious of a sharply defined saving activity of God within the whole of human history, which as a whole possesses no immediate relation to God's salvation at the start. So strong is this consciousness, that the calling of nations to reconciliation and community with God is not inferred from some metaphysical knowledge of God's necessary goodness but is the great mystery of God's free election, hidden from all men yet disclosed contrary to all expectations, God as it were suddenly calling all nations to salvation in spite of the elective, discriminatory freedom of his love (Ac 11:17.18; Eph 2:11 s.; ch. 3).

It is from this experience of God's free personal activity within history that the confession of God as *Creator of the world*, simply speaking, also acquires its specific vitality and clarity (Mt 11:25; Mk 13:19; Jn 1:3; Ac 4:24; 17:24; Rom 11:36; 1 Cor 8:5 s.; Col. 1:16; Eph 3:9; Heb 1:2; 2:10; 3:4; 11:3; Apoc 4:11).

Firstly we may say that in the New Testament (as in the Old Testament) it is never claimed that natural knowledge from the world includes as one of its objects a free creation of a temporal world *ex nihilo*; we leave undecided the question whether and how far the character of the world as *created* in the strict sense is available to natural theology. The New Testament (like the Old) accepts its knowledge of the world's createdness in the strict sense from the God who speaks and reveals himself. Further, man only really learns what *creating* is from God's free and powerful activity in history, unconstrained by any prior obligation. It is here that man experiences concretely the truth that God is ὁ καλῶν τὰ μὴ ὄντα ὡς ὄντα (Rom 4:17), a formula which is on the one hand related to God's free activity in the history of Abraham, and on the other is used by the New Testament as a clear expression for creation *ex nihilo*. Thus knowledge of God's historical activity within the world and knowledge of his creative omnipotence through his mere Word over against everything which is not He, complete and support each other reciprocally. Because he is Lord of heaven and earth he can maintain his sway in sovereign power and freedom over the destinies of the world and of men (Mt 11:25; Ac 4:24 s.; Eph 1:11). And in this sway over history man has a deep impression of God's free and unconstrained sovereignty in action, his creativeness—the ἐνέργεια τοῦ κράτους τῆς ἰσχύος αὐτοῦ, which shows itself with power in the Resurrection, discloses to us in general τὸ ὑπερβάλλον μέγεθος τῆς δυνάμεως τοῦ θεοῦ (Eph 1:19.20), gives us the πίστις τῆς ἐνεργείας τοῦ θεοῦ (Col 2:12), and so allows us to experience concretely and vividly the fact that God is ὁ τὰ πάντα ἐνεργῶν κατὰ τὴν βουλὴν τοῦ θελήματος αὐτοῦ (Eph 1:11).

b. God as He who Acts *freely*.

This God who acts in Nature and in human history is one who acts *freely.* God manifests himself as Person in his activity precisely by the fact that this activity is voluntary and free. Precisely because the activity even *in* his world arises from God's spontaneous resolution, which is not something given along with other ingredients in the original constitution of the world, its tendencies and finalities, it becomes clear that this active God is the God transcending natural and human worlds, that God's Activity is not just another word for the world-process, that his Will is not just another word for εἱμαρμένη. It is on the basis of a concrete experience of free irruptions into the historical course of the world, novel and unexpected and extrinsic to the world's immanent dynamism, that the men of the New Testament recognize God as a free, transcendent Person.

They do indeed know of the *eternity* of God's definitive decree, the purpose of his will to lead all history and the whole world to their definitive goal (Rom 16:25; 1 Cor 2:7; Eph 1:4; 3:9; Col 1:26; 2 Tim 1:9), and go on at once to reflect on it; and what is true of this divine purpose is obviously true of God's historical activity in the world in general. And this is to say that God's freedom has determined from the very beginning a goal for the world and for men which is in fact infallibly pursued and attained in the history of the world. But it is certainly not to say that this final, unified and definitive plan of salvation had always been so deeply imprinted upon the world from the very beginning and objectified there that from the very beginning everything was going to run its course according to a natural law, in such a way that, as in Deism, God would throughout the whole of time merely be the spectator of the immanent unfolding of that reality which he had created in the beginning. God's plan of salvation has rather been an absolute secret of his, concealed from all earlier ages and generations, and which only now, in the last times, becomes objectively real and thereby makes itself known. The reality of salvation in Christ has now emerged in the world for the first time (ἐπεφάνη: Tit 2:11; 3:4), and *in consequence* become manifest (2 Tim 1:10); so that Revelation is not just instruction about something which has always been the case, but the unveiling of the new unfoldings of God's free activity. That this activity of God in Christ takes place precisely now and not at some other time (Heb 1:2, ἐπ' ἐσχάτου τῶν ἡμερῶν τούτων; Col 1:26, νῦν; Rom 16:25, φανερωθέντος δὲ νῦν μυστηρίου); that it emerges over against man lost through sin; that contrary to every human standard it is aimed at the poor, the

eak, the foolish among men (Mt 11:25; Lk 1:51 s.; 1 Cor 1:25 s.),
 men who can lay absolutely no claim to it in justice; that it is thus
ure grace—from all this man learns that this activity is God's really
ew, original initiative, his free doing, βούλημα (Rom 9:19: Jas
:18), βουλὴ τοῦ θελήματος αὐτοῦ (Eph 1:11; Ac 20:27), εὐδοκία
Eph 1:5.9; 1 Cor 1:21; Gal 1:15), προορίζειν (Rom 8:29 s.;
 Cor 2:7; Eph 1:5.11), πρόθεσις, ἐκλογή (Rom 9:11; 11:5.28;
 Thess 1:4; 2 Pet 1:10).

Disciplined by this experience of God's incalculable freedom as
 iown in the basic facts of our salvation, a man of the New Testament
 now capable of seeing God's free activity at work *elsewhere* through-
ut Nature and Grace. What is distinctive in individual natural bodies
 just as much the work of his freedom (1 Cor 15:38 s.) as the over-
 helming and incomprehensible differentiation in his mercy and his
 :probation (Rom 9:13 s.; 2 Tim 1:9; Jn 6:44.65), as the vocation to
ffices and gifts (Ac 10:41; 16:10; 22:14 s.; Rom 12:3; 1 Cor 12:6.28;
 eb 2:4), as the appointing of a time for the End (Mt 24:36; Ac
 :7).

The eternity and immutability of God's free decree on the one hand,
 ad its incalculability in terms of the previous situation of the world
 n the other, belong together and together form the presupposition
 r any proper human attitude to God. On the one hand, man can rely
 faith on the fact that God is faithful (πιστός, Rom 3:3; 1 Cor 1:9;
 Cor 1:18; 2 Tim 2:13; Heb 10:23; 1 Pet 4:19) and true (ἀληθής,
 ληθινός, Rom 3:4; 15:8; Jn 3:33; 8:26), that his decrees are
 ichangeable and without repentance (ἀμετάθετος, Heb 6:17;
 ιεταμέλητος, Rom 11:29). On the other hand, what is still to
 me about by God's act, in its existential concreteness, continues to
 main within God's sovereign power of disposal, and remains for us
 mystery only fully to be unveiled at the end of all the ages; and for
 at reason this free God is never at the power of man's calculations:
 od remains free Lord. Because the God who acts freely is set over
 ;ainst man, and because he has mercy on whom he will and hardens
 hom he will (Rom 9:15.16.18), his free and sovereign dispensation
 first and last for our 'existence' (in the modern sense of the word).

Paul does not even begin to try to formulate a theodicy in respect of
 od's free choice in grace: 'O man, who art thou, that thou wouldst
 spute with God?' (Rom 9:20). The rightness and holiness of God's
 cision rests in itself alone, precisely because it is free; it is not to be

traced back to some necessitating source which has the lucidity of i
necessity.

3. In the third place God shows himself as Person in that he dea
with man in an historical *dialogue*, that he allows man, his creatur
really to be himself too a person. Some brief explanation is needed
what we mean by this. Every purely metaphysical knowledge of Gc
which starts from immediately perceptible reality and penetrates to i
ultimate cause—and calls it God—always at least runs the risk
conceiving the world as a pure function of God, in such a way th
the world becomes a pure expression and objectivization of this caus
merely a derived function of God (as opposed to the risk of makir
God into merely the inner meaning of the world). Thus it is almo
impossible for metaphysics to avoid the danger of forgetting the tw
sided personal relationship between God and the created spirit, t
danger of not understanding that the personal God so transcends t
world that he can allow this world, which is totally dependent on hir
a genuine activity, even with regard to himself; that what is total
dependent on him acquires through his own agency a genuine ind
pendence with regard to him; that God can set man free with rega
to God himself.

Further, this relationship between God and man, which is so obscu
for metaphysics, is seen at its clearest precisely in the *saving* histo
of God's dealings with man. Man takes part in a real *dialogue* with Go
He gives God's Word to him the answer which he, man, wants
give. And his may turn out contrary to God's will. Man can harden
heart (Rom 2:5; Heb 3:13), he can resist the Spirit of God (Ac 7:5
he can obey or not obey God's will (Rom 15:18; 16:19), he c
contradict God (Rom 10:21), he can shut the doors of his heart
God when he knocks (Apoc 3:20), he can set his will in oppositi
to God's plan of salvation (Mt 23:37 s.). The existence of powers
the world which are hostile to God and which are yet creatures of t
one God, cannot be separated from this reality of a personal indepe
dence of the created spirit; the reality of sin, its inexcusability befo
God, God's wrath over sin, his summons to reconciliation, prayer, t
existential genuineness of which depends on man's having a genui
initiative with regard to God—all these realities witnessed to in t
New Testament presuppose the same bi-personal relationship t

ween God and man. God's activity in the course of saving history is
not a kind of monologue which God conducts by himself; it is a
long, dramatic dialogue between God and his creature, in which God
confers on man the power to make a genuine answer to his Word, and
so makes his own further Word dependent upon the way in which man
does in fact freely answer. God's free action never ceases to take new
fire in the activity of man. History is not just a play in which God
puts himself on the stage and creatures are merely what is performed;
the creature is a real co-performer in this humano-divine drama of
history. And so history has a real and absolute seriousness, an absolute decision, which is not to be relativized as far as the creature is
concerned with the remark—at once true and false—that everything
rises from God's will and nothing can resist it. The Scriptural basis
for what has just been said lies in the simple and yet incomprehensible
fact that in the Bible the Almighty, Absolute, the παντοκράτωρ
(Apoc 1:8), through his own personally expressed Word, calls upon
his creature, the work of his hands, to do his will; and that accordingly
this Word which calls upon someone else cannot be meaningless, although it proceeds from him who has the power to do all
things.

Although the creature is given free play in this way, the power to
make a real answer to God, God retains the last word: not only in the
sense that as the stronger physically, so to speak, he finally acts in
such a way that no reaction of the creature can follow his action,
having no further power to withstand it; but also in the sense that even
the creature's sinful act, while it does indeed involve total disaster for
the creature itself, is nevertheless incapable of leaving the field of
God's ultimate will—the will by which God wills his glory. For
God's power is revealed even in those vessels of his wrath which have
fallen into destruction (Rom 9:22.23). So far as we have any knowledge of it from God, the history of the world, from the point of view
of the world and in isolation, closes with a shrill disharmony never to
be resolved. What is exterior to God is never in itself resolved into an
ultimate, all-embracing harmony; and yet, and precisely in this way,
the world proclaims the glory of the God whose ways are unfathomable and whose decisions are inscrutable. A creature can be reconciled
with this end of all the world only if it unreservedly gives glory to
God, and loves him and adores him precisely in the unfathomable,
inappellable freedom of his will; loves him, then, more than itself, so

that solidarity with God's will is more important to it than solidarit
with anything else, like itself created.

d. The *attributes* of God.

It is only after reaching some understanding of the living and fre
personal being of the transcendent God who is able to enter into a
active dialogue with the world, that we can begin to examine th
teaching of the New Testament about God's 'attributes'. For we hav
to know God as Person before we can understand that the decisiv
question for men is not, strictly speaking, *what* God is, but *as whoı*
he wishes freely to show himself with regard to the world. A perso
does not strictly speaking have *attributes* with respect to anothe
person: he has freely and personally adopted *attitudes*. And this ı
above all true of God's absolute, sovereign being as Person with regaı
to his world. Certainly these free attitudes which God has adopteₑ
with regard to the world, have, so to speak, a metaphysical structurₑ
arising from God's necessary nature; but the attitude actually adopteₑ
is not unambiguously laid down in consequence of this structure. H
can have mercy and he can harden men's hearts, he can enlighten theı
and he can send them the ἐνέργεια πλάνης (2 Thess 2:11) or th
πνεῦμα κατανύξεως (Rom 11:8), without thereby ceasing to ŀ
the Holy One (Heb 12:10; 1 Pet 1:15) and his judgments ceasing ı
be true and just (Apoc 19:2). With respect to this God of the Nₑ
Testament, then, everything depends for man on how God in faₑ
behaves with regard to man, not just on how he necessarily is in hiɪ
self. The experiences by which man learns about God in saving histoɪ
are not just exemplifications, instances to show the attributes of Gₒ
as a metaphysical entity which man knows in its necessary characteɪ
they are experiences containing a teaching of which man can onl
become aware through the experience. This experience therefoɪ
always remains new and unexpected; what is learnt from it is nₑ
identified with something always and already there, but itself occuɪ
for the first time. The kernel of what the New Testament declarₑ
about God's 'attributes', then, is not a doctrine about God as ₐ
abstract metaphysical entity, but an announcement about the concretₑ
personal countenance which God shows to the world.

There are of course statements in the New Testament which exprₑ
properly *metaphysical* attributes of God's nature. The Scriptures ₀
indeed speak of a θεία φύσις (2 Pet 1:4), a θειότης (Rom 1:20

If God is called αἰώνιος (Rom 16:26; cf. Apoc 1:4.8; 4:8; 16:5), ἀΐδιος (Rom 1:20), ἀόρατος (Rom 1:20; Col. 1:15; 1 Tim 1:17; Heb 11:27), ἄφθαρτος (Rom 1:23; 1 Tim 1:17), μακάριος (1 Tim 1:11; 6:15), οὐδὲ προσδεόμενός τινος (Ac 17:25), ἀπείραστος (Jas 1:13); or when it is said of him οὐ γὰρ ἄδικος ὁ θεός (Heb 6:10; cf. Rom 3:5; 9:14), ἀδύνατον ψεύσασθαι θεόν (Heb 6:18; cf. Tit 1:2), οἴδαμεν ὅτι ὁ θεός ἁμαρτωλῶν οὐκ ἀκούει (Jn 9:31), οὐδεὶς ἀγαθὸς εἰ μὴ εἷς ὁ θεός (Mk 10:18), μόνος σοφὸς θεός (Rom 16:27), and when his omniscience is praised (καρδιογνώστης, Ac 1:24; Rom 8:27; Heb 4:13; 1 Jn 3:20; Mt 6:4.6)—all these are objective expressions of God's essential attributes, which are also experienced as such: they are axiological statements about God, judgments of essence, not of existence. Inevitably, then, what was said about the relation of 'natural' theology to the revealed theology of the New Testament holds good for these statements too: these properties of the θεία φύσις, the θειότης, can be known and always are known from the world; they are disclosed to sinful man who 'setting aside the Creator shows devotion to the world' (Rom 1:25), and are unveiled anew to anyone who in obedience and faith encounters the living God in his saving history. But these attributes acquire new harmonics in this encounter: he who is αἰώνιος is not only without beginning or end, but is raised up so high above the earthly world that he was able to enter into it and precisely so make it share in his own upliftedness above the eternal up and down, the eternal inconclusiveness of time (2 Cor 4:8 s.; 4:17; 2 Thess 2:16; Heb 5:9; 9:12.15; 2 Pet 1:11). The same is true of God's ἀφθαρσία (Eph 6:24; 2 Tim 1:10) and his invisibility, through which alone we can understand what is meant by saying that we shall see God (1 Cor 13:12; 1 Jn 3:2); the same is true of his holiness and freedom from need, which we shall share (Apoc 21:23); of his omniscience, which no longer signifies strictly the infinite consciousness of the world-cause, containing all things in its being and knowledge, but rather the eye of the personal God, whose discerning, comprehending and provident gaze penetrates man's inmost heart and is felt there by him (Mt 6:4–6; Lk 16:15; Heb 4:12–13; 1 Thess 2:4; 1 Jn 3:20; Mt 6:8.32; 10:29).

It is also important to remember in this connexion that the New Testament does not *systematize* these metaphysical statements about God. Nowhere does it treat of them speculatively; and it remains completely silent about just those expressions which would be even

more important and more central for a theological metaphysics, or at any
rate it has no specialized vocabulary for them: God is never appealed
to in the New Testament as simply Being, his entitative infinity is
never mentioned. It is not so much to the Absolute and Necessary—
and thus easily impersonal and abstract—that the New Testament
turns its gaze in metaphysical contemplation; its eyes are upon the
personal God in the *concreteness* of his free activity.

Everything depends on that. And so the decisive statements of the
New Testament as to *who* God is are an answer to the question, 'As
whom has man experienced God in history?' When God is called the
just *Judge*, this is because of the shattering impression that it was the
God of holiness who first brought men to any consciousness of their
lost and sinful condition in his revelation to the creature, that he
condemned sin in the flesh of Christ whom he made sin for us (2 Cor
5:21; Rom 8:3); that God's wrath broke forth and was experienced
over and over again at other times in the history of salvation (2 Pet
2:3–7; Jude 5–16). Again, we must be careful not to trivialize the
experience of God's wrath in judgment by interpreting it as a mere
reaction of his necessarily holy essence to the sin of the world. For the
same sin suddenly and incalculably encounters on another occasion
God's forbearance and *longsuffering* (Rom 2:4; 3:26; 9:22; 1 Pet
3:20; 2 Pet 3:9; ἀνοχή-μακροθυμία). Further, this ἀνοχή and μακρο-
θυμία of God is not some metaphysical attribute which man can
reckon on as a fixed quantity in planning his life for the future; for that
would be to tempt God (1 Cor 10:9), and the time of God's indul-
gence is suddenly interrupted by the Day of the Lord, which comes
like a thief in the night (2 Pet 3:10).

The existentially personal and active character of God's behaviour
in contrast to some fixed metaphysical attribute of his essence, is just
as clear when he is called *good, merciful, loving*, and so on. He is
forgiving (Mt 6:14; Mk 11:25), merciful (Lk 1:72.78; 6:36; 2 Cor
1:3; Eph 2:4; 1 Tim 1:2; Tit 3:5; 1 Pet 1:3; 2 Jn 3; Jude 2), kind
(Mt 19:17; Lk 11:13; 18:19; Jas 1:5; χρηστός, Lk 6:35; Rom 2:4
11:22; Tit 3:4), loving (Jn 3:16; 16:27; Rom 5:5; 8:37.39; Eph 2:4
2 Thess 2:16; Tit 3:4; 1 Jn 3:1; 4:8–11). He is the God of all grace
(Ac 20:24; Rom 5:15; 1 Cor 1:4; 3:10; 15:10; 2 Cor 1:12; Eph 3
2.7; 1 Tim 1:2; 1 Pet 2:20; 5:10.12; 2 Jn 3), the God of hope (Rom
15:13), the God of peace (Rom 15:33; 16:20; 1 Cor 1:3; 2 Cor 1:2
13:11; Gal 1:3; Eph 1:2; Phil 4:9; 1 Thess 5:23; 2 Thess 1:2; 1 Tim

1:2; 2 Tim 1:2; Tit 1:4; Phm 3; 2 Jn 3), the God of all comfort
(Rom 15:5; 2 Cor 1:3.4; 2 Thess 2:16), the God of love (2 Cor
13:11), the Saviour (Lk 1:47; 1 Tim 1:1; 2:3; 4:10: Tit 1:3; 2:11;
3:4; Jude 25), who in his compassion desires the salvation of all men
(Mt 18:14; 1 Tim 2:3.4; 4:10; Tit 2:11; 2 Pet 3:9). But for the New
Testament God's kind and compassionate love is in its very core
precisely grace, to which no claim can be made, grace, which against
all expectation, encounters the 'atheistic' sinner (Eph 2:12) who has
fallen away from God. That God loves us, that he is 'dear God', is not
a metaphysical matter of course, but the inconceivable marvel that the
New Testament must proclaim, belief in which never ceases to demand
the utmost effort of man's powers of faith. God's love had first to
become objective and to 'appear' ($\dot{\epsilon}\phi\alpha\nu\epsilon\rho\dot{\omega}\theta\eta$, 1 Jn 4:9) in the
sending of his only begotten Son into the world, we had first to
experience in this sending this love as it really is, in order really to be
able to believe it: $\kappa\alpha\grave{\iota}$ $\dot{\eta}\mu\epsilon\hat{\iota}s$ $\dot{\epsilon}\gamma\nu\dot{\omega}\kappa\alpha\mu\epsilon\nu$ $\kappa\alpha\grave{\iota}$ $\pi\epsilon\pi\iota\sigma\tau\epsilon\dot{\nu}\kappa\alpha\mu\epsilon\nu$ $\tau\dot{\eta}\nu$
$\dot{\alpha}\gamma\dot{\alpha}\pi\eta\nu$, $\ddot{\eta}\nu$ $\ddot{\epsilon}\chi\epsilon\iota$ $\dot{o}$ $\theta\epsilon\dot{o}s$ $\dot{\epsilon}\nu$ $\dot{\eta}\mu\hat{\iota}\nu$ (1 Jn 4:16). Until this love
becomes finally manifest, the conviction that it encounters me in my
absolute concreteness must be maintained in this aion by the $\dot{\epsilon}\lambda\pi\grave{\iota}s$
$\sigma\omega\tau\eta\rho\dot{\iota}\alpha s$ (1 Thess 5:8), and never becomes a matter of course; the
triumphant consciousness of being loved by God (Rom 8:39) con-
tinues to be coupled with fear and trembling (Phil 2:12; 1 Pet 1:17);
for even the unburdened conscience is subject to God's judgment.
More clearly still: God's love is so free and sovereign that the effects
in man of its creative, saving Word, its affirmation in faith and love
or its refusal in unbelief, do not in the last resort vary purely according
to man's response in this way or that to God's freedom. On the contrary, its effects depend on whether God himself in his unqualified
sovereignty bestows or withholds his own merciful love (Rom
9:9–11), to which man really consents. God's loving call is always a
call of his $\pi\rho\dot{o}\theta\epsilon\sigma\iota s$, an election (Rom 8:28–33; 2 Tim 1:9; 2 Pet
1:10). Nor is it surprising, in a context like this, that God's *omnipo-
tence*, in spite of its metaphysical quality, is preponderantly seen and
experienced in connexion with his free operations in saving history: he
has the power to raise up children to Abraham from stones (Mt 3:9;
Lk 3:8; Mt 19:26 and par.); he can raise up the dead, and raise them
to a quite new order of life (Mt 22:29 s.; Jn 5:21; 1 Cor 6:14; Eph
1:19; Heb 11:19); his $\dot{\epsilon}\nu\dot{\epsilon}\rho\gamma\epsilon\iota\alpha$ is shown in the raising up of his
own Son (Ac 2:24; 1 Cor 6:14; 2 Cor 13:4; Eph 1:19 s.; Col 2:12);

he is able (δυνατός) even to convert the obstinate and to preserve
those who are true to him (Rom 11:23; 2 Tim 1:12); his power is
shown in his free grace (Rom 1:16; 16:25; 1 Cor 2:5; 2 Cor 9:8
Eph 1:11; 3:7.20; Phil 2:13; 4:13; 2 Tim 1:8; Heb 2:18), in the
performance of his promises (Rom 4:21), in his power to punish
(Rom 9:22). In comparison, metaphysical statements like the assertion
that his δύναμις can be known in the world (Rom 1:20), or which
call him παντοκράτωρ (Apoc *passim*; 2 Cor 6:18—hence only
once outside the Apocalypse!), recede into the background. And
because God's activity is part of a dialogue, his power is not seen as a
magnitude continuously and obviously present in the world, some
thing already realized, but as something which is only slowly realized
by a real struggle, in the drama of God and his world, until his βασι
λεία is actually present and his δύναμις has really appeared (M
24:30; Lk 21:27; cf. Mt 26:64).

It is in the *paradoxical* utterances that we have the clearest view of
God's attitude as personal and existential, to be known concretely no
from the world but only in the enactments of his free activity. For
metaphysical knowledge of God, the summit of the world is itself jus
below God; the world attempts to ascend to God by an intensification
and sublimation of its values and forces; the form of its own immanen
quest for God, which serves as the basis for its knowledge of God'
attributes, always has the form of the Greek *Eros*, which strive
upwards to the supreme fulfilment of human reality and only so to
God; and in consequence the world can only expect a revelation which
would be simply the manifestation of its own power and wisdom. But
the free, transcendent God, who is precisely greater than what is
greatest in the world and is more unlike than he is like the summit of
the world, surpasses all this by his sovereign eminence, and reveal
himself precisely in what in the world seems furthest from him. Not in
the wisdom of the world, not in the glory of the world's might, doe
God reveal himself; but he reveals τὸ ἀσθενὲς τοῦ θεοῦ, τὸ μωρὸ
τοῦ θεοῦ in the foolishness and weakness of the Cross (1 Co
1:18–25). He does not communicate himself to those who are meta
physically close to him, the wise, the strong, the successful, the onto
logically compact, but to the foolish of the world, the weak, th
failures, the inwardly brittle and empty (1 Cor 1:26–9; 2 Cor 12:9
13:4; Mt 11:25). The μορφὴ θεοῦ empties itself in the μορφὴ δοὐ
λου, lowliness, poverty, the death on the Cross (Phil 2:5–8; 2 Co

8:9). The eternal creator Logos becomes *sarx*, temporal, frail, delivered up to the power of sin and death (Jn 1:14). And all this happens ὅπως μὴ καυχήσηται πᾶσα σὰρξ ἐνώπιον τοῦ θεοῦ (1 Cor 1:29). Looked at from the standpoint of the world, there is nothing in the world obviously privileged by nature to serve as God's revelation and representative. Even the highest is infinitely far from God; nor can the lowest of itself drag God down by a voluptuous passion for the base and wretched; *both* high and low in this word are *sarx*, and so all must become dumb before God: strictly speaking, there is no name named in this world and from it, which is really an attribute of God.

Properly and precisely, we know *who* God is, not from ourselves and the world, but only from the activity in history of the free and living God, through which he showed us who he wished to be to us. Consequently the teaching of the New Testament in the ultimate analysis is not an ontology of God's attributes, not a theory, but an historical account of the experiences in which man has come to know God.

3. The God of Love

Of all that man has learnt by experience about God in saving history, the decisive thing is that out of his grace God the Father has called us in his Son to the most intimate community with him: it is summed up in the proposition: ὁ θεὸς ἀγάπη ἐστίν (1 Jn 4:16). But to see what this proposition means we must undertake a somewhat more extensive enquiry. With regard to God's personal activity, the New Testament understands that the free, living God can act differently at different times, can enter into different relationships with man. The decisive feature of this understanding is that it involves a knowledge of the fact which is precisely *not* a matter of course for the New Testament understanding of God, that the free, incalculable God has spoken his last, *definitive* word in the dramatic dialogue between God and man. God is the Free and the Transcendent, whose potentialities could never be exhausted in a finite world, and who in consequence is never really bound by what he has done. But he *has* bound himself: he has taken up a position with regard to man and the finite which he himself freely declares to be definitive, and of which he himself says that he will never go beyond it again and never withdraw from it. And because the only time which really signifies before God does not follow the periodicity of stars and clocks but rather that of God's ever new, free acts in his world, time really stands still when God has spoken his last word. And as this has in fact happened, the *kairos* is in fact accomplished (Mk 1:15), the end of time has come upon us (1 Cor 10:11; 1 Pet 4:7). The inner temporal form of the world, derived from God, is at its end, even if this last *kairos* may last for thousands of years by astronomical measures. We must realize what it means for the Infinite One to say that this deed which he has now done and which inevitably carries within itself the contingency of a free act in the sphere of the finite, is his *last* deed; that of all the innumerable possibilities which remain open to him, none will be realized after this deed; that the mode of his action at precisely this moment shall abide for all eternity.

If we are now to characterize this unique situation, one which can never be surpassed and which has never existed before, we must in the first place distinguish it against God's previous modes of behaviour, and secondly we must determine what is peculiar to it with regard to time and intrinsic content. It was said earlier that in the last analysis the New Testament does not offer a doctrine of God's attributes, but an account of those ever new attitudes of God of which man has had experience in the course of his history; and we have just seen that the *kairos* of the New Testament is characterized by the fact that God's attitude as it is experienced there is the definitive one. Our problem then may be formulated in terms of two questions: firstly, how is this attitude distinguished from God's previous attitudes, those of the Old Testament and in the time before Christ? and secondly, what in fact is this attitude or disposition (*Haltung*) considered precisely in the terminal situation of the New Testament?

a. God's love in the Old Testament.

According to the Epistle to the Hebrews, God expressed himself in the world by his speech and activity in manifold ways. But his last and definitive word, his last and definitive act, which have come to pass in the καιροὶ ἴδιοι (1 Tim 2:6; 6:15; Tit 1:3) of the new and eternal covenant and are now present, are not just the latest in a series but the πλήρωμα of all earlier times (Mk 1:15; Gal 4:4; Eph 1:10) and yet precisely something new with regard to what had gone before. If this is the case, then this final disposition must be distinguished from anything *earlier*, which with regard to it is drawn into a unified order and at the same time this disposition must be understood as the *telos* of all that had gone before, which finds its fulfilment in this disposition. In other words, this ἔσχατον, which is τέλος and πλήρωμα of everything before it, puts all God's previous saving speech and activity—however manifold and various this may be—over a common denominator, and thus stands in essential distinction from the whole of what had gone before; and yet the whole must be resolved into this teleological fulfilment. We must bear this relationship in mind when we ask by what distinguishing features we are to know the God of the New Testament from the God of the Old. After all we have said, it should be clear that we are not just asking the harmless question as to what *man* understood about God in Old Testament and New Testament times; we are not concerned with the subjective conceptions of the men of the two covenants, with the growing knowledge of something in itself unchanging, but with a difference in God's own behaviour (*Anders-sich-verhalten*).

It is of course impossible to set out here the whole doctrine of the New Testament concerning the difference between the Old and New Covenants, between the time before Christ and the time in Christ, although this would be the only really concrete way of showing how the God of the fathers differs from the God of our Lord Jesus Christ. Otherwise we should be committed to the impossible task of discussing all the pairs of contrary conceptions like ἀδικία (ἁμαρτία)-δικαιο-σύνη (Rom 3:5), δοῦλος-υἱός (Rom 8:15; Gal 4:7), δουλεία-ἐλευθερία (Gal 5:1), νόμος-πίστις (Rom 4:13 s.), σάρξ-πνεῦμα (Rom 8:9), κατάκρισις-δικαιοσύνη (2 Cor 3:9), γράμμα-πνεῦμα (2 Cor 3:6), ἔργον-χάρις (Tit 3:5-7), διανοία τοῦ θανάτου-διανοία τοῦ πνεύματος (2 Cor 3:7 s.), διαθήκη παλαιά (πρώτη)-διαθήκη καινή (νέα; αἰώνιος) (Lk 22:20; 1 Cor 11:25; 2 Cor 3:6; Heb 8:6; 9:15; 12:24; 13:20; Gal 4:24), σκιὰ μελλόντων-εἰκὼν τῶν πραγμάτων (Col 2:17; Heb 10:1), ἐπαγγελία-εὐαγγέλιον (Rom 1:1 s.; Eph 3:6), στοιχεῖα τοῦ κόσμου-Χριστός (Col. 2:8-20; Gal 4:3-9). This would be the only way of achieving any real clarity about how God's behaviour in the Old Testament differs from his behaviour in the New. Here we must follow a simpler way. We shall simply start from the usual (and, it would seem, justified) view of this difference, that in the New Testament, and in the strictest sense there alone, God revealed himself as God of *Love*, as Love *itself*. In concrete terms, then, our first question becomes how and why God's love, become manifest in Christ, is distinguished from God's behaviour in the Old Testament and is at the same time its fulfilment.

At first sight the anticipated conclusion does not seem very probable: God seems to have shown himself as one who loves even in the time of salvation *before* Christ. In what follows, only the barest outline of Old Testament teaching can of course be offered, and that with the utmost reserve. Firstly, then, we find references there to what might be called a metaphysical love of God. When we hear that God loves everything that is (Wis 11:24), that Yahweh gives everything its nature and that his mercy embraces all that he has made (Ps 145:9), when the Psalmist celebrates the whole of creation as a work of God's graciousness and goodness (Ps 136:1–9), what we have is the reflexions of a natural theology: the goodness (the value) of reality is traced back to its source in the Source of all being, which in consequence is also conceived of as good. What was said earlier about natural theology in general holds good for this metaphysical goodness of God; it is knowable and in a way familiar, it is hidden because of original sin and is only clearly disclosed when man comes to know God in the supernatural history of salvation. But a 'love' like this does not really set up a personal I-Thou relationship between man and God. Man is aware of being borne by a Will in some way directed to value and the good, but this is not enough to let him turn round, as it were, so as to enter into a personal relationship of community and reciprocal love with this Source of his own ontological value. Again, we often hear in the Old Testament of God's goodness and mercy, as they are shown in his personal, historical activity. God has chosen his people; he has in a special way shown his goodness, his mercy and his love in a special personal guidance, in election and covenant. For the Old Testament, and especially for the prophets, the very fact that he has entered into relationship with man in so personal a way is itself an expression of his inconceivable mercy and grace, a revelation of his love. And the climax of his love in the Old Testament is that he does not allow himself to be turned away by the unfaithfulness of his People, Israel's repeated falling away from its God; that he does not give up his desire for a personal relationship because of the adultery of his People. We could put this more sharply and say that for the Old Testament God's love is shown by the fact that he enters into a personal relationship with his People and that he does not abandon it in spite of man's rejection of him. But that is all this love seems yet to mean. Certainly there is a constant celebration of Yahweh's mercy and graciousness, his compassion and his readiness to forgive, with regard to all creatures in general and the People of the Covenant in particular. But if we are justified in identifying God's goodness with a genuinely personal love, it follows that we cannot really draw any conclusions from language like this as to whether God already loves men there in the sense that as someone wholly personal in his very essence he wants to give himself to man. Goodness, forbearance, mercy, solicitude are still attributes which can characterize the conduct of a master to his servant. Consequently a relationship of this kind still does not mean that this solicitous and just and lenient ruler wishes to have anything to do with the servant in his own personal life. He can continue to be distant and inaccessible. Surely it was the beginning of something new and personal for God to have freely exercised his dominion over all that he has made in such a way as to enter actively into the world and intervene in it by his own personal initiative, as it were surrendering his sovereign upliftedness above everything finite by becoming a fellow-actor with his world. This is a new beginning which, looking back from the New Testatment, we can only understand as a moment in God's movement towards the creature, a movement in which he wished to entrust himself to man in his transcendent identity, in the inner mystery of his own personal life. But this could not yet be seen in the Old Testament. The fact that God in his personal activity takes man into his service, makes him, by a divine historical act, what he already is by nature, the fact that God accepts man as his servant and personally communicates his will to him and has personal dealings with him—all this was already so inconceivable a marvel that it could only be described by using the *image* of paternal or marital love. But that it was already in fact a love which drew men up to God only became evident in the New Covenant. It has further to be remembered that God's loving treatment of man in the Old Testament was intrinsically orientated towards something to come, to a New Covenant. Now this great promised thing remains curiously obscure and ambiguous in the Old Testament. Is this new greater thing only the establishment of God's rule in the world, which is still going to leave man merely God's servant, or is it going to be something more? Is God's law going to be completely established at some time in the future, and is this rule going to be one in which God precisely wills to be more than just the Lord who establishes himself in the world by the jealous affirmation of his own being? Is God going to be beloved Lord or lordly Beloved? All these promises were existential utterances of God, not just predictions; and of their very nature (until God should have bound himself by speaking his last, definitive word), they were held in abeyance so long as it was not known what answer God's free collocutor, man, would give to these promises in the dialogue which forms the history of salvation. In the Old Testament, then, God's love for man (so long as it does not mean just God's metaphysical relationship to his creature, something quite general and unexistential and implying no personal communion at all) consists in the very fact that he desires and makes possible a personal encounter with man, that he seeks this relationship urgently and maintains it in being, and that (provisionally, at least) this relationship was not abandoned in consequence of a turning away from God on man's part. But it was concealed in the Mystery of God's eternal decree that this relationship would go beyond that between a master and his servant and that it would be irrevocable. For God had still not done anything in man's history which would unambiguously and irrevocably open a way for men to the depths of God's own personal life. And in consequence that love for God to which man was summoned, was still provisory, until it should be known how God himself wanted to love man. Man was commanded to love God with the whole force of his being; but it was still hidden in which of two ways this should be. This unconditional assent by man to God in his freedom, would it be the humble love of a servant for his master, who, precisely because by his love he affirms God to be as God wishes to be, remains far from his sovereign majesty and unapproachable light, not presuming to an intimate relationship with God such as would involve really unrestricted personal communion with him? Or does this loving affirmation, which man utters blindly and unconditionally, draw him into the depths of God's inner life? When in the Old Testament man uttered this affirmation of his loving *pistis* to God, he was inevitably swept up into the universal teleology of God's entire redemptive action, even when the *telos* of this activity was still hidden from him. Ready to be just a servant, he was already son; but just this was hidden from him until *the* Son of the Father came, and it thus became manifest in the history of men what the secret of God's purpose had always been.[1]

---

[1] Heinisch, *Theology of the Old Testament* (ET, Collegeville, Minnesota, 1955), pp. 91–101; TWNT I, pp. 29–34.

b. The nature of God's relationship to man in the New Testament.

When we say that God is love, and that this is what finally character-izes God's free, historical behaviour in the fullness of time, in the *kairos* of the New Testament, we mean to say two things. Firstly, this is in fact a free *act* of God in Christ, an Event, not an attribute: the coming to pass of the New Testament in Christ. Secondly, it is the event in which God's inmost life is communicated to men, in his love for them, fully and without restraint. A genuinely personal love always has these two marks. Love is not the emanation of a nature but the free bestowal of a person, who possesses himself, who can there-fore refuse himself, whose surrender therefore is always a wonder and a grace. And love in the fully personal sense is not just any relationship between two persons who meet in some third thing, whether this *tertium quid* is a task, a truth or anything else: it is the ceding and the unfolding of one's inmost self to and for the other in love. The discus-sion which follows will be divided in accordance with this twofold distinction; not that the whole saving reality of the New Testament is to be depicted in this way, but rather that it will be considered only with regard to these two points.

1. That God is Love, that he has received man to the most intimate communion with himself in love—this has become manifest in the Sending and Incarnation, in the Cross and Glorification, of his only begotten *Son*. It has become manifest not merely in the sense that the Christ-reality may be taken as a particular instance, from which may be read off what attitude God has necessarily adopted with regard to man; but it has become manifest in the sense that all God's free activity in the whole history of salvation has been directed to this event from the very beginning and thus rests on this single decision; and that this free purpose of entering into unrestricted personal communion with man first became finally irrevocable and unconditional through God's act in Christ. Christ is the τέλος τοῦ νόμου (Rom 10:4), the ful-filment of the times (Mk 1:15); what became manifest in him is the ἀγάπη τοῦ θεοῦ (Rom 5:8, συνίστησιν δὲ τὴν ἑαυτοῦ ἀγάπην εἰς ἡμᾶς ὁ θεός, ὅτι ἔτι ἁμαρτωλῶν ὄντων ἡμῶν Χριστὸς ὑπὲρ ἡμῶν ἀπέθανεν. 1 Jn 4:9, ἐν τούτῳ ἐφανερώθη ἡ ἀγάπη τοῦ θεοῦ ἐν ἡμῖν, ὅτι τὸν υἱὸν αὐτοῦ μονογενῆ ἀπέσταλκεν ὁ θεὸς εἰς τὸν κόσμον. Tit 3:4, ἡ χρηστότης καὶ ἡ φιλανθρωπία ἐπεφάνη τοῦ σωτῆρος ἡμῶν θεοῦ): God so loved the world that he gave his only begotten Son (Jn 3:16). It is not for nothing that the great argumentative movement of

the Epistle to the Romans on the theme of the new epoch which has just opened, reaches its climax in a hymn which, beginning with a celebration of the love of the elect for God, goes on to the love of Christ and comes to rest in the certainty of τῆς ἀγάπης τοῦ θεοῦ τῆς ἐν Χριστῷ ᾽Ιησοῦ τῷ Κυρίῳ ἡμῶν (Rom 8:28.31 s.).[1] It is in the Christ-reality that God's love is really and truly present for the first time; it is there that it has first really appeared, there for the first time really objectified itself (συνίστησιν, Rom 5:8); and through this real being-present in the world it has become manifest. And it is by this means that a definitive and unsurpassable *fact* has been brought into being; for Christ abides eternally, he has brought eternal redemption into being, he has entered into the eternal tabernacle and sits on the right hand of God. It is by this means that the Promises have first emerged from their existential abeyance and ambiguity, and have been really established (βεβαιῶσαι, Rom 15:8); so that no future epoch and no conceivable stage of development (οὔτε μέλλοντα, Rom 8:38) is ever going to annul this definitive Event of God's love for us.

2. Moreover, God has bestowed his very self upon us in Christ:- ἡ κοινωνία δὲ ἡ ἡμετέρα μετὰ τοῦ πατρὸς καὶ μετὰ τοῦ υἱοῦ αὐτοῦ (1 Jn 1:3; κοινωνία was frequently used in the *koine* for conjugal association); and our fellowship is with the ἅγιον πνεῦμα too (2 Cor 13:13). This fellowship of love is produced by the Pneuma of God, through whom God pours forth upon us his love for us (Rom 5:5; Gal 4:6; 1 Jn 3:24; 4:13); and in this Spirit God's most intimate personal life is unfolded to us. For he is the Spirit who searches the βάθη τοῦ θεοῦ, the depths of God, which none knows and searches but the same Spirit of God (1 Cor 2:10), and so leads us into the deepest intimacies of God's knowledge (Jn 15:26; 16:13; 1 Cor 2:12; 1 Jn 2:20.27). So this Spirit of God, who is the realization in us of God's personal love and in whom God has unfolded to us his ultimate depths, is the Spirit of adoption (Gal 4:4.6), who gives us testimony of our adoption (Rom 8:15). Through him we are children of God (1 Jn 3:1.2), called to know him as we are known, to see him face to face (1 Cor 13:12). In this way we are taken up into the most intimate community of life with the God of whom it is said that no one has seen him or can see him (Jn 1:18; 1 Tim 6:16), whom only the Son knows (Mt 11:27; Jn 3:11.32; 7:29) and in consequence only he to

---

[1] TWNT I, p. 49.

whom the Son reveals it (Mt 11:27) by giving him a share in the nature
and rights of his Sonship (Rom 8:17.29; Heb 2:11.12). It is not our
concern here to inquire further into the nature of this grace and sonship. Even so it is clear enough that this relationship is inseparably
dependent upon the reality of Christ, and owes its existence as a
reality precisely to God's free self-disclosure once and for all in Christ.
'Ο θεὸς ἀγάπη ἐστίν is not primarily, then, a statement, illuminating
in itself, about the nature of God, but the expression of the once-for-
all, undeniable and unsurpassable experience in which mere man has
come to know God in Christ: an expression of the experienced fact
that God has bestowed his own entire self on man. Certainly, in so far
as God's free disposition in the *kairos* of Christ is the unsurpassable
communication of all that God is and can be by essence and freedom, it
is also a communication of the divine nature. But this depends inseparably on the fact that God, as Person, freely wished to love us; and in
the knowledge of this truth the entire reality of Christianity is contained.

4. 'God' as First Person of the Trinity in the New Testament

a. The question formulated.

Biblical and dogmatic theology overlap in a specific way in the last
question we have still to put ourselves. The question is one of dogmatic theology in so far as we presuppose the defined teaching of the
Church concerning the Trinity, and consequently make use of concepts
which are not immediately and explicitly given in the New Testament.
But the question is also one of Biblical theology, in so far as we are
attempting to determine the conceptual content of a word in its New
Testament usage. Specifically, what we are trying to discover is *who*
is meant when the New Testament speaks of ὁ θεός. Thus our task
is not to present the teaching of the New Testament concerning God
as Trinity; this is simply presupposed as a doctrine of faith. We take
it as something given that the content of the Church's teaching concerning God as Trinity in the Unity of one and the same essence, is
present in the New Testament too, though it is formulated there in
different and simpler terms. But we are not concerned to ask whether,
according to the New Testament, the three we find named there,
πατήρ, υἱός, πνεῦμα ἅγιον, are distinct from each other and yet
identical with the divine nature possessed in common. Presupposing

all this, we wish to learn which of these three is meant when the New Testament speaks of ὁ θεός.

Within the conceptual system of scholastic theology, no real question remains once the Trinitarian doctrine itself has been presupposed (i.e. once the linguistic usage of the New Testament has been taken to conform to that of theology): the word and concept 'God' signifies (*significat*) the Person to whom the divine nature is proper; and so 'God' can stand for (*supponitur*) each of the three Persons who possess this nature, or again 'God' can stand for all three Persons together. When, for example, the Logos is called 'Son of God', 'God' in this predication *stands for* the Father, in so far as he is one of the divine Persons, for 'God' can stand for each of the three Persons, while the Father alone has a Son. Or again, in the statement, 'God creates the world', according to the conceptual system of Latin theology 'God' *stands for* the divine Person, this time indeed for the three Persons together, in so far as they are one God by reason of the unity of nature and thus one Source of the world by reason of the unity of their operation *ad extra*. For the theology of the Schools then, 'God' is one with respect to the general concept of personality if we may so put it, and consequently can stand for each of the three Persons individually and for all three together.[1] Once more we do not of course wish to deny that such a view of the concept and the word 'God' is possible, legitimate and in the long run unavoidable. But the question nevertheless remains whether this is also the usage of the New Testament. We may put the matter in the terms of scholastic logic. Is it the case that in the New Testament ὁ θεός only *stands* often for the Father and stands much more frequently for the threefold God in general, in that ὁ θεός signifies simply God's concretely existing and subsisting nature? Or is it the case that in the New Testament ὁ θεός always *signifies* the Father and does not merely stand for him often? We maintain that in the New Testament ὁ θεός *signifies* the First Person of the Trinity, and does not merely stand for him often; and this applies to every case in which another meaning of

[1] Of course the 'generality' of this concept must be understood properly. A concept is truly general only when the form signified *in obliquo* by the concrete concept (the nature) is capable of multiple realization. Further, as regards personality, generality is meant only in the sense in which a 'general' concept can be formed of the ultimate, concrete and irreducible uniqueness of a subsistent being.

ὁ θεός does not become clearly evident from the context. These few exceptions in no way support the opinion that ὁ θεός merely stands for the Father without actually signifying him.[1]

[1] *Translator's Note.* According to Peter of Spain, a representative thirteenth-century logician, signification and supposition differ in that *significatio est per impositionem vocis ad rem significandam, suppositio vero est acceptio ipsius termini iam significantis rem pro aliquo . . . significare est vocis, supponere vero termini iam compositi ex voce et significatione* (*Summulae Logicales*, tr. 6; ed. Bochenski, 6.03, p. 58). For further information on earlier theories see Philotheus Boehner, *Medieval Logic* (Manchester 1952), pp. 27–51. According to John of St Thomas, from whom most modern writers on scholastic logic derive, signification and supposition differ in that the former is 'representative substitution', the latter 'applicative substitution', where the mind applies terms whose signification is already known, to stand for something about which it wishes to make some statement. Thus supposition is the 'acceptance of a term for something to which this term may be seen to refer', *acceptio termini pro aliquo, de quo verificatur* (*Logica*, P. I, lib. ii, c.9; ed. Reiser, p. 29 s.). This 'application' takes place normally in actual statements though it may also occur in everyday life when some object is physically pointed at or addressed.

For those who are familiar with the scholastic theory as well as for those who are not (both may find Fr Rahner's use of the theory puzzling), the following example may help. Suppose we wished to determine what people 'meant' when they spoke of 'the Sun' as opposed to what they 'meant' when they spoke of 'suns'. In the first place 'the Sun' is clearly being used to 'stand for' one determinate object, while 'suns' is used to 'stand for' an indeterminate range of objects. Thus in one sense of the English word 'meaning' (the suppositional or referential sense), 'sun' in *The Sun is shining* differs in meaning from 'sun' in *The Milky Way contains thousands of suns*. But no one would say that the meanings of the word 'sun' are totally unrelated. In fact 'sun' in both cases has the same conceptual meaning (what the scholastics ordinarily call *significatio*), namely 'a fixed star with satellites', though certainly this conceptual meaning is not what ordinarily 'comes to mind' when people speak of 'the Sun'. Thus a third sense of the English word 'meaning' is called for, 'what ordinarily comes to mind' when a term is used; this may be called the *contextual* meaning (or meaning in use) of the term, since it always involves implicit reference to a given context in which the term is used (cf. 'the King', 'the Prior', and the examples on p. 131). It is in a similar way that a proper name can (in spite of most modern logicians) be said to have meaning, by presupposing a context in which the name is understood to be used of a thing *of a certain sort*: by 'Nero' I may mean my bulldog. 'The Sun' in this third sense of 'meaning' means the particular object of a certain sort referred to in a given context of usage. It need hardly be said that this analysis is not meant to be exhaustive.

This is not just a matter of logic-chopping. There will indeed be many cases in which a New Testament expression remains the same as to its material content in whichever way our question is decided; and this for the simple reason that in many or even in most cases a statement containing ὁ θεός, even if it refers explicitly to the Father alone (on the view, that is, that ὁ θεός generally *signifies* the Father and consequently stands for him alone), implicitly states something about the Son and the Spirit. But if statements about ὁ θεός bear explicitly on the Father alone, there is at any rate need of a much closer examination of these statements, and a strict proof that they do really imply something about the other Persons as well. For example, when the New Testament calls us 'children of God', the question arises as to whether this statement already says explicitly that we are children of the three divine Persons, and so in the same breath calls us children of the Son and of the Holy Ghost; or whether the latter can only be inferred from the original statement. No further explanation is required to see that a question like this leads on to the theological problem as to whether we are related in a specific way to each of the three divine Persons in virtue of grace. Although we shall not investigate this point here, the way in which we have formulated our question does indicate an indispensable presupposition of any theological treatment; and this single example is enough to show that the question has a real importance.

But even apart from the solution of this special problem, our question has real importance with regard to the correctness of theological language in relation to the kerygma. Not every objectively

---

Now what Fr Rahner has, I think, succeeded in showing is that ὁ θεός 'means' the Father in this third sense of 'meaning'; but I do not see that this third sense is properly *significatio*. Thus θεός can retain its *significatio* and ὁ θεός yet 'mean' the Father, in a perfectly familiar sense of 'meaning' over and above the suppositional sense. The 'sort' of object here is on the one hand the Persons of the Trinity, and on the other hand anything to which θεός may be applied; but if anyone objects to the notion of 'sort' or genus being applied to the Trinity, he should observe that the logical pattern and the logical difficulties are very similar for 'the Father'. In the last resort, it seems doubtful whether scholastic logic is sufficiently subtle to provide an adequate analysis of the semantics of ordinary language. One of the merits of Fr Rahner's study is that it shows how the sort of linguistic analysis practised in this country after Wittgenstein is not without its relevance for theologians.

true statement is also kerygmatically correct. For example, it is true, objectively speaking, that when Jesus prayed as man, he prayed to the three divine Persons. Yet kerygmatically it would be incorrect to dwell on the fact that Jesus worshipped the Son of God. So if we ask which theologically true statements are also kerygmatic, we shall always have to orientate ourselves by references to modes of expression current in the New Testament (though not to them alone). It is only in this way that we shall avoid the danger of bringing things into the foreground of a human consciousness which is always finite, of emphasizing connexions and relationships, which conceal or at least push into the background the more important view of revealed reality, that which is of ultimate significance for the working out of salvation. For instance, if prayer is always directed only to God in general or to the three divine Persons indifferently, there may perhaps be some theoretical consciousness of Christ's place as mediator, but in the long run it is no longer going to have the significance for the full religious life which in fact is due to it. Taking into account, then, not only the objective truth of a mode of speech but also its kerygmatic correctness, it becomes important to make a close inspection of the linguistic usages of the New Testament. And no long explanation is needed to show that in this respect the use of the word 'God' is consequently of special significance. The detailed examination of what the New Testament means immediately and expressly by calling us children of God, is of particular urgency from the kerygmatic point of view. For in the usual Western sense of the word, the relationship of *filiation* with respect to God has led much more easily to the danger of a moralistic attenuation of this relationship than it would have done if the idea of filiation had from the very start involved a living consciousness of the fact that the Father in the Trinitarian sense is our Father (because 'God' precisely signifies the Father). Thus in this relationship of filiation to the Father of the eternal Son, quite precise relationships to the Son and to the Spirit are included, but they are not directly indicated by the word 'child' in the New Testament, and so ought not to be directly expressed by us in this sense when we speak kerygmatically. If 'God' *signifies* the Father and if we feel ourselves into this mode of speech, we shall become much more clearly conscious 'in prayer to God' (cf. Lk 6:12) that we call upon the Father of our Lord Jesus Christ when, taught by Christ, we say 'Our Father'. And so the Trinitarian structure of our whole religious life will become more vital, and our consciousness of Christ's mediation with regard to the Father become more sharp, than if the word 'God' merely calls to mind in our prayer to God the God of natural theology and the Trinity in general (and hence indistinctly).[1]

b. Questions of method.

In the first place it is of course clear that in the New Testament ὁ θεός often *at least stands for* the Father in the Trinitarian sense, at any rate wherever Christ is called the 'Son of God' or where the Spirit (as Person) is called 'Spirit of God'. For the Son and the Spirit are not Son and Spirit of the Trinity, but Son of the Father and Spirit of the Father. The only question, then, is how we are to know whether ὁ θεός not only *stands for* the Father, but also *signifies him* (all this with reference only to New Testament usage, of course).

It might seem that this question has already been decided in the negative, for the following reasons. 1. Even in the New Testament ὁ θεός occurs in contexts in which the word must signify not the Father but the triune God as such; in those statements, for instance, in which ὁ θεός is used to speak of the God of the Old Testament, the Creator God, God as the object of natural theology. 2. θεός is also used to speak of the Son. If these arguments should turn out not to be decisive for our investigation, we must ask positively how we may in general recognize whether a word merely *stands for* what is meant or *signifies* it in a given type of expression; and how we may know what follows in particular from such general methodological indications for the concrete case with which we are concerned.

From the very nature of the case, the only methodological directive available is that we should simply examine the linguistic usage before us. We may begin with the clearest case. Let us assume that a certain word is invariably used to refer to some one determinate thing and to no second thing, for which the word would also have to have supposition, in case it merely stood for the first thing but did not signify it. Further we suppose that this word occurs precisely in contexts in which, in order to avoid ambiguity, a signifying word, which does in fact exist, might have been expected and not merely a word with supposition. It is clear that in such a case the word would *signify* the

[1] Cf. e.g. J. A. Jungmann, *Die Frohbotschaft und unsere Glaubensverkündigung* (Regensburg 1936), p. 67 s.

thing and not merely *stand for* it. It must of course be noted that in actual usage a word fluctuates between its supppositional application and its signification. This is due to the fact that the application of a word is subject to historical changes. The conceptual content of a word may become broader or narrower; a word may pass from a narrow to a wider meaning, and then to a different narrower meaning. Thus it can happen that a word may at first merely stand for a determinate thing and then signify it, or vice versa; and the signification of a word may become different as a result of an intermediate suppositional usage. It also follows from this that the principle just enunciated (that the significative meaning of a word with respect to a determinate thing may be recognized by the *exclusive* use of the word for the thing) must not be pressed too far. It is quite possible that a word should be significative of a determinate thing (still be or already be), while it may still be applied suppositionally in a few individual cases to indicate some other thing; and this fact would in no way prove that the word has been used for the first thing merely supppositionally. For example, when we are told of Howard in Scott's *Lay of the Last Minstrel* that

> His Bilboa blade, by Marchmen felt,
> Hung in a broad and studded belt

we know of course that the 'blade' here is a sword; but it by no means follows that even for Scott 'blade' means 'sword'. We have here a purely suppositional use of 'blade' for 'sword'.[1] But once a word comes to be used more or less regularly or exclusively for a determinate thing, we must say that it now also becomes significative of that thing. For example, when we speak of a 'torch' in our modern city life, the word has ceased to be strictly a generic concept for our linguistic sensibility. It no longer contains the electric lamp as merely one of its species, so as merely to *stand for* it from time to time. In the context of modern life the signification of the word 'torch' is simply 'electric torch', which is not to say that for modern city-dwellers in exceptional cases, and for others quite frequently, 'torch' may not

[1] Fr Rahner's own example is taken from Schiller's 'Der Graf von Habsburg', where the Count 'auf seines Knappen *Tier* Vergnüget noch weiter des Jagens Begier'. Even for Schiller 'Tier' does not mean 'Pferd' but is used for it in a purely suppositional way.

also stand for an oil or wooden torch, or even signify it.[1] Indeed it is quite possible that the same word should signify two different things and not just stand for them. After the first World War, when we spoke of a 'tank', the word had the meaning 'container' or 'armoured vehicle' according to context, and yet for our linguistic sense there was no question of a single generic concept for the two things. What this shows is that we had no sense of speaking too generally and vaguely when we used the word 'tank' for an armoured vehicle; yet this would certainly have been the case if we felt that *tank* here was a wide, generic concept.[2] It is clear, then, that a word can name several things without eliciting for linguistic sensibility the consciousness of a generic concept which includes them. In such a case we have several significations of the same word and not different suppositional applications. These properties of language must be kept in mind if the following discussion is to be properly appreciated.

c. Arguments against the thesis.

We shall now proceed to examine the soundness or unsoundness of the arguments brought forward to show that, in itself, ὁ θεός means in the New Testament God in general; and that consequently, if it refers in many places to the Father, we have a suppositional application of the word and not its inner signification.

We begin with the first argument. It might be said that even in the New Testament ὁ θεός is used as a name for the object of natural knowledge of God; and this God is not the Father but the one God who is cause of the world in virtue of the numerical unity of his nature: this attribute, then, belongs equally to all three divine Persons since all three possess the one nature. But just this assertion—that what we know from the world is the triune God in the unity of his nature, and not the Father—is open to question. It is obvious that the Father is not known *as* Father in natural theology, i.e. not *as* He who communicates his nature to the Son by an eternal generation; and it is obviously true that the necessary uniqueness of the divine nature is

---

[1] Fr Rahner has, rather more neatly, *Wagen—Kraftwagen* and *Pferdewagen*.

[2] It is to be noted here that 'tank' is not thought of as an accidental homophone for two different concepts, such as 'calf' for the young of bovine animals and for the fleshy part of the leg, or 'ball' for a dance or sphere (Fr. Rahner has *Steuer*, *Dichtung*.—Tr.).

discerned by natural theology. But we can still say that he who is in actual fact known from the world, is concretely the Father and not the Trinity in general and indistinctly. For natural theology itself ascends not just to a divinity but to a God: it knows, that is, that this divine nature necessarily subsists, and subsists, what is more (or at least *also*), in an absolute and unqualified *unorigination* (*Ursprungslosigkeit*). Natural theology is quite capable of affirming the necessity of a pure and absolute unorigination in God, free from any conceivable restriction, even if its statement of this remains wholly formal. Of course it remains utterly concealed from natural theology that this concrete, absolutely unoriginate Origin of all reality is Origin also by communication of the divine nature and not merely by creation *ex nihilo*; that there exists Another originating from it which itself possesses the divine nature; that consequently this absolutely Unoriginate possesses the divine nature and its own absolute unorigination simply in being related *to* its Son; and that in consequence not every origination implies a finite reality, to be classified only as creaturely. All this makes no difference to the fact that when natural theology acquires knowledge of a simple and absolutely first Principle of all reality (not just all creaturely reality), what is so known is the Father. For, as it must yet again be emphasized, the assertion within formal ontology of the necessity of an ἀρχή which is purely ἄναρχος, bears formally and *a priori* on an Unoriginate not just as set over against an origination by creation, but as opposed to *every* conceivable real and hypothetical origination.

It will be seen that our considerations have to do with the topics dealt with in theology under the heading of a *subsistentia absoluta* in God. If we disregard questions of terminology, which sometimes seem to take up most of these discussions, the real problem consists in knowing what (or better, who) 'this God' (*hic Deus*) is: a concept which is on the one hand distinct from that of the divine nature, the divinity; and on the other can apparently be thought and known in disregard (or ignorance) of the three relative Subsistences through which the divine nature alone really acquires unqualified and immediate concreteness. Unless we wish to follow Cajetan and Suarez, among others, in positing a *subsistentia absoluta* (and at least terminologically this does not belong to the Church's teachings), only one course is open to us: to maintain that the concrete Absolute (*hic Deus*) known by natural theology is precisely the Father, although natural theology does not know that this Subsistence is one which is relative to other divine Persons. For in the first place, we know by natural reason that the divine essence must subsist simply and in a way quite peculiar to it as this God, as Person. Secondly, remembering that it is something ultimate and immediate, we do not wish to make this personal subsistence into a concept which would fit more than one individual, or again into something which would entirely fail to bring God's absolutely immediate concreteness into focus (as is the case with the notion of *subsistentia absoluta*). It follows then that 'this God', in whom we are bound to conceive the divine nature as necessarily subsisting, must be the Father, though certainly he is not known by us *as* such.

We may see, then, that where the New Testament interprets 'God' as the object of natural theology, it does not follow as a matter of course that the triune God as a whole is meant, nor, then, that in this context we have a linguistic usage in which ὁ θεός signifies the triune God in his unity and not the Father. The least that can be said of this view of the concept ὁ θεός and its application is a *non liquet*.

There is no difficulty in seeing that the same holds true for the New Testament use of ὁ θεός for the Creator of the world. For on the one hand God can be known naturally as origin of the world and thus at least in the broadest sense as its Creator; and the New Testament does give expression to the idea of God as Creator. On the other hand, this natural knowledge does bear upon the First Person as the radical term of its movement, though not upon the First Person *as* such. It follows that the same kind of thing *can* be said about the New Testament idea of God as Creator of the world. The *absolutely* Unoriginate, which is to say the Father, is Creator of the world too. This is not to deny that objectively this attribute belongs to each of the three Persons in possession of the divine nature, which is the basis of the divine creativity, the *actio ad extra*. On the contrary, it follows immediately from the first assertion; but it need not for that reason be expressly stated there. If it is possible to say without going any further 'The Father created the world', then it is also true of the statement 'God is the creator of the world', that nothing more need be said there expressly. Whether in fact more is expressly said there or just that and no more, is not a question to be decided from this statement in isolation; it has first to be decided whether ὁ θεός merely stands for the Father or also signifies him. The same holds good for those propositions in which ὁ θεός is used to speak of Him who was a work in the saving history of the Old Testament. For in New Testament usage ὁ θεός is precisely Creator *and* the Ruler of the Old Covenant, and so the same thing is true of both expressions; and it is likewise obvious that the other two Persons are included objectively in such an expression, in case this refers explicitly only to the first Person. We may just note here that there are places in the New Testament where ὁ θεός, as God of the Old Dispensation, undoubtedly means the Father, because in the same context mention is made of Christ's being sent by this God.[1]

The second argument to show that ὁ θεός in the New Testament only stands suppositionally for the Father, even in the texts in which he is actually referred to by this word, may seem more weighty. It relies on the fact that in some few texts θεός is also used of the Son. The Jews' reproach to Christ that he makes himself God (Jn 10:33) cannot be counted among these, for in the mind of the hostile Jews there is no intention of making a distinction between the Son and the Father and so making a θεός-statement about the Son with regard to his distinction from the Father. And since we are only concerned here with New Testament usage in its own right, we may also leave out of account the text (Heb 1:8 s.) where St Paul applies Psalm 44:7 s. to Christ. ὁ θεός is certainly applied to the Son here; but this would only supply a convincing proof of the Apostle's usage if it were clear what sense *elohim* itself had in Psalm 44[2] and in what St Paul's messianic application consisted. But other texts of the New Testament are relevant here: in Rom 9:5 s. Christ is called ὁ ὢν ἐπὶ πάντων θεός; in Jn 1:1 the Logos is called θεός; in Jn 1:18 μονογενὴς θεός[3]; in Jn 20:28 Thomas says to the resurrected Christ, ὁ κύριός μου καὶ ὁ θεός μου; in 1 Jn 5:20 it is said of Christ, οὗτός ἐστιν ὁ ἀληθινὸς θεός; in Tit 2:13 we are told of the δόξα τοῦ μεγάλου θεοῦ καὶ σωτῆρος ἡμῶν Ἰησοῦ Χριστοῦ.[4]

---

[1] Ac 3:12–26 for v.26; Heb 1:1–2, God has spoken in the prophets and in his Son; Jn 10:35–6, the Scriptures of the Old Testament are the word of God, who has sent Christ into the world; and so on. Cf. J. Beumer, 'Wer ist der Gott des AT?', *Kirche und Kanzel* XXV (1942), pp. 174–80.

[2] Cf. P. Heinisch, *Theology of the Old Testament*, ET p. 348.

[3] Assuming that we should not rather read ὁ μονογενὴς θεός here, a reading which has been strongly recommended in recent times. Cf. TWNT IV, p. 784, n. 14 (Büchsel) and R. Bultmann, *Johannesevangelium* (in Meyer's *Kommentar*), 1941, p. 55, n. 4.

[4] We cannot count Heb 3:4 among these texts, because θεός here can

Thus we have six texts in which the reality of the divine nature in Christ is expressed by the predicate θεός. In none of them—it is not unimportant to note—is θεός alone, without the addition of modifying clauses but with the article, used to speak of Christ. θεός is either found without the article (Jn 1:1.18; Rom 9:5)[1], and so suggests a kind of conceptual generality; or it is particularized in some way, and so suggests that what is being referred to is not simply to be identified with what is elsewhere meant by ὁ θεός.[2] It is further to be

---

just as well be referred to the Father on account of 3:6, as to the Son on account of 3:2.3; nor can we count 2 Pet 1:1 and 2 Thess 1:12, because θεός here is clearly separated from 'Christ' by the ἡμῶν between 'God' and 'Lord' ('Saviour'), unlike Tit 2:13, and so is to be referred to the Father and not to Christ. Elsewhere St Paul often speaks of the Father as the θεός where he predicates κύριος of Christ; and a mention of the Father as well as the Son is to be expected at the beginning of 2 Peter, in accordance with the usual practice at the beginning of a letter. Nor can we include Eph 5:5; Col 2:2; Tit 2:11; 3:4; in all these it is much more likely that θεός refers to the Father and not to Christ. The same is true of Ac 20:28; for the readings ἐκκλησία τοῦ θεοῦ and ἐκκλησία τοῦ κυρίου are evenly balanced in the manuscripts, and a change from the more difficult, because unusual, reading ἐ.τ.κυ. to the common ἐ.τ.θεοῦ is more easily explained than a change in the reverse direction, especially since from St Ignatius of Antioch onwards the phrase 'blood of God' had ceased to be linguistically unfamiliar, so that a correction of θεοῦ into κυρίου would no longer be suggested from that side.

[1] In itself, the absence of the article in Jn 1:1 and Rom 9:5 is sufficiently explained by the fact that θεός is being used predicatively; but the absence of the article in Jn 1:18 is all the more striking. Lagrange translates correctly, 'Un Dieu Fils unique' (M. J. Lagrange, *Evangile selon Saint Jean*[5], Paris 1936, p. 27). The article in Jn 20:28 is explained by the μου, which normally requires the article before it; by its use with the vocative (Blass-Debrunner, *Grammatik des ntl. Griechisch*[9], § 147, 3); and by its presence in the established formula ὁ κύριος καὶ ὁ θεός (cf. e.g. Apoc 4:11). It should further be noted that ὁ θεός μου, whether it is taken as vocative or nominative, is predicative in sense, and so cannot be used as evidence either way to show whether ὁ θεός in New Testament usage ever appears as *subject* of a statement referring to Christ.

[2] This should be clear from Jn 1:18, where the article is missing again: 'an only begotten God' excludes in advance the danger of simply taking this God for ὁ θεός. In Tit 2:13, θεός—the article is already explained by the ἡμῶν—is protected against any misunderstanding by the conjoined Χριστοῦ Ἰησοῦ, and is found in the context of a specifically Hellenistic vocabulary (ἐπιφάνεια—σωτήρ—μέγας θεός); in a context like this, however, θεός, and especially in the cult-formula μέγας θεός, has a quite different, a much more general ring than ὁ θεός, which against its

bserved that in all these cases (with the exception of Tit 2:13), θεός
tands as predicate or has a predicative sense,[1] and in this way suggests
he more general connotation of the word in the context. But the word
ever appears by itself as grammatical subject, about which something
lse is said, as though it were a characterization of Christ needing no
urther explanation, like κύριος, for instance (Lk 7:13; 10:1; Jn
:11; 6:23; 11:2; Ac 9:10.11; 1 Cor 7:10.12; 1 Thess 4:16, etc.).
ut what is decisive for our inquiry is that these few texts in which
hrist is called θεός are vastly outnumbered by the other texts in
rhich the New Testament intends to express Christ's divine nature in
ne way or another, and yet does not make use of the word θεός, as
ne would have expected if the word had a quasi-generic signification.
hrist is called 'Son of God', the 'true Son of God', κύριος, 'Logos
f God', εἰκών of God, χαρακτήρ and ἀπαύγασμα of God; we
e told of his ἐν μορφῇ θεοῦ ὑπάρχειν, of his 'being-with-God',
f his εἶναι ἴσα θεῷ, of the πλήρωμα τῆς θεότητος that dwells
him. All these are ways of trying to express Christ's divinity, and
hat is more to express it as clearly as possible, without any pedagogic
tempt to withhold the full sense of the affirmation, as may have been
e case when Christ began to reveal himself; and yet in all these texts
e writers avoid the use of θεός for Christ. The only way in which
is can be explained is that for the linguistic sense of the New

---

ld Testament background has much more nearly the character of a proper
me. If 1 Jn 5:20 (bearing in mind that the text here is not entirely certain)
ust be referred to the Son, then this text is without question the summit of
e predication of God with reference to the Son in the New Testament;
r it is impossible to deny that ἀληθινός here does not in itself make the
θεός sound more general, but rather emphasizes still more sharply the
iqueness and exclusiveness of the one God. At the same time it should be
ted that precisely in St John's First Epistle ὁ θεός so often certainly
eans the Father (1:5-7; 4:9.10; 4:15; 5:9-12; and υἱὸς τοῦ θεοῦ
ὗτοῦ] in a good dozen instances) that it must be understood of the
ther throughout the Epistle, unless we are to suppose that some incom-
ehensible change has taken place in the subject referred to by ὁ θεός.
w if at the close of the Epistle Christ is called ὁ ἀληθινὸς θεός in a
t emphatic utterance, this is clearly a conscious and deliberate departure
m the usual sense of ὁ θεός, and we may not conclude from this that
θεός possesses a signification which from the start allows it to mean the
n or the Father indifferently.
As the absence of the article indicates, Jn 1:18 is also to be understood
this sense: an only begotten, who is God.

Testament ὁ θεός originally signified the Father alone. 'Ο θεός does no
start by being neutral in a generic way, so as to be applicable to th
Father and also, without explanation, to the Son. Originally it i
associated with the Father and thus primarily signifies him alone; i
is only slowly, as it were shyly and cautiously, that the expressio
is detached from him and evolves in such a way that a few texts (J
20:28; Rom 9:5; 1 Jn 5:20) venture to use it of Christ. These ar
texts in which an especially profound confession of Christ stirs th
speaker to enlarge linguistic usage, whereas in more everyday languag
the customary signification of terms has to be followed more closel
Θεός is still never used of the Spirit.

Summing up, then, we may say that the arguments against ou
thesis are not conclusive. These arguments attempted to show tha
for the linguistic sense of the New Testament ὁ θεός does not pr
marily *signify* the Father but rather any divine Person or the thre
divine Persons together, so that it only *stands for* the Father whe
it is used of him. It is not to be denied that a development in th
direction is in its initial stages; but it cannot be shown that the signif
cative meaning of ὁ θεός has already evolved so far in the New Testa
ment itself that the unqualified expression ὁ θεός merely stand
suppositionally for the Father there.

d. Positive demonstration of the thesis.

We have already stated the general rule of method for a proof
this kind. This is the principle that a word has significative and n
merely suppositional meaning for a determinate thing when (a) th
word is used always or nearly always to speak only of this thing; ar
(b) when the word is employed for this thing even in a critical co
text, although another word for the same thing is available whic
would be clearer (on the grounds of its signification of the thing),
the first word merely stood for the thing suppositionally. What follo
falls into two parts in accordance with these two requirements.

(a) First of all, ὁ θεός is used so frequently to speak of the Fath
that the few texts already noted where θεός is also used to speak
the Son, have no importance for the question whether the predicati
ὁ θεός of the Father is merely suppositional. Christ is called the 'S
of God' (υἱὸς τοῦ θεοῦ), where, as has been said, 'God' at lea
stands for the Father. Christ himself uses the phrase, Jn 5:25; 10:3
11:4 (cf. Mt 27:43); he expressly confirms it, Mt 16:17; 26:63

thers use it, Mt 4:3.6; 8:29; 14:33; 16:16; 26:63; 27:40.54; Mk
:1 (?); 3:11; 5:27; 14:61; 15:39; Lk 1:35; 4:3.9.41; 8:28; 22:70;
n 1:34.49; 3:18; 11:27; 19:7; 20:31; Ac 9:20; Rom 1:3.4.9; 2 Cor
:19; Gal 2:20; Eph 4:13; Heb 4:14; 6:6; 7:3; 10:29; 1 Jn 3:8;
:15; 5:5.10.12.13.20; Apoc 2:18 (here too belong the texts with
υἱὸς αὐτοῦ directly related to ὁ θεός in the immediate context,
Rom 1:9; 5:10; 8:3.29.32; 1 Cor 1:9; 15:28; Gal 1:16; 4:4; 1 Thess
:10; Heb 1:2; 1 Jn 1:7; 3:23; 4:9.10; 5:10.11).[1] In the same sense
θεός at least stands for the Father when God is called 'Father of
esus Christ', Jn 6:27; Rom 15:6; 1 Cor 15:24; 2 Cor 1:3; 11:31;
Eph 1:3.16; Phil 2:11; Col 1:3; 1 Pet 1:3; 2 Pet 1:17; Apoc 1:6, or
when on the other hand Christ is said to be ὁ λόγος τοῦ θεοῦ
Apoc 19:13), εἰκὼν τοῦ θεοῦ (2 Cor 4:4; Col 1:15), ἴσα θεῷ
Phil 2:7). There is no doubt that the Father is referred to by ὁ θεός
once again at least suppositionally) when ὁ θεός is said to send the
on, Jn 8:42; Ac 3:26; Rom 8:3; Gal 4:4, or when Christ 'proceeds
from God', Jn 8:42; 13:3; 16:27, or when the Logos (Christ) is
poken of as being with God, Jn 1:1; 6:46, or when God is called
the God of our Lord Jesus Christ', Eph 1:17, because one divine
person can only belong to another if it proceeds from the other. But
here are countless other texts in which 'God' actively works upon
Christ or 'God' is the object of one of Christ's actions or in which
God' and Christ seem simply to be put side by side: in all these 'God'
refers to the Father. It is certainly true that according to the purely
neological logic of real attributions, operations of 'God' upon
Christ in his human nature can be attributed to the whole Trinity (St
Thomas, Ia. 43.8), so that somewhat different relationships are found
ere from those found in a 'mission', in the strict theological sense
of this word. But the view that it is in this sense that an operation of
ne triune God as such is also attributed to Christ (not merely
mplied logically) in the New Testament, would lead to linguistic
mpossibilities. For *firstly* ὁ θεός, put next to Christ, is often particularized by the attribute πατήρ (even without ἡμῶν!), and consequently can only be understood of the First Person of the Trinity;
urther, in these combinations of ὁ θεός and Christ, Christ is often

---

[1] 'Son of God' does of course have an indeterminate sense in a number of
places in the Gospels, but this sense does not in itself come into consideration
ere.

characterized as the κύριος, i.e. as divine Person, and once again it
is impossible that the Trinity and one of these three Persons should
be put side by side (e.g. ἐν ἐπιγνώσει τοῦ θεοῦ καὶ ᾽Ιησοῦ τοῦ
κυρίου ἡμῶν, 2 Pet 1:2); and *often* in these statements about an
action of God upon him or vice versa Christ is called 'Son', and
consequently this θεός can only be the Father. Finally, it is quite
inconceivable, bearing in mind the clear and simple language of the
New Testament, that where two subjects are named side by side, the
immediate and explicit sense of what is said should be that one subject
('God') just includes the other (Christ).

We can now go on to interpret a number of expressions in accordance with these presuppositions. Actions relating to Christ are
attributed to 'God': 'God' has raised up Christ from the dead (Ac
2:24.32; 3:15.26; 4:10; 5:30; 10:40; 13:17.33–4; 17:31; Rom 10:9;
1 Cor 15:15; 6:14; Eph 1:20; Col 2:12; 1 Thess 1:10; 1 Pet 1:21.
Ac 2:32 [πατήρ v.33]; 3:26 [ἀπέστειλεν]; Rom 10:9; 1 Cor 6:14
[κύριος!] make it even clearer linguistically that the Father is meant
by this God who raises up from the dead.—Cf. also Gal 1:1, where
θεὸς πατήρ appears as the one who raises up). 'God' has exalted
Christ, glorified him (Ac 2:33; 3:13; 5:31; Phil 2:9). 'God' anoints
Christ with the Holy Ghost (Ac 10:38). 'God' is with him (Ac 10:38).
'God' makes Christ sit at his right hand (Mk 16:19; Lk 22:69; Ac
7:55–6; Rom 8:34; Eph 1:20 [the subject here is ὁ θεὸς τοῦ κυρίου
of v.17!]; Col 3:1; Heb 10:12; 12:2; 1 Pet 3:22; cf. Apoc 3:21,
where the throne of the Father is being spoken of). 'God' has spoken
beforehand of *his* (!) Christ (Ac 3:18). Christ is addressed by 'God'
(Heb 5:10). Christ is attested to by 'God' (Ac 2:22). 'God' gives
Christ the throne of David (Lk. 1:32). 'God' gives Christ all he asks
for (Jn 11:22). 'God' is glorified in the Son of Man and glorifies him
(Jn 13:31.32). 'God' is κεφαλή of Christ (1 Cor 11:3). There are
actions of Christ relating to 'God': Christ ascends to *his* 'God' (Jn
20:17); Christ speaks of *his* 'God' (Jn 20:17; Apoc 3:2.12 [four
times]); Christ is in prayer to 'God' (Lk 6:12); Christ appears in the
presence of 'God' (Heb 9:24); Christ brings us to 'God' (Col 3:3);
Christ delivers the kingdom to 'God' (1 Cor 15:24); Christ belongs
to 'God' (1 Cor 1:24); Christ is an offering to 'God' (Eph 5:2).
There are texts which speak of our relationship to God through
Christ: we are with Christ in 'God' (Col 3:3); we have peace with
'God' through the Kyrios (Rom 5:1); we give thanks to 'God' in

ιe name of Christ (Eph 5:20); we are acceptable to 'God' by serving
Christ (Rom 14:18); St Paul is an apostle of Jesus Christ by the will
f 'God' (1 Tim 1:1; 2 Tim 1:1). In a large number of texts ὁ θεός
ιnd Christ are put side by side: the kingdom of Christ and of 'God'
Eph 5:5); heir of 'God' and joint heir with Christ (Rom 8:17);
riests of 'God' and of Christ (Apoc 20:6); knowledge of 'God'
ιnd of Christ (2 Pet.1:2); the righteousness of our 'God' and of the
aviour Jesus Christ (2 Pet 1:1); servant of 'God' and of the Lord Jesus
Christ (Jas 1:1); servant of 'God', apostle of Jesus Christ (Tit 1:1);
ne 'God', one Christ (1 Cor 8:6; 1 Tim 2:5); commandment of 'God'
ιnd faith of Jesus (Apoc 14:12); testimony of Jesus and word of 'God'
Apoc 1:2; 20:4); love of 'God' and patience of Christ (2 Thess 3:5);
ιe church in 'God' our Father and the Lord Jesus Christ (2 Thess
:1); preaching of the kingdom of 'God' and teaching about our Lord
esus Christ (Ac 28:31); before 'God' and Christ (1 Tim 5:21; 6:13;
Tim 4:1); and all the formulas of greeting, containing wishes of
eace and other benefits from 'God' and Christ (Rom 1:7; 1 Cor 1:3;
Cor 1:2; Gal 1:3; Eph 1:2; Phil 1:2; 2 Thess 1:2; 1 Tim 1:2; 2
im 1:2; Tit 1:4; Phm 3; 2 Jn 3).

'God' at least stands for the Father also in the so-called Trinitarian
ormulas, such as Rom 15:30; 1 Cor 12:4-6; 2 Cor 1:21.22; 13:13;
ph 4:4-6; 1 Pet 1:2.[1] In the same way, 'God' at least stands for the
ather when the Holy Spirit is called Spirit of God (Mt 3:16; 12:28;
Rom 8:9.14; 1 Cor 2:11.12 [ἐκ θεοῦ]. 14; 3:16; 6:11; 7:40; 12:3; 2
Cor 3:3; Eph 4:30; Phil 3:3; 1 Thess 4:8 [πνεῦμα αὐτοῦ]; 1 Pet
:14; 1 Jn 4:2.13 [πνεῦμα αὐτοῦ][2]), when he is sent and given by

---

[1] If we take 'Trinitarian' in the widest sense and consider all those short
ιassages in the New Testament in which all three divine Persons are named,
ιhe Trinitarian texts are as follows: Mt 28:19; Lk 24:49; Jn 14:16.17;
4:26; 15:26; 16:7-11; 16:12-15; Ac 2:32-3; 2:38-9; 5:31-2; 7:55-6;
ο:38; 11:15-17; Rom 5:1-5; 8:9-11; 8:14-17; 14:17-18; 15:15-16;
5:30; 1 Cor 2:6-16; 6:11; 6:15-20; 12:3; 12:4-6; 2 Cor 1:21-2; 13:13;
Gal 4: 4-6; Eph 1:3-14; 1:17; 2:18-22; 3:14-19; 4:4-6; 5:15-20; 2 Thess
.:13; Tit 3:4-11; Heb 2:2-4; 10:29-31; 1 Pet 1:1-2; 2:4-5; 4:14; 1 Jn
:23-4; 4:11-16; 5:5-8; Jud 20-1. In these texts the Father is called simply
θεός seventy times and only nineteen times πατήρ or θεὸς πατήρ or ὁ
εὸς καὶ πατήρ.
[2] For the Holy Spirit as a divine Person can only be called Spirit 'of
God' if he proceeds from this God, as the theologians have always insisted
with regard to the Spirit as Spirit of Christ: cf. e.g. Pesch, *Praelectiones*

'God' (Ac 5:32; 15:18; 1 Cor 6:19; 2 Cor 1:22; Gal 4:6; Eph 1:17; 1 Thess 4:8; 2 Tim 1:7; 1 Jn 3:24; 4:13).

It is further to be observed that the following texts, Rom 1:7; 1 Cor 1:3; 8:6; 2 Cor 1:2; Gal 1:3; Eph 1:2; 5:20; Phil 1:2; Col 3:17; 1 Thess 1:1 (?); 2 Thess 1:2 (?); 2:16; Phm 3, all speak of God our Father; moreover this God who is our Father is clearly characterized as the Trinitarian Father by putting 'the Lord Jesus Christ' immediately after. This alone shows that in New Testament usage it is the First Person of the Trinity who is meant when the writers speak of God our Father and our adoptive sonship. Accordingly Christ himself can speak of 'my' Father and 'your' Father (Jn 20:17), clearly meaning by this one and the same Person, the First Person in God. This may also be seen from the fact that according to St Paul (Eph 1:3.5), the Father of Jesus destined us to be his sons and bestowed his Son upon us, so that we might receive the adoption of sons (Gal 4:5), and Christ so become the firstborn among many brethren (Rom 8:29) and we together with him cry Ἀββὰ ὁ πατήρ (Rom 8:15; Gal 4:5; cf. Mk 14:36). At any rate, New Testament usage allows us to say that we are children of God in the sense that we are children of the Father as First Person of the Trinity, not as children of the triune God (whether the latter statement too is objectively valid or not is not our concern here).[1] Christ himself says that men enter into relationship with his Father (Mt 7:21; 12:50; 15:13; 16:17; 18:10.19.35; 20:23; 25:34; Jn 2:16; 6:32; 14:2.23; 15:8.23.24). The God whom the Jews believed to be their Father, is the God from whom Jesus has proceeded and who has sent him: the Father in the Trinitarian sense (Jn 8:32). Moreover, the heavenly Father, according to Christ's teaching, is not Father of men because he is Creator or because of his providential care for them, so that he could without further qualification be called Father of all men; he is the Father of the followers of Christ, of those in fact who belong to the kingdom of heaven. At least it is only to these

---

Dogmaticae II, n. 529–31. But the God from whom the Spirit proceeds is the Father (Jn 15:26).

[1] How little obvious for scholastic theology this apparently obvious assertion in fact is, may perhaps be seen from the fact that Knabenbauer (*Comm. in Ev. sec. Matt.*[3], Paris 1922, pp. 311–12), citing Maldonatus and Suarez, holds that even in the Our Father it is God in Trinity who is being addressed, because we are children of God and 'God' means just God in Trinity.

that Christ speaks of God as their Father. This fatherhood has its
basis in the free election of the Father, who calls and leads men to his
Son (Jn 6:37–40.44.45). Men are therefore not children of God by
nature, but they can become his children, if they dispose themselves
morally in certain definite ways (Mt 5:9.45: Lk 6:36; cf. Jn 1:12).
According to Christ's own teaching, then, there is no reason to suppose that the adoptive sonship which he preaches is a relationship to
God in general and not to the Father of Christ. All this taken together
justifies the conclusion that in *every* text which speaks of God as our
Father and of us as children of God and of our being born of God,
it is the First Person of the Trinity who is meant. Hence all these
texts are to be counted among those in which $\dot{o}$ $\theta\epsilon\acute{o}s$ at least stands
suppositionally for the Father (Mt 5:9; Lk 20:36; Jn 1:12.13; 11:52;
Rom 5:2; 8:14.16.19.21; 9:8.26; 2 Cor 6:18; Gal 3:26; Eph 1:5;
2:19; 3:14; 4:6; 5:1; Phil 2:15; 4:20; 1 Thess 1:3; 3:13; Heb 12:7;
Jas 1:27; 1 Jn 3:1.2.10; 4:7; 5:1.2.4.7.18; Jud 1; Apoc 21:7).

We may outline our results as follows. Nowhere in the New Testa-
ment is there to be found a text with $\dot{o}$ $\theta\epsilon\acute{o}s$ which has unquestionably
to be referred to the Trinitarian God as a whole existing in three
Persons. In by far the greater number of texts $\dot{o}$ $\theta\epsilon\acute{o}s$ refers to the
Father as a Person of the Trinity. It should be noted here that in the
texts in which $\dot{o}$ $\theta\epsilon\acute{o}s$ is used without its being absolutely clear from
the immediate context who precisely is meant, the expression never
contains anything which is not said of God in other texts; and in just
these other texts, this God may be recognized (directly or indirectly)
as Father in the Trinitarian sense.[1] Besides this there are six complete
texts in which $\dot{o}$ $\theta\epsilon\acute{o}s$ is used to speak of the Second Person of the
Trinity, but still in a hesitant and obviously restricted way (the
restriction is concerned of course not with the reality but with the use
of the word). In addition, $\dot{o}$ $\theta\epsilon\acute{o}s$ is never used in the New Testament
to speak of the $\pi\nu\epsilon\hat{v}\mu\alpha$ $\ddot{\alpha}\gamma\iota\nu$. These findings are sufficient in themselves to justify the assertion that when the New Testament speaks of

---

[1] Thus, for example, the whole Old Testament saving history is ascribed
to the God who sends Jesus, thus to the Father (Ac 3:12–26; cf. Heb. 1:1).
In Ac 4:24 s., Eph 3:9 s. and Heb 1:2, the God who created all things is
clearly characterized as the Father in virtue of his distinction from the 'Son'
('Servant', 'Christ'). Now if creation and saving history are ascribed to
God the Father, there can hardly be a single statement about $\dot{o}$ $\theta\epsilon\acute{o}s$ which
is not included therein.

ὁ θεός, it is (with the exception of the six texts mentioned) the Father
as First Person of the Trinity who is signified. Ὁ θεός signifies him
and does not merely stand suppositionally for him, because a constant
and practically exclusive suppositional use of a word is proof that this
word also signifies the thing for which it stands suppositionally,
especially when it stands for the thing as subject and not just as a
predicative name. The few exceptional uses of θεός, where the
linguistic form itself marks them as exception, do not justify the view
that in the usage of the New Testament ὁ θεός is an expression
which signifies the Trinity in the unity of its proper nature, and so has
always stood suppositionally for each of the three divine Persons in
like manner.

(b) This impression is strengthened when we examine some
critical instances. Where Christ's Person and Nature are to be declared
with the greatest theological strictness and precision, he is called ὁ
υἱὸς τοῦ θεοῦ: so in Peter's confession of faith at Caesarea Philippi
(Mt 16:16), so in Christ's decisive testimony to himself before the
Sanhedrin when he was being threatened with death (Mt 26:63; Mk
14:61; Lk 22:70), so in the final recapitulation of the theological
content of the Fourth Gospel (Jn 20:31), so in the oldest formula in
the New Testament summing up the meaning of conversion to
Christianity (1 Thess 1:9.10, δουλεύειν θεῷ ζῶντι καὶ ἀληθινῷ
καὶ ἀναμένειν τὸν υἱὸν αὐτοῦ), so in the solemn opening of the
Epistle to the Romans, the greatest of the doctrinal texts of the New
Testament (Rom 1:2.4), so in the superscription of the Gospel of St
Mark (Mk 1:1). In all these cases Christ is called 'Son of *God*', the
theological meaning being always, Son of the Father. It must be kept
in mind that the word 'Father' was always available to the New
Testament writers. Indeed it is of the greatest interest that our Lord
himself clearly avoided the form 'Son of God' (at least in general).
In the Synoptics the phrase 'Son of God' never rises spontaneously to
his lips, although he recognizes it as a formula for what he is. He himself speaks of himself only as the 'Son' absolutely (except for the
formula 'Son of Man'); and he speaks of God, the Father, only as the
'Father' absolutely (Mt 11:27 = Lk 10:22; Mt 24:36 = Mk 13:32;
Mt 28:19; Lk 9:26)[1] or as 'his (heavenly) Father (in heaven)'. He

---

[1] Disregarding the parables, in which Christ lets himself be recognized
indirectly as Son in contrast to servants, etc.

never uses the expression ὁ θεός in the Synoptics to speak of 'God', in so far as the latter has a relationship to Christ himself. Even in St John there are only three texts in which it is certain that our Lord speaks of himself as 'Son of *God*' (Jn 5:25; 10:36; 11:4).[1] If it is remembered that St John uses 'Father' 102 times, in 23 of which it occurs as 'my Father',[2] Christ's own avoidance of the word 'God' in characterizing what he is, is no accident; it is even lacking in the baptismal formula.[3] Thus it cannot be denied that when the men of the New Testament wanted to speak of the Father of Christ, they had at their disposal a word which *signified* this Father, a word which was quite familiar to them from Christ's own manner of speech and which they did in fact often (excepting perhaps the Acts of the Apostles) make use of ('Father', 'God Father', 'God and Father'). If, then, in the above-mentioned solemn formulas, where for the sake of clarity and precision everything depended on the use of a word which signified the thing meant and did not merely stand for it suppositionally, these men used ὁ θεός for the Father, this can only be explained by the fact that in these formulas ὁ θεός did in actual fact signify the Father for them and did not merely stand for him suppositionally. For them the expression ὁ θεός was just as exact and precise as 'Father'. Nor can it be said that the word 'Father' would have been imprecise in contexts like these, in that it could not be known which Father was meant; for the New Testament writers would have been able to follow Christ's example and speak of the 'heavenly Father' or of the 'Father in heaven', or they could have used in this context the common phrase 'God Father', like all the Apostolic formulations of faith.

An analogous observation may be made with regard to the Trinitarian formulas. Where this is undoubtedly ternary in form, we find Jesus himself using the group πατήρ, υἱός, πνεῦμα ἅγιον; but for the Apostles the First Person is always signified in these formulas by ὁ θεός or θεὸς πατήρ, never by πατήρ alone.[4] In these formulas

---

[1] Perhaps Jn 9:35 as well. Jn 6:27; 6:46; 8:42; 16:27 should also certainly be noticed. In these texts ὁ θεός is found in the context of other statements of Christ about himself; the use of ὁ θεός is once again quite comprehensible in view of the context.

[2] Only *once* as 'your Father'; and in the 78 occurrences of 'Father' absolutely, the word always refers objectively to the Father of Christ.

[3] How Christ's own manner of speech is itself to be explained is not our concern here.

[4] Cf. 1 Cor 12:4 s.; 2 Cor 1:21 s.; 13:13 s.; 2 Thess 2:13; 1 Pet 1:2;

too, the replacement of Christ's word πατήρ by the Apostles' θεός is only explained if ὁ θεός simply signified the Father.

When in consequence of all this we say that ὁ θεός in the language of the New Testament signifies the Father, we do not of course mean that it always signifies him *precisely in so far as* he is Father of the only begotten Son by an eternal generation. All that is meant is that when the New Testament thinks of God, it is the concrete, individual, uninterchangeable Person who comes into its mind, who is in fact the Father and is called ὁ θεός; so that inversely, when ὁ θεός is being spoken of, it is not the single divine nature that is seen, subsisting in three hypostases, but the concrete Person who possesses the divine nature unoriginately, and communicates it by eternal generation to a Son too, and by spiration to the Spirit.

It may easily be seen that this result is nothing more than a more precise demonstration of the fact that the conception of the Trinity, customarily (if inexactly) known since de Régnon as the Greek view, is closer to Biblical usage than what de Régnon called the Latin or scholastic view. The latter proceeds from the unity of God's nature (one God in three Persons), so that the unity of the divine nature is a *presupposition* of the whole doctrine of the Trinity; while the former begins with the three Persons (three Persons, who are of a single divine nature) or better, with the Father, who is the source from which the Son, and through the Son the Spirit, proceed, so that the unity and integrity of the divine nature is conceptually a *consequence* of the fact that the Father communicates his whole nature.[1] Associated with this Greek view of the Trinity is the fact that the Father is regarded as God κατ᾽ ἐξοχήν. As Schmaus says:

> This is a procedure which goes back to the first Christian communities, because it is based on Scripture itself. Justin Martyr, Irenaeus and Tertullian all witness to this usage. Origen gives sharpness of definition to this view, and distinguishes between ὁ θεός and θεός. . . . This conception, even if not in so sharply defined a form, finds expression in the early Creeds; and it continued to be handed down in tradition. Denis of Alexandria reserved

Jude 20 s. These are the texts recognized as Trinitarian by E. Stauffer, *New Testament Theology* (ET John Marsh, London 1955), p. 326, n. 828.

[1] On these two views, see de Régnon's summaries, *Etudes de théologie positive sur la Sainte Trinité*, I (Paris 1892), pp. 335–40, 428–35.

the name 'God' to the Father. Ὁ τῶν ὅλων θεός and ὁ ἐπὶ πάντων θεός are designations of the Father which are found everywhere in the fourth century. The Cappadocians had a general view of the Father as the absolute God or as the divine *ousia*. Hilary, as a pupil of the Greeks, is speaking of the Father whenever he uses the word *Deus* without qualification. Subordinationist ideas must not be associated with this mode of speech.[1]

Schmaus supports his assertion that this usage, which characterizes one of the two traditional ways of speaking about the Trinity, is based on Scripture itself with a bare reference to one page of de Régnon (I, p. 445); and here the only support offered is a citation from Theodore Abu Qurra (Abucara).[2] We have tried here to establish in more detail what was proposed by de Régnon as a thesis. This thesis may indeed be more or less obvious for someone who comes fresh from the New Testament, and the attempt to justify it may consequently arouse the suspicion that a way is being forced through an open door. Yet for someone who derives from the theology of Western scholasticism, and is accustomed to read the New Testament under the *a priori* of the conceptual patterns prevalent there, the thesis may well have its significance. We may leave aside the fact that the thesis which we have established in this way shows that the Greek conception of the Trinity is to be taken seriously on the authority of Scripture. But it is also important for a question such as what exactly is involved in our being children of God. If ὁ θεός in the New Testament is the Father, then we are children of the Father of Christ by participation in the eternal sonship of the only begotten Son. And it remains an open question whether we can characterize as sonship the justified man's relationship through grace to the Son and the Spirit (so that this fatherhood by grace is merely appropriated to the First Person of the Trinity); or whether, strictly speaking, it is *not* possible to interpret this relationship to the Son and the Spirit as sonship, so that each of the three divine Persons has its own proper relationship to the justified man,

---

[1] M. Schmaus, *Die psychologische Trinitätslehre des heiligen Augustinus* (Münster 1927), p. 19.
[2] In Petavius, *De Trinitate*, lib. IV, c. xv, n. 14: Ὅθεν οἱ ἀπόστολοι καὶ ἅπασα σχεδὸν ἡ ἁγία γραφή, ὅτ' ἂν εἴπῃ ὁ θεός, οὕτως ἀπολύτως καὶ προσδιορίστως, καὶ ὡς ἐπίπαν σὺν ἄρθρῳ, καὶ χωρὶς ἰδιώματος ὑποστατικοῦ, τὸν πατέρα δηλοῖ.

not merely an appropriated one. Furthermore, this question is signifi
cant not only for a closer understanding of the nature of justifying an
sanctifying grace, by providing what is in the last resort the only mean
of deciding whether 'uncreated grace' is merely something subsequen
upon created grace, or whether it must be recognized as an independen
element in the total concept of sanctifying grace. The question i
significant also for the problem of the connexion between the Trinit
as immanent and as economic, the entitative Trinity and the Trinit
of Revelation; if man really has a special relationship to each of th
three divine Persons,[1] the opposition between the entitative Trinit
and the Trinity of Revelation is resolved at its very root: God *stana
in relation* (*verhält sich*) to the justified man as Father, Word, Spiri
and *is* this too, in and for himself.

We may note finally that in the official prayers of the liturgy, it i
the Father to whom we pray through the Son, and this Father i
simply called *Deus*.[2] We have seen that this is also the usage of th
New Testament. The kerygmatic significance of our enquiry wa
briefly touched upon earlier in this study.

---

[1] Because grace in its full sense cannot be reduced to the concept of a
effect of God's efficient causality, an effect which is worked by the thre
divine Persons in common. See below, pp. 319–46.

[2] de Régnon, I, pp. 495–9.

5

CURRENT PROBLEMS IN CHRISTOLOGY

ONCE theologians and the ordinary magisterium of the Church have begun to pay attention to a reality and a truth revealed by God, the final result is always a precisely formulated statement. This is natural and inevitable. In no other way is it possible to mark the boundary of error and the misunderstanding of divine truth in such a way that this boundary will be observed in the day-to-day practice of religion. Yet while this formula is an end, an acquisition and a victory, which allows us to enjoy clarity and security as well as ease in instruction, if this victory is to be a true one the end must also be a beginning. It follows from the nature of human knowledge of truth and from the nature of divine truth itself, that any individual truth, above all one of God's truths, is beginning and emergence, not conclusion and end. In the last resort any individual human perception of truth only has meaning as beginning and promise of the knowledge of God. But whether the latter is conceived of as *visio beatifica* or otherwise, it can only be genuine, only make blessed, in the knowledge of his incomprehensibility: at that point, then, in which comprehension and the determining limits of what is known are jointly transcended in the Incomprehensible and the Unlimited. Because every truth of the God who reveals himself is given as an incitement and a way to the closest immediacy of communion with him, it is all the more an opening into the immeasurable, a beginning of the illimitable. The clearest formulations, the most sanctified formulas, the classic condensations of the centuries-long work of the Church in prayer, reflexion and struggle concerning God's mysteries: all these derive their life from the fact that they are not end but beginning, not goal but means, truths which open the way to the—ever greater—Truth. The fact that every formula transcends itself (not because it is false, but precisely because it is true) is not due just to the transcendence of the mind which apprehends it and, in apprehending it, is always off beyond it after the greater fullness of Reality and Truth itself. Nor is this self-transcendence due merely to the divine grace of faith, which always transforms the perception of a truth in propositional form into a movement of the mind towards the apprehension of God's ontological truth in itself. This transcendence is at work precisely in the movement of the formula itself, in that it is itself surpassed with a view to another. This certainly does not mean that the first formula has to be given up or abolished in favour of another, as though it were antiquated or another could take its place. On the contrary: it preserves its significance, it remains precisely living, by being expounded. This is so true and so obvious, that whole books can and must be written about the principle of identity, that is to say, the simplest, clearest, most necessary and undeniable formula of all, because it cannot really be said with much confidence that someone who monotonously keeps on repeating it—dressed up with a few 'clarificatory' phrases—has in fact understood it. Anyone who takes seriously the 'historicity' of human truth (in which God's truth too has become incarnate in Revelation) must see that neither the abandonment of a formula nor its preservation in a petrified form does justice to human understanding. For history is precisely *not* an atomized beginning-ever-anew; it is rather (the more spiritual it is) a becoming-new which preserves the old, and preserves it all the more *as* old, the more spiritual this history is. But this preservation, which recognizes the true uniqueness of something which has taken place once for all, is only historical preservation when—the history goes on, and the movement of reflexion departs from the formula which has been reached in order to discover it (just this old formula itself) again.

This holds good of the Chalcedonian formulation of the mystery of Jesus too. For this formula is—a formula.

Thus we have not only the right but the duty to look at it as end *and* as beginning. We shall never stop trying to release ourselves from it, not so as to abandon it but to understand it, understand it with mind and heart, so that through it we might draw near to the ineffable, unapproachable, nameless God, whose will it was that we should find him in Jesus Christ and through Christ seek him. We shall never cease to return to this formula, because whenever it is necessary to say briefly what it is that we encounter in the ineffable truth which is our salvation, we shall always have recourse to the modest, sober clarity of the Chalcedonian formula. But we shall only really have recourse to it (and this is not at all the same thing as simply repeating it), if it is not only our end but also our beginning. We must say something here about this incompleteness which the formula does not resolve but in fact preserves.

Anyone who speaks of incompleteness in a matter like this must be prepared to be dismissed with contempt. This sort of language is hardly 'scientific'. It has to try to get a hearing without the help of the apparatus of learning; inevitably it sounds a little vague, rather like the cheap political programme which promises the emergence of a New Age, although the new Government is probably going to be just as bad as the old. It cannot by itself put into practice what it demands, and that is what is most questionable about it. For if someone says that this matter or that must be considered or investigated, or should be freshly analysed and treated of more comprehensively and profoundly, and yet this does not come about immediately in reality, he speaks like a man who proposes a route by which he himself has never travelled. It may very well be that many of his wishes and conjectures do not touch upon the essential, that the really decisive point will be overlooked. Nevertheless preliminary reflexions of this conjectural and tentative kind are unavoidable, and can only be despised or rejected in principle by someone who thinks that as far as Christology proper is concerned we have already reached the end. But if we are always at the beginning, then the first step is always the uneasy feeling of a need to ask whether it might not be possible to give this or that matter closer attention and find a better solution.

The object which this anxious seeking for the question (it is nothing more) has in view is not of course simply the whole plenitude of the objective Spirit'[1] of Revelation and theology in their long history. If we had clearly before us the plenitude of what was once perceived in faith and meditated upon in theology throughout its entire history, we should already in great part have found the question we are looking for and its answer too. For it is the bitter grief of theology and its blessed task too, always to have to seek (because it does not clearly have present to it at the time) what, in a true sense—in its historical memory—it has always known. The history of theology is by no means just the history of the progress of doctrine, but also a history of forgetting. That is the only reason why historical theology and history of doctrine have a real, irreplaceable and necessary task within

---

[1] In the Hegelian sense.—Tr.

dogmatic theology itself. What was once given in history and is ever made present anew does not primarily form a set of premises from which we can draw new conclusions which have never been thought of before. It is the object which, while it is always retained, must ever be acquired anew, by *us*, that is, we who are just such as no one else can ever be in all history. So that when in considerable uncertainty, we set about asking—and the question itself has to be found first—what it is that we must bring back to mind so as to be able to make our own what we believe, the starting-point of this attempt to ask questions cannot be the whole of Revelation and its history in theology. It is the *answer* which lies there. The starting-point can only be the generally accepted position in theology today (meaning here Christology), as it is found in modern textbooks, in the conception which everybody would agree is the ordinary one, in what appears really clearly in our ordinary theological consciousness today. Any attempt to describe this starting-point is inevitably going to give the impression of being ill-informed, of generalizing unjustly and of distorting current theology. For this 'current theology' cannot easily be detached from its entire past; because along with the average it always offers—thank God—something deeper and closer to the sources of life; because when it is attacked and defends itself, it can always surpass itself and relate what it holds to the past and the future. And so it is impossible to avoid the danger of seeming to caricature current Christology when one attempts to describe what it finds clear and what would have to become still clearer to it in the future. Just because in theology everything is connected with everything else, it is always going to be the case that anyone who is sensitive to the reproach of not having examined this or that question sufficiently or given it a satisfactory answer, can impatiently, but with a good conscience, hold that he has always really been aware of the question in point, and 'basically' even discussed it and analysed it sufficiently. One can only ask such a theologian why he has only discussed so briefly and casually what clearly deserves precise and detailed treatment, and whether he has not forgotten in other places what he—so he claims—regards as 'obvious', and whether this does not show that after all what everybody knows and what has long since been cleared up doesn't perhaps count for much. One has only to consider how few really living and passionate controversies there are in Catholic Christology today which engage the existential concern of the faithful (is there a single one?). Unless

omeone is inclined to regard this fact simply as a mark of superiority,
 proof of unruffled orthodoxy and crystal-clear theology, he will
sten with patience and good will to the most modest attempt, under-
aken with the most inadequate means, to depart from the Chalce-
onian formula in order to find the way back to it in truth.

We should also observe the following point. The degree of theoreti-
al precision and existential vitality with which man understands what
e hears depends on the degree to which he comprehends it within
ne total content of his spiritual being. If this were not the case, there
vould never have been Councils of the Church with their definitions,
ecause a new age would always have been able to live on in the old
larity; or we should have to suppose that the *only* reason for these
Councils was the fact that there had been evil heretics who maliciously
bscured what in itself had been said with quite sufficient clarity and
vhat in itself would have been quite sufficient for later ages in spite of
heir unlikeness. If then the ordinary theology current today is to be
sked why what it has told *us* is insufficiently clear, by 'us' is meant
ve as we must be today; for man's unique standpoint in history is
nescapably given him in advance and helps to determine the perspec-
ive within which we have to consider God's eternal truths too, if we
re really going to let them become a reality of mind, heart and life
n our personal existence. This is not to say that it is in general par-
icularly profitable for theology to take as the explicit starting-point
f a critical consideration of the average Christology current today, any
haracteristic features of just that spiritual situation which has been
mposed upon us, in so far as they are apprehended *reflexively*. Such a
nethod is seldom successful, if only because these reflexively appre-
ended characteristics of the time are probably signatures of a time
vhich is on the way out; it is unlikely that we should discover from
hem postulates big with promise for the Christology of tomorrow.
t is preferable simply to look at the facts, that is to say at Christology
self—always providing that one has the courage to ask questions, to
e dissatisfied, to think with the mind and heart one actually has, and
ot with the mind and heart one is supposed to have. One can then be
onfident that after all something will perhaps emerge which we ought
o be thinking today. For it is quite meaningless to want to be modern
n purpose. The only thing one can do in this situation is not to
uppose that it is necessary to deny who one is (out of anxiety or dis-
rust or falsely understood orthodoxy), but rather allow oneself

honestly to have one's say, and really build on the fact that God can give his grace to this age of ours too, as he once gave it to sinners.

Let us then begin by going to the heart of the matter. This is primarily Biblical theology. There is no question here of practising Biblical theology in its own right; our intention is much more modest. We propose to show by means of a kind of transcendental hermeneutics[1] starting from dogma that the Church's Christological dogma never claims to be an adequate condensation of Biblical teaching, and so that there does remain from the viewpoint of dogma a place for further Christological Biblical theology. It is only in this sense that we shall speak of Biblical theology in what follows. It should be the source of dogmatic theology and so also of Christology. Without it, according to *Humani Generis*[2], dogmatic theology becomes sterile. And here we are already faced with a serious problem. How are we to pursue Biblical theology for Christological purposes, both generally speaking and in dogmatic theology in particular? Is it rash or unjust to say that among Catholic writers, the professional exegetes in this field do not practise Biblical theology, and that the dogmatic theologians know or make use of only those parts of the Scriptures which they require in order to prove Christological theses which have been laid down in advance in a canon already become traditional? Or, in case the first suggestion seems too hard, what noteworthy influence has modern Biblical theology had (so far as it is practised) upon the structure and content of the traditional scholastic theology?[3] Of course the theses of this scholastic theology are true and important, so far as they are dogma. Of course these theses are the concise, condensed expression of the fundamental testimonies in Scripture concerning Jesus Christ, an expression achieved by the immense labour of an irreversible spiritual and cultural history under the guidance of the Spirit of God in the Church. But is it true that the Chalcedonian dogma, and what little else has been acquired for the theology of the schools in the history of dogma, is a condensation and summary of *everything*, without

---

[1] An expression reminiscent of Kant, Dilthey, Heidegger.—Tr.

[2] Pius XII, *Litterae Encyclicae 'Humani Generis'* (12 August 1950), AAS XLII (1950), pp. 568–9; Denz 3014.

[3] 'Traditional' here refers to the actual practice of recent centuries especially since the Enlightenment and the (fruitful and perilous) restoration of scholastic theology after the theology of the Enlightenment.

remainder, of which we hear in Scripture about Jesus the Christ and about the Son, or, again, of what we *might* hear if only we were to speak once more of what has still not entered into scholastic theology? Anyone who answers this question in the affirmative would deny that the Scriptures are the *inexhaustible* source of truth about Christ.[1] But is this conviction noticeable as an active force and a holy disquiet in the ordinary practice of Christology today? For example, let us take L. de Grandmaison's undoubtedly great work on Christ; after all its minute historical investigations, does it not, looked at *theologically*, simply arrive once again at the scholastic position in Christology? Is this to be explained merely by the fact that it has an apologetic end in view and not an immediately theological one?

Let no one say that nothing more is really possible in this field any longer. Something is possible, because something *must* be possible, if it is a matter of the inexhaustible riches of God's presence with us and if we honestly admit that we often find traditional Christology difficult to understand (we shall return to this point later) and so have questions to put to its source, the Scriptures.

For example, let us take so central an assertion of the Scriptures as the statement that Jesus is the Messias and as such has become Lord in the course of his life, death and resurrection.[2] Is it agreed that this assertion has simply been made obsolete by the doctrine of meta-physical Sonship, as *we* recognize it and express it in the Chalcedonian declaration, and that its only real interest for us now is historical, as a first formulation, important merely because Jesus found it useful for the Jews? Is the Christology of the Acts of the Apostles, which begins from below, with the human experience of Jesus[3], merely primitive? Or has it something special to say to us which classical Christology does not say with the same clarity? Is there nothing more to say about the historical self-consummation of the Lord after we have said: *meruit glorificationem corporis sui* (and yet this is by no means peculiar to him)? Is Phil 2, for instance, really covered by this? It does indeed follow from the Incarnation of the Word of God through Mary (in the Chalcedonian sense) that he is the 'Mediator'

---

[1] '*Humani Generis*', AAS, p. 568; Denz 3014.
[2] This is true of the Synoptics and also—though in different words—of St Paul.
[3] Ac 2:21–36; 3:12–26; 4:8–12.27; 5:29–32; 7:56; 9:22; 10:34–43; 13:28–41; 17:31; 18:28.

between us and God, *provided*, of course, that the real initiative, in some true sense, of· the man Jesus with regard to God is given its *genuine* (anti-monothelite) meaning, and Christ is not made into a mere 'manifestation' of God himself and ultimately of him alone, such that the 'appearance' has no independent validity at all with respect to the one who appears. Such a 'Mediator' would be one in name alone. A Christology which fundamentally failed to see this would end by becoming a mythology.[1] But the fact that we have to add this proviso, in order to draw out the full sense of the concept of the mediator and thus (?) of the Messias from the theology of the Incarnation as it is currently taught in the schools, shows that the Bible can contribute something to this classical theology. In particular, if the human 'nature' of the doctrine of Two Natures[2] is seen merely

[1] Thus mythology in this connexion could be defined as follows: The representation of a god's becoming man is mythological, when the 'human' element is merely the clothing, the livery, of which the god makes use in order to draw attention to his presence here with us, while it is not the case that the human element acquires its supreme initiative and control over its own actions by the very fact of being assumed by God. Looked at from this point of view a single basic conception runs through the Christian heresies from Apollinarism to Monothelitism, sustained by the same basic mythical feeling. The persistence of this idea even in theoretical formulations ought to make us realize that although it may have given up announcing itself in such a theoretical fashion today, the idea probably still lives on in the picture which countless Christians have of the 'Incarnation', whether they give it their faith—or reject it.

[2] It is not the Council's doctrine of Two Natures that is in view here, but a 'customary' curtailed form of this doctrine. We have not the slightest intention of suggesting that the Council should be blamed for this curtailed form or indeed that it represents the Council's teaching. What we have in mind is that this reduction of the Mediator to a mean term between God and man does exist in the common mind, when *nature* is seen as a mere instrument of the person, and consequently has no significance for a *divine* Person. The actual existence of such a reduction is not disposed of by the fact that it cannot find conceptual expression within orthodox Christianity in the form of obstinate error (and so is not even easy to grasp conceptually), nor by the fact that it is rejected by other doctrines which are maintained explicitly (Redemption as satisfaction). To establish this point is not to deny that the teaching of the Council, when it is taken in its full, historically ascertainable sense, was concerned to use the doctrine of the Two Natures to elucidate Christ's genuine, human role as Mediator. In the period just before Chalcedon, the recognition of a twofold *physis* in Christ certainly made it possible to locate the decisive mediatorial act, as against Apollinarism, within the reality of this world, in the very human nature of

in the customary sense of a pure 'instrument', the possessor of this instrument can no longer be thought of as Mediator. He would simply be Mediator to himself. Any attempt to deal with the question by discussing it in terms of two 'moral subjects' would still only provide a verbal solution, because a 'nature' conceived of in this way could not provide any foundation for a second moral subject—in relation to God, what is more—in that everything pertaining to a subject in this moral subject (= human nature) would be precisely the Logos himself, with respect to whom the Mediator is supposed to mediate. But is it possible today to keep sharply before our minds Jesus' true initiative in his human history with respect to God and before God and consequently its immediate empirical subject (in distinction from the metaphysical Person), by using *only* the word 'nature', and that in sharp distinction from the divine Person? Or is it not true that the Redemption thereby becomes for all practical purposes simply God's act among us, and no longer the act of the Messianic Mediator between us and God? And is it not true that the almost unavoidable consequence of all this is a conception, which undoubtedly dominates the popular mind (without of course reaching the stage of consciously formulated heresy), and which could be put rather as follows: 'When our Lord (= God) walked on earth with his disciples, still humble and unrecognized . . .'?

Now it may and indeed must of course be said that the doctrine of

---

Christ. Although there are many who refuse to accept this view, there is a good deal to show that Athanasius located the act of redemption in the Logos as Logos; Apollinaris elevated this into a principle, by deducing the absolute hegemony of the Logos from his concept of *physis*. If nevertheless —in spite of Cyril's mia-physis formula—the Two-Natures formula was finally successful, all it was intended to emphasize was the fact that Christ's humanity was a $\phi \upsilon \sigma \iota s$, i.e. an $\alpha \vartheta \tau o \kappa \iota \nu \eta \tau o \nu$, and so that the intrinsically redemptive act was an act of genuinely human freedom. This formed the basis of a genuine soteriology over against the over-emphasized Logos-sarx schema. Clearly it was the Mediator concept which was involved here. Once all this has not only been 'granted' but also clearly and explicitly maintained, it is surely permissible to proceed to a distinction between the *full* sense of the Chalcedonian formula, as this *sensus plenus* emerges according to the evidence of the history of dogma from the mind of the Council, and the perfectly true but curtailed version of the formula, as this can be drawn from the concepts of the formula alone when these are interpreted in conformity with the watered-down version of the schools. What we shall go on to say applies to this latter version alone.

the unconfused and unchanged real human nature implies, as the struggle against monothelitism after the rejection of monophysitism shows, that the 'human nature' of the Logos possesses a genuine, spontaneous, free, spiritual, active centre, a human selfconsciousness, which as creaturely faces the eternal Word in a genuinely human attitude of adoration, obedience, a most radical sense of creaturehood. Indeed it is emphatically maintained that this sphere of consciousness proper to a subject, a sphere enclosed in itself in creaturely fashion by reason of the gulf that distinguishes and separates God from the creature, only knows and only could know of its hypostatic union with the Logos in virtue of an objective communication. This communication is said to depend on the *visio beatifica* of this human consciousness, and cannot be a datum of Jesus' *human* selfconsciousness—if by selfconsciousness is understood the simple being-present-to-itself of an independent entity [1] (in the identity of the act and object of knowledge). Thus by maintaining the genuineness of Christ's humanity, room is left within his life for achievement, and the possibility of a real Mediatorship and thus—if you will—of a real Messiahship is preserved.

Let us first set aside the question whether this account of the matter, which Paul Galtier is trying to urge on theologians today as the unmistakable voice of Tradition, is in itself free from objection. Let us set aside the fact that the opposition which Galtier encountered, and the controversies which have continued since then, show that there still remain obscurities in orthodox theology, although both parties claim the support of the Chalcedonian doctrine. Our first concern *here* is this: is it possible from the basic Chalcedonian doctrine itself actually to evolve the account given us above in reply to the question how far Jesus can be the Mediator between us and God? Although this requirement is not strictly necessary, it seems nevertheless to be justified, because in fact the formula 'One Person and two natures' is the basic formula of Christology. If it is replied that we are quite certainly bound to take into account the fact that other truths, witnessed to in Scripture, must be *added* to this basic formula for a full understanding of the Lord as Mediator, although strictly speaking they are not found in this basic formula and cannot be *derived from* it —then the question with which we began arises *implicite* with even

---

[1] *Das schlichte Bei-sich-sein einer Seinswirklichkeit.*

more urgency. Is it in fact possible to *derive from* the formula 'One Person—two natures in the possession of the one Person' that characteristic relationship to God in the sphere of Jesus' human reality, a relationship apparent in Scripture and indispensable for the understanding of Christ's function as Mediator (for it makes it possible for him to act freely towards and before God)? That is to say, is it possible to recognize this relationship as contained in the formula *implicite*? Or is it in fact open to one to doubt this? It is well known that at the last moment it was decided to make an omission, verbally slight but theologically important, from the text of the Encyclical on Chalcedon: instead of rejecting a doctrine which held that there were two subjects in Christ 'saltem psychologice', the Encyclical rejected the (Nestorian) doctrine of two (ontological) subjects, by omitting the phrase 'saltem psychologice'.[1] One thing at least becomes clear from this little episode in the history of the Encyclical's redaction: that there were and are theologians who cannot see that the doctrine of two natures involves a duality of even a merely psychological and relative kind between an existentially[2] independent I-centre (*Ichzentrum*) in the man Jesus and the Logos; indeed they believe that anything of the sort is excluded. And there are theologians who hold that something of the kind is a fact which can be demonstrated theologically and historically. But what must be granted is that the concept of *person* is always at least in danger of being understood in such a way that the 'independence' in view here seems to be excluded. It is not merely since the nineteenth century, with Günther's modern concept of *person* and Existentialist philosophy, that this has been the case. The concept of *person* as the ontological principle of a free[3] active centre, selfconscious, present to itself and through itself in being, is a concept which, in the sense just indicated, has always played round the edge of the most static and objective concept of *person*.[4] We cannot prove this here. But if it were not the case, monothelitism would

---

[1] Cf. Pius XII, *Litterae Encyclicae 'Sempiternus Rex'* (8 September 1951), AAS XLIII (1951), p. 638. On the above-mentioned emendation of the text of the Encyclical, cf. P. Galtier, 'La Conscience humaine du Christ', *Gregorianum* XXXII (1951), p. 562, n. 68.

[2] *Existential*: see Introduction.—Tr.

[3] I.e. a freely responsible active centre, which merits even before God and in distinction from him, because before him.

[4] I.e. substantial unity and distinction involving incommunicability.

have been quite inconceivable; for it was not just a political device for making a concession to monophysitism, but persisted with such vigour that today it is still a widespread 'heresy' among Christians— all verbal orthodoxy notwithstanding. In the customary teaching about sin, untouched by any kind of Existentialism, a distinction is made between *peccatum personale* and *peccatum naturae*; in this terminology too we see that existential[1] ideas about the *person* are simultaneously at play. If these come to the fore, a connexion obtrudes itself upon the mind: where there is a *single* person, there is a *single* freedom, a *single* unique personal active centre, in relation to which any other reality (=nature, natures) can only be in this person the material and the instrument, the recipient of commands and the manifestation of this single, personal centre of freedom. But this is precisely not the case with Jesus. Otherwise he would only be the God who is active among us in human form, and not the true man who can be our Mediator with respect to God in genuine human freedom. It would of course be utterly false to say that the conceptual pair 'Person-nature' *involves* this monothelite interpretation (it would be better and clearer to say today 'mono-existentialist conception'). But the concept of *person*, as it is in actual fact understood,[2] in fact

---

[1] *Existentiell.*

[2] We shall later have to discuss at some length why it is that such a misconception or the danger of it cannot be removed simply by terminological exactitude. Clearly it can be laid down that by 'person' we shall understand only the ultimate substantial unity and completeness of a subject which is incommunicable and whose reality as one in this sense can only be expressed by this subject itself. But as soon as the concrete person understood in this way exhibits a plurality in its real being, the question must arise as to how and in virtue of what the plurality is combined with the personal unity: what is sought is just the unique unifying centre of this plural unity, the unique point prior to the instituted plural unity; we want to make clear to ourselves *in terms of its actual content* what the function of this prior unity is in establishing unity in plurality, not just in terms of the *communicatio idiomatum*, which is only a *consequence* of this unity. Consequently when we are thinking, in connexion with this unity, of a person as *ens rationabile*, we tend to think that the function of the person which consists in establishing unity is not the actual, centralized, existential control and direction of the plural realities of the person, but rather their ontological foundation, which most clearly emerges to view *in* this control and direction. How little permissible it is simply to exclude this position out of hand may be seen from the defined doctrine that Christ's 'human nature', on account of the *unio hypostatica*, is wholly subject in its freedom to the Logos, and thus was

insistently suggests this interpretation, and it is again and again taken unreflexively in this sense, though the interpretation is never reflexively thought out and formulated (for that would be heretical). Inevitably the question then arises: how can the whole complex of Christological dogma be formulated so as to allow the Lord to appear as Messianic Mediator and so as true Man, as soon as possible, or at any rate with sufficient clarity? As true Man, who, standing before God on our side in free human obedience, is Mediator, not only in virtue of the onto-logical union of two natures, but also through his activity, which is directed to God (as obedience to the will of the Father) and cannot be conceived of *simply* as God's activity in and through a human nature thought of as purely instrumental, a nature which in relation to the Logos would be, ontologically and morally, purely passive? The ordinary doctrine of two natures just by itself is quite insufficient as a ground from which to derive this insight into Christ's mediation as something which arises from the inner tendency of the doctrine. For if someone says that a human nature has a free will and that *eo ipso* this gives us all that is required, he overlooks the point that the question arises just here as to how freedom can belong to someone[1] with whom it is not identical, whose intrinsic core it does not consti-tute; why this freedom is neither subjugated to the 'person' distinct from it nor in a position to rebel against it.[2]

---

essentially sinless. But once again, how little this doctrine offers us by way of an answer to the problem with which we are concerned, may be seen by putting the following question. Is it the case *either* that the *unio hypostatica* just in itself as such is the *immediate* real ontological ground for the realiza-tion of this sinless subjection of the humanly free spontaneity of Christ's human nature to the other will (that of the Logos)? *Or* is it only the medi-ately operative requirement in order that the Logos should effect this sub-jection by the use of means which elsewhere in the domain of creatures God is also capable of using as sovereign master over creaturely freedom, without thereby injuring it—indeed precisely realizing it? Or finally does the question itself in its disjunctive form show itself to be a false one, once the *unio hypostatica* is set quite generally in the wider context of the ontological relationship between God and the free creature?

[1] A person in the traditional ontological sense.

[2] There is no need to spend any time here in showing that the following approach provides no solution. Someone might say: The will is an accident of the substance of the soul (=nature), and freedom is its modality; conse-quently this cannot be conceived of in such a way that the question should ever arise as to how the freedom could be 'eccentric' to the person. The

It is easy to see from all this that only a *divine* Person can possess as its own a freedom really distinct from itself in such a way that this freedom does not cease to be truly free even with regard to the divine Person possessing it,[1] while it continues to qualify this very Person as its ontological subject. For it is only in the case of God that it is conceivable at all that he himself can constitute something in a state of distinction from himself. This is precisely an attribute of his divinity as such and his intrinsic creativity: to be able, by himself and through his *own* act *as such*, to constitute something in being which by the very fact of its being radically dependent (because *wholly* constituted in being), also acquires autonomy, independent reality and truth (precisely because it is constituted in being by the one, unique *God*), and all this precisely with respect to the God who constitutes it in being. God alone can make something which has validity even in his own presence. There lies the mystery of that active creation which is God's alone. Radical dependence upon him increases in direct, and not in inverse, proportion with genuine self-coherence before him. Measured against God, the creature is precisely *not* to be reduced unambiguously to the formula of merely negative limitation. Our problem here is only the supreme application of this basic truth concerning the Creator-creature relationship (a truth which at least historically has never been reached in non-Christian philosophy). And it immediately follows once again that the purely *formal* (abstract) schema *nature-person* is inadequate. We must conceive of the relation between the Logos-Person and his human nature in just this sense, that here[2] *both* independence[3] *and* radical proximity[4] equally reach a unique and qualitatively incommensurable perfection, which nevertheless remains once

---

starting-point of this answer is sound enough in certain respects; yet 'freedom' remains in its intrinsic ontological root supremely central to the person, and thus the question we have tried to put remains. If anyone doubts this, he should consider the fact that this modality of the second act of this accident is simply speaking master of the destiny and the decision of the *whole* reality of the free being, and that the free act can thus never be made 'central' enough.

[1] It is just this which is meant when Christ's merit as a man before God is spoken of.

[2] Corresponding to the general creature-Creator relationship.

[3] Freedom of the human 'nature'.

[4] Substantial appropriation by the Logos of this human nature and its freedom.

and for all the perfection of a relation between Creator and creature.[1]
But in view of the fact that this simultaneous perfection can only be
realized in a creature with regard to *God*, it becomes even clearer that
the abstract concept of a 'person who has a nature' is not enough to
allow us to infer this characteristic feature of Christ's human liberty
with respect to God, a feature which is of such decisive significance
for him and which characterizes him as Man and Mediator. This liberty
is possible only when the person who has this free nature is either
identical with this nature or is the *divine* Person as divine. And in this
way it becomes clear how necessary it is to go beyond this 'Two-
natures-one-Person' formula. In so far as this assertion (as predicate)
'one Person who possesses two natures' is made of the Logos (as
subject), the subject must be introduced into the predicate, if we are
to avoid the danger of saying too little and of conjuring up a—monothelite—error of interpretation. The metaphysical formulation of the
truth 'This human history is the pure and absolute revelation of *God*
himself' in terms of the formula 'This human nature is hypostatically
united to the Logos', could very well be supplemented by a metaphysical formulation of the truth 'This human history, by the very
fact of being God's own pure and radical revelation, is the most living
of all, the most free before God from the world towards God, and thus
mediatorial, because it is the history of God himself *and* because it is
supremely creaturely and free.' But where are we to find the formula
which expresses this latter truth with the same clarity as that with
which the Chalcedonian formula expresses the former one?

Here we have entered upon a train of thought which it may seem
profitable to pursue. Christological considerations have led the way
back to the more general doctrine of God's relation to the creature and
allowed Christology to appear as the clearly unique 'specifically'
distinct perfection of this relation. Does this fundamental perspective
not permit of being extended and built upon? In order conceptually

---

[1] If in the Incarnation the Logos enters into relationship with a creature,
then it is obvious that the ultimate formal determinations of the Creator-
creature relationship must also hold in *this* particular relationship. Hence the
question remains entirely open as to whether the special character of the
Incarnation, in so far as it is *distinguished* from all other relationships of God
to a created thing, may be derived as a special case of this general property
or not. A negative reply may be given to this question without its necessarily
following that what we have said would have to be or could be contested.

to express the mystery of Christ, classical Christology makes use of concepts of formal ontology, the content of which recurs at *every* level of reality, according to the distinct mode of each: nature, person, unity, substance and so on. Would it not be possible to go further, without abandoning classical Christology, and make use of the concepts in terms of which the relation of created things to God is conceived?[1] The fact that this relation reaches its absolute peak in the case of Christ does not exclude such an application in advance. Such an analogical application of *general* concepts (and states of affairs) to a *unique* case occurs in classical Christology too. An attempt to carry out this suggestion would be of great importance if it were successful. The fact that the reality of Christ is intrinsically unique and cannot be derived from anything else, that it is a Mystery, does not mean that we may not regard it in a perspective in which it appears as peak and conclusion, as the mysterious goal of God's plans and activity for his creation from all eternity. Indeed this is not something new in theology. The fundamental lines of this perspective are in fact to be found in Scripture. But if this perspective is a valid one, we could try to express this inclusion of the reality of Christ in the total reality of all that is not God, not merely by stating it of him subsequently, after having spoken about Christ himself merely in the fashion of classical Christology; we could try to use this view in order to express the very essence of Christ. The advantage of this would be that the Incarnation of the Logos would no longer appear merely as something subsequent, a particular event *in* a world already *finished* (and hence in danger of seeming to be something mythological), a world into which God suddenly introduces himself by his action and to which he

---

[1] It goes without saying that it is above all the relationship of the *spiritual* creature to God that we must keep in mind, and that in a special way, as we have learnt from Existentialist philosophy. For it is the spiritual creature which in a special way, as person constituted by transcendence and freedom, enters into relationship with God. We shall be speaking in what follows about 'creation' in general; but this should not be allowed to obscure the fact that it is at men above all that we must look in order to learn what the Creator-creature relationship is. It should thus appear—and this is the point of all that follows—that Christology may be studied as self-transcending anthropology, and anthropology as deficient Christology; that Christology is the 'primitive conception' (although 'for us' in part subsequent) of anthropology and the doctrine of creation, as Christ is the πρωτότοκος πάσης κτίσεως (Col 1:15).

makes corrections as a kind of afterthought and which he consequently presupposes as already given. The Incarnation of the Logos
(however much we must insist on the fact that it is itself an historical,
unique Event in an essentially historical world) appears as the *ontologically* (not merely 'morally', an afterthought) unambiguous goal of
the movement of creation as a whole, in relation to which everything
prior is merely a preparation of the scene. It appears as orientated from
the very first to this point in which God achieves once and for all both
the greatest proximity to and distance from what is other than he
(while at the same time giving it being); in that one day he objectifies
himself in an image of himself as radically as possible, and is himself
thereby precisely given with the utmost truth; in that he himself
makes most radically his own what he has created, no longer the mere
anhistorical founder of an alien history but someone whose very own
history is in question. Here we must remember that the world is something in which everything is related to everything else, and that
consequently anyone who makes some portion of it into his own
history, takes for himself the world as a whole for his personal environment. Consequently it is not pure fantasy (though the attempt
must be made with caution) to conceive of the 'evolution' of the world
towards Christ, and to show how there is a gradual ascent which
reaches a peak in him. Only we must reject the idea that this 'evolution'
could be a striving upward of what is below by its own powers. If
Col 1:15 is true, and is not attenuated in a moralistic sense; if then in
Christ the world as a whole, even in its 'physical' reality, has really
reached historically[1] through Christ that point in which God becomes
all in all,[2] then an attempt like this cannot be false in principle. But if
it is in fact possible to attempt something like this, we can make use
of the general categories of the God-creature relation (distance-
proximity; image-concealment; time-eternity; dependence-indepen-
dence) in their radical, sharply differentiated form in order to make
fundamental statements about Christ, and regard all other realities in
this field of what is distinct from God as deficient modes of this primary
Christological relation.

[1] Though in a history which is at the same time essentially spirit, freedom,
'moral'.
[2] And this must be understood in an essentially Christological sense, not
as something abstractly metaphysical, 'permanently valid'; because God in
Christ really *became* world, and so 'All' in all.

The fact that classical Christology makes permanently valid statements about Christ which attribute to him an entitative determination [1] already (relatively) fixed and familiar (such as 'He is man'—so that we must already know what 'man' is) is no argument against this view. We may not say that it is illegitimate to try to take Christ as the starting-point in order to define these entitative determinations, and that consequently a 'Christian' ontology must necessarily be false in principle. For it will be clear on reflexion that our presupposition is that statements about Christ himself (even though they are intended to serve as a point of departure for the more general statements of a theological ontology) are made with the help of a general doctrine of creation (and the ontology contained in it). Christology most certainly cannot and should not form an absolute point of departure for an ontology (and hence still less for an anthropology). Nevertheless the parallels in philosophical knowledge of God and the world show that a retrospective use can be made of Christology for ontological and anthropological assertions: God is known from the world, and yet we can start from God in order to say what the world is. It is neither necessary nor possible here to discuss more fully the general epistemological presuppositions of this shifting back and forth of initial and terminal points in the process of acquiring knowledge.

The only point with which we were concerned was to investigate the suggestion that other categories than those of classical Christology might be used to make the basic, initial statement of what Christ really is, categories, moreover, taken from a truly *theological* doctrine of creation. If such were the case, even the bare appearance that what was offered in orthodox Christology was an anthropomorphic myth might perhaps be more easily avoided from the start.

A further question, to which classical Christology has given no very clear or far-reaching answer, is contained *implicite* in this question of a possible task for the future. The static categories of formal ontology employed by this Christology do not locate Christ in saving history in the narrower sense (or better: they do not locate the history with respect to him as goal and origin). The question suggests itself whether there might not be a formula for saving history as God'

---

[1] *Sachverhalt.* This can ordinarily be rendered 'state of affairs'. The word has however a technical philosophical usage, in which it means something like 'the objective content of a proposition'. 'Entitative determination' is offered as a rough approximation.—Tr.

progressive taking possession of the world in history, as the manifestation, ever clearer and more hidden at once, of God in the world as his quasi-sacramental *mysterium*. The Christ would appear as the summit of this history and Christology as its sharpest formulation, just as inversely saving history would appear as the prelude to and the extension of Christ's own history. Perhaps the ancients had a better idea of all this than we usually have today, with our still very pale and vague idea of the time before Christ as the preparation for the fullness of times. The old speculation about the Logos, which ascribed to him an activity and history in creation 'before Christ but Christ-like' distinct from the invisible Father, would be well worth rethinking, after being purified of its subordinationist elements. It is still by no means established that the extraction of this waste matter would inevitably lead to the ruin of these early speculations. The Logos did not merely become (statically) man in Christ; he assumed a human history. But this is part of an entire history of the world and of humanity before and after it, and, what is more, the fullness of that history and its end. But if we take at all seriously the unity of this history as centred upon Christ, it follows that Christ has always been involved in the whole of history as its prospective entelechy. We have then to ask how to conceive of history so that this result should follow from it. But if we do think of it in this way, it should then be possible, inversely, to learn from it who the Christ is to whom it is orientated and whom it has brought forth from its womb. What do we mean by Time, History, the Evolution of Humanity, if the Christ is to be the fullness of this time? Can all this be ascribed to Christ merely as an afterthought *after* he has been expressed in terms of the Chalcedonian formula? Or can it also be stated from the starting-point of a theology of history itself with such directness that the Chalcedonian formula in its abstract formality may rather be *derived from* this? Is it not possible so to conceive of Time and History *theologically* (not merely in terms of the philosophy of history) that one has conceptually stated the Christ of Chalcedon when one has said of him that he is the fullness of times, who as their Head definitively comprehends and recapitulates the aions and brings them to their end? We must not nurse the tacit yet active prejudice that conceptual exactitude and compressed formulas can only be found in those concepts which the Fathers and the scholastics worked out from Greek philosophy with their eye upon—*conversio ad phantasmata*—individual things of a physical and static kind and their individual processes of change. Anyone who does not share this prejudice, anyone who is convinced that the conceptual apparatus of scientific theology can be enlarged beyond the bounds of the traditional pattern, will not immediately assume that there is no prospect of carrying out the task which has just been proposed.

A Christology which derives from Biblical theology might set us a further task. If anyone were to attempt to discover the Biblical foundation of scholastic Christology, he would reach the conclusion, which does not seem false or unjust, that it contrives to get along with a handful of texts from the Bible. Its predetermined goal is the dogma of Ephesus and Chalcedon and nothing more. The only texts from Scripture, whether they are sayings of Christ himself or appear in the teaching of the Apostles, in which it is interested are those which can be translated as directly as possible into the terms of classical metaphysical Christology. The method is a legitimate one; but it cannot cover the whole ground. A whole body of Christological statements remains unused in this way, statements which describe Jesus' relationship to the Father (God) in the categories proper to conscious experience (existentially)[1]: Jesus as the only one to know the Father, Jesus who brings tidings of him, does his will at all times, is always heard by him and so on. The question, then, is whether it is possible on this basis to construct a Christology in terms of Christ's consciousness. We shall not attempt to offer a complete solution to this question here; but we may make some remarks about its meaning and significance.

When it is said of a spiritual substance that it is 'simple', what we have here is an *ontic* statement (as we shall call it). When we say that it is capable of a *reditio completa in se*[2], we are making a statement which belongs to the metaphysics of knowledge: an onto-*logical* statement, or one which belongs to the philosophy of Existence.[3] We need not delay here to explain the connexion between these two state-

---

[1] *Existentiell.*

[2] This phrase, deriving from the *Liber de Causis* and thus ultimately from Proclus, is made considerable use of by St Thomas in order to analyse the ontological status of beings capable of self-knowledge. See, for example Ia.14.2 ad 1, where St Thomas quotes the proposition of the *De Causis* 'Omnis sciens qui scit suam essentiam, est rediens ad essentiam suam reditione completa', and concludes that since to subsist in himself is proper to God above all, therefore he above all returns upon himself and knows himself.—Tr.

[3] *Existential-philosophische.*

ients *in re:* they correspond to each other; the same asserted entitative determination is explained on the one hand by a characteristic feature of selfconsciousness (and thus by a concept applicable to a field in which the only entities are spiritual ones), and on the other by a metaphysical concept[1] which can be verified positively or negatively in *every entity.* Anyone who has grasped the metaphysical meaning of the scholastic axiom 'ens et verum convertuntur', 'ens est intelligibile et intelligens, in quantum est ens actu', will know that *in principle* at least, every ontic statement (whether positive or negative) is capable of being translated into an *ontological* one, however difficult or impossible this may often be 'quoad nos'. The higher an entity (in the widest sense of this word, including then entitative determinations and so on) in its grade of being, compactness of being, 'actuality', the more intelligible it is and present to itself (*bei sich selbst*). Clearly this axiom of scholastic metaphysics would require closer analysis if it is to be applied correctly in particular cases. Nevertheless we may say that the fact that Christ's humanity is substantially united to the Logos, in so far as this is a determination ('act') of the human nature itself, cannot be simply 'subconscious'. For as something ontically higher, this determination is something real which cannot be simply unconscious at least in the case where its subject has attained that grade of actuality in being which involves a presence to itself (*Bei-sich-selbst-sein*) of this entity. At least in the case where this presupposition is satisfied, it is metaphysically impossible that this actuality of the subject should be simply unconscious, when we remember that this actuality is entitatively higher in comparison with the level of actuality proper to the subject, and that this subject is present to itself; it is impossible that the immediate subject of the human presence-to-itself should not also be present to itself precisely in so far as it is wholly and substantially made over to the Logos. Here we must be careful to note that this 'presence to itself' is not to be confused with a 'knowledge of an object'. Presence-to-itself is the inner being-illuminated of actual being for itself; more precisely, for the subject which possesses this being in its own self. From this it follows that it is opposed to the true teaching of the scholastic metaphysics of knowledge to say that Christ's human soul knows of the *unio hypostatica* only in the way in which an object is known (and so through the 'visio immediata' as in

---

[1] *Seinsbegriff* ('Concept of being').

the vision of an object). Inasmuch as the *unio hypostatica* implies or involves an entitative determination, namely the being-united (*Vereint-sein*) of the human reality with the Logos, as an ontological determination of this human reality, Christ's human soul is 'with the Logos'[1] in an immediately ontic and conscious way. The 'visio immediata'[2] is (if we may be allowed to make our point in this way for the sake of clarity) the consequence and not the presupposition of the conscious being-with-the-Logos of Christ's soul. It is not (in the last resort) a *donum*, conferred as a moral 'title' on the human soul on account of its being united hypostatically to the Logos, for reasons of *convenientia* or *decentia*; it *is* the hypostatic union itself, in so far as this is necessarily an 'intelligibile actu' in the *intelligens actu* of Christ's human soul. Once again: in the measure and manner in which the *unio hypostatica* is (or includes) a real ontological determination of the human nature, and indeed its ontologically highest determination; further, in the measure in which this human nature is by itself 'present to itself': the union must also be a datum of the selfconsciousness of this human nature of its very self, and cannot simply be part of the content of its object-knowledge given 'from without'. The Chalcedonian ἀσυγ-χύτως must not be taken in a sense which would result in the denial in fact of a union between the Logos and his human nature which was still being affirmed verbally.[3] But this would be the case if neither or

---

[1] *Beim Logos.* This being *with* is at a level of being which necessarily involves conscious presence (*bei sich sein*). For the phrase *bei sich sein* ('being with oneself') compare Marcel's *être chez soi*.—Tr.

[2] We prefer to say 'visio immediata' because this phrase expresses with greater exactitude and caution than 'visio beata' the 'theologically certain content of the doctrine concerned here, in that the 'immediacy' of the possession of God follows from the considerations just proposed, while the 'beatitude' of this vision in Christ need not be experienced so nearly and immediately as something necessarily always 'beatifying'; after all, is it not conceivable that the vision may be undergone as a 'consuming fire' in certain situations proper to a 'viator'?

[3] All 'unconfused' says is that the same One is truly God and truly man and not some third thing in between. It does not however deny the unity the human nature's state of having given itself away (*das Sich-selbst-weg-gegeben-sein*) to the Logos. It is precisely the task of theology (one which i set by the Chalcedonian formula but has not yet been performed) to throw light on (which does not mean 'to dissolve the mystery of') why and how this thing, which has suspended itself in this way, not only remains what it was, but in the most radical sense, unsurpassably and definitively ratified

the side of the Logos (because he is immutable) nor on the side of the human nature there were present a real ontological determination other than that which would exist even if there were no unity. But if such a determination does exist on the side of the human nature, really and truly determining it, then it will also be a datum of the presence to itself of this nature in consequence of its being what it is (*des Von-sich her—bei-sich-seins dieser Natur*).[1] It is not our concern here to see how this may be harmonized with the data of our *a posteriori* empirical knowledge of the 'inner life' of Jesus and his psychology. The task is not an impossible one. In fact—given careful thought—it is considerably simpler than when traits, apparently postulated quite arbitrarily, are ascribed to Christ's inner life on the basis of argumentation *ex convenientia, ex decentia*. It only seems difficult to harmonize these traits with what we are told by Scripture about Christ's thinking and willing because these postulated 'traits' and 'endowments' are thought of as existing in the dimension of Jesus' everyday consciousness, on the surface of his awareness of objects. But our Lord's self-consciousness, which we have here inferred metaphysically from the *unio hypostatica*, is—in its source and primarily at least—a given quantity which must be thought of as being situated in that substantial depth of Christ's created mind which becomes aware of itself in the act of knowledge, pointing ontically beyond itself to that with which it is united, the Logos.

These are only brief indications, and we have no intention of taking

---

becomes what it is: a human reality. But this only becomes possible once it has been shown how in the essence of man this tendency to become self-suspended upon the absolute God (in the ontological, not just the moral sense) belongs to his most basic constitution. Thus the *highest* actuation (unobliged, only once and for all realized in event) of this obediential potency (and this is no purely negative determination, no purely formal non-repugnance) makes the self-suspended thing all the more man in the most radical sense, precisely unites it thus with the Logos. And it needs to be shown too how this self-suspension can be a datum of man's selfconsciousness, because it belongs to his selfconsciousness to have, ontically and existentially, a disponibility open to God's disposal and the absolute mystery, that disponibility towards becoming self-suspended which is supremely realized and brought to consciousness in the *unio hypostatica*.

[1] This is not the place to show how the approach outlined here—very briefly, of course—bears upon the controversy between P. Galtier and P. Parente.

up the problem in its own right. All we wish to suggest is that a Christology using categories appropriate to the description of consciousness need not be false *a priori* or impossible. If there is an ontic Christology, there can also be an existential[1] one (or however one may wish to describe statements about the way in which a spiritual being is present to itself). Thus we may confidently ask whether an absolutely exact understanding of our Lord's statements about his 'spiritual' relationship to God (the Father) could not lead to statements which would be equivalent, as *ontological* (existential)[1] statements, to those of an ontic Christology. The fact that this existential[2] relationship of Christ as man to God is not immediately available in our own experience, thus where *our* concepts have their origin, does not absolutely forbid our making such statements. For the ontic relationship of his human nature is not immediately available to us either, and yet it can be stated in an analogical, indirect and asymptotic way. Otherwise there would be no Christology at all which could say something about what Christ really is. It is true that there have been attempts in this direction in modern Protestantism which, owing to hostility to the metaphysics in the 'Greek' theology of the Fathers and Scholasticism and the use of philosophically inadequate instruments, have led to heresy, because they reduce the mystery of Christ to the level of our own religious experience and our own relationship to God; but this is still no proof that such attempts are impossible and false *a priori*. Suppose someone says[3]: 'Jesus is the man whose life is one of absolutely unique self-surrender to God.' He may very well have stated the truth about the very depths of what Christ really is, *provided* that he has understood (a) that this self-abandonment presupposes a communication of God to the man; (b) that an absolute self-surrender implies an absolute communication of God to the man, one which makes what is produced by it into the reality of the producer himself; and (c) that such an existential statement does not signify something 'mental', a fiction, but is in the most radical way a statement about being. It may be objected that a Christological statement like

[1] *Existentielle.*
[2] *Existential.*
[3] This example is not meant to anticipate the successful performance of an undertaking which has here only been postulated. It is only intended to illustrate, in a case which is clearly highly problematic and in need of cautious treatment, what the task proposed would in general involve.

this, bearing on Christ's mind, either remains outside the limits of Christological dogma and its ontic formulation (and thus is heretical), or must appeal to ontic formulations in order to characterize the uniqueness and specific otherness of this relationship to God in distinction from any religious experience of our own or of the prophets. The second alternative[1] may be granted, though it does not follow from this that such existential statements are superfluous. It is true that these statements (so far as we possess concepts for them) may perhaps[2] not be capable, without the help of formal ontic concepts, of distinguishing precisely enough from other relationships a conscious existential relationship to God which is not available to our immediate experience. Yet they are extremely useful in filling out the formal emptiness of a *purely* ontic Christological statement, which would otherwise be in danger of being filled out in some other way, namely by interpretations of Christological formulas which are not indeed formulated explicitly, but which only too easily crystallize round the formulas without being noticed; these interpretations then make Christ out to be nothing but God clothed in a human form. If this danger is really avoided by asserting a conscious relationship of the man Jesus with respect to God, and by asserting it in such a way that the assertion of the distinctively unique character of this relationship is *eo ipso* an implicit or explicit assertion of the *unio hypostatica*; then the Scriptural accounts of Jesus' conscious dispositions to the Father would really be translated into theological Christology. We need only consider the following two statements to see this.

a. 'The Logos, who possesses in identity the absolute divine being, assumes a human nature as his own and thus becomes man while remaining himself.' b. 'This man—who, as we have said, is God—can pray, adore, be obedient, feel in a creaturely way to the point of abandonment by God, can weep, receive the wonderful gift of "being heard", experience the claims of God's will upon him as something authoritative and alien,' and so on. Does the second statement always come immediately to mind as soon as the first, which is a formula of faith and, it goes without saying, a true one, is uttered? Or do we know all this, but in a different compartment of our minds,

---

[1] As something not wholly avoidable 'quoad nos'.

[2] This question, which would lead us into general considerations belonging to the metaphysics of knowledge, cannot be treated of here, and must be allowed to remain open.

as it were, so that we have to 'switch over' from the first formula, almost entirely forgetting it, in order to make real to our minds what is also witnessed to by Scripture and what we find so difficult to think 'about God'? How would it be if we thought and spoke about the second, the human side, in such a way that it simply remained clear that all this was only possible in a man, and it became clear that this is only conceivable as a *human* happening if it is wholly the Happening of God himself, in all truth and in the most radical way?

Here we shall cease to pursue our investigations into Biblical theology, or more accurately, the transcendental hermeneutics for a Biblical Christology. We shall try to investigate the Chalcedonian formula itself, and make clearer to ourselves the problems it sets us. The formula speaks of two natures: it puts them clearly before our eyes in the characters proper to each. For we have some knowledge of what a man is, and our experience in this matter grows daily. And so we can make a fair estimate of what is really involved in being a man. What God is we only know by going beyond any information we may possess, in a *docta ignorantia*. But in this very way the Being whom we recognize as unknown is set apart from human nature. And now the Chalcedonian formula bids us conceive of the unconfused unity of the 'natures'. Isn't that hard? Of course we have at least a vague idea of what unity is. Someone may even like to call it a clear idea, and say that the apparent vagueness is not an indistinctness but is merely due to the formal generality and abstract emptiness of the concept. But that is just the point: here is the supreme particularity, the incomprehensibly profound, unique *Mysterium*, which decides my destiny and that of the world, on which absolutely everything in heaven and on earth depends because it declares God's own destiny and takes up into this the destiny of the world; and I am supposed to see this mystery expressed in a concept which is one of the most general concepts of formal ontology, like that of *entity*, something which is itself always one thing and thus gives rise to the concept of unity from this emptiest of all abstractions. One should suffer the heavy burden of obscurity before running up with an answer. And please let no one say just that the concept of unity is indeed highly formal and abstract, but that in this case it acquires density and fullness from what is united. No doubt this is true in a certain respect: as the concurrence of two things, a unity consists of what is united.[1] But this is precisely on the assumption that something is known of the distinctive character of the concurrence which unites what is to be made one. Now it could be said here (as was done earlier) that what is being spoken of is not just any unity of divine and human reality in Christ. What faith really makes profession of is a substantial, lasting, indissoluble, hypostatic unity, the belonging of the two natures to one and the same Person as its very own in virtue of its being the selfsame.[2] So this unity is not so empty, it does not allow the united natures to stand 'isolated' before the spiritual eye of faith, as though the duality were clearly given while the unity is as it were unverifiably situated on the side turned away from the eye of faith. The unity reaches the highest point of clarity for our understanding in the fact that, precisely because it is hypostatic, we must and can state of one and the same Person both what is divine and what is human, because precisely *both* are really and truly proper to one and the same Person. All this is true, and belongs to the essential core of meaning of the *mysterium* which we are toiling to understand. But does it say everything which can be said towards an understanding of the unity in the twofold reality of Christ? We do not propose to show that this is open to doubt by pointing to the old controversies between Catholic theologians which have once again been revived today. This would be too long a way of clarifying the question which still remains. Let us put the question in a different way; let us start from a few of the usual notions of scholastic Christology, which we shall presuppose. God the Word of the Father, so we are told, 'changes' in no way when he assumes the human nature as his own. The change, the novelty, is entirely on the side of the human nature. We have no desire at all to make the usual objection that in spite of this proposition it must remain simply true that it was the Word of God himself who became man; nor do we wish to inquire how this divine truth can remain valid if the former proposition,

[1] This sentence illustrates the wider sense of the German *Einheit*, which means 'union' as well as 'unity'. Fr Rahner rarely uses the ordinary German phrase for 'hypostatic union', which is *hypostatische Vereinigung*: instead he either uses the Latin *unio hypostatica*, or speaks of the *hypostatische Einheit*. The English reader should bear in mind this wider sense of the word *Einheit* when he finds the phrase 'hypostatic unity' in the text.—Tr.

[2] *Die Angeeignetheit der beiden Naturen durch die Selbigkeit der einen und selben Person.*

deriving from human metaphysics, is soundly based.[1] On the contrary, the immutability of the Word in the Incarnation will be our pre-supposition. Thus as far as the Word itself is concerned, nothing is held to have happened, nothing emerged which has not always been there. It is purely on this side of the abyss between God and the creature that the new, emergent Event takes place.[2] Thus what we have to learn here is what happened when the Word became flesh. This flesh, this human reality, does not belong to itself, then, in that it came into being as united to the Logos. But what does it mean to say, 'It does not belong to itself', what does it mean—we keep falling back on the same formulas of the Tradition, a sign that we don't really understand them—what does it mean to say, 'This human reality is united to the Word of God'? The reality can be predicated of him, someone may answer; what takes place here in this world in his flesh is most personally his own affair, someone may explain. That is all very well, one might reply, almost in despair; but *He* is not a man as *I* am a man. For I am a man in such a way that the I, the person itself, becomes human through my human-being; this is its own lot, it does not itself remain untouched. And that is just what one cannot say about the Logos of God, according to just this doctrine of faith. Nor is that all; according to the theology current in our schools, this humanity of the Logos is, without injury to him, not only created by the one God (not by the Logos alone); but every influence upon it

[1] This metaphysics would need rethinking; and that would naturally lead to the problem, in what sense God does not alter when he creates the world. Here it would be necessary to say that he does not in himself become other to himself when he himself becomes other to the world as what is other than he and derived from him, and *vice versa*. This same formula would have to be applied in Christology. In fact the whole of Christology could be seen as the unique and most radical realization of this basic relationship of God to·what is other than himself, measured by which all else in creation would be only a deficient mode, fading away into indistinctness; it would be the sharpest realization of this basic relationship, which lies in the self-alienation of the God who remains with himself, and thereby radically unchanged. However we have already alluded to this connexion between Christology and the doctrine of creation above.

[2] But what takes place on this side of the ἀσυγχύτως is precisely and exactly the history of God *himself*! Primarily at least in the case of Christ. So something of the sort is possible. Anyone who suspected that we were practising Hegelian and not scholastic metaphysics in the preceding note, might well reflect on this point.

which it undergoes, either because it is a creaturely human reality or because it is precisely the humanity of the Logos, is the object of the operation of the whole Trinity as a single efficient cause *ad extra*, just because it belongs to the dimension of what is created from nothing. Thus all that this humanity possesses (in the highest measure, of course) in the way of tangible, expressible reality, is what can be given to any man: grace, knowledge, virtue, the *visio beatifica*. From this point of view again, the unique distinguishing feature which belongs just to it and to nothing else, is simply the formal unity which gives it the reality of the Logos without affecting the Logos itself. An example will show us what this means. How many sorrowful souls have been comforted and have seen through their tears the everlasting stars of love and peace because in their faith they knew, 'He, the eternal meaning of the world, the Word, has wept with me, He too has drunk of the chalice!' How many have died 'piously in the Lord' with the thought that this common and general death must mean something just because the Uncommon, the uniquely important, the absolutely Indiscutable, the incommensurable Measure, the coherent Meaning at the heart of being, because He—really He himself—died! 'One of the most holy Trinity has suffered', the Scythian monks used to say, with that brutality of faith which takes not only death but its hidden divinity with the same seriousness, so that hundreds of years after Ephesus and Chalcedon we are still startled by it, though it is perfectly obvious that we are bound to speak like this and that the whole truth, the single unique truth of Christianity, is contained in it. But— the same orthodox faith may now say—how do you understand this saying? Be careful not to take it too literally! God died, certainly. But he did so in precisely the same reality whose hopeless tears and death you believe are redeemed when you say, 'He wept too, he died'. But so doing he only made just *another* human reality weep and die, and thus himself remains the Holy One, serenely exalted above death, as he always has been, is, and will be. He wept only in the *flesh*, died in the *flesh*. When what is to be redeemed happens to the Redeemer, then it is itself redeemed. But does it really happen to him, when he remains untouched by the lot of what is to be redeemed? 'Non horruisti virginis uterum', we sing to him! As orthodox Chalcedonian theologians, are we not bound to say: 'You could not and need not ever have dreaded it, because it left you untouched in your real being; and why should your humanity have dreaded it, if it began like everyone else's in your mother's womb?' Or where is your kenosis, which the Apostle adoringly celebrates, if you remained in plenitude, and the emptiness which we have been from the first and which you assumed, need not itself first be emptied but has never known anything but itself—emptiness, tears, death, the whole misery of man? Are we ever to escape from this hopeless dialectic? When we say, 'He has remained eternally the same, untouched, immutable, glorious', we say it not only under the tyranny of a rigid metaphysics of infinity, about some pure, unspotted, uninterrupted Being; we say it because we need someone who is not as we are, so that we may be redeemed in that which we are. But if that is why we say it, as soon as we say it the door beyond which we who thirst for redemption sit, seems finally to shut, and there the matter seems to end: he is in heaven and we on earth, he is not where we are, and we are not where he is. Suppose we say: he came to us; he too wept; he too died; he too is flesh; he too is the emptiness, the infinity of which is immeasurable hollowness—then the Redeemer seems to be with us, but precisely a captive with us, one who shares our fate. But what good does it do us, if he too is truly— just what we are? Yet suppose we say: the finite is good: it is by no means one pole of a tragic opposition, from which we have to be redeemed; that which makes redemption necessary is merely 'accidental' to the finite, something from which the finite must be cleansed; the finite has always been finite and yet always as a simple matter of course *capax infiniti*—what need is there then of the Lord, of the God who became flesh? Is the Redemption anything more than a small repair job to something which was good and basically has always remained good? Has he who became man still an eternal function, if it is the prior goodness of the world which supports him and not he who really gives it its foundation and completion? Of course the world is good; obviously there could be a world which would be good and so possible, even if He had not come who stands free in relation to a world already in existence and so has freely come. Of course the stock of meaning and goodness cannot be just consumed without remainder by darkness, death, guilt and damnation. But it is wrong from the start to divide up the meaning and goodness of the world and its need of redemption in this quantitative way. Because it is still good, it can be redeemed. But all this goodness, all this meaning, needs redemption, from the meanest atom to the highest spirit. All is to be redeemed, because as good it is capable of redemption, because

apart from Christ it is all lost, as a whole, with all its goodness. All.
But how does this happen, when he shares the appearance and the
concreteness of this lost state, when he himself becomes what is in
need of redemption? He could have done this in another way? He
could have saved the world even without this, and redeemed it *into*
his freedom and infinity? Certainly: but *in fact* he did so by becoming
himself what was in need of redemption, and in this way, this way
alone, must take place that one Redemption which really exists and is
the only one we know. And that is what is so difficult to understand,
because it seems in fact not have helped us at all, both when we take
seriously the proposition that he became flesh, and when we take
seriously the proposition that by becoming flesh he remained immutable and intact. The dilemma becomes still more acute if we think of
the ascended Lord. He must be present in heaven as the *God-man*, we
reflect, in the plenitude of his redemptive function, in its complete
actuality. As Son of Man in his eternity, can he be more than—let no
one take offence at our boldness—more than the conservation of an
instrument of past times, a meaningless instrument long since antiquated, fit only for a museum? No wonder textbook theology has
nothing to say about Christ in the tractate *de Novissimis*! Thus the
dilemma becomes more acute: God would be the Blessed One even
without this humanity, and the humanity has strictly nothing more to
do than to enjoy a *visio beatifica*, which could also be present in someone who was mere man. The Christ is split into two possibilities,
held together only by the formal and empty assertion of their hypostatic unity.

We may put the whole question formally. What remains of the
ἰδιαιρέτως, when the ἀσυγχύτως is taken seriously with all its
consequences, and how are we then to interpret the ἀχωρίστως?
Can it be analysed merely in terms of the *communicatio idiomatum*,
and what does this mean if the actual human reality predicated of the
Logos as Person does not change the Logos, and so does not make
him something which he would not be without this humanity? Can
the 'average Christian' only get on by allowing the ἀσυγχύτως to
slip into the background of his consciousness in faith in favour of the
ἰδιαιρέτως, by tacitly thinking in a slightly monophysite way, to
this extent at least, that the humanity becomes something merely
operated and managed by the divinity, the signal put up to show that
the divinity is present in the world—a world which is only concerned

with this divinity and where the signal is put up pretty well for our sakes alone, because we wouldn't otherwise notice the bare divinity? Must it be an inevitable feature of our everyday religious life and practice that the Chalcedonian formula should be tacitly cut short like this, so that—here we must weigh up the matter for ourselves honestly —the 'average' non-Christian feels called upon to protest in his unbelief, refusing to admit that God has become man 'like this' and thus believing that he must reject the Christian doctrine of the Incarnation as a myth?

Our discussion of the problems of the Chalcedonian formula cannot set out to offer a precise and detailed answer to the question which has been raised; we shall merely make a few brief observations. Obviously what we should have to do would be to work out a fresh concept of unity (of a substantial, hypostatic kind, clearly). This concept would not *merely* analyse the unity in terms of a logical predication of idiomata (however indispensable this may be), because by itself this would either only be understood 'monophysitically' in the form of a cryptogamic heresy (*sit venia verbo*!), as we have pointed out above; or, while the immutability of the Logos and the Chalcedonian ἀσυγχύτως remained clear, the emptily formal abstractions of the unity (for all its being hypostatic[1]) would take on no real fullness of meaning for us. We cannot escape from this trap by looking at the unity as the (even merely logically) subsequent unity of two things to be united, already

---

[1] We repeat: anyone who is tempted by our speaking of a formal emptiness of the unity to maintain that on the contrary, the unity in question is a *hypostatic* one, and thus a perfectly 'full' and close unity, must be warned that he should consider what precisely it is that he is saying. He will then realize (supposing that he has taken the average Christology as his starting-point) that his explanation of the hypostatic unity is conceived of in terms of a *communicatio idiomatum*. And then he will have to ask himself what it means for the Logos to remain 'unchanged' by this unity, when any sort of history which it implies takes place on this side of the abyss between God and creature, and what is more, without confusion. He is bound to indicate what remains of the former given the latter. If he says that this is just the mystery (and that we ought not to let go of one end of the famous chain because we don't know how it is linked with the other end, which we also hold), then we must ask with all moderation whether this mystery might not permit of being formulated more clearly, so as to come before the eye of faith as a whole; in this way the impression would not arise that the one truth must be utterly blotted out 'quoad nos' when we turn to look at the other.

existing independently as two prior to the unity. The Logos may be regarded in this way; but as soon as the humanity is so conceived of too, the position becomes untenable. It is not enough to say that the humanity has never existed apart from the hypostatic unity *in fact*, that is to say temporally. Nor is it permissible to suppose that it may *merely* be conceived of as always combined *in fact*, on the grounds that its nature is the same as ours, and we certainly exist apart from the hypostatic unity and yet are 'men'.[1] The only way in which Christ's *concrete* humanity may be conceived of in itself as diverse from the Logos is by thinking of it *in so far as* it is united to the Logos. The unity with the Logos must constitute it in its diversity from him, that is, precisely as a human nature; the unity must itself be the ground of the diversity. In this way, the diverse term as such is the united[2] reality of him who as prior unity (which can thus only be God) is the ground of the diverse term, and therefore, while remaining 'immutable' 'in himself', truly comes to be *in* what he constitutes *as* something united (*geeinte*) with him *and* diverse from him.[3] In other words, the ground by which the diverse term is constituted and the ground by which the unity with the diverse term is constituted must as such be strictly the same. But if what makes the human nature ek-sistent[4]

[1] It will appear from what follows that this consideration is at any rate lacking in force. Everyone who is a Thomist in Christology must grant this. Further, it must be borne in mind that a purely *de facto* unity in the strict sense would be an accidental one.

[2] *Geeinte*. Fr Rahner gives *einen* (to unite) the sense of an act by which one of the two terms of a unity is the cause of this unity. It is difficult to make the English 'to unite' bear this sense: in English it is usually some *third* term which unites the other two, a suggestion which would be quite unsuitable here. *Einen* here means simply and solely 'to one'.—Tr.

[3] It follows from this statement that the assertion of God's 'immutability', of the lack of any real relation between God and the world, is in a true sense a dialectical statement. One may and indeed must say this, without for that reason being a Hegelian. For it is true, come what may, and a dogma, that the Logos himself has become man: thus that he himself has become something that he had not always been (*formaliter*); and therefore that what has so become is, as just itself and of itself, God's reality. Now if this is a truth of faith, ontology must allow itself to be guided by it (as in analogous instances in the doctrine of the Trinity), must seek enlightenment from it, and grant that while God remains immutable 'in himself', he can come to be 'in the other', and that *both* assertions must really and truly be made of the same God as God.

[4] See Introduction.

as something diverse from God, and what unites this nature with the Logos, are *strictly* the same, then we have a unity which (a) cannot, as uniting unity (*einende Eienheit*), be confused with the united unity (*geeinte Einheit*) (this is not permissible)[1]; (b) which unites *precisely by* making existent, and *in this way* is grasped in a fullness of content without any relapse into the empty assertion of the united unity; and finally (c) which does not make the ἀσυγχύτως look like a sort of external counterbalance to the unity, always threatening to dissolve it again, but shows precisely how it enters into the *constitution* of the united unity as an intrinsic factor, in such a way that unity and distinction become mutually conditioning and intensifying characteristics, not competing ones. Properly speaking, we should now go on first to examine the question whether this position is in harmony with the Thomist theory of the unity of Christ, and how far it is so (we shall

---

[1] The weakness of the Christology associated with Scotus and Tiphanus is that it cannot distinguish these two concepts: it declares that the human nature and the divine nature are united in the Person of the Logos. When it is asked by what (i.e. by what uniting unity) they are united (in the united unity), the original formula is repeated, so that in fact no answer is forthcoming. If someone goes on to maintain that it is impossible to provide a further answer because it is precisely a mystery with which we are dealing here, it would be necessary to reply that this account would suffice *provided* that the mystery given expression in the original formula remains clear in its meaning (though not in its explanation) even when no answer is offered to the further question. But if this is *not* the case, i.e. if the united unity in the sense intended (a sense which, though undetected, must be there even in a mystery) does not permit of being thought unless the uniting unity comes into sight, then the *docta ignorantia* of Scotus and Tiphanus is simply not appropriate here—no matter how far the ancient tradition provides or fails to provide a further explicit question and answer as to the uniting unity. Someone may object that it is in fact the one hypostasis which is the uniting unity for the two natures. To this we must reply that this may well be true, so far as it is a matter of the two natures in their mutual concord. But the question here is to what extent the divine hypostasis unites the human nature to himself. When the question is formulated like this, the hypostasis, *in so far as* it is just the static concept of *ens per se et in se* which is involved, is something to be united—one 'part' of the united unity, and not the uniting unity. Thus it must be asked *by what* (i.e. by what uniting unity) the hypostasis unites to himself the human nature. Putting the same thing in another way: unity (as a formal transcendental property of an entity) is never something which can be set up as such, but is always the result of some other state or process among entities. Thus one has neither explained nor even understood what one is saying, when one elucidates unity by—unity.

not pronounce any final judgment on this matter here); secondly, to consider how far and in what way such a position makes it necessary to go back to a *more general* theory of the relationship between God and his world, of which the relationship 'Logos-human nature' would appear as a special case. Unfortunately this is not possible here either. All we shall do is to offer the following brief note. It might be supposed that any attempt to connect the general relationship of God to the creation with the relationship of the Logos to his humanity would immediately come to grief owing to the fact that the creation is the work of the efficient causality of the *one* God, while the hypostatic union is a relationship of the Logos alone. Before this is taken as finally settling the question, it would be necessary to offer a solution to another question: is it really agreed that another divine Person could also have become man? Or could it not be that—when the unity of the created with the Creator given in creation itself attains by God's free act that unique height in which an existence as distinction from the Creator is bestowed upon a creature, an existence through which the distinct term becomes absolutely and supremely God's very own— could it not then be that this God is necessarily the Logos and no one else? What theological considerations would suffice positively to exclude this view? But if they are in fact produced, the suggested objection ceases to be so obviously compelling as it seemed to be at first.

Now, if the positing of Christ's humanity in its free distinction from God itself becomes in this way the act of unification (*Einigung*) with the Logos, it further becomes clear why this humanity, in its concrete existence as such, is *eo ipso* the mysterious manifestation, the quasi-sacramental presence (*Anwesenheit*) of God with us. We have constantly to remind ourselves that human-being is not some absolutely terminated quantity, which, while persisting as a quite self-contained whole indifferent to all else, is combined with some other thing (in this case the Logos) by a wholly external miracle. Human being is rather a reality absolutely open upwards; a reality which reaches its highest (though indeed 'unexacted') perfection, the realization of the highest possibility of man's being, when in it the Logos himself becomes existent in the world. The fact that there is human being which is not of itself the presence of the Logos existing into the world, is no more a proof of the falsity of this view than the proposition, 'The *visio beatifica* is the most perfect realization of (pure) human nature', can be objected to on the ground that human being is also to be found without the *visio beatifica*. The fact that an ('obediential') potency is only fulfilled by a free act from above is no argument against the view that this act is the pure fulfilment of just this potency for what it is in itself. It is quite true that *we* first become acquainted with human being in a less significant realization, and consequently derive our concept 'man' from this (and so can look forward from *our* point of view to a higher actualization of this concept only by way of an empty anticipation of the range, as yet undetermined, as yet open upwards, of our transcendence as a possibility perhaps possible). But this does not mean that we are not entitled to sketch the outlines of a theological anthropology from the starting-point of Christology, now that this has been revealed to us—no doubt by using our terrestrial concepts; nor is it perverse to conceive our human selves in terms of that Man who as such is God's presence for us, existent in the world. Only someone who forgets that the essence of man (although in a specifically human way, which is to say, in accordance with the point of departure, in terms of a point in space and time) is to be unbounded (thus in this sense, to be un-definable) can suppose that it is impossible for there to be a man, who, precisely by being man in the fullest sense (which we never attain), is God's Existence into the world. But if this is the case, we only radically understand ourselves for what we really are, when we grasp the fact that we are existential beings because God willed to be man, and thereby willed that we should be those in whom he as man can only encounter his own self by loving us. The fact that God could have had a different will for us, that he *freely* willed us 'so', does not necessarily mean that he has not in fact precisely willed us 'so'. This 'so' is not just something mental, external to what is willed and without significance for its real consistency; it is a genuine 'existential', a mode of our own existence, without which we can indeed grasp ourselves as question, but never as the answer which it alone gives to the question which we are.[1]

---

[1] *Translator's note*. The reader may find it helpful to bear in mind the notion of existence as 'self-realization', a 'coming to the light', and this as eminently realized in *human* existence. It might be said that God, as supremely actual, cannot in this sense 'exist', cannot come to be himself: the Incarnation is what allows him to 'come to the light', 'existent into the world'. In this last paragraph, I take it that Fr Rahner wishes to point out

At the beginning of this section it was said that our rough knowledge of what man is, when we used the formula of Chalcedon, was
due to the fact that we daily learnt what it is to be human by experience
of each other and of ourselves. The slightest of discussions of the
problems of this formula has shown that the attempt to advance our
understanding of what this unity (unconfused and undivided) is which
makes the human nature that of the Logos itself, would also further
our understanding of who man is; we see that Christology is at once
beginning and end of anthropology, and that for all eternity such an
anthropology is really theo-logy. For God himself has become man.
The less we merely think of this humanity as something added on to
God, and the more we understand it as God's very presence in the
world and hence (not, all the same) see it in a true, spontaneous
vitality and freedom before God, the more intelligible does the abiding
mystery of our faith become, and also an expression of our very own
existence.

In this third section we shall discuss in more detail, though without
any attempt to treat them systematically, the problems of a modern
Christology; and for this purpose we shall go beyond the immediate
range of the Chalcedonian formula.

1. Would it not be possible and appropriate to look for some sort
of Transcendental Deduction[1] of faith in Christ? What we have in
mind is an inquiry, more explicit than is usual, as to why man is
capable of faith in the Christ of Christian dogma. Someone may answer
'He is the hearer of a message which is of itself credible, a message
which exhibits its credibility by means of ascertainable facts.' But this

---

that we are existential beings (*wir die sind, die existieren*) because of God's
will to be an existential being himself, and thus to achieve self-realization
in common with other beings defined by their capacity to realize themselves,
in a communion, a common 'presence', of love. For the meaning of the
noun 'existential', see Introduction.

[1] In the Kantian sense.—Tr.

would be to overlook the fact that it is not only the knowability of the *object* which must be examined, but also the distinctive nature of the *subject* and *his* specific openness with regard to just that object. If this object is something indifferent and contingent, which has incontestably always been found within the region of this subject's experience, the transcendental deduction of the subject's capacity to know with respect to *this* object is simply that of the meaning and extent of his knowledge *in general*. But just in so far as Christ is the freest and in this sense (but also only in this sense) the most 'contingent' fact in all reality, so it is true that he is also at the same time the most decisive and important, and moreover that which is the most clearly related to man (... *propter nos homines*). *His* subjective knowability cannot tacitly be thought of as simply subsumed under the conclusions of a general metaphysics and critique of knowledge. He is too unique for that, too mysterious and existentially significant. It cannot be objected that such a 'transcendental deduction' of Christ's knowability by man would be to prejudge the question of what is contained in Christ, who can in fact be known only by obediently listening to a message which has gone forth in history. Nor can it be objected that such a deduction would imply the *necessity* of the fact of Christ, for this was something freely established by God. Both these considerations are unacceptable. An *a priori* sketch of the 'Idea of Christ' as the correlative object of the transcendental structure of man and his knowledge, even if it came to anything *purely a priori*[1], could never decide the question as to where and in whom this 'Idea' is reality (and without this reality this 'Idea' is of less existential significance than any other). It is only from the message of 'fides ex auditu' that this question could ever be answered. If and in so far as such an abstractly formal, *a priori* Christology were to offer a kind of formal schema of Christ to the Christology which hears the message *a posteriori*, we should reflect that such an *a priori* Christology is wholly capable of taking shape in the illuminating light of the grace of the real Christ (one need neither reflect on this nor be able to reflect on this and yet one's thought can move within the space enclosed by Christ's grace); we should thus consider that the *a priori* schema can owe its existence to the real object *a posteriori*,

---

[1] It did not come to anything *before* Jesus Christ. And now it is no longer capable of coming to anything, because he exists and it would be a delusion to suppose it possible—even in a purely methodological way—to abstract from him entirely.

and thus by no means implies a mastery of it. The question whether God might not wish to show us his grace, and what is meant if he did wish to show it, the deduction of a 'desiderium naturale' of the *visio beatifica*, neither makes the message from without superfluous nor restricts its content a priori, although these objects belong to the same strictly supernatural order as the *unio hypostatica*. Anyone who understands that an *a priori* openness to something is far from making this 'something' a *debitum* in a conceptually necessary way[1], will not say that such a deduction stands or falls with the affirmation of the necessity of the Incarnation.

A deduction of this kind must aim at showing that man is at once a concretely corporeal and historical entity on earth and an absolutely transcendent one. Accordingly he looks out—and looks out in the course of his history—to see whether the supreme fulfilment (however free it may remain) of his being and his expectation is not on its way to meet him: a fulfilment in which his (otherwise so empty) concept of the Absolute is wholly fulfilled and his (otherwise so blind) gaze can 'see through' to the absolute God himself. Thus man is he who has to await God's free Epi-phany in his history. Jesus Christ is this Epiphany. It can, therefore, remain a completely open question whether the content of the *a posteriori* dogma simply 'coincides' with the Idea of Christ, which is the correlative object of this transcendental deduction, or whether this correlative only 'corresponds' to the real Christ declared to the hearing of faith and is essentially surpassed by him, although in its own axis.

An undertaking of this sort would be an important one. By means of it a religious *a priori* which lives today in every man who believes in Christ would achieve reflexive self-awareness. For this religious piety can only draw its life in fact from the historical Christ (from him and from no one else, from him and not from an Idea!) because man is continually kept in movement by the existential need to possess God concretely, to 'have to' possess him. Without such a deduction, and unless it is brought home to man as something really achieved, the historical message concerning Jesus the Son of God is always in danger of being dismissed as a mere piece of mythology. A deduction

[1] This proof can only conclude if the potency, the openness, etc., were to be purely and simply meaningless without just the act which is in question and which is itself foreshadowed in the potency. But that is by no means the case with the potency in question here.

of this kind might also contribute to the conceptual equipment used
by Christology proper.

2. A theological phenomenology of the religious attitude with
regard to Christ is greatly to be desired. It cannot be denied that in
the ordinary religious act of the Christian, when it is not referred
precisely to the historical life of Jesus by way of meditation, Christ
finds a place only as God. We see here the mysterious monophysite
undercurrent in ordinary Christology and a tendency to let the
creaturely be overwhelmed in face of the Absolute, as though God
were to become greater and more real by the devaluation and cancella-
tion of the creature. Another sign of this is to be observed in the fact
that Christ's humanity no longer has any part to play in the theology
of the *visio beatifica*, as this is ordinarily presented. Theology is only
concerned with the One who has become man in so far as he appeared
at the historical time of his life on earth as Teacher, Founder and
Redeemer. There is hardly any developed doctrine of his abiding
function as man; and correspondingly, the doctrine of the specific
character of our abiding relationship to him as Man-for-all-eternity is
extremely fragmentary. Something is said about the adoration which
is due to him even as man. But no one seems to have much to say
about the fact that our basic religious acts, which are continually
effected through the mediation of Christ, have an 'incarnational'
structure. There is hardly any mention of Christ in the tractate *de
Virtutibus Theologicis*: the discussion moves merely in the thin atmo-
sphere of pure theological metaphysics. Reflexion on the permanence
of Christ's humanity according to Chalcedon, which alone really
brings God within the reach of our acts, has not yet penetrated as far
as these tractates on the theological virtues or on *religio*.[1] The Council
of Chalcedon has still to conquer here. The anti-Arian reaction, the
special character of the Latin doctrine of the Trinity and the existential
undercurrent of monophysite tendency in Christology, have all
delayed this victory. But this very fact, that Christ more or less vanishes
for an act momentarily directing itself to God, has led to a situation
for which there are other causes as well, in which the Incarnation

---

[1] Cf. K. Rahner, 'Die ewige Bedeutung der Menschheit Jesu für unser
Gottesverhältnis', *Geist und Leben* XXVI (1953), pp. 279–88 (which appear
in vol. III of the German edition of these studies).

appears to be almost a transient episode in God's activity in his world and is thus unreflexively felt to be a myth unworthy of faith. In view of this situation, a theological phenomenology of an 'incarnational' piety, valid now and always, would not only have significance for the doctrine of the spiritual life; it would also be important as a means of removing the basic causes which have led to a demand for 'demythologization'.

3. The first proposal (no. 1) would further suggest that dogmatic Christology might pay a little attention to the general history of religions. There is no intention here of proposing a 'hunt for parallels' to the doctrine of the Incarnation in other religions, nor ultimately of showing that such parallels do not really exist. In the last resort the point of such a study would be to examine the history of religions from the standpoint of our knowledge of the historical Incarnation, and from this standpoint alone, the only one to offer a really illuminating interpretation of a history otherwise unintelligible in itself: and to examine this history with a view to seeing whether and how far man in fact shows himself in history for what he unquestionably is in the depth of his concrete nature: a being who in the course of his history looks out for the presence of God himself. When the early fathers kept a lookout for such an activity of the Logos, the beginnings of his Incarnation as it were, in saving history before Christ (at least in the Old Testament), they were better advised than we are, for whom God rules there simply from heaven. It may in general be allowed that the history of religions[1] as a whole only escapes the mortal danger of infecting Christians with some sort of relativism when it is integrated (as Yes or No) in the single history of the dialogue between God and the world, a dialogue which flows into the Word become flesh, and when it is not interpreted merely as the product of a purely terrestrial religiosity of rationalism and as a human perversion. If this is true, it holds good also of the history of religions in so far as they were an unconscious Yes or No to the Word of God who was to come in human flesh.

[1] For the first time since the patristic era, this history is becoming a reality for the West again, in the perichoresis of all cultures and historical movements which is in fact taking place today. Cf. H. de Lubac, *La Rencontre du Bouddhisme et l'Occident*, Paris 1952.

4. Would it be a delusion to suppose that the abstract formalism of Christology has also contributed to a decrease of interest in a theology of the mysteries of Christ's human life? There is still a lively theological (and not just pious) interest in the mysteries of the Life of Jesus in St Thomas and even in Suarez. In the ordinary textbook-Christology current today, one has to keep a pretty close lookout to find anything about Christ's Ascension, as if this was a matter primarily for *theologia fundamentalis*. The Passion is treated of from an exceedingly formal viewpoint in soteriology, which seems very little interested in the concreteness of the Passion on the ground that some other moral deed of Christ's would have redeemed us 'just as well' if God had so pleased. What do we hear of Christ's Circumcision, Baptism, his prayer, the Transfiguration, the Presentation in the Temple, the Mount of Olives, the abandonment by God on the Cross, the descent into the under-world, the Ascension into heaven and so on? Nothing or pretty well nothing.[1] All this is left to piety, and it is rarely that we find anything more than applications of a moral and edifying kind here. The mysteries of Christ, which precisely in their once-for-all character and indissoluble historicity form the law of once-for-all world history, are all too easily misconceived as mere illustrations and examples, as 'instances', in which general moral laws, which are just as clear even apart from Christ's life, are exemplified. Instead of a genuine theology of Christ's life, we find that the theology (not in itself unjustified) of certain abstract privileges enjoyed by Christ has forced itself into the foreground; and that this theology draws attention to certain features (in the field of knowledge, for instance, Christ's *visio* in the course of his life on earth, his infused knowledge and so on) which distinguish

---

[1] The Biblical exegetes proper often seem today to be intimidated by the dogmatic theologians and their true—and often presumed—office as censors. They take the utmost care to avoid going a single step beyond the letter of the text and getting down to the real theological issues involved. What really happened at the Transfiguration? What took place at the Ascension? What did eating involve for Christ after his Resurrection? What really happened when he descended into Hell? What is Mt 27:51 s telling us about the saints who rose from the dead, and what is its theological significance? What took place when Jesus was tempted? What are we to think about his remaining behind in the Temple as a boy? How are the postulates of dogmatic theology capable of being harmonized with Jesus' wonderment, his 'ignorance' and so on? It cannot be said that the exegetes have given much sign of theological heart for these questions and others like them.

him from us, and even these features it does not always postulate for reasons which are really illuminating. This development is conditioned (if not perhaps with a very high degree of self-awareness) by that purely formal understanding of the unity of Christ as united, of which we have spoken above. In a conception like this an event in the field of Christ's humanity only has 'interest' in so far as it is digni-fied by being adopted by Christ's person, and thus precisely not in itself; or again in so far as it possesses special features not to be found elsewhere among human beings. Once attention has been turned in these two directions, the only soteriology to be expected is of that single type which (perfectly correct in itself) we do in fact find even today. This still contains a section on certain permanent 'consectaria unionis hypostaticae', but lacks any theological consideration of the history (which is in itself theological in the highest degree) of the particular, once-for-all events of the life of Christ as man, born of a woman, subject to history, law and death. This human reality as human (not as something abstract, of course) in its 'bare' humanity can only be of theological importance if it is as such (as just this) the manifestation of God in the world, not just as something joined on in a logically subsequent way; if, that is to say, it is one with the Logos in virtue of being the reality of the Logos itself, and not the reality of the Logos in virtue of being 'one' (how?) with the Logos. If we are to have a true theology of the human life of Jesus (not merely a theo-logy of the extraordinary in Jesus' life) we must recover that right view of things which does not (by 'abstracting') overlook just that which cannot be really separated from what is human in Jesus: we must learn to see that what is human in Jesus is not something human (and as such uninteresting for us in the world) and 'in addition' God's as well (and in this respect alone important, this special character however always merely hovering above the human and forming its exterior setting, as it were). On the contrary, in this view the everyday human reality of this life is God's Ek-sistence, in the sense cautiously determined above: it is human reality and so God's, and vice versa. Then it will no longer be necessary to ask the question: What is there exceptional about this life over and beyond ours as we are already familiar with it, whose heights we have already climbed and into whose depths we have already plunged, what is there about it (still strictly only as a plus-quantity) which could make it important for us too? But the question we must ask is: What does our life mean, this life which we ultimately fail to understand when we examine ourselves, however familiar with it we may be, what does it mean when it is first and last the life of God? It is because we need this ultimate interpretation of our lives, one which is not to be had elsewhere, that we must study the theology of Christ's life and death. Why does this happen so seldom in current Christology?

5. Thus we have reached the point of laying down requirements for *soteriology*, and have indicated why and how the average textbook-Christology leads to inadequacies or omissions in this field. The gravamen of our charge may be simply formulated as follows: as far as soteriology is concerned, the average theology current in our schools today is only interested in the formal value of Christ's redemptive act. not in its concrete content, the inner structure of the redemptive process in itself. Now the account usually given of the infinite worth of Christ's act as regards satisfaction and merit, on account of the infinite dignity of the Person, is a perfectly correct one. But it would be false to suppose that this accounts for all that is essential in soteriology. Yet this is in fact what is supposed. The simplest proof of this statement is found in the fact that the satisfaction theory in soteriology not only assumes tacitly but also explicitly maintains that Christ would equally have been able to redeem us by any other moral action, provided only that God had so willed it and had accepted this action as vicarious satisfaction. The inner content of the redemptive act (i.e. the Cross death, obedience, abandonment by God, death due to the action of sinners themselves) thus only has significance for the Redemption as such in its abstract moral quality, which as it were gives up its substratum and its matter for the value which this action acquires in virtue of the dignity of the divine Person; the precise content of the action makes no difference. Now we have no intention of denying that God would have been able to forgive us our sin in regard to any one of Christ's acts at all, and that this forgiveness would be 'Redemption' and what is more Redemption on account of a 'satisfactio condigna' But if the matter is so regarded, essential facts and problems of a really adequate soteriology are overlooked, in that a soteriology is bound to say how *we* were redeemed in concrete fact. The view which we have just described supposes that it has already proved that all the concrete particulars of the redemptive act really do not belong to the cause a

uch of the Redemption as such. But in fact all it makes clear is that
n *abstractum* of Redemption can be achieved by means of various
pecies of one generic redemptive cause. *If* it is true that the Redemp-
ion consists *only* in God's purpose of forgiveness, conceived of in
uridical and moral terms, or is considered only under this single
formal and abstract) respect, the view we have described may be
ccepted as the correct one. But what reason is there for saying that
his presupposition is correct? Strictly speaking, one and the same
ffect can only be brought about by a *single* cause. If the causes *as such*
liffer, they cannot have the same effect. Thus when it is said that we
ould have been redeemed 'in another way', one of two things may
e meant. *Either* it is meant that these differing causes do not in fact
liffer *as such*, that they are distinguished from each other in their
ubject only by modalities which are simply indifferent so far as their
ausality as such is concerned (as two knives, for instance, which are
listinguished from each other only by the colour of their handles, can
eally cut in 'exactly the same way'), and consequently can really
ring about the same 'Redemption'. *Or* it is meant that these causes
iffer even as such; thus they do not bring into being exactly the same
Redemption, even if these different Redemptions can be conceived of
ubsequently in a conceptual unity of an abstract, generic kind such
hat in *this* sense it is possible to say that God could have effected 'the
ame' Redemption through some other redemptive action of Christ's.
t would be necessary to prove that the first sense of the proposition
s the right one; it cannot simply be presupposed. In fact no proof can
e offered. This means that when Scripture says, 'We have been
edeemed by Christ's death (with all that death, and death alone,
nplies) and by his obedience (his concrete obedience, realized pre-
isely in death, and capable of being realized only in death)', we must
ssume, until the contrary is proved, that *this* is what characterizes the
edemptive action *in so far as* it is cause, and not other characteristics,
undamentally unimportant as far as its causality is concerned, as the
sual version of the theory of satisfaction assumes. This is not to deny
hat this death in obedience, which is *as such* the cause of our Redemp-
on, is precisely cause in virtue of being the death of the Logos become
man and thus of participating in the infinite dignity of the Person. If
he death as such is the cause of Redemption, it naturally follows that
his cause has not brought about exactly the same Redemption as
ould have been achieved if we had been redeemed in some other way.

These are primarily considerations of an abstract, methodological kind. But they do point to the fact that the soundness of the moral and juridical satisfaction theory, with regard to what it says positively, does not serve as a proof that there is nothing more to be said in soteriology.

There are various points at which any attempt to complete positively and give real content to the abstract formalism of the average treatment of soteriology would have to begin. (a) We could first enquire whether the various theories of the *unio hypostatica* have any significance for the foundations of the satisfaction theory, and what that significance might be, for the doctrine, that is, that the infinite Person endows with infinite value even the actions he performs in his human nature. It is certainly not obvious that these theories about the hypostatic union are of little importance for this soteriological doctrine. If we do not wish to defend any sort of juridical and moral Idealism or a modern theory of 'values', and if the principle 'ens (reale) et bonum convertuntur' is true, then in the last resort every 'value', every 'dignity' (just to use another word and to look at what is involved from another point of view) *is* a reality, a real entitative determination, and does not merely 'rest upon' such a determination. Transposing our proposition into the ontological order, then, what does it mean to say, 'The Person endows its action with a certain definite dignity'? The variety of theories concerning the *unio hypostatica* cannot be without importance for this question, the answer to which again is of decisive significance for the precise meaning of the proposition to be transposed. Both the inquiry as to the uniting unity, the essence of the intrinsically hypostatic function of the Logos with respect to the human nature, as well as the inquiry as to the independence of Christ's human reality given precisely by this unity, must, if they are properly conducted, be capable of giving the satisfaction theory new depth. (b) It would then be necessary to work out in greater detail a theology of death in general and of Christ's in particular. Only then would it be possible to give a really adequate answer to the question: Why is it that we have been redeemed by Christ's *death* (and by nothing else), and what exactly does a redemption of this kind look like, which is brought about in just this way and no other? It is no exaggeration to say that a theology on these lines is still entirely lacking in our average modern treatment. Nothing is said about it in soteriology, and pretty well nothing in the tractate *de Novissimis*. Death would have to be

een in its indissoluble unity of action and passion.[1] Only so can it
become clear that the Redemption takes place in virtue of Christ's
obedience (action) and yet in virtue of his death (itself); not, however
(as is generally said in a minimizing and superficial way), in virtue of
the 'Passion bringing death in its train', for then once again this
Passion would as such remain outside the redemptive act and would
form merely the matter 'in which' obedience is actively engaged—
something in the last resort accidental and for which substitutes may
be found at will. Death would have to be set forth as the connatural
manifestation of alienation from God by sin (and not just as the externally inflicted 'penalty', something for which God could just as
well have found some substitute) *and* at the same time, as the manifestation and constitutive sign of absolute obedience to God (at least
when Christ dies this death or someone with him).[2] It would further
have to be shown that in spite of the separation of body and soul,
death does not simply withdraw man from the world and make him
acosmic; rather it transposes him into a new and more comprehensive
relationship to the world, freed from the limitation to a single point in
space and time characteristic of his earthly existence.[3] This result
(together with much else which would also have to be considered)
would make it possible to achieve a better understanding of the
significance of Christ's descent into hell, as something which does not
merely signify a phase of his historical existence made void by what
happened after. More searching questions could then be raised about
the possibility of reaching a more concrete understanding of the
lasting efficacy of Christ's humanity with regard to grace than is

---

[1] On what follows, see the short sketch: K. Rahner, 'Zur Theologie des
Todes', *Synopsis* III (1949), pp. 87–112. (Also, by the same author, 'Zur
Theologie des Todes', ZKT LXXIX (1957), pp. 1–44.—Tr.)

[2] It is not possible here to show that death has a basic nature open to
further determination, such that it becomes the death of sin or the death of
redemption according as it is undergone in disobedience or obedience. Nor
is it possible to show here that this is why death is 'natural', indeed that this
is the fact on which is based the possibility of the above-mentioned existen-
tial-ontological dialectic of death as Adam's death and Christ's death.

[3] That the soul is not in consequence of this 'everywhere' is illuminating.
This would certainly imply a more extensive relationship to the world in
that dimension precisely which is abandoned in virtue of death (until the
resurrection). Thus the theory indicated above has no connexion with
Luther's doctrine of the ubiquity of Christ's resurrected body.

allowed of in the rather thin formalism of the Thomistic teaching of the instrumental causality of Christ's humanity.[1] But it would then once more be necessary to show how all this is connected explicitly with the proposition that the humanity and the human events in the history of this humanity in Christ are the ek-sistence of God himself in the world.

In thus attempting to give a deeper meaning to ordinary soteriology, we should take account of another point of view, which could also have found a place in an earlier stage of our discussion. Scripture speaks to us in many places of Christ's σάρξ.[2] We ordinarily take this to be a reference to Christ's human nature or to his body. This is quite sound; but it clearly fails to exhaust the Scriptural meaning. What *we* involuntarily think of when we speak of Christ's humanity and his human nature is nearly always just that element in the meaning of sarx which belongs to the necessary and permanent constitution of the entities so characterized. But sarx is intended to characterize man or his corporeality precisely in so far as this possesses a quite definite character arising out of an historical development within a history of salvation and damnation. Flesh is the weak, the corruptible, consecrated to death, the dimension within which sin becomes manifest and tangible: it is man's essential reality in so far as it did in fact become flesh at the beginning, yet in free history, and so in primordial history The Logos assumed the 'flesh of sin'. We must take this phrase seriously, and we must say what exactly 'flesh of sin' is. Only then can we understand why it is in Christ's flesh precisely that we are redeemed. Only then can we see that the Event of the Redemption has taken place precisely in that dimension of man's personal existence which is capable of being simultaneously the dimension in which his personal guilt becomes historically tangible *and* that in which his guilt is overcome. A really adequate soteriology cannot renounce the task of laying as its foundation a sharply defined theology of what is meant by 'flesh'. We should then see more clearly that Christ had not only to be 'like us in nature' so as to be our Redeemer, but with us had to spring 'from one' (Heb 2:11), our brother according to the flesh For he could only possess this flesh, which was to be redeemed and in

---

[1] Cf. K. Rahner, 'Die ewige Bedeutung der Menschheit Jesu', pp 279–88.

[2] Jn 1:14; 6:51; Rom 8:3; Eph 2:14; Col 1:22; 1 Tim 3:16; Heb. 5:7 1 Pet 3:18; 4:1; 1 Jn 4:2; 2 Jn 7.

which we were to be redeemed, if he who was 'born of woman' shared our origin as well as our nature. Here again we see that a satisfaction theory of a purely formal and juridical kind does not exhaust the Biblical truth of Redemption. For in such a theory the Logos would have been able to redeem us whatever creaturely form he assumed, and not only in a flesh derived from a single origin and stamped by the history of man's sin.

What has been said in this fifth section only has any real importance for our purposes in so far as the usual soteriology too shows the same kind of formal and almost juridical abstractness which we have noticed in ordinary Christology today, and for the same basic reason. Any progress beyond Chalcedon, and thus really any further insight into the meaning of its definition, would then be to the advantage of both tractates. We intend to offer only a few brief indications here.

6. There are two distinct points as regards which the problems raised by the old Christology deserve fresh consideration.

. The *single* Christ.

The question as to whether the Logos did not also become *angel* was raised as early as Origen. Today it is less possible than ever to dismiss as an idle speculation the question why there is and will be only *one* Christ, and one Christ as man, simply by appealing to 'God's decree'. There are indeed decrees of God and ultimate dispositions of his free choice. But free acts of this kind do not exclude the possibility of our asking what they mean. On the contrary, it is precisely God's field of action that is the field of the greatest intelligibility, more so than the field of a mechanical and meaningless 'necessity'. And so we should not appeal to God's decrees and his 'unsearchable' will in order to lighten our theological labours or dispense with them altogether. Anyone who wishes to proclaim the Incarnation as something worthy of faith, that is, who wishes to make it possible for modern man to assimilate this Truth of all truths, must find a place for it in his *single* historical world. But it is no longer a simple matter for modern man to accept as worthy of faith the position that the event of the Incarnation should have taken place just once. Why is there no Godmanhood in general? Or better: why does this exist in fact (as regards grace and eternal life) in such a way as precisely to 'require'[1] that the *unio hypostatica* in the strict sense took place just once? How are we to understand the inner connexion and unity of the cosmos as a whole, the nature of man and angel, in such a way as to make it comprehensible that the Logos became 'only' man, and yet that as such he is Head and End of the whole cosmos (including the angels), and this not only in respect of a higher dignity (than that of the angels) but also in respect of a real function which he exercises with regard to the angels as well? We have to offer a picture of the world in which the *one* Christ, the one Christ as *man*, seems meaningful. This point is of kerygmatic importance today. A clearer and more explicit treatment of it would help to show (and this itself is important) that the classical Christology of the dogma is in no need of demythologization.

b. The same is true of the *time* of the Incarnation.

The Fathers took a more active interest in this question than the thinkers of later times. Today it has become important again: on account of the prolongation in time both of human history *before* Christ, as well as of possible history *after* Christ. Both are more extensive, stirred by more various movements, than the Middle Ages used to think. In the expectations of many men, the higher development of humanity seems only to reach its ultimately intended realization in a mastery of the material world, the unification of men in society and their planned, i.e. rationally ordered life in common. It is of the first importance to show, with a sympathetic and yet critical regard for current patterns of thought, why this expectation does not contradict the fact of faith, that the finally decisive Event of history for all time to come has happened already: God's becoming man. To the stature of this Event all humanity can only asymptotically grow, in all its cosmic and moral dimensions, in the dimensions of grace and eschatology, whatever conceivable 'evolution' it may undergo. It can never surpass this Event, because the summit of all 'evolution', the irruption of God into the world and the radical opening of the world to the free infinity of God in Christ, has already been realized for the whole world, however true it may be that what has already taken place definitively in this Event must still reveal itself within the world

---

[1] It need hardly be said that the question is left open here as to how far this 'requirement' signifies a pure *convenientia*, i.e. a genuine connexion of meaning obtaining in objective reality, or a strict necessity.

n the reflexion and image of all history still to come, in an eschato-
ogical climax.[1]

7. It would be to the benefit of both Christology and the other
dogmatic tractates if both were more clearly aware of their unity. The
fact of this unity has already been touched on more than once in the
foregoing discussions. The division and structure of the tractates in
the textbooks of dogmatic theology available today is a problem in its
own right, and a much more serious and important problem than is
generally recognized. Perspectives and existential allocations of
attention are very nearly as important as the question, 'Is what is said
here correct?' We shall say nothing about these matters here. But
even within the customary framework of a modern treatise of dogmatic
theology more Christology could be studied in the other tractates than
is actually the case; it would be highly beneficial for these tractates.
We have already discussed the way in which the truth and richness of
content both of a 'protology' as well as of an eschatology essentially
depend on its becoming clear that man and his environment and his
history are from the first devised with a view to Christ, and that the
man Christ at the end of all history still retains his fundamental
significance. The tractate *de Gratia* is commonly entitled *de Gratia
Christi*. Commonly it contains little else about Christ. And yet we
only have a Christian understanding of grace when it is conceived of
not only in the most metaphysical way possible, as a divinization, but
rather as assimilation to Christ. And the existential transposition of
this is the following of Christ, something about which moral theology
ought to say rather more, although it offers a schema less handy for
casuistical purposes than the Ten Commandments or other schemata
of natural moral law. Furthermore, why is it only in Christology that
Christ is said to have sanctifying grace in his soul? Why is it not
stated conversely that grace is the unfolding within human nature of

---

[1] In such a theology of time in Christ, it would naturally also be necessary
discuss the question to what extent the grace of Christ, the communica-
on of the Spirit, justification, could exist *before* Christ; and again, why, for
example, there was no *visio beatifica* before Christ, and why, then, in the
former case the 'post Christum' became in the historical development of
theology a 'propter Christum', 'intuitu meritorum Christi futurorum',
while this is not possible in the latter case.

the union of the human with the Logos (in the sense mentioned above
and is therefore, and *arising thence*, something which can also be ha
in those who are not the ek-sistence of the Logos in time and histor
but do belong to his necessary environment? Sacramental theology i
again becoming more Christological today, so too the theology of th
Church as a doctrine of the 'Mystical Body of Christ'. A theology c
history, and what is more a Christocentric one, is almost entirel
lacking.

8. Would it not be fitting for someone to make a systematic stud
of the ways in which the real teaching of faith about Christ is unre
flexively misconceived? This is not a question of the 'official' heresie
from the earliest days up to the liberalism of our time, or if these, onl
in so far as behind them a profound misconception of the real dogm
is at work. It would rather be a matter of investigating with exactitud
and system what sort of idea the average Christian and non-Christia
really has of Christ, whether it be to 'believe' this idea or reject it ;
not worthy of belief. It would probably emerge that the content c
this idea by no means coincides with the real dogma, or at any ra
renders the dogma with really serious, that is disastrous, distortio
and omissions. We should then have to ask which misunderstoc
formulations of the dogma, either in solemn pronouncements or (wh
is of more practical importance) in the normal catechesis and preachin;
have given rise and continue to give rise to such pre-theoretical ar
cryptogamic heresies in Christology. Such an investigation could l
of use not only for apologetic and kerygmatic ends. It could mal
clear to academic theology that what are apparently very ticklis
questions of theology could be of the highest missionary significanc
provided that they are properly put and answered. For a true theolog
of proclamation is nothing else than the one theology, which takes i
religious task so seriously with all the scientific means at its dispos;
that it becomes at once more scientific and more kerygmatic.

6

THE IMMACULATE CONCEPTION

ON December 8, 1854, Pius IX made the following solemn declaration, which the appeal to his supreme teaching authority in the Church shows to have been infallible: 'The doctrine which holds that the Blessed Virgin Mary, in the first instant of her conception, has been, by a special grace and privilege of Almighty God, and in view of the merits of Jesus Christ, the Saviour of the human race, preserved and exempted from every stain of original sin, is revealed by God, and consequently is to be believed firmly and inviolably by all the faithful.' Since then a hundred years have passed; and to mark the occasion Pius XII, in his encyclical 'Fulgens Corona' of December 8, 1953, has announced a Marian Year.

The first thing which this centenary celebration and the announcement of a Marian Year would seem to demand is an attempt to understand more deeply this truth of Catholic faith. The fact that the supreme Pastor so explicitly desired the celebration of this centenary, more so than in the case of similar commemorative feasts (such as those of Ephesus, Chalcedon and Trent, in recent times), makes it immediately clear that a true Catholic's attitude in faith and love to this definition cannot be one of 'minding one's own business'. 'We desire', the Pope says, 'that sermons and lectures should be delivered on this subject in each diocese, so that this Christian doctrine might be made clearer to men's minds.'[1]

A truth of faith can be brought home to the understanding in various ways: we can find out what Scripture says about it; we can trace the historical course of the doctrine with the passage of time, and learn what is involved, both as regards its content and as regards its binding force on faith, from the examination of this long and often fluctuating history in which the Church's consciousness in faith has come to maturity. We can observe the influence of such a doctrine on

[1] AAS XLV (1953), p. 587.

piety, liturgy and art, study that mutual interaction between life an
official authority, theology and devotion, God's eternal truth and th
preoccupations of succeeding ages, in which the conscious grasp c
this truth slowly reaches maturity. We can also quite simply try to se
how the particular truth fits into the whole of Christian faith, how
derives its life from this whole and how its meaning and content ca
be clarified by reference to the whole.

The last procedure is specially valuable for truths of the kind wit
which we are concerned here. For truths like these, which have ne
always been in the stage of a reflexive and explicit presence for th
mind in their own right, have grown out of the totality of the Christia
understanding of faith, or else they would not exist at all. The develop
ment of a particular theme of knowledge in the Church, stimulated ar
watched over by the Holy Spirit, takes place rather in the way
which a man's knowledge grows in the course of his historical life:
is out of the whole of his being that his knowledge apprehends th
particular, although this whole may in certain circumstances l
available only unreflexively. Thus it is not surprising that any attem
to understand a particular truth out of the whole of faith must inev
tably have recourse to propositions and points of view which do n
so certainly form part of the traditional deposit of the faith—as th
is determined by reference to the Church's official teaching—as t
proposition to be explained, which in a given case has already be
defined. This must be borne in mind, when we now set out to see hc
the *de fide* proposition concerning the Immaculate Conception of t
Blessed Virgin allows of being made intelligible in terms of the who
of Revelation.

Mary is only intelligible in terms of Christ. If someone does n
hold with the Catholic faith that the Word of God became man
Adam's flesh so that the world might be taken up redemptively ir
the life of God, he can have no understanding of Catholic dogma abc
Mary either. It may indeed be said that a sense of Marian dogma is
indication of whether Christological dogma is being taken rea
seriously; or whether it is being regarded (consciously or unco
sciously) merely as a rather outmoded, problematic, mythologi
expression of the fact that in Jesus (who is basically just a religic
man) we undoubtedly feel God (here again a cipher for an unexpress
mystery) particularly close to us. No, this Jesus Christ, born of Ma

Bethlehem, is at once, as One and Indissoluble, true man and true
ʹord, consubstantial with the Father. And so Mary is in truth the
other of God. It is only to someone who truly and unreservedly
ɔnfesses this that the Catholic Church can continue to speak meaning-
lly about her other Marian dogmas. And if anyone protests against
rther Marian dogmas, either explicitly or by passive indifference, he
ust expect to be asked whether he believes and confesses what the
hurch solemnly confessed at Ephesus in 431 as the faith of the one
ıd undivided Church, and what the Reformed Church of the sixteenth
ntury believed too, though it did not really raise the question
hether this was necessary in order that one could as a sinner be
ɔnsoled by faith in a gracious God.

Now according to the testimony of Scripture, this divine Mother-
ɔod is not simply identical with the biological fact that Mary is the
other of Jesus, becoming this 'passively' as it were, while Jesus is
fact the Son of God. St Luke's witness goes further than this: this
otherhood is a free act of the Virgin's faith. One comes about by
e other, and both together form a unity. Mary's consent in faith, as
Luke relates it, cannot be regarded merely as a fragment of the
essed Virgin's private biography, one which consequently should
ive no further interest for us. It is rather an Event of public ('official')
ving history as such, more so than Abraham's faith or the Covenant
ı Sinai. It is for this reason that St Luke relates it: it is part of the
ving history of humanity, not a pious, edifying idyll from someone's
·ivate life. Mary is blessed because she believed; and she is blessed
:cause her sanctified womb bore the Holy One. Thus her consent at
e Annunciation must not be regarded as a merely external pre-
ɔndition of an Event which as human (and this is something more
an biological and physiological) would be exactly what it is even
this consent had not been given. She is Mother personally, not just
ɔlogically. Looked at in this way, her personal divine Motherhood
·ecedes—this is rather a bold way of putting it, admittedly—her
ɔn's divine Sonship. It is not as though some biological process in
:r reached its term in a divine Person, without her having taken any
ırt in it. It is perfectly true that it is of fundamental significance for
e Christian understanding of the divine Motherhood as a deed per-
rmed by the Virgin, that her obedience in faith, without which she
ould not be Mother of God, is itself a pure grace of God; but it makes
ɔ difference to the fact that she became Mother of God in the freedom

of faith. That is why we must say with all truth that for us and for ou
salvation she opened the way into our flesh of sin for the Eternal Word

Catholic theology is often reproached with making an absolute o
the official, the institutional, whatever can be applied by process o
law or administrative authority, whatever has become detached fron
freedom, charisma, faith, to the detriment of free grace, the uniqu
the creative act not subject to administrative discipline, the charis
matic. This is why she is said to have combatted Montanism, Donatisr
and so on, and the Reformation too, as so many outbreaks of fanati
cism; thus she has glorified spirit-less officialdom and declared it to b
God's authentic representative in the world. To this it must be replie
that sacrament, office, law possess their own consistency, quite inde
pendently of the holiness, the pneumatic endowment of the dispense
or bearer. And this is necessary, for otherwise office or law would nc
exist at all, or man would have to be able to establish with certaint
someone else's grace or holiness, and judgment on this point woul
cease to be God's secret. And further it must be pointed out that th
distinction between sacrament and grace, law and pneuma, office an
holiness, exterior and interior hierarchy within the Church, does nc
in general mean that there could be an ultimate and absolute dis
crepancy between them. Otherwise the Church would be a provisiona
synagogue, and not the Church of the Last Times, which are the time
of the victory of grace over sin and defection. Thus the Church a
such and as a whole can no longer escape from God's truth, fall awa
from his salvation, no longer lose the Holy Spirit, no more cease to b
the Holy Church even 'subjectively'; she can no longer become merel
an official, emptily institutional Church. And this is not because th
men by whom she is borne are no longer free, but because their free
dom remains comprehended within the predominance of grace. Thu
the Church is not only the Event of the victory of God's *Yes* ove
man's *No*; it is just this become historically tangible too (allowing fc
all that God's grace can do by way of making things perceptible in th
light of faith). In the last resort, then, the realm of the official, of savin
history, in the Church cannot be sundered from the realm of the per
sonal and the pneumatic; for the Word has definitively and for all tim
become flesh, and overcome in death the power of darkness. That i
why the Church has always seen clearly that the Apostles' office wa
exercised not only while they lived here on earth, but that they sit i

judgment on heavenly thrones in the heavenly city too, the gates of which bear their names; and the Church has seen that we must say this and confess it. So too she has always seen that the witnesses to her faith before the tribunals of earthly history, to the point of death, are also really the delivered. So too she could be sure that the very heroes of her own prehistory in the Old Testament belong eternally to the number of those who have power with God, the redeemed. Office (= essential function in the public saving history of God's People) and personal holiness coincide at the decisive points of saving history, so that each supports the other and makes it possible. Such is the Church's conviction according to the Scriptures, in spite of her unequivocal rejection of Donatism.

We are now better able to understand what was maintained above, that according to the Scriptures Mary is Mother of the Incarnate Word in and through her free obedience in faith.

Her divine Motherhood, then, belongs to that utterly decisive Event of saving history in which the Word of the Father came into the flesh of sin, and thus also, fundamentally and inevitably, to the death which redeemed us. Her motherhood is an event of authentic, public (i.e. engaging God's People as such in its historical tangibility) saving history. In fact, so far as such an act of saving history can be performed by a mere human being, it is the decisive Event of saving history, and an eschatological one. From this time on (as opposed to all previous acts of saving history) the dialogue between God and humanity (even in this world) is no longer open, because in reply to this assent of the Virgin, God spoke his definitive word to the world as a Word of salvation and not of judgment. This eschatological and decisive Event of public saving history, through which Mary dealt in the name (= for the salvation) of all humanity, is at the same time her personal act in faith. At this point if at all there clearly coincide office and person, position in the Church and situation before God, dignity and holiness. Mary is the holy Mother of God, as necessarily as the Church is the holy Church, as necessarily as God's grace is stronger than man's power to deny him. Her life is the free act (maintained right up to the moment when she stood below the Lord dying on the Cross) through which she received God's Word in faith and in her womb, for her own salvation and the salvation of all men. This was the moment for which she existed; then it was that there took place the covenant between God and humanity, which is eternal and definitive.

Here we must give more explicit consideration to the fact that this act of unconditional faith performed by the Blessed Virgin was God's grace and Christ's, and only so of saving significance for her and for us. A man's free performance of a salutary act and God's grace are by no means things which tend to exclude one another: grace rather bestows the power to act and the actual performance, and the creature's answer is itself the work of God's effective call. If Mary opens the door of the world for the definitive coming of the redeeming God into the flesh of humanity, she does it freely, because God wishes to come, and on account of this unconditional will to save the world, himself gives her the power to realize the condition under which God's Word wished to come: in the freedom of those who were to receive him, because the Word wished to come freely. Her word is pure answer in the strength of the Word directed to her: nothing else, but this wholly. That reception in acceptance of the grace of the world is itself grace. As her act, her conception of the Word is just as much grace as what was so received and conceived. He gives not only himself, but also his conception, on the human side, in free faith and in the very corporeality of the Virgin's Motherhood. But he wished to give himself only by giving the Virgin too the free word of faith.

If we were to try and sum up what we have so far said about Mary in a concise formula, which expresses it all at one stroke by means of a concept whose theological validity requires no preliminary proof, then all we need say is: Mary is she who is most perfectly Redeemed. What this formula means will appear from the following simple considerations. Redemption as one person's grace is always another's blessing; redemption takes place as the reception of Christ in the act of faith, which is itself grace and—for faith—establishes itself as something historically tangible in the world. Then the most perfect redemption is the conception of Christ in faith and in the body for the salvation of all in the holiest act of freedom, which is grace. Because Mary stands at that point of saving history at which through her freedom the world's salvation takes place definitively and irrevocably as God's act, she is most perfectly redeemed. It may be felt that these propositions take away from the significance of Christ's death; that they do not may be seen from the fact that the descent into the flesh is already the beginning of the descent into death, because the flesh assumed is dedicated to death. Thus the Incarnation is not just a condition for a redemption still open, still to come, but its inception, with which the whole, however much it has still to grow, is set upon its own proper way. As Mother of God, Mary is most perfectly redeemed, and *vice versa*. The Church has always been aware of this, however little explicit that knowledge may have been in itself and in its consequences. But it is only possible for the Church always to have been aware of Mary as holy before God, as redeemed and delivered, and to know this from her divine Motherhood alone, if in the present regime of salvation there is found in her some real, objective connexion between her task in saving history and her personal holiness. If this is so, then it includes a perfect correspondence between Mary's unique task in saving history and her personal holiness. In short, for the faith of the Church Mary is she who is most perfectly Redeemed, the example and exemplar of redemption simply speaking.

We have now reached a position from which we may look directly at Mary's Immaculate Conception, but before we do this, two points still have to be considered.

The first of these may appear if we ask ourselves what we as Christians really think about the unbaptized infant. We say that it has original sin, it is not justified, possesses no sanctifying grace, is not yet a temple of the Holy Spirit and so on. We say all this without hesitation, and none of it calls for further discussion. But if we go on to say that it is under the dominion of the Devil, that it is a child of God's wrath, a lost and rejected creature, then we hesitate with some justice. And yet we must grant that these assertions are identical in content with the former ones, or are their simple logical consequences. Why do we hesitate? We notice that we have abstracted from certain things in making the first set of assertions, and still more the second. This child, of which we can and must make both the former and the latter assertions, is already, as unbaptized, an object of God's infinite mercy, in spite of original sin; it is included in God's vision of his only-begotten Son, and thus it has, if not yet a realized, at least a 'remote' claim to inheritance with the Son. Looked at from this point of view, its condition as first described is basically—I do not say *in itself*—already annulled, or, if this formulation seems doubtful, already comprehended within God's grace and love. We should remember that in original sin (and so in all its formulations: enmity, wrath, damnation, dominion of the Devil and so on) we are dealing with a 'sin' which is essentially different from personal sin as the act of that freedom which permits of no deputization, a sin, then, which only falls under the same concept 'analogically'. We should not then be wholly astray if—to exercise our minds a little and clarify matters—we were to say that in this case (as opposed to personal guilt or freely received justification) Luther's 'simul iustus et peccator' had something to be said for it.

This coexistence of God's true saving purpose and of original sin in the unbaptized infant forms as it were a supratemporal region within which the infant has its existence. It is only because God's gracious love in Christ already belongs to the infant that the perceptible history of its salvation takes a sacramentally visible form, that history in the temporal succession of which a sinner becomes one of the just by baptism. Now this grace, given in the lifetime of this individual, derives from the former grace, which already comprehends his whole lifetime, and pretty well amounts to its temporal deployment; one might have the impression that it is not after all very important exactly when the temporal realization should take place—has anyone ever seriously regretted having been baptized after a fortnight instead of as a two days old babe in arms? That is why the whole mystery of Mary's Immaculate Conception cannot simply consist in the fact that she was graced a little earlier, temporally speaking, than we were. The distinction must lie deeper, and this deeper distinction must condition the temporal difference. And this for the primary reason that it would otherwise be impossible to see why God, whose saving purpose has reigned in unspeakable power over the holy Virgin 'from the first moment of her existence', of her 'conception', as it does in every case, for us and for all things, why God did not want this difference between natural beginning and the temporal realization of his purpose in her case too, though she too is redeemed. Would it not have appeared more clearly in history that she too is redeemed, as we are? If the mystery of our dogma were merely this difference of time, it would not be easy either to understand how the Church could have come to know it, since she has not always grasped this mystery explicitly. For it would always be possible to hold that what Tradition tells us about Mary's unsurpassable holiness did not bear strictly upon a condition of grace in her, but upon God's saving purpose from the beginning.

Consequently a second point must be taken into consideration if we re to make any progress. We have a rather more difficult theological oncept to consider here, and the reader must be asked to be as patient s he can. In what follows we wish to discuss the free actions per-ormed by creatures, and morally good ones, since the question of God's causal relationship to evil actions does not arise here. God can of imself, i.e. prior to a man's actual decision, absolutely and effectively vill a definite good act of a man's freedom, and yet this act does not hereby cease to be free, nor does it follow that on account of the reature's freedom God merely has foreknowledge of this free action ust because it happens and not also because he wills it. In this way God attains his will, and man does freely what God of himself has inconditionally willed. For God is He who as God can bestow free-dom itself upon the creature, freedom even before Himself. Why he an do this, how he does it—this is a mystery of blinding darkness. Let us for convenience call this fact predestination, carefully excluding everything fatalistic, unfree, deterministic from this theological con-ept. Thus we may say: Mary, as the Holy one and she who has been nost perfectly Redeemed—her personal free consent includes both hese—is already predestined in God's will with respect to Christ, the incarnate Redeemer of the generation of Adam. If in the last resort God's grace is the cause and not the effect of man's actions; if conse-quently the redemption of sinful humanity proceeds from God's free aving purpose alone; if according to this saving purpose, which rises from God's free yet absolute initiative, the redemption through he Incarnation of the Son was to take place by the assumption of an Adamitic human nature and its destiny: then it is immediately clear hat in God's predetermining will for this Christ an earthly Mother of he Son was likewise predestined, i.e. was willed absolutely and prior o any human decision, like the Incarnation itself. And so her free con-ent to this Motherhood is already given too. For human motherhood nust be free, if it is not to injure the dignity of the human person, vhich is unthinkable with God. Yet in this election is also included the hoice of Mary as the Holy One, as she who has been most perfectly Redeemed. That is to say, in that God's absolute and unconditional vill is that the Redeemer should come from Mary and her free *Fiat*, is will is that she should be the most perfectly Redeemed in this free Motherhood itself. For here 'office' and personal holiness must co-icide. If, then, God wills Christ and his Mother in the plan of pre-estination, he wills her as the Holy one in this single predestination:

not just in any similar predestination, but in Christ's, and thus in his first, original plan.

Now what does all this imply for the 'Immaculate Conception'? We have already said above that even prior to any actual eradication of original sin by baptism or any non-sacramental justification, God's saving purpose as First and Last embraces each human being; and that consequently man is never the sinner he would be if God's free grace were not to support his existence from the beginning. We can now say: this divine purpose of salvation, which embraces Mary in this way from the very beginning, indeed from all eternity, and thus precedes all other possibilities (in reality, at least, if not in time), is for her the predestination of Christ himself. That is to say, if she had not been willed as the Holy one and the perfectly Redeemed, then Christ himself, as we know him in actual fact, would not have been willed by God. This cannot be said of any other of the redeemed. It is true that a divine predestining purpose of salvation of this kind reigns over everyone who is going to find salvation; it is true that God wills this salvation as an effect of Christ the Incarnate, Christ who was crucified in obedience to the Father. And yet, so long as we are here below, this saving decision of God remains hidden from us for everyone except Mary—at least in general. In general we can point to no event in the experience of our own history which will allow us to read off this divine predestining decision for any individual as such. And further—and this is the decisive point—in every other case Christ could exist and be predestined by God without its being necessary for the individual concerned to be one of the redeemed. Any individual apart from Mary who is predestined to salvation, is not simply included in God's predestining will in respect of Christ, but relies upon a divine decision which must proceed for his especial benefit. Otherwise everyone would be certain of his own salvation by the mere fact that Christ exists. But that is a position which is forbidden to us, we who have to work out our salvation in fear and trembling, in firm hope, and not intellectual certainty; we who must always say, whatever may be our humble, acquiescent trust (and no one is forbidden to hope in the unlimited extent of this for each of us): 'I do not know whether I belong to the elect'. As perfectly Redeemed, Mary stands—in reality and for our knowledge in faith—within the circle of Christ's own predestination. And thus it is that she is different from us not merely by having become graced at a temporally earlier point in her existence. It is much more the mystery of her predestination we must look at: this is the mystery which first gives its real meaning to the temporal difference between her and us in the mystery of the Immaculate Conception.

But does it follow from what has been said that Mary, from the beginning of her existence, was not only the object of a specifically unique predestining purpose of salvation on the part of God, but also possessed sanctifying grace; that in this sense she was preserved from original sin, redeemed by being preserved and not just by being freed from original sin? For this, after all, whatever may have been said about her predestination, is what is immediately contained in the Marian dogma. Is the latter statement something which we have to say 'as well', 'additively', or does it follow as a consequence and a more explicit articulation of what was said earlier? We hold that the second alternative is the true one.

Firstly, then, we have already said that Mary is the perfect, exemplar, pure case of redemption in general. Now one of the points of faith on which the Church has slowly reached a reflexive clarity of insight with the assistance of her Spirit, is that redemption does not necessarily and in every case presuppose a temporally earlier condition of being unredeemed, of sin and alienation from God. Someone who is preserved in grace is just as radically delivered and redeemed, if not more so. The fact that of ourselves we are nothing and have nothing, that nothing could come from our hearts but a malice which ultimately God alone overcomes at its source and not we: all this is something which he who is preserved can and must acknowledge in praise of grace, just as much as he who is delivered with regard to his deliverance. If in the Our Father we are bound to pray to be preserved from temptation, the thanks we offer for this grace of protection is no less in praise of redemption than the thanks for deliverance from the consequences of giving way under temptation. Both standing fast and standing upright again are his grace. If this is true, then the redemptive preservation from original sin is the most radical and most blessed mode of redemption. It must necessarily have been her lot who is the most perfectly Redeemed, because she alone, by reason of her office and person, stands precisely at that point at which Christ began the definitive and victorious redemption of mankind. Thus it is that the dogma of the Immaculate Conception of the holy Virgin belongs to the doctrine of

Redemption itself, and stands for the most radical and perfect form of redemption.

There is a second point to consider. Why do infants first obtain Christ's grace only at baptism? Why not earlier, at the very beginning of their existence? If someone were to adopt the latter view (which won't do), this would not necessarily be in flat contradiction with the fact that the Immaculate Conception is a unique privilege of the Blessed Virgin. For we have already seen that this privilege involves more than just the temporal difference between her justification and ours, especially as still other differences remain, such as freedom from concupiscence and so on. Nor would such a view necessarily do away with the Redemption and the character of justification as grace; for these remain in Mary's case too. Nor again would such a view put in doubt the necessity of baptism. Although justification by faith and love is normal in the adult, and in the normal way takes place before baptism or the sacrament of penance, these sacraments retain their necessity and their meaning. Nor can such a view be disposed of simply by a reference to the lot of infants who die unbaptized. For we have absolutely no real knowledge of what happens to them, and the controversy over the 'limbus puerorum' is once more quite open today. And yet this view must be rejected, because Tradition and the official teaching of the Church too clearly presuppose and speak of original sin in Adam's posterity not just as a condition due in itself (if it were not hindered by God's redeeming grace), but as one which has come about in fact. But why does God permit it to come about, if on the one hand the reasons for it which people tend to offer immediately are not free from objection, and on the other, a divine purpose of salvation reigns over man, directed as redemption and forgiveness against the hereditary guilt? Why is this purpose not realized from the beginning of any individual's existence? It would certainly remain grace, the Redemption of Christ, and even infant baptism would remain meaningful and necessary.

Unless one is prepared to be satisfied simply with an arbitrary 'decree' of God, which is too cheap an answer, however frequent it may be in a theology infected with nominalism, the only possible answer to this question is as follows. The interval of time between the beginning of existence and the commencement of justification is not an expression of the bare need for redemption as such. Rather, what becomes visible here is the fact that man may not in general be regarded even in the Regime of Christ as simply one redeemed, predestined, as someone who is absolutely and unconditionally taken into God's grace simply because God's mercy has become, absolutely and unconditionally, an irrevocable and victorious fact in the world in the flesh of Christ. The fact that our salvation and our attained blessedness are not simply predestined simultaneously with the predestination of Christ acquires historical manifestation in the temporal interval between the beginning of existence and the commencement of justification. And thus the converse holds good: Mary is she who is taken into predestining grace in Christ's becoming flesh as the victorious and definitive presence of God's mercy in the world, overcoming all sin; and therefore in her case this temporal interval has no meaning. Not because she did not require redemption, but precisely because she is the one member of the redeemed without whom it is impossible to think of the Redemption as victorious. The dogma of the Immaculate Conception belongs to the very heart of the doctrine of our Redemption by the one unique Mediator Jesus Christ, the Son of God, who became man, died and rose again 'propter nos homines et propter nostram salutem'.

If this Marian Year which has been proclaimed should make us specially bear in mind the dogma, proclaimed a hundred years ago, of the Immaculate Conception of the Blessed Virgin and Mother of God, such a commemoration, rightly understood, is a celebration of the mystery of our Redemption and a praise of the grace of the one Lord in whose name alone there is salvation. Ultimately we can only praise him by saying what he has done among us. If we want to speak of this as his deed, how can we do it better than by acknowledging what he has done in Mary, and in this way fulfil the saying that the Spirit put on her lips: All generations shall call me blessed.

7

THE INTERPRETATION OF THE DOGMA OF THE ASSUMPTION

IN this short study we shall attempt to discuss what is actually meant by the new dogma of Mary's bodily assumption into final perfection, and not its theological foundations. Thus we shall not ask in what way precisely it can be 'based on' Scripture (this is how the *Constitutio Apostolica* promulgating the definition cautiously formulates it). Nor shall we ask how the dogma is contained explicitly or implicitly in the tradition of faith, nor how one can reach the conviction that the 'new' dogma is a truth which belongs to that Apostolic Tradition which never changes, although it was not always taught in the Church so expressly and with such binding force as is the case today. These questions too do indeed have their own, by no means small, importance; and they too must be answered in a theology of this dogma. Indeed they are even more important theologically. But everyone has the right to choose his own subject; and what we choose is not the latter but the former. Moreover we believe that an exposition of the *content* of the new dogma of Mary's 'bodily' assumption into 'heaven' is not only of importance in itself (for ultimately one has also to know *what* one believes); we also believe that it is of use in answering the questions not dealt with here. For many of the difficulties of an epistemological and psychological kind which seem to show that this doctrine does not belong to Revelation as it is handed down to us, arise rather from a misconception of its content than from any special difficulties in establishing the fact. What is more, as far as one can see, among the almost countless studies of the question today, there is hardly one which attempts to enter more deeply into the inner meaning of the new dogma. Writers are content to demonstrate the fact of what is asserted as something given in the case of Mary, and obviously take it tacitly for granted that Christians are sufficiently familiar with the truths of Christ's Resurrection and of the future general

resurrection to understand what is really meant by saying that someone is corporeally glorified in heaven.

Thus if we wish to know what is really involved in the substance
of this defined proposition, our best plan is to ask first of all in what
wider context of Christian truths it really belongs. The true meaning
of any individual proposition of revealed truth does indeed contain an
'item' of new knowledge, which is added on to the other truths, en-
larges and completes them; yet a proposition of this kind is itself only
really intelligible in the totality of the one saving Truth. We may
regard this totality as plainly set out for the first time in the Apostles'
Creed. Our question then runs as follows: To which article of faith
does the new dogma belong as its consequence and organic unfolding?
The question seems simple: it belongs to the article 'Born of the
Virgin Mary'. The answer is correct but insufficient, and that in two
ways. Firstly, for the connexion we are seeking, everything depends
on how exactly 'Born of the Virgin Mary' is itself understood.
Secondly, this is by no means the only article of the Creed to which
the new dogma is essentially and immediately related.

As to the first point we may say this: by itself, i.e. if the words are
simply taken in their most primitive sense, 'born of the Virgin Mary'
could mean that Mary has given the Word of the Father his body
from her own (as every mother does her child), and that she is for this
reason, and in this way alone, his mother, the mother of the Son of
God, and nothing more. But according to the Scriptures and the
testimony of the Church from the most ancient times, the phrase says
more than this. It is not just of an event belonging to the private life
of Mary and Jesus that the phrase speaks; even by itself (and not only
in consequence of the actions performed later in his life by this child
born of Mary) it means a *saving* event, an historical happening, which
makes a fundamental difference to the situation of the whole world
before God. For the Father's eternal Word has become flesh in Mary,
God has already indivisibly assumed the world in the flesh of this
Virgin's Son; God's eternal Son has already made his own the destiny
of the world in the 'flesh of sin' (Rom 8:3) (i.e. in flesh dedicated to
death), so that this personal existence in the world's sinful flesh led
undeviatingly (in this wise or that) to the death in which the guilt
of the world is endured to the end and overcome. Thus this Event of
becoming man is an 'eschatological' event: the definitive salvation of
the world, irrevocable and unsurpassable, by God's grace in the Word

of the Father become flesh, is already definitely in the world in virtue of what took place in and through Mary, and had to and still has to merely work itself out in what we call the Cross of the Son, his Resurrection and the history of the world *post Christum natum*. This eschatological Event of saving significance for the whole world took place in Mary: in her flesh and through her faith. In her flesh: for our whole salvation depends on the fact that the Son shares not only our 'specific' human nature but also our very generation, entering into that community of us all in which no one lives for himself or dies for himself. The Son of God had to be a son of Adam. And this he became in Mary, so that our salvation depends upon his having been born of woman, that is to say, quite concretely, of Mary. Through her faith: however true it may be that the Event took place and had to take place in the flesh, we know from the testimony of Scripture that it did not fail to engage the Blessed Virgin's 'private life', her freedom and her faith. No, what took place in the flesh, took place there through the 'Let it be done to me according to thy word', through her faith; so that because of this she might be called holy, by Elizabeth at that distant time and since then by all generations. Her objective service, by means of which her bodily reality is delivered to the Word, is also her subjective action, one in the other. Her faith is called blessed because it admitted the Word into the region of the flesh, and her bodily motherhood is not only a biological occurrence but the supreme action of faith, through which she becomes blessed. She lets the Son of God into the world; and she does it only by his power and in virtue of his grace. She can only let him into the prison of the sinful and mortal world because *he* wishes to come, and because her letting him in is itself again the work of the grace of his coming. But it is *she* who does it. She could do nothing if he did not grace her by his coming. But he graced her in just such a way that in her (flesh and faith together) the salvation of the world has definitively begun, and that in her God spoke his final, because total, word in the dialogue between him and humanity which had till then remained open. And so, when we make confession in the words 'born of the Virgin Mary', we do not merely say that the 'biological' happening of the Incarnation of the Son of God has made use of the Virgin's womb; we say that in her and through her (both) Christ's salvation (his alone!) was bestowed upon the world. She does not thereby become 'Co-redemptrix' *'by the side of'* Christ, as though the Son and the Virgin 'shared' in the redemption of the world in a kind of 'synergism'. But she co-operates in the redemption of the world, in so far as she does, for the salvation of the whole world and not only for her own, what a human being can and must do in the power of grace and for grace: receive it. She has received in her flesh the salvation of the world from the Holy Spirit through the consent of her faith, she has received for all men and in the most 'corporeal' way the whole Christ.[1] That is why, however, the Church has always believed that in her the redemption which took place in her and through her in the world has reached its fullest and most radical perfection. When the Church confesses of her that she remained 'preserved' from original sin (an expression which is easily misunderstood) and always sinless, this does not mean that she 'privately' by herself, and in contrast to the rest of humanity, has not lost man's original grace in Adam (this was lost to her too in Adam); it means that she is the radically Redeemed, in whom Christ's single and unique grace exhaustively surpassed man's sinfulness, even 'temporally' in a certain way, so that she can in no way (not even as to sin) call anything her own which is not the gift of the incomprehensible grace of the Father in the Son of her womb. And that is how she is the second Eve, the Mother of all the living, the type of perfect redemption and the perfect representation of what redeemed humanity, what the Church can be.[2] God's grace achieved its most incomprehensible and unsurpassable work where it laid hold of the world most closely and in the most 'fleshly' way: in Mary.

Before we attempt to unfold the full meaning of the article 'Born of the Virgin Mary' as it concerns the new dogma, we have yet to discuss the second point made above. We said that there were other articles of the Creed to which this proposition was essentially and immediately related. We have in mind the 'descent into the kingdom of death' and the 'resurrection of the flesh'. First of all, these two articles belong together. Because He descended among the dead and rose again there exists a resurrection of the flesh. It is only because he

---

[1] No more seems to be claimed for Mary's position in saving history, as it is briefly indicated here, than what the Lutheran theologian, H. Asmussen, presents as a completely Biblical teaching about Mary. See his book *Maria. Die Mutter Gottes* (Stuttgart 1950), esp. p. 51.

[2] Cf. here O. Semmelroth, *Urbild der Kirche. Organischer Aufbau des Mariengeheimnisses* (Wurzburg 1950); H. Rahner, *Maria und die Kirche* (Innsbruck 1950; ET in preparation).

himself arrived at that furthest point of human existence which we call being dead, which was limitless and implies something deeper and more dreadful than what modern man thinks of in terms of a cessation of biological life, that a Resurrection exists, that alone is why man is saved through and through, and is capable of God's beatitude with his whole undivided being. The heart of the earth has accepted and received the Son of God; and it is from a womb so consecrated, this womb of the 'hellish' depths of human existence, that the saved creature rises up. Not just (not even temporarily) in the Son alone. It is not that he alone descended and so rose again as victor because death could not hold him captive. 'Even now' he is not the firstborn among the dead in the sense that he is even now the only human being to have found the complete fulfilment of his whole human reality. By his death salvation has come to be definitively. Then what is there in principle to prevent any man from finding this definitive salvation? When the early Church confessed her belief in Christ's descent, victorious over death, she had in mind other dead ones, who 'already' share in the definitive character of the total victory over death and sin.[1] Let us remember (and this is something Althaus[2] has said too— quite rightly, in itself, though his approach is wrong), that it is quite impossible for the Resurrection to be an individual event, because our bodily condition' (whether glorified or not) is simply the outward aspect of the spirit, which the spirit forms for itself in matter so as to be open to the rest of the world, and which in consequence necessarily includes a community of a bodily kind with a bodily Thou (and not just with God's Spirit). If this is so then the Son of Man 'cannot' have risen alone. What, we may ask, is really to be understood by his glorified bodily condition (if we take it seriously, and don't spiritualize it into another way of talking about his eternal 'communion with God') right up to the 'Last Day', if meanwhile it should persist all by

---

[1] Cf. e.g. K. Gschwind, *Die Niederfahrt Christi in die Unterwelt* (Münster 911); K. Prümm, *Der christliche Glaube und die altheidnische Welt* II Leipzig 1935), pp. 17–51 (esp. pp. 29–31). It should be noted that the conclusion arrived at in these works—that the overcoming of death in others is *also* contained in the ancient Christian confession of the *descensus*— was reached wholly without an eye to the modern doctrine of the Assumption or any apologetic concern for it.

[2] The Lutheran theologian from Erlangen. Cf. P. Althaus, *Die letzten Dinge*[6] (Gütersloh 1949), p. 141; pp. 156 s.

itself—something which is precisely unthinkable for the bodily condition (though glorified)? So when we find in Mt 27:52 s.[1] that other bodies too, those of saints, rose up with him (indeed even 'appeared'—as he himself did—to show that the end of all the ages has already come upon us), this is merely positive evidence from Scripture for what we would have expected anyway, if definitive salvation has already been unshakably founded, death conquered, and a man, for whom it is never good to be alone, has entered upon the fulfilment of his whole being. Hence to try to set aside this testimony from Matthew as a 'mythological' intrusion, or to argue away its eschatological meaning with ingenious evasions—such as that it is merely a matter of a temporary resurrection or even of 'phantom bodies'—would not be in accordance with the authoritative voice of Scripture. It is a fact that by far the greater part of the Fathers and the theologians, right up to the present day, have firmly maintained the eschatological interpretation of the text as the only one possible from the exegetical point of view. In this connexion it is not without interest that most of the Fathers and theologians adduced as witnesses for Mary's Assumption in the Bull of the definition also gave explicit support to this eschatological interpretation of the text.[2]

But how are we to conceive of a bodily condition like this, perfected and glorified, as an essential element in the total perfection of the single, whole human being? What kind of existence is this? And where? It is not easy to answer these questions and others like them. But can we who are imperfect ever form an idea of what has been brought to perfection? Even in the risen Lord, who showed himself

[1] On the exegesis of this text and its history see H. Zeller, 'Corpora Sanctorum. Eine Studie zu Mt 27:52–3', ZKT LXXI (1949), pp. 385–465. We still maintain that Zeller's exegesis is correct and convincing in spite of the objections made to it by A. Winklhofer, 'Corpora Sanctorum', *Tübinger Theol. Quartalschrift* (1953), pp. 30–67, 210–17. It is clearly impossible here to go into the exegesis of this text in greater detail. So too we must renounce any attempt to evaluate works like that by W. Bieder, *Die Vorstellung von der Höllenfahrt Jesu Christi. Beitrag zur Entstehungsgeschichte vom sog. Descensus ad inferos* (Zürich 1949).

[2] Daniélou's view, in *Etudes* 267 (1950), p. 291, that it is no longer admissible after the bull to interpret Mt 27:51 s. in terms of a definitive, eschatological resurrection of these saints, is quite without foundation. There can be no question of this. The bull nowhere affirms that Mary's privilege of 'anticipated' resurrection is to be understood as being unique in itself simply, as well as in its cause and title.

to appointed witnesses in his manifestations, we see little more than the fact of his Resurrection. For the inner nature of his glorified bodily condition could only be made deeply evident for 'what it is in itself' to those who themselves live in this new mode of existence. What the Apostles saw and touched of the Risen One was the Risen One himself in his 'flesh and bone', as he himself said; and yet this was necessarily in the manner in which something glorified can appear to the unglorified, it was an appearance 'for us' which permits us to say little about him 'as he is in himself'. We need only remember how seriously this in itself obvious fact ('quidquid recipitur, ad modum recipientis recipitur', runs a scholastic axiom) must be regarded if the idea is not to arise that, for instance, our Lord's 'Ascension into heaven', as the Apostles saw it take place, is something which continues rectilinearly 'in itself' after his being taken up by a cloud from their eyes, and in *such* wise ends in heaven. And when St Paul insists that an absolutely radical 'transformation' of our bodily condition must take place in order that we, who will no longer then be 'flesh and blood', may be able to inherit the Kingdom of God, what is being said at the same time is how little capable we are of 'forming an idea' of the new condition of the body. All we really know of it allows of being stated only from the 'outside', from two points of view: we ourselves shall be in this condition, we with all the reality we had and all our experience; and again, we shall be transformed, be quite different. Beyond this we shall say what St Paul said, that an incorruptible, a glorious, a spiritual body will rise in power (1 Cor 15:42 s.); and we shall read the blessed visions of the Seer of the Apocalypse, visions of a new heaven and a new earth (Apoc 21 s.), in which image and reality for us now are inseparably intertwined. Ancient man (who in this respect continued to exist in Catholic theology into the eighteenth century) could be easier in mind about the possibility of representing the definitive fulfilment of the whole man and of the world corresponding to him. For him (in his unreflexive, underlying, 'world-picture', not in the convictions he held in faith, even if the one passed without distinction into the other), Heaven, as the region of the glorified condition of the body, was a spatial setting which existed even before the saving Event of the Resurrection, towards which this event moved as the 'uppermost part' of its cosmos. Time ran its course (one might have said) in space; in virtue of being glorified the body came to its new place, a place connatural to it, existing prior to it and possessing the 'properties of glorification'. Today we can no longer use this imaginative picture to explain an 'ascent into heaven'. Consequently it is usual for theologians today to reply to the question as to the 'place' of heaven by merely saying that it is above all a 'condition'; and that, if one must allow for some spatial location on account of the bodily condition of a man who has been saved totally, it is in fact impossible to say just 'where' this heaven is. Certainly this modesty is in large measure justified, and yet it sounds a little unhappy. Especially so, because the attempt is made, instinctively and yet without any real reason, to conceive of this spatiality, however indefinite its Where, as a portion of this 'physical' world of space, something infinite and in itself homogeneous, which we are acquainted with as the space of our experience. Today we should say something more like this: the new 'spatiality' is a function of saving history, of the time which *shapes* this space; it comes to be by the fact of Christ's rising from the dead, and it is not given in advance as the possibility and the place of this glorified state. The ancients may have conceived of the happening of historical event (i.e time, thought of as 'local movement' up to and including Christ's Ascension) as a function of space, *in* which it moved; we today on the other hand think of it rather differently: 'space' and 'place' arise through the happening of historical event; space is rather a function of time; in virtue of an event as radical as a transforming glorification, a spatial and local condition (of a quite new kind) arises which is no longer a portion of space as it was known till then but is incommensurable with it; and hence it is no longer capable of being 'represented', but has to be 'postulated' for the single reason that the true 'bodily condition' of someone who has risen in glory must not be dissipated by a false spiritualization. What is more, Christ's body remains in this way eternally a piece of this world, bound up with it in its deepest and inmost ground; otherwise the mortal would not have attained to eternal life or the unity of the world would be split asunder. Beginning with Christ's body, this very world thus achieves even now a new mode of being by means of its history in Christ, which is a history of the material and the spiritual at once, of flesh and person in the one Spirit of God which renews all things. The world acquires a new heavenly 'dimension' (not of course to be thought of as added to previous ones as a 'fourth', but one which for the first time gives the whole of the world a new order, its all-embracing 'heaven' in fact, by means of the originating Event of

Christ's Resurrection). Here too and here above all is it true to say that time and history shape 'space' and do not intrinsically presuppose it. None of this makes heaven easier to 'imagine'. Yet it becomes conceivable that heaven is not deprived of 'place' by the mere fact that we are no longer capable of accommodating it in a 'caelum empyreum' by a homogeneous extension of the world of our experience. Our own representation of the world in terms of space and time is itself, as a part of this world, necessarily confined within the structures of this world and our senses. But speculation and above all faith testify to the fact that reality does not simply come to an end where our representation of it does.

Everything depends on the fact that our own reality itself is transformed and not simply replaced by another, one which could no longer be our own selves and our world. There follows, then, a twofold consequence, in so far as the new reality which has come to be through Christ's Resurrection and the space which is proper to this reality continue to cohere with our world in its ultimate ontological root. Firstly, there will be not only a new heaven but also a new earth, and the new earth will be no other than the perfection of the 'heaven' which will have wholly and exhaustively transformed into itself and its mode of being the reality of the world. Secondly, we may grant that the new heaven and the old earth are radically and necessarily connected, and that the heavenly form of existence does indeed involve a migration from the mode of being proper to 'flesh and blood', the earthly, perishable manner of being characteristic of the body and its environment, under sentence of death; but it does not involve a migration from the world itself (there cannot be a 'beyond' like this, if in fact man is ever to 'rise again' and this is to involve his intrinsic fulfilment). If this is so, then the reality beyond (so far as it already exists in the glorified Christ and those 'saints' who follow in his train) cannot be conceived of as lacking all objective bonds with this world, as lacking a cosmic bond with the unglorified world which objectively coheres with the glorified reality and is really capable of being used to express it; though this does not require the application to it of categories which because of their cosmological limitations could not be used to speak of things 'beyond'. Reflexion on this point will show that it is meaningful to say, for example, that one man has 'already' risen again while another has 'not yet' done so, for this does not involve any application of limited categories to an object which wholly transcends them. The eternity in glory of the earthly and historical is not simply identical with God's eternity, which is equally immediate and equally near to every point in time, and to which consequently temporal statements cannot be applied. Rather, the eternity in glory of the earthly is a fruit of time and history itself. Saving history transforms the temporal itself into eternity, by means of a process which on the one hand does not necessarily run its course 'simultaneously', owing to the plurality of our earthly reality; and on the other does not in its parts and their outcome lose its connexion with the process as a whole, so that the part can be really determined 'temporally' from the point of view of the whole. What is glorified retains a real connexion with the unglorified world, it belongs inseparably to a single, ultimately indivisible world; and that is why an occurrence of glorification possesses objectively its determinate place in this world's time, even if this point in time marks precisely the point at which a portion of this world ceases to endure time itself, in so far as it is different from all others while remaining in unity with the whole. Furthermore, the Christian has a guarantee that statements of this sort, open to temporal qualification, can be made meaningfully about something 'beyond'; for Scripture makes them about the Risen Lord. Of him it is said that he has 'already' risen, while just this statement cannot yet be made of us and also of many of the dead. Supposing that this distinction may be meaningfully and justly applied to statements about the 'moment in time' in which there is possession of the resurrection-body in Christ's case and in the case of many of the dead who have not yet risen, it follows that the distinction cannot be meaningless in Mary's case either, on the alleged ground, perhaps, that the transcendence of God and of the eternity of the man who has been saved touches *every* point of our time with equal immediacy.

We can now resume our consideration of the phrase 'born of the Virgin Mary'. As we said, this proposition of faith concerning Mary has in view not only the fact that she *is* the Mother of the Lord, in so far as she *has* bestowed upon the Son of God his earthly existence from her flesh; but also above all the fact that she *becomes* Mother, i.e. that in her and through her, in her flesh and through her faith, the eschatological Event of salvation takes place, drawing after it everything else as its inner consequence, so that Mary appears as herself the perfectly Redeemed and the representation of perfect redemption. The concept of the 'perfectly Redeemed' may in certain respects be a 'dynamic' one (if we may so put it), i.e. a concept the contents of which cannot be simply enumerated, in terms of fixed, given notes, one which cannot be 'defined' like mathematical and geometrical concepts. It has a life of its own, so that it is never possible to avoid the apparent difficulty that more is found in it when it is expounded than it originally contained, or that one can find quite arbitrarily in the concept of '*perfect*' Redemption whatever one chooses to find. However, the objection does not touch us very nearly. It has already been shown that that End of time has begun already, although thousands of years may still draw out this single End in Christ; it has been shown too that that End of the whole history of salvation which has already become Event and Presence in Christ's Resurrection includes not only his Resurrection but that of the saints as well, however little it may be in our power to say *in general* who precisely these first fruits of complete redemption may be. But it follows from this that the total redemption in body and soul 'already' achieved is not something which has been arbitrarily invented or merely postulated *a priori* as characteristic of a perfect redemption. And what this means is that if Mary is the ideal representation of exhaustive redemption because of her unique place in saving history, then she must 'even now' have achieved that perfect communion with God in the glorified totality of her real being ('body and soul') which certainly exists even now.

Thus it is that the two articles of the Apostles' Creed from which we started fuse into one and provide us with the meaning of the new dogma: She who by her faith received salvation in her body for herself and for us all, has received it entire. And this entire salvation is a salvation of the entire human being, a salvation which has already begun even in its fullness. Mary in her entire being is already where perfect redemption exists, entirely in that region of being which came to be through Christ's Resurrection. When we speak of 'Mary's Assumption' into heaven, the 'privilege' of the Blessed Virgin implied here is simply that she has a special 'right' to this Assumption in virtue of her divine Motherhood and her unique position in saving history. It is also possible to speak of a special privilege here in so far as the temporal interval between death and bodily glorification in Mary's case must clearly be thought of as being shorter than in the case of those 'saints' in Mt 27:52 s., 'who had seen corruption'; though here of course it must not be forgotten that this distinction is conditioned not so much by the difference of the persons in themselves as by the progress in the general situation of salvation in consequence of Christ's Resurrection, before which it was precisely impossible that anyone else should rise, because the 'space' of the world's glorification could only be opened up by Christ. But a 'privilege' is implied here not in the sense that Mary alone enjoyed it or that what is involved is in a real sense an 'anticipation' of a perfection which in every respect and in every instance could only 'really' emerge later. On the contrary: salvation has already advanced so far historically that since the Resurrection it is completely 'normal' (which is not to say 'general') that there should be men in whom sin and death have already been definitively overcome. Christ's victorious descent into the kingdom of death is precisely not just an event belonging to his private existence, but a saving Event, one which affects the dead (not merely and not in the first instance those who lack the vision of God). And his entry into the eternal glory even of his body does not open up an 'empty space', but institutes a bodily community of the redeemed: however far from being complete the number of the brethren may be, and however little we may be able, with a single exception, to call them by name as those who have been redeemed even in their bodies.

Because the 'future' of the Church is the presence of the glorified Son of Man, and because this future is already present even for the Church in Mary as her most perfect representation, the Church too is already redeemed totally, not in all her members certainly but already in reality in some of them. The salvation of the flesh too has already begun in its final form. The world is already in transition to God's eternity, not only in the 'spirit' of those who have gone to their everlasting home and not only in the body of the Son who came 'from above', but also in the bodies of those who are simply 'from below'. Even now there belongs to the reality of the entire creation that new dimension which we call heaven and which we shall also be able to call new earth once it has subjected all earthly reality to itself and not just an initial part of it. Perhaps the deepest reason why Protestantism rejects the new dogma is because really it is only aware of a theology of the Cross as a formula for reality here and now, and not a theology of glory; for Protestantism this is ultimately only a promise, and not something which exists 'even now', although it has not embraced everything yet and for us here below has not yet become apparent. But for anyone who believes that counter to all appearances the forces of the world to come have already seized hold of this world, and that these forces do not consist merely in a promise, remaining beyond every sort of creaturely existence, for a future still unreal; for such a one the 'new' dogma is really nothing more than a clarification, throwing light on a state of salvation already in existence, in which he has always believed. That this state of salvation should be attributed to Mary in its entirety and fullness will not seem an impossibility to someone who knows that this salvation was born of her in virtue of the consent of her faith and in consequence has had its most perfect effect in her. The 'new' dogma has significance not only for Mariology but also for ecclesiology and general eschatology.

8

THEOLOGICAL REFLEXIONS ON MONOGENISM

THIS inquiry proposes to treat of a restricted number of questions relating to monogenism in the strictly theological sense of that word. There is no intention of undertaking a systematic and exhaustive treatment. No attention will be given to that aspect of the problem concerned with the natural sciences. And even apart from this, many things which would form part of a comprehensive treatment of the topic will be omitted or merely touched on. Nor will there be any detailed examination and assessment of modern theological literature dealing with the controversy between monogenism and polygenism.[1] Occasional references will be made to this literature only

[1] We give here a conspectus of recent literature in alphabetical order. This survey makes no claim to completeness (the writings of Catholic 'polygenists'—in the widest sense—are indicated later on). It is noticeable how small the German contribution to this literature is.
J. M. Alonso, 'La encíclica "Humani Generis"', *Illust. Cler.* XLIV (1951), p. 16; L. Arnaldich, 'Historicidad de los once primeros capitulos del Génesis a la luz de los últimos documentos eclesiásticos', *Verdad y Vida* IX (1951), pp. 385–424; F. Asensio, 'De persona Adae et de peccato originali riginante secundum Genesim', *Gregorianum* XXIX (1948), pp. 464–526; '. Ayuso Marazuela, 'Poligenismo y evoluzionismo a la luz de la Biblia y e la Teología', *Arbor* XIX (1951), pp. 347–72: J. Backes, 'Die Enzyklika Hum. Gen." und die Wissenschaft', *Trierer Theol. Zeit.* LIX (1950), pp. 26–32; J. Bataini, 'Monogénisme et polygénisme. Une explication hybride', *Div. Thom.* (Piac.) XXX (1953), pp. 363–9; A Bea, 'Die Enzyklika "Hum. Gen." Ihre Grundgedanken und ihre Bedeutung', *Scholastik* XXVI (1951), p. 36–56; C. Boyer, 'Les Leçons de l'encyclique "Hum. Gen."', *Greg.* XXXI (1950), pp. 526–39; G. Castelino, 'La storicità dei cap. 2–3 del Genesi', *alesianum* XIII (1951), pp. 334–60; J. Carles, 'L'Unité de l'espèce umaine. Polygénisme et Monogénisme', *Arch. de Phil.* XVII-2 (?), pp. 4–100; F. Ceuppens, 'Le polygénisme et la Bible', *Angel.* XXIV (1947), p. 20–32;—*Quaestiones selectae ex historia primaeva.*[2] (Turin 1948);—'Rilievi ad una nota sul poligenismo', *Sapienza* II (1949), pp. 107–9 (*contra* . Prete in *Sap.* I (1948), p. 420); G. Colombo, 'Transformismo antropo-gico e teologia', *Scuola Catt.* LXXVII (1949), pp. 17–43; P. Denis, *Les*

as a help to our own exposition. Our examination is divided into three parts: 1. The official teaching of the Church; 2. The possibility of proving monogenism from Scripture; 3. The possibility of proving monogenism metaphysically.

It will be clear from this programme alone that we have no intention of setting out explicitly the teaching of Tradition, its content, its force and its limits. This is not to say that it is of no importance. But it is not difficult to see the reason for this omission. An investigation of this kind would probably compel one very soon to take up funda-

Origines du monde et de l'humanité (Liège 1950); M. Flick, 'Il poligenismo e il dogma del peccato originale', *Greg.* XXVIII (1947), pp. 555–63; J. de Fraine, 'De Bijbel en het ontstaan van de Mens', *Streven* VI (1952), pp. 215–23; M. García Cordero, 'Evolucionismo, Poligenismo y Exegesis biblica', *Ciencia Tom.* LXXVIII (1951), pp. 465–75; 477–9; R. Garrigou-Lagrange, 'Le Monogénisme n'est-il nullement révélé, pas même implicitement?' *Doct. Comm.* II (1948), pp. 191–202; J. M. Gonzalez Ruiz, 'Contenido dogmático de la narración de Gen. 2:7 sobre la formación del hombre', *Est. Bibl.* IX (1950), pp. 399–439; J. Havet, 'L'Encyclique "Hum. Gen." et le polygénisme', *Revue dioc. de Namur* VI (1951), pp. 114–27;—'Note complémentaire sur l'encyclique "Hum. Gen." et le polygénisme', *ibid.*, pp. 219–24; C. Hauret, *Origines de l'Univers et de l'Homme*[3] (Paris 1952); M. M. Labourdette, *Le Péché originel et les origines de l'homme* (Paris 1953); C. Lattey, 'The Encyclical "Hum. Gen." and the origins of the human race. An answer', *Scripture* IV (1951), pp. 278–9; H. Lennerz, 'Quid theologo censendum est de polygenismo?' *Greg.* XXIX (1948), pp. 417–34; J. Levie 'L'Encyclique "Hum. Gen."', NRT LXII (1950), pp. 785–93; V. Marcozzi, 'Poligenismo ed evoluzione nelle origini dell'uomo', *Greg.* XXIX (1948), pp. 343–91;—'Le origini dell'uomo secondo l'enciclica "Hum Gen." e secondo la scienza', *Doct. Comm.* I (1951), pp. 26–39; B. Mariani 'Il poligenismo e s. Paolo (Rom 5:12–14),' *Euntes Docete* IV (1951), pp 120–46; E. C. Messenger (ed.), *Theology and Evolution* (London 1952); C Muller, *L'Encyclique 'Hum. Gen.' et les problèmes scientifiques* (Louvain 1951; on the Index); G. Picard, 'La Science expérimentale est-elle favorable au polygénisme?', *Sciences Ecclésiast.* IV (1951), pp. 65–89; J. Renié, *Le Origines de l'humanité d'après la Bible. Mythe ou Histoire?* (Lyons 1950) J. Rojas Fernandez and M. de la Cámara, *El Orígen del hombre según e Génesis y a la luz de la ciencia* (Madrid 1948); J. Sagüés, 'La encíclica "Hum Gen." Avances teológicos', *Estud. Eclesiast.* XXV (1951), pp. 147–80 M. Schulien, *L'Unità del genere umano alla luce delle ultime risultanze antro pologiche, linguistiche ed etnologiche*[3] (Milan 1947); E. Stakemeier, 'Di Enzyklika "Hum. Gen."', *Theol. u. Glaube* XL (1950), pp. 481–93; G Vandenbroeck and L. Renwart, 'L'Encyclique "Hum. Gen." et les science naturelles', NRT LXXIII (1951), pp. 337–51; G. Weigel, 'Gleanings fron the Commentaries on "Hum. Gen."', TS XII (1951), pp. 520–49.

mental theological considerations of great generality, and these cannot be undertaken with sufficient thoroughness in a short essay. For the question would soon arise as to what constitutes a 'unanimous' witness of 'Tradition', i.e. whether the tradition is a really *theological* one in the strict sense. It is not easy to answer this question. For it must be borne in mind that another 'tradition' which is at least as unanimous exists in regards to the creation of the first man, a question which is very closely related to our own. And yet we know from the most recent pronouncements of the *magisterium*, which leave the question of some sort of transformism open to the free investigation of theology and the other sciences, that a unanimous 'tradition' like this is never sufficient of itself as a conclusive argument for a definite view which it represents; and we know then that in the case of transformism there is no certain agreement as to whether the tradition is a really theological one which binds the theologian. If we were to investigate Tradition in our case, then, we should either have to go into the difficult question of what sort of tradition was involved and what principles of discrimination were applicable, or we should have to consider not Tradition as such but the objective arguments proposed in it (on the basis of Scripture or other dogmas). It is the latter course which we shall in fact pursue in the following reflexions.

I. MONOGENISM AND THE OFFICIAL TEACHING OF THE CHURCH

1. The Encyclical 'Humani Generis'

For reasons of method we begin with the *latest* utterance of the *magisterium* to do with our question. It is not only in a purely temporal sense that it is the latest. The reason why it forms the proper starting-point of our investigation is that it is the only one to treat of the topic *ex professo*, and treat of it in the context of the latest controversies; thus it is the latest by reason of an acquaintance with the questions and results of modern science, which were not available in earlier times to set the background of the problem. In addition, by leaving the question of anthropological transformism open to theological discussion, 'Humani Generis' has—in appearance at least—made the theological problem more difficult. For one thing is clear from the start. It was once usual to offer a simple and direct theological proof of monogenism. Applied to the corresponding question of anthropological transformism, this would inevitably lead to its condemnation as obviously false theologically. Now such a simplicity and directness cannot be correct. For if it were (just as the practice really used to be once in both questions without distinction) the Church would not be able even temporarily to leave the question of transformism free for theological dispute. We should thus be well advised to make a start with 'Humani Generis'.

We find the following statement in the encyclical 'Humani Generis' of 1950:

> Cum vero de alia coniecturali opinione agitur, videlicet de poly-genismo quem vocant, tum Ecclesiae filii eiusmodi libertate minime fruuntur. Non enim christifideles eam sententiam amplecti possunt quam qui retinent asseverant vel post Adam hisce in terris veros homines exstitisse, qui non ab eodem prouti omnium protoparente, naturali generatione originem duxerint, vel Adam significare multi-tudinem quandam protoparentum; cum nequaquam appareat, quomodo huiusmodi sententia componi queat cum iis quae fontes revelatae veritatis et acta Magisterii Ecclesiae proponunt de peccato originali, quod procedit ex peccato vero commisso ab uno Adamo, quodque generatione in omnes transfusum inest unicuique pro-prium.[1]

There is little to be said as far as the letter of the text is concerned. The opposite opinion called 'polygenism' which the encyclical rejects is first of all formally characterized as a *coniecturalis opinio*. This is a way of saying that even within the natural sciences and anthropo-logical paleontology the view is no more than a hypothesis; so that it is not *a priori* impossible even from this point of view that the opinion should be rejected as false because of information derived from a source *other* than the sources of natural science. The description of polygenism which follows does not regard it purely as an hypothesis of natural science; it is taken up from the only viewpoint which could be of interest to theology. In this sense (i.e. looked at from the point of view of the 'Adam' of theology) polygenism is the doctrine which either leaves room for the existence, after the Adam of theology, of other men who do not belong to his bodily posterity; or which holds that 'Adam' is a collective concept which combines into one the totality

---

[1] Denz 3028. Cf. also the encyclical 'Summi Pontificatus', in which the same teaching seems to have found an earlier expression, AAS XXX (1939), pp. 426 s.

of human progenitors. By taking polygenism in this sense the encyclical clearly intends to avoid the question of the so-called Pre-Adamites: whether, that is to say, other human groups might not have existed before 'Adam', the sinful progenitor of the whole human race which was going to exist on earth after him, those earlier groups having died out. This view is not sanctioned, nor again is it rejected; it simply remains outside the theological discussion of the encyclical. This is not of course to say that a theologian may not hold that Pre-Adamitism is a theory which is scientifically speaking arbitrary, as well as being absurd and dangerous theologically.[1]

What is said of polygenism formally and substantially characterized in this way is that it is not a free opinion in the Church, it cannot be held. Thus it is not permitted positively to defend polygenism even as a possible theory or scientific hypothesis, the grounds of this inadmissibility being of course theological and not derived from natural science. Quite intentionally, a more precise theological *qualification* (for instance, 'This opinion is heretical') is not given. Thus the only theological qualification of monogenism which may be derived from the encyclical just by itself is that it is theologically certain.[2] That is to

---

[1] I hold that it is not sufficient to qualify this theory with Vandenbroeck and Renwart (p. 349) as merely 'antiquated and lacking in interest'. Cf. also Levie (p. 789). This seventeenth-century theory is a characteristic product of an attempt to reconcile theology and secular science (so-called) in an external and basically nominalistic way. Could anyone but a nominalist, for whom reality consists of an atomized sum of divine decrees, conceive the idea that God calls one man to a supernatural end, and another of exactly the same nature, simply to a natural end? And the angels again are joined together with one part of humanity in being given a supernatural end. Again, it would be necessary in the case of these Pre-Adamites who have come into being in this polygenistic way, that they should have died out just at the time of Adam—an arbitrary postulate. It would be improper on this view for Adam to have descended from them—another arbitrary postulate. The whole position is contrary to the way of looking at things we find in Scripture: Adam is the Man, not the surviving representative of human group. If there had been Pre-Adamites, God can 'become man' more than once. On the basis of what calculations does this possibility cease to be realized once Adam comes into existence? No, Adam was the first man; and where for the first time a man is to be found in the metaphysical and theological sense, that is where we must look for Adam, even if this is in the late Tertiary period.

[2] We are aware of the kind of discussion this concept requires, its 'general problematic'. It is often said that something is 'theologically certain' if it

say, according to the current state of the Church's consciousness in faith, of the doctrinal pronouncements of her *magisterium* and of theology, monogenism must be affirmed with inner (but not in itself irreformable) assent. And this assent must be given for two reasons: because on the one hand it has not been possible, at least up to now, to say that polygenism is without danger for assured truths of faith; and on the other because monogenism itself seems to be at least contained (*mitgesagt*) in doctrinal statements; and our assent must be given in so far as this is the case. Consequently opposition to monogenism—without sufficient grounds—would threaten to deprive these statements, in which monogenism is contained, of their sense, and would imply the denial of a statement of which it can be said with good reason (though not with absolute certainty) that it is to be found in the sources of Revelation. No stronger qualification—as far as the encyclical goes—can be given. For if any such attempt were made it would be easy to reply by asking why the encyclical itself does not give this stronger qualification. It would not have been difficult. And we have no right to assume that the encyclical has been lacking in courage and in theological decision.

Now it is indeed *theoretically* possible that a pronouncement of the *magisterium* should in fact allow only of a weaker qualification, while a theologian could on other grounds decide for a stronger one.[1] But

---

can be inferred from a revealed truth only with the help of a truth of natural reason. By qualifying monogenism as theologically certain we naturally do not wish to say that the truth of monogenism cannot itself be revealed. We use this problematic theological concept in a more general sense: by 'theologically certain' we mean anything of which on the one hand it cannot be said with absolute certainty that it is revealed by God and is indubitably taught as such by the Church; and which yet on the other hand can legitimately claim our interior assent, in such a way that a contrary doctrine is not tolerated by the Church.

[1] J. F. Sagüés (*Sacrae Theologiae Summa* II, Madrid 1952, n. 545) reviews the usual qualifications of the monogenistic thesis in these terms: 'etsi non constet thesim umquam explicite magisterio sollemni definitam, theologi eam expresse vel aequivalenter habent (a) aut communius ut de fide vel simpliciter (Pesch, Flick, Card. Ruffini), vel divina (Lahousse, Minges) vel etiam catholica (Janssens, van Noort, Beraza, Hugon) vel etiam saltem implicite definita (Boyer, Lercher, Pohle-Gierens, Muncunill, Daffara, Lennerz, Huarte, Bozzola); (b) aut saltem ut fidei proximam (Tanquerey, Garrigou-Lagrange)'. For Sagüés himself, 'de fide divina et catholica, imo implicite definita (Denz 788–91)'. Concerning these qualifications i

this is highly improbable in the concrete case with which we are concerned. The clear intention of the encyclical is to exclude polygenism from theology. The simplest and most radical way of doing this would have been to declare that such a teaching was in direct contradiction to the teaching of faith, or to have branded it explicitly as heretical. If however the encyclical did not do this, it may very well be taken as a sign that the Church's *magisterium* does not (or does not yet) suppose such a qualification possible in the current state of her consciousness in faith and of theological reflexion. Consequently it is

---

must first of all be noted that nearly all of them belong before 'Humani Generis' and before a moderate transformism was permitted. Further they all belong to that period of exegesis which believed that it was possible immediately to extract the historical content of Gen 1–3 without taking into consideration its specific literary genus; on this view it was possible to hold that monogenism was stated with complete explicitness, and was thus *de fide divina*. Finally, transformism is rejected by many of the authors cited with a correspondingly higher theological qualification. Beraza, for instance, held that every kind of transformism was temerarious in the highest degree, and cited authors who regarded the creation of man out of inorganic matter as *fides catholica* (Suarez, Valentia, Perrone, Katschthaler, Jungmann, Mazzella, Lahousse). Huarte held that any kind of transformism was temerarious. Hugon regarded its contrary as guaranteed by the literal sense of Scripture. For Pesch the rejection of transformism is 'evidently' taught in Scripture. Minges and Janssens hold like views A critical revision of the methods which led to this over-emphatic qualification would doubtless show that polygenism by no means deserves exactly the same qualification as transformism; rather it would seem that the revised methods would conduce to a greater restraint in allotting theological qualifications than was practised by the authors whom Sagüés cites. Further, it would not do to get the impression that the certainty of the monogenistic doctrine is as highly qualified by all theologians as it is by Sagüés and his authorities. He himself cites Tanquerey and Garrigou-Lagrange as giving a lower qualification. To these should be added, for the period before 'Humani Generis', Diekamp-Hoffmann (*fidei proximum*), and in recent times C. Hauret, J. de Fraine, L. Ott (*sententia certa*: *Fundamentals of Christian Dogma*[2], ET. Patrick Lynch (Cork 1958), p. 96), A. Gelin (*Problèmes d'Ancien Testament* (Lyons 1952); cf. *Eph. Theol. Lov.* XXVIII (1952), pp. 285 s.), C. Muller, J. M. Alonso, J. Havet, Labourdette. The last-named says quite rightly (p. 204): 'On sera autorisé à dire en théologie que des assertions inséparables de celle qui a été définie ne peuvent pas être niées; mais on ne le serait pas à prétendre que, du moins en vertu de ce texte-là, elles sont définies aussi. C'est ce qui nous a paru être le cas du "monogénisme".' Furthermore Sagüés himself says in regard to the qualification which may be derived from 'Humani Generis', *saltem theologice certa* (n. 543).

hardly probable that an individual theologian by himself and on his own account should see more deeply than the *magisterium*. At any rate a theologian who claims no greater certainty in this question ought not to be accused of minimalism or indecision.

Many people may find this situation unsatisfactory. But it is undoubtedly an essential part of theological conviction and its growth that there should exist theological certitudes and obligations to a positive inner assent which are not 'in themselves' those proper to a definition and the assent of *fides divina et catholica*. If this is so, the 'per se' in the *assensus per se non irreformabilis* of a theological certitude ought not to be expounded so as to give the impression that this revision of assent could never occur at all. For this would be to continue verbally to grant the existence of a distinction between a theologically certain proposition and a proposition of faith (*fides divina e catholica* or *fides ecclesiastica*) while annulling it in fact: so when a theologian declares that what is involved is an *assensus per se reformabilis*, he must not be reproached with wanting to dissolve or to throw doubt upon the certitude of the proposition concerned. All he is doing is to apply to a given proposition what is maintained in theory by all theologians in *theologia fundamentalis*, and furthermore what the history of theology requires us to say.

Corresponding to this assessment in the light of 'Humani Generis' of the degree of theological certainty to be attributed to monogenism we should note the way in which the encyclical provides grounds for its teaching. In the first place (and this is remarkable) it does not appeal to the texts of Scripture and the *magisterium* which speak *directly* of the one Adam as progenitor of all men. Had it been the view of the *magisterium* that it was certain that monogenism was unambiguously stated in these texts, it would simply have cited them and perhaps laid it down in an authentic interpretation that monogenism was in fact the true meaning of these texts. But in reality the encyclical merely refers us to an indirect argument: monogenism is logically presupposed by the dogma of original sin, unless this too is given an inadmissible interpretation.[1] But this connexion is itself asserted in the

---

[1] This is obviously what the phrase 'ex peccato vere commisso' points to. One tendency in modern Protestant exegesis, which has found favour here and there even among Catholic theologians (though this sympathy has not manifested itself in a literary form), has been to deny the 'act'-uality (*'Tatsächlichkeit'*) of a once-for-all historical process at the beginning of human

most cautious way: the encyclical does *not* say: *cum appareat nequaquam componi posse* ... ; it says *neququam appareat quomodo* ... *componi queat*. ... We may well suppose that this milder and more cautious formulation was chosen deliberately. What is being stated is not a positive declaration of the irreconcilability of polygenism and the Catholic doctrine of original sin, but a denial of the obviousness (not in fact to be had) of a possibility of reconciliation. It goes without saying that a formulation of this kind neither offers the slightest indication nor makes any positive affirmation as to whether at some later date this reconcilability might not or could not be recognized. Thus it cannot be said that the encyclical positively 'leaves the door open' for some future polygenistic theory. Nor, on the other hand, is any positive statement made to the effect that something of the sort is always going to be impossible. Thus the attitude adopted is precisely that which theology describes with respect to the propositions which it calls theologically certain. Of course the fact that the encyclical restricts itself to this indirect probative procedure with a reference to the dogma of original sin does not mean that the theologian is prevented from bringing other arguments to bear in favour of monogenism. Admittedly it would hardly be modest if he wished meanwhile to claim for such an argument—looked at theologically and in view of a theological qualification—a greater degree of stringency than for the argument briefly sketched by the encyclical.

In view of the firm attitude of the *magisterium* in this matter and its wise restraint, one is bound to conclude that its previous utterances as regards our question cannot be regarded with absolute certainty and clarity as a formal definition of monogenism. It is clear first of all that up till now (leaving aside the decree of the Biblical Commission, which is not a definition) the Church has never imposed her anathema on polygenism as such in a decision having the form of a definition, directly and explicitly taking up a stand with regard to it. For up till now it has not been a centre of theological interest, and a definitory

history, and to make of original sin (as *peccatum originale originans*) the mythological expression of a condition 'always and everywhere' to be found because of what man himself is as such: thus original sin takes place always and everywhere. On this view of original sin there could obviously be no question of presupposing monogenism. (It is often important to remember that the ordinary German expression for original sin, *Erbsünde*, means literally 'hereditary sin'.—Tr.)

intention of this kind, formally directed against polygenism, is nowhere to be demonstrated. Moreover, in view of the attitude adopted by the encyclical, it is not even possible to speak of monogenism as *certainly* contained in the Tridentine doctrine of original sin in virtue of so *formal* an implication that it would have to be called an implicitly defined truth of faith (granting that there was no intention of defining it directly). For the question precisely arises as to whether the single sinful ancestor of all men, of whom the definition speaks, must *necessarily* be understood in the sense of monogenism alone; and this not merely as an idea belonging in historical fact to the mental background of the Fathers of the Council, but as something which the intention was to teach in the form of a definition. It is possible to show (as we shall try to do) that an objective connexion holds between monogenism and the Council's teaching on original sin, in such wise that to contest the former is implicitly to deny the latter. But at the moment at any rate, the demonstration of this connexion is by no means so immediately obvious *quoad nos* that one can speak without hesitation of a formal implication of monogenism in the Tridentine teaching on original sin, and could thus claim for it the status of something in fact already defined in substance. If that were the case, the encyclical would not have stated the connexion with such prudent restraint.

We need not here go into detail about the occasion of this teaching of the ordinary *magisterium*. It is well known that there were individual theologians in the years before the appearance of 'Humani Generis' who believed that the polygenist theory was an open question in the same sense as transformism, the solution of which could be left to the natural scientists.[1] And in individual cases polygenism was

---

[1] The names of a few writers may be mentioned here, not so as to brand them as 'polygenists', but because they raise in their writings, more or less circumspectly, the question whether polygenism might not be an open problem for the theologian: E. Amann, 'Préadamites', DTC XII (1933), col. 2799 s.;—'Transformisme', DTC XV (1946), col. 389 s.; J. Batain, 'Monogénisme et Polygénisme', *Div. Thom.* (Piac.) XXVI (1949), pp. 187–201; A. and J. Bouyssonie, 'Polygénisme', DTC XII (1933), col. 2520–36, esp. 2534 s.; J. Chaine, *Le Livre de la Genèse* (Paris 1948), p. 54 s. A. M. Dubarle, *Les Sages d'Israel* (Paris 1946), p. 21 s.;—'Sciences de la vie et dogme chrétien', *La Vie Intell.* XV (1946), p. 624; J. Guitton, *La Pensée moderne et le catholicisme* (Aix 1936), p. 39; A. Liénard, 'Le Chrétien devant les progrès de la science', *Etudes* CCLV (1947), pp. 299 s.; A. Mancini, 'Monogenismo e polygenismo. Informazioni', *Pal. del Clero* XXVII (1949), pp. 904–8; B. Prete, 'A proposito del poligenismo', *Sap.* I (1948

positively maintained. Other theologians were doubtful about the theological certainty of monogenism. Consequently attempts were made here and there to assess the possibility of reconciling polygenism with the Church's doctrine of original sin: the assumption relied on here was that a plurality of ancestors could jointly act as the cause of original sin, and this plurality of ancestors was combined in Scripture in the idea of the one Adam.

2. The Decree of the Biblical Commission of 1909 (Denz 2123)

However readily one may grant that the more recent declarations of the *magisterium*[1] permit of, or authorize, a wider interpretation of the decree of the Biblical Commission of 1909, no one can doubt the force of this decree even today.[2] As regards the matter with which we are concerned, the decree teaches that among other things the *generis humani unitas* too belongs to the historical content of Gen 2–3. The expression may in itself be undefined and vague, but it cannot be doubted that what is meant is the monogenistic unity of the human race, and not some merely specific or other conceivable unity. For the specific unity is not in question; and any other unity (apart from the two just mentioned) is not easy to grasp. It would, as it were, have to be discovered or invented first; so that the decree cannot have had it in mind. Thus a concept not yet available would first have to be found; and it would further have to be shown of this concept that it does as much justice to the ultimate theological intention of the decree as monogenistic unity, which the decree without any doubt had primarily in mind. Thus it can be said that in virtue of the continuing force of this decree monogenism is theologically certain, as the single

---

p. 420 s.; H. Rondet, 'Les Origines humaines et la théologie. Problèmes pour la réflexion chrétienne', *Cité Nouvelle* (= *Etudes*) I (1943), pp. 973–87.
[1] It is expressly said in the reply of the Secretary of the Biblical Commission to Cardinal Suhard, a reply sanctioned by Pius XII, that this decree should be understood and interpreted in the light of the Pope's recommendations, in which exegetes are encouraged to make a *fresh* approach to difficult problems in such a way that their solution might be in full harmony not only with orthodox doctrine but also with the assured results of modern science. Thus it is emphatically maintained that the decree in no way prohibits a more searching examination of the problems in question in accordance with the results of research over the last forty years (Denz 3002).
[2] Cf. Denz 3002; 3029.

tangible point so far as we are concerned here: a result which takes us no further than 'Humani Generis'. It is stated in the decree that this *unitas* belongs to the *sensus litteralis historicus* of the first three chapters of Genesis. We may ignore the fact that the concept of the *sensus litteralis historicus* has undergone a sharpening of definition—and in some respects a restriction—as a result of the declarations already mentioned. Even so, the conclusion we have reached leaves an important question open: do purely exegetical means allow us to establish the fact that the monogenistic unity of man is contained in Gen 2–3? Nothing is stated on this point. We cannot simply take it for granted that it was the intention of the decree to indicate the possibility of doing so as something which goes without saying. For then we should also have to say, for example, that purely exegetical means (without the help, therefore, of the rest of Scripture and of Tradition) would allow us to derive with certainty from Gen 3:18 the *Reparatori futuri promissio*. It may well be doubted whether all exegetes would undertake such a task.[1] In other words, the decree of 1909 does not require us to maintain that the monogenistic unity of the human race is not only contained in Gen 2–3, but also that it can be derived from this text by purely exegetical means and thus can be known from it *quoad nos*. Thus a theologian who is not prepared to admit the stringency of such a proof does not go counter to the decree. Obviously this is to say nothing *against* the possibility of such an exegesis: the question is left open. Thus the encyclical's approach has already been preformed, as it were, inasmuch as it does not prove monogenism simply by a Scriptural citation (say Gen 2:6 s. 18.21; 3:20; A 17:24–26) but by a process of theological discussion. We can sum up, then, by saying that the decree of the Biblical Commission of 1909 takes us no further than the teaching of 'Humani Generis', either as regards theological qualification or by way of supplying fresh ground of proof.

3. The Council of Trent

In the canons of the Council of Trent on original sin many theologians see an implicit definition of monogenism.[2] Clearly it is in

---

[1] Flick says (p. 558): 'Anche sei testi biblici dell'Antico Testamento potessero, considerati astrattamente, non repugnare assolutamente poligenismo. . . .'

[2] See above, p. 234, n. 1: all the theologians who hold that monogenism (at the very least) implicitly defined have the Council of Trent in mind.

possible here to examine more closely what is really meant by 'implicitly defined'; whether such a concept allows of being reconciled with CIC c. 1323 §3, or whether 'defined' (and so 'manifeste' ascertained to be defined)[1] and 'by way of inclusion' (and so, while not perhaps 'manifeste', yet ascertained to be defined) do not cancel each other out.[2] Let us adopt as simple as possible a way of establishing what the Council of Trent has to say to us.

We should first remind ourselves of two obvious points which are easily forgotten. On the one hand, it is possible for a Council to teach or to define something even when it has no knowledge of the problems which only arise later in connexion with its teaching. Thus it would be wrong to say or to assume that, because the Council had no knowledge of polygenism and monogenism as a problem of secular science, therefore it is *a priori* impossible that it should have said anything of importance on this matter. On the other hand, it is not *a priori* impossible that a Council should formulate a doctrinal statement in such a way that one could see in the light of historical studies that the statement has been reached under the influence of a presupposition which turns out later to be false or unnecessary. The essential proviso here is that the presupposition actually made is not itself expressed (and so is no more than an actual presupposition of the mode of expression), and that what is really expressed has its own objective validity apart from the presupposition. We may take an example from a field quite

---

[1] One might well ask if something can be ascertained to be defined 'manifeste' except when the *intention* of the definition is known. But this is precisely not given in the case of something *implicite definitum*. (The text of CIC c. 1323 §3 runs: 'Declarata seu definita dogmatice res nulla intelligitur, nisi id manifeste constiterit.'—Tr.)

[2] If *implicite definitum* means no more than 'implicitly contained in a definition', such that this being-contained can be brought to expression by logical operations, then there is of course no doubt that something of the sort exists. What *is* doubtful, however, is whether it can be said to be 'defined'. One would have to go on to ask what the various ways are in which a proposition may be implicitly contained in another (defined) statement, and what degree of certainty the implicit proposition has, compared to that of the other proposition, according to which of the ways it is contained (formal or virtual implication; two concepts, again, whose meaning it is not easy to set out clearly and sharply). The controversies, still not settled, over *fides divina* and *fides ecclesiastica* and their relationship in the matter of what can be defined as revealed by God, show how many obscurities remain in the apparently simple concept of something *implicite definitum*.

close to our own. The Council of Carthage, followed by many other Councils and doctrinal pronouncements, says (Denz 102) that original sin is incurred *generatione*. Speaking as historians, we must say that the Fathers of the Council thought of *generatio* in an Augustinian way, as involving *libido*; in other words, they thought of generation as communicating original sin because and in so far as it is bound up with sexual desire; and we must say then that this idea was one of the reasons which made them formulate their statement in just the way they did. But this does not prevent us from saying today (any more than it did in the Middle Ages) that what was stated in the definition of Carthage retains its validity even without this idea[1], and that what is presupposed by the formulation (not the formulation itself) is false. In other words, not everything which can be learned from the text of the definition as belonging to the mind of the definer is by that very fact defined. It may be said, conversely, that something is co-defined (*mitdefiniert*) which, although it is not directly intended by the definer as properly speaking to be defined, fulfils the two following conditions. Firstly, it must have been certainly compresent to the definer's mind (*mitgedacht*); and secondly, which is more important, it must stand in so immediate, so immediately evident and indissoluble a connexion with the proper and direct matter of the definition, that it is impossible in fact or in thought that it too should not bear the whole weight of the affirmation given to the proper content of the definition.[2] If this is not the case, i.e. if the connexion between what was compresent to mind and what was properly intended by the definition is not seen quite directly and quite explicitly as such, although it is quite objectively given and even demonstrable, then what was compresent to mind cannot be spoken of as defined. We could say that it can be derived from a definition as a presupposition or a consequence of what is contained in the definition; but it cannot be said to be affirmed by the definer with that absolute affirmation which he gives to the proper content of his definition. For suppose one were to ask the definer if

---

[1] This idea is still very clearly to be seen at work in the discussions of the Council of Trent.

[2] One could ultimately in this case speak of something 'implicitly defined' But in our view it would seem preferable to say that what we have here i something (expressly) 'co-defined', something clearly and unavoidabl 'co-expressed' in the definition, possessing the same theological grade a that upon which the intention to express directly bears.

such a case, 'Are you affirming what was in fact compresent to your mind just as absolutely as what you properly defined, and are you doing so for the very reason that this latter is what you are defining?' Then in this given case he would have to reply, 'I must think about this first, i.e. I must first reflect on the connexion between what is defined and what was merely compresent to my mind (as a matter of fact, first and foremost).' But what he is saying here implicitly is that he has not defined what was compresent to his mind at the time, but only that he *might be* in a position to define it on some future occasion, when in fact there emerges on further explicit reflexion an indissoluble connexion between what was defined and what was compresent to mind at the time. Thus this affirmation of the *possibility* of definition depends (so far as the individual theologian is concerned) on the stringency of the knowledge of this connexion.

If we apply what has been said to the canons of the Council of Trent, the following conclusions would seem to be true.

a. The Fathers of the Council had no intention of defining monogenism, nor does anyone in fact assert this. The definition and so its substance are directed against the Pelagian denial, renewed by Erasmus[1], of the existence of a hereditary sin; in this heresy the condition of sinfulness prior to personal sin is replaced by personal sins which each person commits for himself in his own lifetime, though certainly in imitation of Adam. Because the Council's intention was to define the existence of hereditary sin over against personal guilt, we cannot say that the phrase 'origine unum' (in the sense of a chain of causality derived from a *single* individual) is as such defined. If this were the case, we could obviously say that monogenism was defined implicitly. But is this the case? That precisely is the question.[2] It is a question which cannot simply be answered in the affirmative without further proof, if it was indeed the intention of the Council to establish the existence of a state of guilt prior to personal sins against the teaching

---

[1] Cf., e.g., S. Ehses, *Concilium Tridentinum* V, p. 212. References will also be found here to Erasmus's teaching on original sin as an *imitatio* of Adam's sin.

[2] Lennerz (p. 421) seems simply to assume this. This makes it very difficult to see why the only use he makes of the consideration that polygenism does away with the unity of origin of hereditary sin is to show that monogenism is not a matter of indifference to dogma (p. 423).

of Pelagianism (and of Pelagian essays at the time of the Council, such as that of Erasmus). Certainly no one denies that the Council *could* have taught more and even defined more than what is necessarily posited in the mere contradictory opposite of the rejected heresy. But the question is whether it has in fact done so, that is (in our case), whether as well as just teaching the unity of origin of hereditary sin it also defined it; and further (this too) defined it in such a way that a 'moral' unity of origin of hereditary sin is not merely something which did not enter the Council's field of vision but has been objectively excluded by means of an authentic definition. But the proof of this is so complicated as itself to serve as a proof that there can be no question of a definition here but rather of an inference from what was defined.

b. There is no doubt that in this definition there is contained a statement (*mitgesagt*) that a single individual stands at the beginning of human history, who as 'first man'[1] and as ancestor of all men handed down original sin to his posterity by means of the natural bond of generation (Denz 788, 789, 791, 793). Original sin is spoken of as *origine unum* (Denz 790), in saying which the Fathers of the Council once again had in mind the single deed of a single historical ancestor. It cannot be doubted that the Conciliar Fathers had in mind only a single, numerically individual person at the beginning of human history, who by means of his unique historical act instituted the sinfulness of the race, a sinfulness which becomes each individual man's own in so far as he is connected with his fellows and so with the first ancestor by a bond of natural, biological generation. It cannot be doubted that the whole Tridentine teaching on original sin is formulated on this presupposition. Nor is it a matter for doubt that something contained (*mitgesagt*) in this way in the solemn definition of a fundamental dogma is of great theological weight, even if it is not defined.

---

[1] If Adam is the *primus homo* (Denz 788) in relation to *omne genus humanum* (Denz 789), to *omnes homines*, then the defenders of an implicit definition of monogenism would also have to say (if they are consistent) that the falsehood of any Pre-Adamite theory is equally defined implicitly. The fact that they do not do so, but rather expressly reject this view, puts the affirmation of the implicit definition of monogenism in an unfavourable light.

c. Yet it may be doubted whether monogenism is itself implicitly defined or, better, co-defined (*mitdefiniert*). The question here is no longer whether it is clearly a necessary presupposition of the Tridentine teaching. To demonstrate this would still be far conceptually from demonstrating that what we have here is an implicit definition. This would only be demonstrated once it had first been shown that what was *concurrently* asserted (Mit-*gesagte*) by the Conciliar Fathers about monogenism was for them so precisely and *immediately* a composite part (*mitgesetzt*) of their doctrine of hereditary sin that their absolute affirmation of the one had to extend with the same force and unambiguity to the other—and this is doubtful. Once again we have to start from the fact that the Conciliar Fathers *did not want* to define monogenism. But then the burden of proof does not fall upon those who doubt the status of monogenism as something defined but on those who assert it. This proof is not effected by demonstrating that monogenism is *concurrently* asserted by the Fathers in the definition of the doctrine of original sin, nor even when it is clear over and above this that the Conciliar Fathers did not engage in reflexion as to the possibility or impossibility of separating what was defined and what was concurrently asserted, or that the Fathers knew nothing of such a possibility, or (had they turned their minds to this question) would have rejected it. All this can in certain circumstances prove that anyone who defines the Conciliar doctrine of original sin or affirms it absolutely must *logically* do this in respect of monogenism, but not that he has already done so.

The question ultimately amounts to this: does what the Council defined concerning original sin stand in an objectively indissoluble and *immediate* connexion with monogenism? If the connexion exists, *and* exists immediately and so is clearly to be seen immediately and at once, then it is possible to speak of an implicit definition. If the connexion does indeed exist, but the demonstration of the indissoluble connexion requires relatively involved consideration which, looked at in itself, is not entirely free from doubt, then we can speak of a possibility of definition (definability) and of a theological certainty, but not of a definition already (implicitly) achieved. We shall be concerned in Section II with the demonstration of this connexion, and it will appear there that a demonstration is not as simple as it might seem at first sight. In other words the doctrine of a state of sin pertaining to a number of men in virtue of an historical event prior to an individual act of sin committed by each one of them does indeed imply mono-genism (as we shall see); but it does not imply it with that immediacy which would be necessary for an implicit definition.

It might be objected that instead of 'historical event' in the previous sentence what should have been said (as in the Council) was precisely 'through the historical act of an *individual*', which would have made the whole matter clear and clearly in favour of an implicit definition of monogenism. The answer to this is twofold. (a) In this case too, monogenism would unquestionably be defined if the 'generatione (propagatione)', so far as it means more than just the contradictory opposite of 'imitatione', were regarded as defined in the sense of a mode in which hereditary sin is handed down. That is, it would have to be *defined* not only that a guilt derived from someone else exists prior to the personal decision of the individual (*non imitatione*), but that this can be inherited only by a *biological* bond of generation with the historical cause of this guilt ('generatione' as more than 'non imitatione'). De Fraine for example contests this.[1] In other words it could be asked whether the 'generatione' (in so far as it is the object of the *definition*) means more than 'non imitatione'.[2] If this were not the

---

[1] Pp. 57–62. (If this is a reference to the article cited at the beginning of this study, it is obviously wrong, but I have not been able to check it.—Tr.)

[2] Not much information on this point is to be gained from the Conciliar discussions. It is generally evident that the precise point of our question was not under consideration. There was a desire to repudiate the Pelagian error, which instead of original sin only admitted an *imitatio* of the first sinner. Ideas about why and how *generatio, propagatio* handed on original sin were pretty confused. There was still a widespread idea that the cause of the handing down of original sin was an infection of the flesh due to *generatio*, and theologians were still fairly far from regarding *generatio* as a pure, non-causal condition under which original sin was passed on (cf., e.g., Ehses V, p. 174: *propagatione et libidine inordinata transfunditur*; p. 176: the *caro corrupta* causes original sin in the soul infused into it; similarly p. 180; p. 166: *contrahitur ex carne infecta*; p. 181: *transfunditur in omnes ex carne infecta ex generatione*, offered as a summary of the view of the Conciliar Fathers!). This fact alone warns us of the need for a certain caution. If we were to take 'propagatione' as defined even in so far as it says more than 'non imitatione' (it is often spoken of in the acts of the Council as a pure opposite of 'imitatione'), then it would be strictly consistent to say that it should be taken in the sense in which most of the Conciliar Fathers took it: in the Augustinian sense of the corruption of the flesh due to 'libidinous' generation as the immediate cause of the soul's infection with guilt.

case, the fact that the Council speaks of the guilt of an individual does not lead in this case either to any clear consequence in the direction of monogenism. However, we do not intend to examine this question here. (b) But that is not the main answer to this objection. As we shall see, it may be shown with sufficient certainty that the 'individual' of which the Council speaks as the originator of hereditary sin must really be an individual, because otherwise the defined doctrine of hereditary sin would no longer retain its force. But what is not proved by this is that this unique individuality of 'Adam' is itself thereby defined.

4. The Vatican Council[1]

In the original schema of a 'Constitutio dogmatica de doctrina catholica contra multiplices errores ex rationalismo derivatos' monogenism was included as a doctrine of faith, and the polygenism which opposed it was branded as heretical. Appeal was made for this purpose to the explicit testimony of Scripture in the Old and New Testaments (Gen 1:28; 3:20; Wis 10:1; Ac 17:26), and it was pointed out that the denial of monogenism infringed (*violatur*) both the dogma of original sin as well as that of the redemption of all men by the one Christ, and thus came into conflict with Rom 5:18.[2] The

---

[1] For the following see: *Collectio Lacensis* VII, col. 515 s. (the theologians' schema, chiefly due to Franzelin, 'De doctrina catholica cap. 15: de communi totius humani generis origine ab uno Adamo'); col. 544, n. 3 (a note on this chapter of the schema); col. 555 (*Schema reformatum constitutionis dogmaticae de doctrina catholica*, cap. 2: 'De hominis creatione et natura'); col. 566 (canon II, 4 of the canons of the revised schema: 'Si quis universum genus humanum ab uno protoparente Adam ortum esse negaverit: anathema sit'); col. 1633 (cap. 6 of the schema as revised by Martin and Kleutgen); col. 1637 (the corresponding canon of the revised schema: 'Si quis universum genus humanum ab uno protoparente ortum esse negaverit: anathema sit'). As is well known, only the first four chapters of this schema were thoroughly discussed by the Council's *Deputatio de fide* (January–March 1870) and laid before the Council in the form of a proposal for a *constitutio dogmatica de fide catholica* in its own right (col. 69 s.). The *Deputatio de fide* did indeed continue to discuss the second part of the original schema; but this part never reached the General Congregation of the Council, still less was it voted upon in a public sitting.

[2] The annotations to the first schema (col. 544) still further developed this indirect argument. It is said there that doubt was cast upon monogenism 'nostra aetate ab hominibus quibusdam ex levissimis rationibus geologicis et ethnographicis'. Labourdette himself (p. 158) remarks: 'On ne pourrait

discontinuation of the Council prevented any further treatment of the schema.

The first thing to strike one about the much-revised schema is the fact that neither chapter nor canon make allowance for any kind of Pre-Adamitism. Had the text been defined in the form proposed, this theory, which 'Humani Generis' prudently avoids, would have been heretical, which suggests the need for a certain prudence in our estimate of the schema. And this is independent of the fact that it did not achieve the status of a definition, that it is not the last word for theology: we must not be in too much of a hurry to wonder how things might have gone, if... Otherwise one could also pronounce sentence on Molinism, for example, in view of the fate it suffered at the hands of the theologians during the congregations *de Auxiliis*.[1] Nor ought the general parallels between the decree 'De Doctrina Catholica' of the Provincial Council of Cologne in 1860 and the Vatican schema to be overlooked. These are especially noteworthy as regards the title, purpose and choice of matters dealt with. Chapter 14 of the Cologne decree[2] rejects equally transformism (even in

---

plus parler aujourd'hui avec cette hauteur'. In the revised schema the direct argument is brought more into the foreground; here it is said (col. 555) that polygenism does injury to (*laeditur*) the dogmas of original sin and redemption. In the note it is further added: 'tertium dogma, quod statuitur, est unitas generis humani, de quo nulla est difficultas'. In the further revision by Martin and Kleutgen (col. 1633) recourse is had only to the direct argument with the help of Wis 10:1 and Ac 17:26. Not much was said on this question in the course of the Council. The American Bishop of Savannah, A. Vérot (who in his speech sought, let it be noted in passing, an explicit rehabilitation of Galileo), took it up in the sixth general meeting (3.1.1870). He objected to the phrase 'ex *levissimis* rationibus' of the theologians' annotation: the reasons, he maintained, were much more serious, and it was only the authority of Scripture which prevented him from giving them his assent. In his view the schema (on this point) laid undue emphasis on German errors, and overlooked French and English representatives of erroneous teaching, as well as American polygenism in the form of a theoretical justification for racial discrimination. (Cf. Granderath, *Geschichte des Vat. Konz* II, p. 100 s.; Hauret, p. 174 s.)

[1] Rabeneck says, quite rightly, 'neque quidquam iuvat illuc confugere librum concordiae aegerrime tantum condemnationem sedis Apostolicae evasisse. In eiusmodi rebus quod paene accidit pro nihilo habendum est (*Archivum hist. S.J.* XIX (1950), p. 140). Of course we do not wish to suggest that the two cases are simply parallel; there is, nevertheless, a certain analogy.

[2] *Coll. Lac.* V, col. 292.

respect of the body only) and polygenism. Now it is indeed worthy of note that the Vatican schema touches on the question of transformism with the utmost caution, by using Biblical expressions (*formavit de limo terrae*; *corpore de limo terrae formato*) to describe the genesis of man, so as to turn its full attention to the other error against which the Council of Cologne protested. Perhaps this may be taken as an indication that the two points in question were not regarded as entirely equivalent even then. But on the other hand the parallels between the Cologne decree (which was confirmed by Rome in its rejection of moderate transformism too) and the Vatican schema show that a certain prudence is in place with regard to an opinion of theologians (even if it is a general one) in questions of this kind. From the point of view of the *magisterium* the Vatican schema is no more than an unofficial product of the labour of theologians. It can only have a theological weight over and above the weight of the arguments it adduces if and in so far as it can be said to reflect the general teaching of the theologians of the time, and so serve as a token of something of more importance than this theological labour purely by itself. But precisely this general view of the theologians, as it takes clear shape in the schema, hardly justifies a higher theological qualification than that we have already arrived at on the basis of more definite pronouncements of the Church. For the case of transformism, with regard to which the theologians of the time, generally speaking, took up the same attitude as with regard to polygenism, shows that an irreformable position is by no means reached by simply establishing the fact of a consensus of opinion (even when this consensus claims to be related to a theologically relevant question).

The results of this investigation into the doctrinal pronouncements of the Church may be summed up by saying that monogenism is to be qualified as theologically certain. Neither a higher nor a lower theological qualification would seem to be justified in the present state of the question. In view of the fact that the pronouncements we have examined or at least the most recent of them taken from 'Humani Generis' are extremely explicit, it is not to be expected that an appeal to the ordinary *magisterium* in its usual teaching would produce a different result. For it is not to be supposed that the Church's *magisterium* at the moment wishes to have this question treated in ordinary instruction and preaching and so on otherwise than in its own most explicit treatment in 'Humani Generis'. There is no need to

repeat here the other observations and positions at which we have
arrived.

Nevertheless a general remark will not be out of place here. Some
readers may have had the impression that we have as it were haggled
about the Church's doctrinal pronouncements, practising the utmost
theological minimalism and juridical formalism, always concerned to
make their demand on us nothing more than is absolutely unavoidable.
As regards such an impression it should be remembered that we
Catholics rightly insist that the Scriptures can only be read rightly in
and with the living Church, and under the guidance of her *magisterium*
as it is actually exercised in a given situation at any particular moment;
it should be remembered that the historical letter of the Bible by itself
does not fully guarantee the assimilation of the truth therein expressed
by a spiritual subject who belongs to another age and whose historical
perspective is unavoidably different. If this is true of the Scriptures as
God's Word, it is obviously true too of the historical letter of an
earlier Council or of some other pronouncement of the Church of
earlier times. We Catholics, then, have neither the duty nor the right
so to conduct ourselves with regard to an earlier doctrinal pronouncement of the Church—like the old Protestants with regard to the Bible
—as if from it alone, independently of the *magisterium today*, all the
teaching we need, the answer to every problem which afflicts us for
the first time today, could unambiguously be obtained. For a Catholic,
then, who believes in the guidance of the *magisterium* today by the
Holy Spirit, the prudent and restrained appraisal of what may be
obtained with certainty from *old* pronouncements of the Church for a
question of *today*, is simply a consequence of a twofold conviction.
Precisely as a Catholic he holds that every age has its own questions,
because it is not always simply the same thing that happens in history
—even in the history of the Spirit; and he holds that the living *magisterium* of the moment so preserves the old that a real advance in knowledge is possible, and that what is said is not just an exact repetition of
what has always been said. Consequently when the *magisterium* today
adopts a clearcut and yet restrained attitude with regard to our question, there is still less ground for saying that more is to be learned from
old declarations of the *magisterium* than from modern ones. To establish the fact that this restraint exists is not even remotely to insinuate
that the present attitude is perhaps going to be revised in favour of
some form of polygenism, just as little as if someone a few centuries

ago were to have qualified the Assumption as 'merely' certain theologically (and it was to this and no more that he would have at that time been obliged).

II. MONOGENISM AND THE SCRIPTURES

The subject of this second section falls naturally into two parts. First we must discuss the question as to whether it may be said, and with what certainty, that Scripture testifies directly to monogenism. Secondly we must consider whether other Scriptural doctrines postulate monogenism as a necessary presupposition. In this second matter we shall proceed first by presupposing the teaching of the Church as an authentic interpretation of the given Scriptural doctrine; then try to show that monogenism is really presupposed by this doctrine. The method may not be that of 'pure' Biblical theology, but it has much to recommend it here. We are by this means relieved of a task which we should otherwise be incapable of fulfilling in this context, the task of opening out and establishing according to the methods of Biblical theology the doctrines of original sin and redemption in the Scriptures, and of doing this *in extenso* and taking all the pains required by such a task. We are specially justified in adopting this method here because the Church's doctrine of original sin presents itself not only as true in itself and revealed, but also as an authentic interpretation of Scripture itself.[1] In this way we can carry out what we have so far omitted from our consideration of the Church's doctrine concerning monogenism, and that is to ask ourselves whether the Church's doctrine of Original Sin does not necessarily contain monogenism objectively, even if it cannot be said to be implicitly defined there. Nor does this method prevent us from making ourselves clear about whether the certainty we seek does not vary, both as regards the starting-point of the deduction and as regards the process of inference,

---

[1] Cf. Denz 789, 791. When it is said that Rom 5 contains the Church's doctrine of original sin and that this too is expressed in the canon just cited, the question obviously still remains open as to how far this content may be extracted by purely exegetical means. It is not easy to hold the proper mean here between an exegetical semi-agnosticism and an attitude in which one behaves as though the Biblical theologian had no real need of the Church's understanding in faith and her *magisterium*. Cf. the study by J. Levie, taking precisely our question as an example, 'Les limites de la preuve d'Ecriture Sainte en théologie', NRT LXXI (1949), pp. 1009–29.

according as we regard Scripture alone or together with the utterances
of the Church's *magisterium* bearing on our question.

A. *The Direct Proof, its possibility and limits*

1. The Old Testament

a. *Gen 2–3.* Because there is no doubt that Wis 10:1 looks back to
Gen 1–3, while there are no other Old Testament texts of importance
we must begin by considering the doctrine of Gen 1–3.

It is of course impossible to develop here all the hermeneutic
principles which must be presupposed if we are to establish what the
inspired author of these chapters wishes to tell us, the real content of
his teaching so far as it is binding theologically. We have to take these
principles for granted. There is no difficulty in assuming them in so
far as they are generally acknowledged; where differences of opinion
persist, we shall content ourselves with the mere application of those
principles which seem to us to be correct and which we believe to be
in harmony with the principles which according to the Church's
magisterium hold good for everyone in the interpretation of this
chapter.

There is no doubt that in Gen 2–3 [1] an individual man is set before
us; before him there was no man who could cultivate the earth, he
was 'alone', and it was only by a fresh divine intervention that he was
given a companion of the same rank who did not exist before and who
was to become the mother of *all* the living (cf. Gen 2:6.7.18.21 s.
3:20). The Adam who is portrayed as the ancestor of all men is portrayed as an individual. Does this mean that according to the testimony and in the intention of the author of Genesis he was *eo ipso* an
individual? What we have just established merely gives rise to this
question but as yet provides no answer to it. For the question precisely
arises as to what the author meant to say by this portrayal in symbolic
and dramatic terms. Anyone who says that the question has already

---

[1] We may ignore Gen. 1:26–8. Ceuppens (p. 25), Hauret (p. 162) and
others have justly declared that monogenism could not be proved from this
text. All that is said here is that God created 'man' ('*den* Menschen'), in two
sexes. We have a statement of the origination of the species and of the duality
of the sexes by God, and nothing more. Lennerz leaves the question open
(p. 429).

been answered by what has been established is asserting that we have before us an historical report in the modern sense of the word: a statement, that is, whose *genus litterarium* itself is historical[1] in the modern sense, and not just a statement the *content* of which—in a sense to be more sharply defined—is constituted by an historical state of affairs. In other words, what we have to ask is whether, in the intention of the author of Genesis, Adam's individuality belongs to the mode of expression or to the (historical) content of these chapters. This question must in any case be *put*, in the present state of hermeneutic principles regarding the literary genre of the first chapters of Genesis. A mere citation of the sentences from Genesis in dispute, together with the assertion that monogenism is in fact unmistakably and palpably referred to there, is simply not possible any longer. By methods like this one could equally prove that the creation of the world in six days or God's immediate formation of man out of the slime of the earth were 'acknowledged facts'. For it is really not at all clear at first sight why one rather than the other should belong to what is 'expressed' or 'meant'. And yet, while granting the methodological necessity of putting the question, people are quite prepared today to say that monogenism belongs to the content and not to the mode of what is expressed, because otherwise the statement would no longer have any historical content at all.[2]

[1] A statement may be (a) historical in its *mode of expression* (and yet in certain circumstances be unhistorical as regards its content, namely when it is erroneous). It is historical in its mode of expression when it describes the historical object in the categories proper to it as an observable phenomenon. A statement may (b) have an historical *content* (and be unhistorical in its mode of expression), i.e. describe the historical object intended in categories which are not those which an observer and reporter would arrive at by an examination of the historical event in the mode of manifestation proper to it. Expressions like 'the falling to earth of the stars', 'the coming of the Son of Man on the clouds of the air', 'the sounding of the archangel's trumpet' do refer to a (future) historical event (not a supra-temporal truth); but if the historical event intended were portrayed as an observer then in existence would be able to observe and narrate it, presumably there would appear in the portrayal neither the sound of a trumpet nor a cloud nor a star falling to earth. The historical content and the historical mode of expression (=historical *genus litterarium*) are two different things.

[2] Cf., e.g., Lennerz, p. 431, Sagüés, n. 546. I must admit that both these eminent theologians seem to me to reach their conclusions rather too abruptly. 'Nam,' says Sagüés about these texts, 'ea, nisi negentur aliquid historice verum continere, saltem monogenismum docere putanda sunt'.

But is this really so certain? First of all, what is said about the one Adam and the one Eve is found in a narrative context of a symbolic and dramatic kind. Is the distinct individuality of the persons put before us an independent element of the account, for which as such by itself an historical content must be sought? One cannot just arbitrarily detach a single element from its total context and ask what its particular content may be. If one were to do this, could one not also consistently look for the historical content of 'God's walking in the cool of the day' and 'the sound of his feet' in Gen 3:8? Must we suppose that the first man was a husbandman, because otherwise Gen 2:15 would lack historical content? It is by no means asserted that the former case and the two latter are equivalent. But where is the strict and positive proof that they are not? Even if we ignore this preliminary difficulty, the question remains: is it true and above all is it *proved* that the account of the one man would cease to have any historical content if it were not understood 'literally' in a monogenistic sense? From the purely exegetical standpoint, is it agreed that this account is certainly intended to *give expression to* ('to teach') more than the real and genuine community of all men among themselves, who, being created by one and the same God, are meant to possess, in spite of their great mutual differences, a single nature, a single goal and a common history of salvation and damnation? We should recall the tendency of the Oriental mind to think in concrete and personalistic terms and to see the foundation of every sociological unity in a single king or a single ancestor.[2] Is it not conceivable that

---

And Lennerz says, 'Non iam apparet quid in tota illa narratione veri remaneat de origine generis humani. Si ergo hoc loco aliquid de origine generis humani dicitur, non potest esse nisi monogenismus'. No more is said on this capital point; all we hear is this one assertion. But is it so certain from the first that the whole narrative of the first human pair could have no historical content apart from that of monogenism? The matter is still simpler in the case of Ceuppens (p. 25). After going through the texts (Gen 2:5-7, 18-23) he says simply, 'De ce passage il ressort assez clairement, je pense, qu'à l'origine Dieu ne créa qu'un homme et une femme'. In this way the exegesis of the texts is disposed of. It is really not clear why by such methods one could not also prove that any kind of transformism is 'assez clairement' in contradiction with Scripture; yet Ceuppens will not allow this for Adam, although for Eve again he maintains it strictly.

[2] Cf. e.g. Gen 9:19.22; 19:37 s.; 25:1-4. Finally it should not be forgotten that even in the New Testament (Mt 2:3; 3:5; 4:24) 'all', 'the

the mutual community based upon the single divine origin of man and the unity of his nature, the family relationship of all men should be given expression by putting it before our eyes in the form of an image of a unique clan with a unique ancestor? From the purely exegetical point of view, is it immediately certain that this is insufficient as the historical content of the 'description populaire des origines du genre humain' (Denz 3002)? Nor can it be said that this content is insignificant and obvious. The fact that all men of the most diverse peoples are children of the one God and form one family was not even at that time simply a matter of course. How should this specific and historical unity be expressed in a 'langage simple et figuré, adapté aux intelligences d'une humanité moins dévelopéc' otherwise than in the image of a unity of origin giving rise to relations of kinship?

Anyone for whom monogenism is simply expressed in an explicit and indubitable way in Gen 2–3 has to face the question of the sources of such a knowledge. Simply to introduce here an appeal to a recent revelation is rather too simple. Inspiration and Revelation may by no means be confused, especially since today 'it is no longer doubted by anyone' that these reports make use of extra-canonical sources both oral and literary. However if it is proposed to refer the knowledge of these sources to the primitive revelation, the following considerations must be borne in mind. 'Adam' could not know in virtue of his human experience that he was the one and only man. He could at most ascertain that no others were to be found in his environment. But God could inform him of this? Certainly, that is possible. But did this possibility become a fact? Had he to know this with certainty in order to be able to be and to do what he in fact was and did as ancestor and sinful head of humanity? Are we to suppose that this knowledge, supposing it existed, was handed down over a few hundred thousand years? It may be true that in other narratives of the Near East which describe the emergence of man several human pairs are created simultaneously[1]; that is still no reason why the Genesis narrative should be a deliberate contradiction of these other narratives so as to make monogenism the content of what it has to say. For on the one hand these other narratives and the enumerations peculiar to them (7 pairs, 4

---

whole', need not imply more than a great number, which need by no means include every relevant case.

[1] C. Hauret, p. 119 s.; R. Labat, *Le Poème babylonien de la création*, p. 51.

men) may only wish to state the same thing as the unitary number of Genesis: the totality of men. On the other hand one would have to ask whether the intention of these other narratives was not to symbolize an essential distinction between different men (and of the peoples springing from them) by speaking of a plural number. The intention of the unitary number in Genesis would then be to combat *this* view by emphasizing the fundamental likeness of men; but this would not necessarily mean that monogenism in the strict sense was being taught here in objective fact. Ultimately this too must be borne in mind: it is not immediately clear why an essential distinction should be held to obtain between the story of the single human pair and the story of Eve's origin from Adam in respect of a 'literal'[1] interpretation of the two stories. In connexion with the question of Biblical monogenism Ceuppens, for example, does in fact hold that Eve's physical bond with Adam is expressly taught in the Scriptures.[2] But if one is not prepared to grant this[3] it does not seem immediately intelligible how monogenism may nevertheless be presented as an explicit and unmistakable declaration of Scripture. It is not clear how one can consistently associate this conception of Eve's origin with the admission that Gen 1–3 is not necessarily in contradiction with a moderate transformism.[4] Thus from this point of view too it seems more in accordance with the facts not to assert that it is certainly possible for someone to show by

[1] We make use of this term only for the sake of brevity and so as to be understood quickly. In itself it is misleading: a statement is taken most literally when it is understood to have the meaning proper to it on the basis of the literary genre employed in the given case. Someone who holds that God created the world in six times 24 hours has not really taken Gen 1 'literally'; he has misunderstood its meaning.

[2] *Le polygénisme*, p. 26.

[3] There appears to be an increasing number of writers who in this matter too take the literary genre of the first chapters of Genesis seriously, and see in the formation of Eve from Adam's rib a dramatic symbolization of her likeness to the man and her subordination to him, the question of the physical mode of her origination being left open: so Cajetan, Hoberg, Hummelauer, Nickel, Holzinger, Peters, Lagrange, Junker, Göttsberger, Schlögl, Lusseau, de Fraine, Hauret, Premm, Colungs, Chaine, Bartmann, Cordero, Remy. Naturally there are considerable differences of detail between the views of these authors into which we cannot go here. The same is true of the extent to which they go in rejecting Eve's physical and material extraction from Adam.

[4] In fact it has been one of the 'classic' arguments against transformism in any form (Pesch, Lercher, Sagüés, etc.) that since it is not applicable to Eve, it cannot be asserted in Adam's case either.

purely exegetical methods that monogenism is contained in Gen 1–3 as a direct statement.

It goes without saying that this is neither to throw doubt upon monogenism in itself nor positively to contest the fact that it is in actual fact contained in Gen 1–3. Thus what has so far been said in no way conflicts with Denz 2123. For all that is declared there is that the *unitas generis humani* is objectively contained in Gen 1–3, against those who deny the fact itself; no position is taken up with regard to the question of how this fact of being contained may be recognized by the use of purely exegetical methods.[1]

If we have restricted the bearing of Gen 1–3 for monogenism in this negative way, our task is by no means done. We can and must now go on to add positively: what Genesis says is *positively open*[2] to a revealed doctrine concerning monogenism arrived at elsewhere and

---

[1] *Sensus litteralis historicus* is precisely not the same as the *sensus litteralis historicus* which can be extracted from the passage concerned taken by itself. Denz 2124 itself points out that the *analogia fidei* must be observed in the interpretation of Gen 1–3. This would be superfluous if everything a text contained objectively could be extracted from it without recourse to anything else. Certainly we must as far as possible proceed from the text itself if we wish to find out what the human author has necessarily stated as a minimum, or else we shall be dragging into *this* literal sense things which owe their origin to a later and more developed revelation.

[2] 'Positively open' is intended to imply more than 'does not exclude', 'is not in contradiction with' (but indifferent as regards any further statement). What Genesis says, rather, is so formulated that its human author did not indeed have to be conscious of its entire bearing, but so that it can nevertheless be understood without hesitation as an expression of this fuller content; and it is God's will too (as later Revelation shows) that *we* should now understand it positively like this in this 'sensus plenior'. In this case at least it cannot be objected that God wishes to say to us in the given passage what the human author wished to say, and thus no inspired 'sensus plenior' exists. This objection to a 'sensus plenior' may be justified (we need not go into the matter here) in many cases where appeal is made to it, but that is not the case here. For here it is not a matter of some new idea which is affixed additively to one which has been really expressed as its 'sensus plenior'; what we have here is a proposition (and they are countless) which exhibits marginal indistinctness, so that it was neither necessary nor possible for the human author (as opposed to God) to be reflexively clear about how far the proposition does in fact go, although he was quite capable of seeing that it *could* imply the 'sensus plenior'. In a case like this it is quite possible to say that the 'sensus plenior' is inspired, for the human author affirms it in the sense meant by God even when he is incapable of giving a reflexive

by other means and guaranteed by the *magisterium*; and in this sense
it is now possible to say that monogenism belongs to the content of
Gen 2.

Let us clarify this point a little more. First of all it can be said that
all we have so far said in no way excludes the fact that monogenism
is part of what is actually stated, its content. We take it that there is
no question of explaining what is said in Gen 1-3 arbitrarily and without resort to really clear hermeneutic principles, finding a literal sense
here and a symbolic one there; we take it that the *whole* is a great,
complex image with an historical content which is meant to be the
kind of content proper to a unified, symbolic utterance. But then there
is nothing to prevent this plastic image of a human pair from giving
expression to the reality of a unique human pair as the ancestors of all
men, over and above what was said to be the minimal sense above.

But it is permissible to go further. The author of Gen 2-3 intends
to tell the story of the beginnings of humanity, and by means of this
reflexion upon the Beginning to speak of what is 'original' in his own
existential situation, provide a theological interpretation of his own
existence, by referring it to its origin. In fact one can say that the past
is regarded from the point of view of the writer's religious situation.
The author sees himself faced by an ethnological and cultural plurality,
and he reduces this to a more primitive unity. It is very far from our
intention here to examine the exact terms in which he determines this
original unity, whether he speaks quite certainly there of the strictly
numerical unity of our terrestrial origin or only of a transcendent
unity in God or of what is indeed a quite tangible unity of a terrestrial
but not of a strictly monogenistic kind.[1] The reduction to an original

---

account to himself as to whether everything which even he sees as a possible
sense of his own statement really belongs unmistakably to what is affirmed.

[1] It would not indeed be excluded *a priori* that a terrestrial, original, historically tangible unity of humanity might be conceivable for the author of
Genesis, a unity which is not precisely that of a unique original pair and for
which such a pair would serve as a plastic medium in which the unity could
be visualized. To portray *a priori* possibilities of this kind would serve no
useful purpose here. In order to see that they are not *a priori* impossible one
need only reflect on what this unity is meant to be opposed to in the mind of
the author of Genesis. Looked at from the viewpoint of the whole theology
of the first chapters of Genesis, what this unity is contrasted with is not
simply a purely numerical multiplicity, but the qualified multiplicity of a
humanity rent asunder into peoples, races and religions, a humanity which

unity of an historical and cultural plurality belonging to his own living-space, a unity which guarantees the mutual community today of the many in a common whole of meaning and a common history of salvation and damnation—to see this and to say it is already in itself an astonishing phenomenon, especially as the author's field of vision embraced a number of peoples extremely unlike each other in race, culture and religion, in respect of whom this original unity was hardly a matter of course for the religious philosophy of this simple man. We can realize how particularly hard it must have been for him when we remember that the distinctions in Gen 1 among plants and animals, the *differentiae* of which in themselves must have seemed no greater throughout their entire range than those among men, were seen without the slightest hesitation as original in a 'fixist' way (Gen 1:11. 21.24.25). It is impossible to say that the Yahwist arrives at this essentially bold idea of unity *merely* from the observation that men have children and multiply (Gen 1:28). Modern rationalist ideas (inter-racial fertility in spite of diversity, etc.) were certainly still further from his mind. The fact that he nevertheless sees the riven plurality of his own living-space as sprung from an (at least larger) unity of a terrestrial ('Adam') and transcendent kind (the one Creator of all), is the mark of a profound mind, especially since generation for him elsewhere means the generative cause of the like (Gen. 5:3). Admittedly the Yahwist feels this need for unity even where the plurality of individual peoples each for itself is involved: this plurality too he refers back to a unique ancestor for each (to this extent what was said above about the certainty of a strictly monogenistic statement holds good). But let us not be in too much of a hurry to say that therefore no more lies behind the former statement than behind the latter. For in the latter case we may have a secondary, inexact application, not wholly accurate objectively, of a *valid* metaphysical principle (though of a relatively unreflexive kind), which is wholly justified in the former case.

We may describe this basic metaphysical conception by which the author must be actuated in the following terms. A. In spite of their variety men are basically the same, and are thus sharply and (even

---

is no longer at one in anything, so that the various peoples themselves no longer acknowledge a common God as their joint origin. It is against this empirical plurality that the Yahwist writer sets his portrayal of what was 'in the beginning': the one Man from the hand of the one God as a unique pair of man and woman.

from a purely terrestrial point of view) unconditionally separated from the animal kingdom; they are the same by nature: perishable in their earthly substance (like the animals) and yet moral creatures addressed by Yahweh in a special way, for whom everything else exists as the environment of their own existence; over all of them there reigns in grace and judgment the one God of their origin, so that they all belong to a single history of salvation and damnation in spite of their differences; where they are found to be not merely different but divided by enmity, this is not of the origin but the result of their guilt (the history of Cain, the Tower of Babel). Thus men form ('now' primarily) a solidary community of nature and history, and this is something belonging to the origin, created by God. B. This unity in the now, which is theologically disclosed behind the surface of dismembered existence as an existential[1] willed by God, now in force and prior to all guilt, has a beginning and an origin; this beginning is as early as men themselves (and not the effect of an historical decision of the guilty choice of men themselves), and it is primordial just because it arises from the real unity of an identical origin. For in the first place the larger plurality arises from the more restricted one, as everyday experience teaches: men multiply (Gen 1:28). But over and above this, if they are able to multiply in this way, there need only have been *one* human pair in the beginning. For if there were another cause of human multiplicity, independent of generation, why should it no longer be active now, why should there be another cause as well? And above all, would these men who have been independent of each other from the origin really form the unity and solidary community which they now are—or ought to be? Or would they not precisely stand over against each other in the same alien way as the animal species which God created? May one suppose that the Yahwist's theological reflexions moved in this direction, and occasioned that portrayal of the beginning and one origin of all men which he gives us in plastic imagery? If one can credit him with something of the kind (and there is a good deal to be said for this), then it becomes apparent with what justice we may say that his statements are—even 'quoad nos'—at least *positively open* to a genuine monogenism. Yet this is not to say that it becomes probable, purely exegetically, that monogenism belongs to what is expressed in the strict sense. Nor do

[1] See Introduction.—Tr.

we wish to assert that this view that the unity of the whole of human reality is prior to its plurality, even terrestrially, is so consciously thought out by the Yahwist that his intention to act as guarantor of absolute monogenism is unmistakable.[1]

We may put this in slightly different terms. The account of the single primordial pair is first of all an element in a figurative account, and we have next to *inquire* what in its total context it is meant to express by way of historical content. It states without doubt that from the beginning humanity forms a unity of nature and of destiny in saving history, in virtue of a divine disposition (and not by its own 'choice'). Over and above this, it is quite probable and at least positively open (from the purely exegetical point of view) that Genesis means to say that this primordial unity possesses a terrestrial foundation in a strictly physical unity of generation. It is not, however, possible to decide purely exegetically whether the image of a single primordial pair can *only* possess its historically intended content in a physically unique primordial pair, because the reality aimed at might in certain circumstances have been conceived of in terms of a different kind of original unity, also terrestrial in kind. For this reason, from a purely exegetical point of view we regard monogenism as a Scriptural doctrine which is only probably expressed in Gen 2-3.

We must add a few notes to what has just been said. It might be objected that we have forgotten that it is a question of Revelation here, and that consequently any attempt more sharply to determine what strictly was meant in the statement by reconstructing what the author must have thought is bound to go astray. The objection is unsound. It is nowhere laid down that what is said in Gen 1-3, over and above its character as inspired, must have been revealed throughout in just such a way that in regard to what it really certainly states—not in regard to what we arbitrarily suppose for such—it could only be known by genuinely new revelation. What the Yahwist tells us he could at least in many cases have known without new revelation (woman's equality of nature, the creation, even probably, according to the great medieval theologians, the fact of some kind of guilt at the beginning of humanity). The fact that he did see what can be known in this way, and see it and express it with such purity in spite of the obscurity of his existence, remains a marvel of the God who reveals

---

[1] In his theological aetiology he does not, for instance, expressly extend his reflexions beyond the surrounding history of his field of vision.

himself[1], and remains inspired. It may even be said that until the contrary is proved, that is, until it is shown to be impossible, we should presume that the *immediate* source of the human author's statements in many individual cases in Gen 1–3 is his own theological reflexion, not a revelation the content of which is communicated sheerly by God from above without any intermediary. Otherwise one would have to look for this revelation in concrete form in the Yahwist's sources, or postulate an oral tradition going back to the beginning[2]; expedients, these, of a highly questionable kind, to say no more. If this view is correct, it is metaphysically entirely justified and even imperative to try to find out first of all what the author's thoughts may have been and how he arrived at them; and then by following his train of thought in this way we should have a more exact knowledge of what he really intended to say and what possibly he did not. These reflexions show how necessary it is for us to reconstruct for ourselves reflexively those metaphysical and theological considerations which moved him to form his image of original humanity; then we should see how far these considerations of his and ours will carry us. But this is something we can only turn to later.

Let us provisionally establish as our only result that in view of the literary genre it is impossible to be sure by exegesis alone that monogenism is found in Gen 1–3 in the form of an authentic and binding statement. However, the whole presentation is at least positively open to a monogenistic interpretation; this lies minimally in the author's theological tendency to explain the religious situation of his own existence by reflecting theologically on the (really historical) origin. In any case the narrative of the single ancestor is a declaration about the original, divinely willed unity of all humanity and its history of salvation and damnation. For it follows from all that has been said that this is the minimum statement made by this narrative.

[1] Especially as this theological reflexion on the Beginning proceeds from the author's experience of God's dealings in his own period of saving history thus the point of departure of the reflexion is by no means simply 'natural' but contains God's Revelation in the strict sense through his deed and the word accompanying it.

[2] This is not to contest the genuine possibility of such a tradition. But it may fairly be said that if one tries to form a concrete idea of it one begins to suspect that all it is capable of preserving through thousands of years of history is what is simultaneously kept alive by man's metaphysical reflexion and his needs; just as conversely the latter is continually stimulated by the former

b. *Wisdom 10:1*. We find it said of Wisdom in a review of her activity in the history of the chosen People: 'She protected the father of the world, the first creature to be formed, when he alone was created, and delivered him from his fall. She gave him power to exercise dominion over all things.' There is no doubt that the text has in view the Adam of Gen 2–3. We have a survey of the saving history of Genesis, in which Cain, the Flood, Abraham, Lot and so on are also mentioned. It is to be observed that the subject of the statement in 10:1 is not Adam but Wisdom. In chapters 10–12 her powerful sway over her lovers in mercy and blessing is celebrated. Historical examples are provided to show how active Wisdom is, and these are simply taken in a freely poetic way from Genesis as a didactic aid in making vividly clear what the writer really wishes to state: the blessings acquired by the followers of Wisdom. One may set up a principle for the interpretation of such statements: where a report belonging to an earlier book of the Old Testament is simply taken over without further commentary, the content and bearing of what has been taken over in the later book is to be assessed according to the content and bearing of its source, provided that the purpose to which it is put demands nothing further. In virtue of this principle, what may be derived from Wis 10:1 is just what can be derived from Gen 2–3 and no more. Nothing new is said except that Wisdom has protected and delivered that Adam whose story we find in Gen 2–3, in the way in which that story relates and in the way in which what is there related of him is to be interpreted. Wis 10 s. mentions no proper names (neither Adam nor Cain nor Abraham nor Lot nor Jacob nor Joseph nor Moses are spoken of in chapter 10 by their own names, although it is they who are being spoken of); and so the only purpose of the statements which are made about Adam as ancestor is to distinguish who is being talked about at all, without having to use his name. Thus the author of Wisdom could with a tranquil mind leave it to his source to determine and to guarantee the bearing of the characterization taken from Gen 2–3. Thus the text possesses no independent significance for the question of monogenism.[1]

[1] A parallel case may help to make this clear. The Vatican schema, already cited, speaks of the *corpus (Adae) de limo terrae formatum*, of Eve *e costa eius (Adae) divinitus formata* (*Coll. Lac.* VII, col. 1633). It is clear to everyone that what we have here is a citation from Gen 2, and that the author of the schema relies on the source of his citation and its interpretation for the

2. The New Testament

Ac 17:24–26. It must first be noted that St Luke is reporting one of St Paul's speeches. Inspiration as such with the inerrancy proper to it is thus referred primarily to the fact that this speech with this content was actually delivered, not to the correctness of what was said. Thus the content of the speech can only be guaranteed true in so far as the speech is an Apostle's sermon and is *for this reason* true in its content and exacting for faith, and in the measure in which the content of a single Apostle's sermon raises such a claim. An Apostle can err where his preaching does not exact the absolute obedience of faith[1]; and so it would have to be proved that St Paul uttered this proposition as an absolute demand of his preaching of the faith, as the indispensable content of his Gospel.

But we may peacefully disregard this question. St Paul says that the one God unknown to the Athenians whom he preaches, formed the entire race of men 'from one'[2] so that it might inhabit the whole face

---

bearing and *precise* content of the citation and its delimitation; thus the text offers no conclusive argument against transformism or in favour of the physical reality of the rib. This remains true even though it is practically certain that the author of the schema was at that time convinced that Adam's body was formed directly from inorganic matter, and that Adam's rib as the matter out of which Eve was formed was a physical reality. But all he wished to *state* was what the cited text really covered with its authority. The same example in more recent times is to be found in Pius XII's address to the members of the Papal Academy of Sciences, AAS XXXIII (1941) p. 506.

[1] It is quite unnecessary to attribute any wider range of infallibility to an individual Apostle as such (i.e. when he is not at the same time an inspired author) than to the successors of Peter. In other words the limits of the latter infallibility are those of the former. For a practical example, see Ac 20:2 compared with 2 Tim 4:20.

[2] It seems to me to make no real difference whether one prefers the old reading ἐξ ἑνὸς αἵματος instead of ἐξ ἑνός or goes to great pains to find a way of completing ἑνός. For in every case this εἷς or ἕν seems to imply a unity which according to the context is other than God and is a unity of *origin*. Even if with de Fraine (p. 55) one reads 'out of one blood' and refers to Jn 1:13 and the Old Testament significance of blood as bearing life, it is still a unity of origin (ἐξ) and not the unity (=identity) of the mode of origin of all men that is in question. For even then the translation 'from the lineage of a single individual' would be the most obvious one (cf.

of the earth. All he does is to repeat, as every preacher is allowed and expected to do, the account given in Genesis (and the ideas of Deut 32:8). And he does this to make the Athenians realize that their piety and their religious observances cannot be nationally autochthonous but must be determined by the one Lord of heaven and earth; their religious existence is not dependent upon a private God peculiar to their nationality and their history. In accordance with the principle formulated above, we must say that St Paul is simply repeating his source, giving it the meaning and the bearing which it has in itself. For the context in which St Paul repeats this teaching of Genesis demands no more either. He wishes to draw attention to the unity of humanity in its saving history due to the one living God of Israelite and Christian saving history, and so he makes it arise 'out of one' just as in Genesis and with the same intention. Genesis teaches an historical unity of origin as the ground of the unity of men and of the solidarity of their history; this is what happens in St Paul's speech too, in the same measure and with the same limits and the same certainty. Nothing more can be said with certainty. St Paul is certainly concerned in the context of his speech with a unity of origin; nor can one say that this is merely a rhetorical element without significance for the central point of his speech. But all he says in regard to Genesis is simply what is said there already. Just because a unity of origin is spoken of there

---

Bauer, *Wörterbuch* (ET Arndt and Gingrich) s.v. αἷμα). One would have to translate 'make out of the same blood' and give this the meaning 'make out of the same (= homogeneous) matter' (as the ἐξ in Jn 1:13 refers to the material cause and not strictly to the origin).' But is this interpretation possible? What would then be the purpose of ἐξ ἑνός? The homogeneity of men would be expressed, even without this clause, by the statement that the one God created all peoples. Surely the reference to Adam is much more obvious, since it appears elsewhere in St Paul in similar contexts (Rom 5:12 s.; 1 Cor 11:7 s.; 15:22.45), since the whole passage from the very beginning is a summary of the first chapters of Genesis, since Rabbinic theology too (Strack-Billerbeck II, p. 7, etc.) taught the descent of all men from Adam for reasons which are closely connected with those with which ultimately St Paul is concerned here: the justification of the unity of nature and solidarity of all men. We believe (in spite of de Fraine) that Lennerz is right in saying (p. 428) that he knows of no exegete who would not interpret the text as referring to the one Adam; and we are of the opinion that this is the most obvious interpretation for the unprejudiced exegete. Only we hold that this still does not dispose of the problem in regard to monogenism; it is just the beginning of the problem, exactly as in the exposition of Gen 2–3.

which would suffice for his argument in any case, he does not need to
have reflected on the precise limits and bearing of the statement in
Genesis with regard to the alternatives of monogenism and poly
genism. But this statement taken in itself provides us with no fina
and unambiguous information about monogenism in the strict sense
over and above what it says about an original, historical unity of th
human race, and this unity can be conceived of *a priori* in various ways
nor can we then find this information when St Paul repeats the accoun

Thus what was said above about Gen 2–3 might be said here abou
Ac 17:26, both negatively and *positively*, too. For we have here th
same ἐξ ἑνός which we find in Heb. 2:11. It may be true that th
same thing must be said about this ἐξ ἑνὸς πάντες, taken purely i
itself, as about Ac 17:26 and Gen 2–3, read in isolation (and also di
regarding the fact that it is formally set in opposition to all ἁγιαζόμ
νοι not to all men). And yet, in the framework of the whole Paulin
theology of redemption, the objective context of Heb 2:11 shows th
a genuine unity of origin of all men must be understood in St Paul i
a really monogenistic way if it is to retain its meaning. However, w
must postpone to the next section these considerations drawn from th
whole Pauline doctrine of original sin and redemption, since they g
beyond the exegesis of an isolated text.

A certain prudence and caution is very much in place with regar
to these New Testament citations from the Old Testament.[1] Man
exegetes today are no longer prepared to grant that 2 Pet 2:5 make
it certain that the Flood extended to all man.[2] Is it necessary th
Jonas' stay in the belly of the whale should have been historical fa
because of Mt 12:40?[3] Does Jude 9 guarantee the historicity of th

---

[1] Another example of this sort of thing is to be found in Ex 20:11; th
six days of Creation do not become 'more literal' because they are spoken
in a passage which, compared to Gen 1, is extremely unpoetical and sobe

[2] It is contested by Vaccari and others, and an increasing number
writers after him.

[3] The following comparison would seem to be a fair one. Someone wh
says 'I shall be as brave as Siegfried was' no more vouches for Siegfried
historicity than Jesus did for the historicity of this event. J. Schildenberg
too finally admits this (*Vom Geheimnis des Gotteswortes*, Heidelberg 195
p. 316, n. 212). It is not here in debate whether Jonas' fate is necessari
historical on other grounds. Catholic exegetes like A. Calmet, A. v
Hoonacker, H. Lesêtre, M. Tobac, A. Condamin, Dennefeld are amor
those who doubt this. There is no reason why the text of the encyclic

struggle between Michael and the Devil for Moses' dead body, which is taken from *The Ascension of Moses*, or is it still possible and meaningful to say what the Apostle wishes to say when the example which is meant to explain something else—what is really stated—has only a literary existence? Is it really possible to use 1 Cor 11:8.12; Eph 5:28–30; 1 Tim 2:13 s. to prove the 'literal' interpretation of the story in Genesis of the formation of Eve from Adam's rib? The Catholic exegetes mentioned above[1] are clearly not of this opinion. What St Paul wished to inculcate about woman by making this reference is still meaningfully illustrated by the reference even when a less 'literal' interpretation of Eve's origin 'out of' Adam is assumed beforehand. What historicity does 2 Tim 3:8 guarantee to the names Jannes and Jambres for the sorcerers mentioned without their names in Ex 7:8–12, since St Paul took these names from an apocryphal writing? What historical particulars about Melchisedech can really be got from Heb 7:3? It might be said that citations, especially when the writing being cited is an authoritative one, form a literary genre of their own. This is not to say, with the theory which received so much discussion a few decades ago, that a writer need not identify himself with what he cites; what is meant is that a writer, when he makes a citation, knows from the first, precisely because of the authority of the source accepted beforehand, that one can and must speak 'to this effect', and consequently need have no reflexive knowledge of the exact bearing of the quoted statement. This is something which belongs to the plain and unavoidable rights of human speech. It holds good for Scripture too. But precisely for that reason it is ordinarily to be presumed that one should assess a citation by its source; the cases mentioned above are examples of this. This is not to say that Ac 17:26 is simply an instance of exactly the same thing as we find in the other examples. By no means. But if this principle derived from an examination of the examples given above is applied to Ac 17:26, it will not be found easy to prove that this passage, taken in isolation, is

---

Spiritus Paraclitus' of Benedict XV (AAS XII (1920), p. 398) should be seen as contradicting this view. It is merely being explained there by examples that the Old Testament in all its parts was an absolute authority for Jesus. But Pope Benedict gives no decision as to how one should interpret the texts which Jesus cited in this sense, in themselves firstly, and consequently in Jesus' intention.

[1] P. 256, n. 3.

capable of providing more in favour of monogenism than is said by Genesis.

B. *The Indirect Proof (from Scripture and the Church's Magisterium)*

The indirect proof of monogenism consists in the demonstration that it is an indispensable presupposition of the doctrines of redemption and original sin as these are contained in Scripture and in its interpretation by Tradition and the Church's *magisterium*; and that in this sense it is taught by Scripture. That this proof must be regarded as the most important of all may also be seen from the arguments with which 'Humani Generis' justifies its rejection of polygenism, though with the utmost brevity.

1. The usual form of the indirect proof

The proof is usually presented by taking the unity and universality of original sin as point of departure.[1] On the basis of these two points as taught by the Council of Trent, the argument proceeds as follows. On the polygenistic hypothesis, unless original sin is to be rejected outright, several ancestral pairs who were in possession of original justice would have to have sinned at various times and in various places; and they would have to have transmitted their sin, i.e. the loss of original justice, to their posterity. Firstly, it is argued, it is arbitrary to assume that all these men should have sinned, and, what is more, sinned at considerable intervals of space and time, independently of each other—for otherwise the polygenistic hypothesis could no longer meaningfully be maintained. It is not clear why none of these pairs should have had children before its fall or the fall of another, so that the question arises as to how these stand with respect to original sin. Nor is it clear *when* this original sin, which—as *peccatum originans*— would need to be conceived of as the one act for the whole earth of a collectivity, really came into existence. Only when *all* the pairs have sinned? But *ex suppositione* the last of these pairs exists it may be a few thousand years after the first pair. How do matters stand with the earlier pairs and especially with their children, if, while there have been personal sins of the earlier primordial pairs, original sin still cannot

---

[1] For what follows see among others Lennerz, pp. 419–24.

be handed down to their posterity (although this arises by generation) because original sin does not yet exist, and does not exist because the last primordial pair belonging to the constitution of this sinful collectivity does not yet exist? Or does original sin come into existence with the sin of the first pair? But then the other pairs do not yet exist, or if they do exist, have not yet sinned. How do matters stand in this case with the children they perhaps already have? When these later pairs first come into existence, after the first pair has sinned, will they be created with or without original justice? In the first case they would not have original sin, which would not then be general; in the second case, the withdrawal of original justice on account of the fall of the first pair would not be original sin, which is transmitted 'generatione', nor would the fall of the later pairs when it takes place have anything further to contribute to the constitution of this 'original sin'. Supposing that these pairs are not conceived of as a juridical unity for the purpose of administering the original justice intended for humanity, and that each of them is thought of as having sinned 'on its own account' and only transmitting its own loss of original justice to its own posterity, then original sin would not be 'origine unum' and there would be instead be several original sins, which will not do either.

There is no doubt that these arguments show that polygenism is far from being in harmony with the doctrine of original sin. But is it completely excluded by this kind of argument?[1] It is, I hope, permitted to express some doubts as to the absolute stringency of this procedure.

Admittedly no difficulty remains if one regards both the 'origine unum' as well as the 'propagatione' of the Council of Trent as an unambiguous and defined statement to the effect that the *peccatum originale originans* was the sole act of one physical individual and that every transmission of original sin can *only* take place in virtue of a generative connexion with this *unus*. For then every form of polygenism is straightforwardly opposed to the doctrine of original sin, for only a physical individual can be the primordial sinner. If *everyone* else is to have original sin, and this can *only* be had through a generative connexion with this primordial sinner, then everyone else must

---

[1] The whole series of acute arguments in Lennerz (p. 423 s.) seems in the end only intended to prove that polygenism is not a dogmatically indifferent, purely secular affair, although the whole argument is aimed at wider conclusions.

descend physically from this one individual. A postadamite polygenism cannot be reconciled with a defined doctrine of universal postadamite original sin caused by a physical individual and only capable of being transmitted by generation.

One may also regard this particular doctrine of original sin, with all the details to which attention has been drawn, as a general and obligatory teaching, though not indeed defined. In this case one will be bound to regard this proof of the irreconcilability of polygenism and this version of the doctrine of original sin as formally stringent, and will merely have to add that monogenism acquires that theological qualification which is proper to the premises of the proof on this valuation. Thus it would not be defined *implicite*, but would have to be given a lower qualification.

But if all this (or the latter at least) may be granted, all the questions concerning this indirect proof in its usual form are by no means disposed of.

First of all, we have already shown above that it is not beyond all doubt that the '*propagatione*', in so far as it signifies more than the contradictory opposite of 'imitatione', is defined by Trent. If the doubt is admitted and one then assumes (something which is far from being implied in the first admission) that the 'propagatione' is a theological explanation, not a doctrinal statement in the strict sense,[1] it is possible to conceive of the following hypothesis. The first man created in the state of original justice is nominated by God as the trustee, in respect of the justice compulsorily intended by God for all men, for all the men who follow him, whether they descend from him physically or not.[2] This first man loses original justice for himself and all other men. Thus all are subject to original sin. The universality of original sin and its unity of origin are preserved. It is through Adam that all are subject to original sin, the other first pairs not indeed *generatione*, but *per inoboedientiam primi hominis, non imitatione*. Soon,

---

[1] This seems to be de Fraine's assumption.

[2] This supposition need meet with no ultimately insoluble difficulty in the average theory of original sin. Grace is God's free gift. Thus he can make its possession dependent (so it might be said) upon any meaningful condition. The preservation of grace by the first man would be a meaningful condition even for the men who do not descend from him, because these other men and their posterity are intended to form a community of goal and history with the descendants of the first man.

one could go on, all these men became so mixed that there was no longer a single man left who did not go back to Adam *generatione* as well. Hence *generatione* would continue to be the expression for what now holds good generally (descent from Adam as well) and what was always the chief point at issue, namely that men's likeness of nature and the consequences of this were God's reason for making the justice of all men dependent upon the action of the first man. Would it be possible to show that this view clearly runs counter to the dogma of original sin as *defined*? It seems doubtful. We have of course made an assumption which is very far from being proved. The possibility of a communication of original sin in individual initial cases without a generative connexion need not be clearly and unmistakably counter to a definition, and yet be quite untenable theologically. We have in no way proved that it is *not* untenable or even shown it to be only positively probable. The general doctrine that original sin is transmitted by generation is in truth unfavourable to this assumption. But if this doctrine is to be a simply peremptory argument against the assumption, it would still remain to be shown: (a) that 'generatione' in Tradition, and furthermore with the obligatory character of a doctrinal statement, certainly implies more than 'non imitatione'; (b) that the expression is not chosen as a theological interpretation of the authentic dogma of original sin merely because monogenism has been *pre*-supposed without thereby being absolutely guaranteed; (c) that *generatione* cannot signify, 'by reception of human nature after Adam' (the question then being left open as to whether it was received *from* Adam or elsewhere, while after Adam and in consideration of his stock). It is obvious that this investigation cannot be carried out *here*. And so a kind of question-mark must be left *here* against the result of the ordinary indirect proof.

To this it must be added that what was said earlier about the doubtfulness of whether 'propagatione' was defined, holds good also of the 'unum' of original sin. Certainly original sin is 'one' in so far as all men born by generation are born without original justice, the privation of which is of the same kind in all of them; in so far as in all of them this privation arises in the same way owing to the guilt of the man or men not brought into being by generation; in so far as no further increase of this original guilt occurs once there exist only men brought into being by generation. Original guilt is thus 'one' in many respects, in virtue of which it is distinguished from personal sins, which differ specifically among themselves, may be increased at will and are performed by each individual self. Thus it cannot be said without further qualification that the 'origine unum' of Trent would lose all meaning if the agent of the loss of grace in men born by generation were not a numerical individual. It would be possible to translate 'origine unum' by 'a hereditary state of guilt of the same kind everywhere owing to the mode of its reception (from another)' in contrast to personal sins. Of course the Fathers of the Council had more in mind than this; but did they wish to define this plus, when in fact they only wished to define the existence of original sin against Pelagius and Erasmus? We must repeat: even if the 'origine unum' is not certainly defined in its traditional fullness of meaning it may still be binding as a doctrine of tradition. At any rate proof of the contrary has never been produced. And that surely means that the Catholic theologian cannot *tuto* or *sine temeritate* depart from the traditional meaning of 'origine unum'. But if he retains it, it follows as a consequence that he must either deny *this* traditional unity in polygenism or must postulate the juridical hypothesis of a collective guilt of primordial pairs, which once again comes into conflict with the doctrine of the hereditary transmission of original sin as the unique means by which it is handed on. Nevertheless, let us for the moment suppose that the 'origine unum', in its traditional fullness of meaning, is not defined, and let us make the (wholly unproved) assumption that the plus of the full meaning over and above the sense proposed in the hypothetical interpretation above is not necessarily demanded by a tradition binding upon faith. Then we could say that when all the original pairs (only a few, after all) have sinned [1] and transmitted their privation of grace to their posterity in each case, all born men would be subject to original sin and would have the like original sin from the origin, in so far as the same grace was lost to them all for the same reason. A true collective guilt of a true collective subject would then not be necessary. All the difficulties of such a view would cease to arise. A collective subject would only have existed in the sense that these pri-

---

[1] If we say that without God's special help not one of the countless millions of men could observe the natural moral law for any length of time and yet sins by not observing it, this assumption ceases to be as arbitrary as it may seem at first sight. For the same reason the assumption of a guilt which appears very *soon* (hence before the generation of children) among several pairs is not quite so arbitrary as one might otherwise suppose.

mordial sinners were brought together under the name of Adam in a symbolic and plastic way. It must once again be emphasized that even apart from 'Humani Generis' it may *not* be asserted that the restrictive interpretation of 'origine unum' can be classified as unobjectionable. No proof of this has been produced; and the weight of the tradition which points in the opposite direction cannot be denied. It would thus be temerarious to depart from it. But is it absolutely certain that this tradition which takes the full meaning of 'origine unum' for granted and hands it down, is indubitably binding upon faith? And so, is the argument against polygenism, in so far as it is based on the 'origine unum', free from every possible objection?

The following point should also be borne in mind. Let us suppose that in virtue of Tradition, the 'propagatione' and the 'origine unum' in the original sin *common to all* is quite certainly binding upon faith (though not directly defined) in the full and strict meaning upon which the usual indirect proof of monogenism relies. It can then still be asked whether this traditional interpretation of the unity and mode of transmission of original sin can be derived from Scripture itself, and how far this may be done, such that in this way it can be made the basis of an indirect argument for monogenism.

All we have so far said about the traditional form of the indirect proof is only intended to show one thing: that there is no need to feel that the endeavour to provide this indirect proof has yet reached its term. Something still remains to be done. Clearly the most important thing to do would be to examine carefully the theological weight of that whole tradition which forms the basis of the indirect proof of monogenism in its usual form. This is of course impossible in a slight essay like this.

We have a much more modest contribution to this indirect proof in mind here, which is simply to offer a small study of the teaching of *Scripture* in this matter. We are not so much concerned with the formal conclusiveness of the considerations to be put forward in favour of monogenism, with an effort to retain the desired result in as few and as 'clear' syllogisms as possible (what usually happens here is that the real difficulty remains hidden away in one of the premises classified as obvious). We hope rather to extend the field of vision by showing how closely monogenism coheres with the fundamental Biblical conception of a history of salvation and damnation. It is in this sense that the following discussion must be understood. If we succeed in showing that monogenism is not simply a marginal idea in Scripture, the only function of which is to elucidate something which would remain in just the same form without this elucidation, we should have fulfilled the task we have set ourselves here in this section.

2. The community of a stock as the basis of the community of salvation and damnation

A difficulty concerning our question meets us at the very start. In this connexion it should be noticed that the fact of the redemption of *all* men by the *one* Christ from whom we are not physically descended in no way shows that an individual and his action for others can be morally significant before God independently of whether he stands with regard to the others in an ontologically real relationship of membership or not. For the question is precisely whether Christ can only be Head and Mediator of humanity because and only because he is a member of a humanity monogenistically one from the origin.[1]

However obvious it may be in itself, one thing must be made perfectly clear from the start: it is utterly unacceptable from the viewpoint of Catholic theology to regard some object (or the inquiry into it) as dogmatically or theologically irrelevant just because it is also to be found in the field of the profane sciences or has such a scientific aspect or consequence. One cannot allot their respective competences to theology and the sciences simply by telling them to 'part and be friends'. One cannot begin by tidily banishing the objects of theology to an 'existential' beyond, the sphere of 'the events of faith', with the result that they are no longer even capable of disturbing the profane sciences or being disturbed by them. If God's word has gone forth and the Redemption has taken place, they have done so for Christianity

---

[1] Hence I do not fully understand what de Fraine is trying to prove by appealing (p. 61 or 223) to the statements of Cornelius Mussus at the Council of Trent (Ehses V, p. 175; 'omnes eramus in Adam, cum ipse peccavit antequam nasceremur, cum nascimur, Adam in nobis est. Quemadmodum cum Christus pro nobis passus est, omnes in eo eramus . . .'). The parallel may show that not every moral consequence necessarily presupposes a relationship of *descent* precisely between the cause and the subject of the effect. But it does not prove that such a consequence can dispense with the presupposition of an ontologically real connexion, based on the physical unity of the stock.

ust where we exist in other respects, in the one space of existence in which we live in other respects with our experience and our science. Of course we *know* of this decisive event for salvation which took place here because we have been *told* of it and have believed what we were told, but it took place and is heard of just where we are in other respects. Hence theology can never admit that the object of a profane science could lie utterly outside its competence. The one identical reality is the object of faith and of profane science under *essentially* different aspects, but it remains one and the same for all that. In the last resort it is theology alone which can decide whether in a particular case something falls within her competence and is theologically significant or not. Hence if an object of theology penetrates into the realm in which the profane sciences pursue their way (as for instance happens with the existence of Jesus, the historicity of a definite statement made by him, the empty tomb), it cannot be totally untheological to want searchingly to examine the statements of faith intellectually, i.e. logically and metaphysically, in respect of their meaning, their presuppositions and their consequences. This is indeed a matter of course for Catholic theology generally speaking, but one cannot help having the impression that in the question of monogenism a kind of juridical theology has been practised with undue exclusiveness: a few individual propositions are interrogated in the way in which a jurist interrogates a paragraph of a statute and takes as indisputable in themselves propositions from 'positive law'; thus he looks at the propositions and not properly at the reality meant by them, making little attempt to discover the one meaning of the whole so as to grasp it in terms of the whole of reality.

But now to our real business. In the Scriptures Christ appears as our Redeemer, not (only) because he is man (1 Tim 2:5) and thus of 'specifically' the same nature, but because he is the 'firstborn'[1] among

---

[1] It does not concern us here in what sense Christ is called firstborn in Rom 8:29 (in the sense of Col 1:15 or Col 1:18; Apoc 1:5; 1 Cor 15:49; Phil 3:21). Nor is it denied that the 'brethren' in question here are those who are being conformed to Christ, and that a close kinship with the Son is based upon the spirit of adoption. But they are not just 'brethren' because they are conformed to him, but because they are brethren they are destined to become conformed to him (in glory). *This* brotherliness cannot be simply that of a community of disposition, of a supernaturally ethical kind. For in view of the irreducible distinction maintained by Jesus and the whole New Testament elsewhere between our filiation and his Sonship, it would be

many *brethren*, and we are his brethren according to the flesh (Rom
8:29; Heb 2:11.12.17). He is of the seed of David according to the flesh
(Rom 1:3) and thus has assumed just that flesh of sin in need of
redemption (Rom 8:3), he is 'of' the fathers according to the flesh
(Rom 9:5); he the Sanctifier and we who are sanctified are all of the
same origin: ἐξ ἑνός (Heb 2:11). This verse means 'that Christ and
Christians are descended from one like children of a common flesh
and blood (v. 14). In view of the emphasis laid upon the bodily kinship
this one is not God but Adam.'[1] Because our connexion with him is of
this kind we justly lay claim to the inheritance of his glory with the
Father (Rom 8:17.29).[2] The emphasis laid upon the identity of origin
and on the assumption of a human nature precisely as historically
incriminated (the σὰρξ ἁμαρτίας: Rom 8:3; Eph 2:14; Jn 1:14
Col 1:22; 1 Tim 3:16; Heb 5:7; 10:20; 1 Pet 3:18; 4:1; 1 Jn 4:2
2 Jn 7) shows clearly that Christ's brotherhood with us can be neither
a mere community of disposition or of grace, nor one based purely
upon the specifically identical human nature. Rather he enters redemp
tively into our *one* common history of guilt, which is one because it
is the history of our physically real common stock.[3] That σάρξ which
is his is not just a quidditative but an historical concept: that which
has become what it is and belongs to us as the inheritance of the stock
it is that historically evolved situation of our existence which became

---

peculiar if these two things were now being subsumed under the one con
cept of brotherhood. The reason why we can speak of a brotherhood at all
must lie at that point at which we are really 'consubstantial' with him, in
such a way, then, that those who are like each other are really 'brethren'
hence in virtue of a common stock. This train of thought finds confirmation
in the Epistle to the Hebrews.

[1] Procksch in TWNT I, p. 113.

[2] To repeat, it is the possession of the Spirit of Christ that gives us our
immediate right. But that his Spirit can be in question for us at all (and this
must keep on happening if we are to lay hold of it) is due precisely to the
fact that he belongs to our flesh. For when it is asked why the condemnation
of sin in Christ's flesh should mean anything at all for us, the only possible
(though not yet adequate) answer according to the mind of the New Testa
ment is: because his 'flesh' is 'our' flesh. This answer puts us new questions
fails perhaps to 'explain' very much. Nevertheless it is the answer which
must be given first and foremost, although it may itself be in need of theo
logical clarification.

[3] Cf. on this point E. Stauffer's analyses in TWNT II, pp. 432–40 (εἱς)
which are instructive for the whole problematic of the categories employed

is in that he precisely came to be as we come to be flesh (Jn 3:6), by birth in a generative series: he is of woman and *therefore* has an origin κατὰ σάρκα (Rom 1:3; 9:5). The unity of the community of redemption, and thus of the community of salvation and damnation of humanity in general, is not a purely juridical one, rising out of the coincidence of the actions of originally isolated individuals; it is not a 'universal' formed subsequently from individuals thought of as alone being real: it is a community of a stock. Because and in so far as Christ entered into this community by being 'born of woman' (Gal 4:4) he is solidary with men and they with him.[1] We have here a use of the concept of the unity of a stock as a theological concept independent of the Genesis account. This use (in the doctrine of Redemption) may indeed be preformed by the Old Testament doctrine of the one historical origin of the human situation of condemnation which extends to us and in which we come to be as members of this common stock. Nevertheless the *new* use shows that the New Testament takes up the doctrine independently and uses it on its own responsibility. And that again shows that it is not just 'making a citation' in this case, leaving the meaning and bearing of the idea, as well as its limits, to the Old Testament.

The objection is naturally to be expected here that even in the New Testament the whole thing arises out of a typically Semitic and anyway archaic or even 'mythological' kind of thought, which is only capable of thinking of a community of destiny and a similarity of kind in terms of the community of a stock. To this it must be replied that nowhere is it laid down that such 'archaic' thought does not see more truly than our atomistic and individualistic thought today. One would have to ask whether it was methodologically and objectively sound to push off lightly on to some alien 'thought-form' a conception which does not strike us immediately as obvious (as though this were to explain anything, since it is only to replace one question by another, provided that one does not simply regard a thought-form, in a mechanistic and biological way, as a matter in no need of further explanation and accessible to none), instead of allowing this thought

[1] We should remind ourselves of the theological sense of the genealogy in Luke, who takes it back to Adam (Lk 3:38). It becomes all the more necessary to ask what the genealogy really means if it is held that the last part before Adam has no historical content in the modern sense.

to draw our attention to something which would otherwise escape our notice but which is usually capable of being comprehended by us. Clearly it is methodologically necessary in such a case to look at the reality itself with the eyes of Scripture, to make this object present in its own intelligibility, which is to practise theology and not just historical philology. This will allow us to see clearly that Scripture does not merely 'elucidate' and 'illustrate' something (namely the human unity of destiny and kind) 'in this way' (by a unity of stock); it justly sees in this and expresses through it an objective and essential presupposition[1] of the former truths. One might be tempted to say that a little 'blood and soil mysticism' would be beneficial here and would teach us to see what *is*, not merely what is 'thought' by one but what is overlooked by the other. We shall have to take this up in the third part of our discussion, returning meanwhile to our examination of Scripture.

This unity of saving history resting on the unity of a stock in which all men are solidary with Christ because he is of their stock[2], becomes still clearer as a reality for Scripture (and Tradition) in the doctrine of original sin.[3] It is true that the handing down of original sin (or putting it differently, the extension to further human subjects prior to their personal decision of that situation of pneuma-less ungodliness realized independently of Christ) in virtue of *generation* precisely is not expressly declared in Scripture. We have also seen that the assertion that this is a defined doctrine is not entirely free from doubt, while it is of course a doctrine general and undisputed in the Church. But the doctrine is in reality attested in Scripture. We are 'flesh'

---

[1] We say '*a* presupposition' not 'the adequate justification'. In the ordinary scholastic doctrine of original sin the question is for instance certainly treated of, without a final decision, as to how far the fact that Adam is the physical origin of the stock suffices to establish the possibility of hereditary guilt, or whether anything else is necessary. Unfortunately parallel questions in Christology are not submitted to a sufficiently careful examination.

[2] It would be interesting perhaps to reflect on how the unity of community with Christ in the one stock was gradually weakened by its Greek equivalent, that he is *consubstantialis* with us. The historical perspective is displaced by one which is confined to the static quiddity. 'He has the same nature as we have' says less than 'He is of our stock'.

[3] It goes without saying that we have no intention of providing here a general Biblical theology of original sin. The greater part of it has to be assumed here.

fleshly' (in the sense of a condition of hereditary guilt, i.e. Spirit-less, subject to death as the manifestation of this guilt-incurred abandonment by the Spirit, in the servitude of the law which provokes us to personal sin) because we are *born* of flesh (Jn 3:6), because we are flesh from our very origin (φύσει: Eph 2:3; cf. 1 Cor 15:44–9). Death, which for St Paul is the manifestation of the sin which entered into the world in the beginning, is for him an *inherited* death (true though it is that it can also be an expression of personal guilt). We die in Adam' (1 Cor 15: 21 s.), because it is from him that we bear his earthly image (1 Cor 15:48 s.).[1] But if this is true of death, it is true of death's inner essence, original guilt itself: it really is *hereditary* guilt, a guilt-situation which is ours because we human beings belong to a common stock: *born* of flesh and therefore flesh.[2]

All we have said about the situation of salvation and damnation may be summed up as follows: Scripture knows of such a common situation of salvation and ruin only in so far as men are of one stock.

3. The institution of the community of salvation and damnation by the act of an individual

This general situation of salvation and damnation having the unity of a stock for its presupposition is not however simply a static exisential which is just there. Rather it has come to be historically by a personal action. Such an act, if it is to be of significance for all, i.e. for those too who have not posited it, presupposes that the agent and those jointly affected by his act are of a single stock. But the reverse is true too: the fact of being affected by salvation and damnation is caused

---

[1] We have still to see that this general guilt-situation was established historically, by the trespass of an individual. For the moment the important point is that it is general and that its generality extends as far as the common stock by means of which it is spread.

[2] The overcoming of this guilt-situation can consequently be conceived of as a re-*birth*: Jn 3:3–5; Tit 3:5 s.; 1 Pet 1:3.23. While the 'new creation' might be conceived of as 'birth' without reference to another birth, the emergence of the pneumatic man can only be called 're-birth' in regard to a birth which puts the one born into fleshly existence; what is more, this latter birth clearly does not just put him there because without birth he would not exist, and when he exists he is precisely fleshly: it is because the birth *as descent* from fleshly man brings forth the one born into the fleshly common stock.

by a unique act which took place once for all within this community. This is clear with Christ in the first place. In the flesh which he shared with us, he, the concretely and historically one, abolished sin by his obedience, and our situation became that of the redeemed, of the redeemed by God.

But it is true of Adam too. That is to say, the one Adam and his act are not the plastic, symbolic simplification of a process in itself 'complicated', which St Paul merely sketched out (in imitation of the symbolic speech of the Old Testament) so as to have a smoothly working parallel to the one Christ. This we shall now try to show.

Let us ask first of all: what, according to *Scripture*, Tradition and the Council of Trent, is the minimum[1] if we are to continue to speak of original sin at all? The answer must run as follows: by 'original sin' we must at least mean a general situation of damnation[2] embracing all men prior to their own personal free decision, a situation which is nevertheless historic and not an essential condition, one which has come to be through man and is not simply given in the fact of creatureliness. If there were no situation of damnation prior to the sin of the individual, it would be impossible to speak of an hereditary original sin, a cosmic sin (Rom 5:12), the 'generatione' of Trent even as the mere opposite of 'imitatione' would be false and Pelagius would be

---

[1] The word 'minimum' does not of course mean that the minimum ascertained in this way is sufficient in fact for the teaching of the Church. It is a minimum agreed to for purely methodological purposes, which if it were absent would make it impossible, as *everyone* must see at once, to speak of original sin in the Church's sense.

[2] This concept should not be allowed to obscure the character of the state of guilt, in the strict sense, in original sin. Nevertheless it is in our opinion capable of indicating the distinction between original and personal sin, and also of making a point of view clear in a way which concerns us here: this is the universality of original sin, which is precisely not that of a subsequent conceptual unification of the actual sinfulness of many individuals, but is something prior to the individuals as such. And this 'prior something' is not only Adam's one sin as a once-for-all, temporally punctiform happening, but a real *universal* unity, which may best be appreciated by being called a *situation*. This is not exactly the same as what is called in scholastic theology the *debitum contrahendi peccatum originale*; yet the latter expression too draws attention to a state of affairs which is prior to the existence of the individual and the original sin which is inwardly his, and yet cannot simply be identified with the *peccatum originale originans* as Adam's sinful act.

in the right. If the origin of this universal situation were not historically human, what we should have would be Manicheism (as Augustine
would say) or a conception which saw inevitable sinfulness in the very
fact of being creaturely. Here we must bear in mind what has already
been shown: in so far as this situation of damnation is general, i.e. is
binding for every individual, it is based upon the community of the
stock. We may then go on to ask the following question. Is it possible
to conceive of and to maintain this universally pre-personal and yet
historically realized situation of damnation proper to the stock as such,
if its historical origin did not lie in a single real individual in the
beginning and in his act? The answer is in the negative.

A *universal* situation of damnation is only conceivable, supposing
it to be based upon the community of a stock, if it was historically
established at the *origin* of this community. A later member *within*
such a community can certainly become, by his being and actions, of
saving significance for the *whole* community, as we see in the case of
Christ's act, which is salvation for the pre-Christian world too.[1] But
a later member cannot establish a situation of *damnation* for all. For
the temporal priority of many of the members of this community
would make possible and enforce a personal decision by them which
would precede such a situation of damnation not only temporally but
also in reality, which could, in other words, make it impossible in
advance. For a situation of *damnation* can only be brought about by
one who himself belongs totally to this temporal history.[2] But if the
founder of damnation belongs totally to time and if this time is
genuine time, i.e. irreversible, and not merely a reflexion of an intem-
poral 'simultaneous' network of relations of dependency which can

[1] The ancient Church was exercised by the question of how this was
possible (e.g. 'Christ's preaching in the underworld'; the doctrine of faith
in the Redeemer to come as a cause of salvation). In later times people have
been rather too easily satisfied with the statement that the redemption of the
pre-Christian world took place *intuitu meritorum Christi*. This is perfectly
correct, but it is an abstractly formal answer which tells us nothing about
how this single divine purpose of salvation embracing the totality of the
world in Christ so produces its effect upon the pre-Christian world that the
grace given to this world is really Christ's; for surely this means more than
the acceptance in God's eyes of Christ's action as the 'juridical' title for this
grace. But we cannot go further into this question here.
[2] In Biblical terms: a second individual who is still an 'Adam' is only
possible if he is more than the son of Adam and his other ancestors.

run as well in a reverse direction as in their merely apparently temporal exposition[1]; then the later cannot be the ground of the earlier's situation of damnation. To assert the opposite would be to degrade time and the temporal to mere appearance. But it is one of the basic presuppositions of Christianity that time is a reality, created by God, and that in this genuine time itself salvation and damnation come to pass. Thus the historical act which establishes the one situation of *universal damnation* of the one stock must necessarily have been established at the *origin* of the stock.

This historical origin of the situation of damnation at the beginning of the stock can only proceed from an *individual*: in other words, it cannot there and then have been posited by a multitude. The plurality of those to posit the situation of damnation is something which is in direct contradiction with what we are here concerned to maintain: that a situation of damnation is to be found prior to the freedom of any individual you like. Whether it were many (if original sin did not exist) or few (if a polygenistic 'explanation' of original sin were justified) who decide independently of each other, without presupposing in their decision an historically realized situation of damnation already there, would make no difference to the facts of the case: there would be *many* who do not act out of the solidarity of an historically realized disposition of things in their regard. But if this could be the case in this order of salvation, and with men who give being by generation[2], then original sin ought not to exist at all. If it did indeed exist for many, who would nevertheless form only a part of men,

---

[1] The eternal God's timeless knowledge of the whole of the genuinely temporally structured (i.e. objectively irreversible) Whole of the world and its history may not simply be used as a substitute for a terrestrially impossible relationship between a temporally later cause and a temporally earlier effect, when the precise question at issue is how the cause-effect relationships lie in the temporal world itself. We do not in fact pray for the happy issue of past events too, which would be perfectly possible on the contrary assumption. God can indeed, in so far as he wills the totality of a definite world, will every part so far as it is a part and hence stands in correspondence with everything else; and so everything can be of significance for everything else (no matter what point of time it occupies). But this does not signify any terrestrial causality of the later on the earlier; and that is all we are investigating here.

[2] We shall speak later in more detail about this point, that it is always a question of men who have the active power to *form* a plurality.

although men form an historical community of goal, it would split the
history of the salvation of all humanity into two wholly disparate
(though unequal) parts. The situation, that is, which forms an
intrinsic factor in man's creaturely freedom, i.e. his *externally* conditioned freedom, would be essentially different in the two parts: the
situation of Paradise[1] and the situation of deliverance as a liberating
redemption.

The fact that it is not at all easy to visualize this clearly is the result
of a *lusus imaginationis*: one thinks of the one original member as a
random, variable member of a multitude. One argues to oneself: if
there has been *one* 'Adam', who in spite of the radically different
situation from which he set out to make his free decision can nevertheless form a unity of personal community and history with his posterity
then there could have been two or three or more, and each one of
them can (by himself or together with the others) hand down an
'original sin', if this is still to be the way of things. But this precisely
will not do, or at least this 'idea' in no way proves that this is how
things are or can be in reality and that the proof of the contrary already
provided must be false. For these many would already constitute—
prior to their decision—humanity as a multitude, the 'members' of
which share no common situation (no matter whether, each for himself, they were to produce a somewhat similar situation for their
posterity in each case). The fact that there is one instance by no means
proves the possibility of a multitude of them. The first is precisely not
necessarily one of a multitude with the index '1' but it is in our case
the whole in its original unity.[2] Thus it is lacking in cogency to argue

---

[1] What use is made of this situation is another question, with which we
have nothing to do here. Let it be noted in passing that Mary's case is not
the one in mind here, the case of a paradisal supralapsarian situation of
freedom; it is the supreme and the most radical case of the infralapsarian
situation of redemption, which presupposes the situation of damnation. This
may be seen simply from the fact that Mary finds her salvation and works it
out *in carne passibili*.

[2] The whole in its original unity does not make the whole which arises
out of it superfluous, neither is it merely the first member of the latter.
Otherwise one would have a series, but no stock and no genuine time, in
which the later is no longer capable of reaching back behind the origin but
remains enduringly committed to it. The idea of a mathematical series, in
which one term proves the possibility of another, is out of place here. For
one term does not really arise out of the other in such a series. The problem

that if there can be one Adam who is not bound to act on the basis of an infralapsarian situation of 'flesh' but on the contrary posits this situation, then there 'can' (at least) be many such. For if the one Adam is humanity in the sense of its origin and not merely the first of a series, it is no longer possible to say that there has once been a supralapsarian situation open to decision, then it 'can' exist more than once (which is impossible, as we have shown). It is not every unit that can be multiplied in every respect. Any one of these many individuals not subject to original sin would be only one *among* many in relation to the many subject to original sin who do not descend from him (not their origin, which essentially forms a primitive and not a special case) and yet of an essentially different kind: the situation of damnation would cease to be the common one. And yet this commonness of the situation of damnation is presupposed by every Christian interpretation of existence: you, I, all of us here below, begin as the lost[1], so much so that we know from the start that everyone we come across in the course of our history, with whom we have to do as 'neighbour', is of this kind. The fact that this common situation came into being 'historically' makes no difference. It shows rather how this very historical origin is to be conceived of if it is not to do away with the universality of the situation of damnation. This origin in its proto-historical character must lie wholly behind us, it has a kind of historical transcendence, it cannot be encountered as one factor alongside another in our history. But that is what it would be if (speaking quite concretely) a sinner in the course of his history could encounter another primordial man who was ('so far', at any rate) in a state of justice.

It becomes clear from these considerations that we cannot interpret Rom 5:12 s. as a plastic simplification and stylization of the plural occurrence of more than one Fall. We must either take the text as it stands, the one Adam as one[2] has made all into sinners; or we must

---

of the multiplicability of the origin is thus different from that of the multiplicability of what arises from it and of the terms of a purely quantitative series. It should be observed that the proof offered here is purely negative: we do not prove that the *possibility*, apparently obvious in itself, of a multiple human origin is more than—a confusion.

[1] Someone who thinks of Mary too and of the divine purpose of salvation embracing the situation of lostness would perhaps do better to say 'as those who are to be delivered and the one delivered by anticipation'.

[2] 'One' is really better here than 'individual'. The old problem of

simply reject original sin and understand the text as the existentialist analysis of man in general as a sinner in terms of the purely mythological image of 'Adam'. Every other explanation is a hybrid. But if original sin did not exist, then the redemption of many by one would be superfluous too; and we should have to reject it for the same reasons as those for which St Paul's doctrine of original sin is rejected *a priori* by an atomistic Existentialism based on the uniqueness of the isolated conscience and a guilt which always transcends history. St Paul was therefore completely right when, taking as his starting-point Christ and the knowledge of his Redemption, he gave new depth to the Old Testament doctrine of a situation of death inherited from Adam by making it into a doctrine of original sin, and setting the one Adam and the one Christ in strict parallel to each other.

One result at least ought to have emerged from these considerations: monogenism is a doctrine which is closely connected with the whole basic conception of saving history found in Scripture. It is not something barely attested marginally by this or that brief text, a pure matter of fact which could quite 'possibly' be otherwise. This last point may now serve as the occasion for some discussion of a few matters of principle.

---

humanity's 'being contained' in Adam should be taken up again from the standpoint of Adam's never to be repeated 'uniqueness' ('*Einmaligkeit*'), which becomes more intelligible in the course of such considerations. It is to miss the point either—as is usual today—to make Adam merely the first individual in a series, or to try to grasp the ontological realities involved here in terms of a Platonic universal, in the Patristic manner. The transcendence of primeval history in our regard could give new life to our understanding of the ancient traditional doctrine of the privileges of Paradise, an understanding which is in danger today (cf. H. Rondet, *Problèmes pour la réflexion chrétienne. Le Péché originel. L'Enfer et autres études*, Paris, 1945). All one has to see is that the historicity of the primeval history is not simply a piece of our history with its structures, structures which in spite of all the variety and diversity of what takes place in it remain homogeneous with those of primeval history; that it is and seeks to be a history with its own structures (if it is taken seriously), granting the identity of what exists in both historical regions. Once this is seen, no insuperable reserves will be felt towards the portrayal of Paradise found in classical theology. It is to be expected, indeed postulated theologically, that this portrayal should not 'fit in with' *our* conceptual world and its science.

III. THE POSSIBILITIES FOR A METAPHYSICAL PROOF OF MONOGENISM

1. We assume that from the point of view of the natural sciences polygenism even as a scientific hypothesis possesses no greater probability than monogenism. We assume that monogenism in the strict sense (i.e. one unique original human pair) cannot be proved scientifically, i.e. that from the purely empirical standpoint many original pairs might be possible 'in se'.

2. However it should not simply be assumed as obvious that monogenism can *only* be known by us here and now in virtue of a positive revelation. Not as though this were impossible *a priori*. But we have here to do with realities which on the one hand belong in themselves to the natural order, or at any rate are not mysteries in the strict sense, and of which on the other hand it is extremely difficult to say just when and how they formed the express object of a revelation. One only endangers the appropriation of such realities in faith by being in too much of a hurry to banish this object from the realm of natural knowledge and erect the knowledge of it solely upon the basis of this text of the Bible or that. There is a theological positivism too, and it is dangerous. Clearly the only way in which one can answer the question whether monogenism can really be proved philosophically (i.e. within the framework of a theological metaphysics) is by trying to do it and seeing how far one succeeds.

3. *Notes for a metaphysics of generation.* Such an attempt would have to presuppose an analysis of the essence of generation in terms of natural *philosophy* if it is to be firmly based. It is not a rash judgment to assert that there is nothing adequate in this field within the framework of scholastic philosophy[1], although the subject is of course

---

[1] It is impossible that such a metaphysics of generation should exist for the simple reason that *generatio aequivoca* was taken for a fact, so that from the first generation was looked at as being on the same level as other processes of change, all of them being conceived of after the manner of human production of a form in matter. Where *generatio aequivoca* is regarded as possible and real, monogenism must always have the look of a mere fact which could just as well not be. Consequently, the effort thoroughly to

treated of according to the lines laid down in Aristotle's *De Generatione*. Clearly it is impossible to make good this neglect here. Nevertheless we shall try to offer some remarks on this theme, in an attempt to show that such an ontology of generation might perhaps be of use in the discussion of monogenism. In full consciousness of the questionableness of such a procedure we shall omit all discussion of generation in living things in general and turn our attention at once to human generation. What is offered is merely a sketch for a route which might perhaps be followed.

a. Man is to be conceived of as spirit, and as a bodily spirit: both together, so that he is body in order to be spirit, and only is a spiritual person as such (in the concrete) by incorporation. 'Corporeality' is understood in the first place as spatio-temporal determination. Thus man has a world, i.e. he is a here and now in the one continuum of space and time and is himself a spirit who has a space-time. He is not a personal spirit first 'and then' also an entity with a body. But bodiliness is the necessary mode in which alone he can reach the achievement of his spiritual being.

b. The personal spirit is a spirit referred to others. An absolutely lonely spirit is a contradiction in itself and—so far as it is possible at all—is Hell. If (a) is correct, then what (b) means is that the bodily spirit which is man exists by necessity of nature (also) in relation to a Thou, which is itself present in its own spatio-temporal world as such. It is not only as an isolated person but also as isolated *man* that an individual man is incapable of perfection—or is Hell. Where there is man, there is necessarily—not only in fact—*human* community, i.e. bodily personal community, personally spatio-temporal community.

c. Spatio-temporal order (the basic structure of bodiliness too) is not a subsequent, purely conceptual summation or abstract of individual spatio-temporal entities; it is the single and, as single, exhaustively distributed, prior real condition of the possibility of the individual spatio-temporal entity. Both the scholastic ontology of *materia prima*, when it has reached an understanding of its own nature, and tendencies

---

analyse monogenism philosophically is paralysed from the start. It seems as though this medieval attitude is still active in theology today.

in modern physics point in this direction. Thus every material entity is co-determined in its real concreteness by the totality of material reality.

d. The *living* spatio-temporal entity must exhibit this dependency of the individual upon the whole (its whole) as something itself living, if life is to be on the one hand a new, irreducible order (dimension) above the inorganic, and on the other hand a higher dimension precisely of the spatio-temporal order and not something 'alongside' it. The individual living thing is thus an entity which is necessarily determined *as* living by the totality of the form of life to which it belongs and whose concrete individuality it displays, just as the individual, merely spatio-temporal thing is determined by the prior real spatio-temporal order in general. The institution of such a form of life itself takes place quite concretely in the institution of the first living thing of this species: this is not merely the first instance of a purely ideal multitude which arises by the emergence (no matter how) of the individuals; it is the institution of the totality in its origin.

e. The real dependence of the individual spatio-temporal living thing upon the totality of its form of life reaches its real completion and concrete manifestation in generation. Hence this is not just *one* possible way in which an individual spatio-temporal living thing (as such) and a living spatio-temporal thing as such may 'also' come to be: it is the only possible way. Generation must be conceived of transcendentally as *the* exclusive genesis (not one of the possible ways of coming to be) for the living individual as such within a species. Just as sensibility is not just *one* of the possibilities of receptive (spiritual) knowledge but the only one, so the coming to be of the living individual within a single species (i.e. in a characteristic living spatio-temporal unity) is generation and nothing else. Where a living thing arises differently, what takes place is not the coming to be of an individual within a species but the institution of the species itself. Anyone who contests this conception of generation and treats it as a merely contingent possibility among many other, at least conceivable possibilities, denies that the individual spatio-temporal thing and the living thing as spatio-temporal are contained within a real *a priori* unity which forms the condition of the possibility of the spatio-temporal individual as such; or he refuses to allow that this holds also for the living thing as such, i.e. in so far as it displays being of a higher order than the merely inorganic material thing.

f. If and in so far as man is and must be a spatio-temporal personal spirit in a spatio-temporal community of like beings, he is a spirit living in matter: *animal rationale*; living animately so as to be spirit and to be spirit in human community.

g. But then it is true of man too that generation is the one necessary way of forming community; where the human species has already been instituted in its origin, no other way of man's spatio-temporal extension in community than that of generation is possible. The institution of a new origin would be the institution of another species. Monogenism and the unity of species allow of being distinguished conceptually but not of being separated in reality. Conversely, wherever 'polygenistic' phenomena are really to be found, what we are in presence of is the genesis of a metaphysically new species, not the multiple original coming to be of the same one; or (if this is not the case) not the genesis of a new species in the metaphysical sense but merely accidental spatio-temporal variations of the same species (in the metaphysical sense).

4. *Monogenism and the transcendence of the divine creation of man.* We may look at the metaphysical problem of monogenism from another point of view. This will give us an opportunity of replying to an objection which may easily arise to what we have just said. It will probably be objected to no. 3 that it is surely beyond all doubt that God can create many men on this earth independently of each other. To doubt this would be to restrict in a quite absurd way the divine omnipotence, which must be able to do more than once what it once could and has done (thereby proving that it is intrinsically possible). Our second mode of approach may also perhaps be more easily intelligible in view of the extremely sketchy character of what has been said above.

a. Before attacking the new question itself we have once more to draw attention to an established position. Man is a being distinguished in a strictly metaphysical sense from everything below him. However difficult it may be to say where natural boundaries of a really meta-physical kind run in the realm of things below man, man knows that a radical boundary of nature lies between him and everything below and near him, because he is spirit, person, selfconsciousness, transcendence opening in knowledge and freedom upon the unlimited, beyond the inevitable particularity of his environment. He is not just a combina-tion in a different pattern of what is to be found elsewhere in the material world. What he is cannot be conceived of as a modification of other realities. He has an essence really distinct from any other, which is one and entire, irreducible to another. Hence he must be an original institution; not a modification of what was there already, taking place through its own powers, but an original reality newly instituted by God. It may well be that inanimate and animate elements already present in the world are drawn upon and united in this original new beginning, and that man thus has a real genetic connexion with the animal kingdom in the one dimension of organic life. But this makes no difference with regard to the really decisive point: the one entire man as a whole is God's original institution and not the *bare* product of terrestrial forces, conceived of as having produced man solely in virtue of potentialities permanently inserted in other terrestrial beings. We need not attempt to decide here whether this irreducible novelty of nature may only be recognized in the field of the spirit and of the humane sciences, or whether it is also manifested with sufficient clarity in man's bodily and sensitive life, and thus in the field of the natural sciences too.[1] It makes no difference to the estab-lished fact, though it may make some difference in the method by which the fact is exactly established.

b. A certain caution is in place when reference is made to some 'potentiality' in God in virtue of his omnipotence. The abstract possibility of an entity or a fact, when this is regarded in itself and in its own isolated relationship to God's power, is to be distinguished from a concrete possibility of whatever is in question when it is related to the totality of things in the world which already exist, to the one world in which they are to exist, to the intelligibility of the divine action (*potentia ordinata*), to the mode of action proper to God as creator of the world, i.e. to the transcendent creator of a self-consistent

[1] Cf. the investigations of Gehlen, Portmann and others.

world of which God and his action are not a portion but the background, the meta-physical condition of the world's own reality.[1] In
relation to one and the same whole, for example, something which is
possible 'in itself' because it exists in this whole can both be impossible a second time[2] and can also be contradictory as an object of
God's meaningful action. The possibility of an imaginative reduplica-
tion of the same thing at two different places and-or times, both being
thought of as brought about by the same divine cause, affords us proof
that something of the sort is a genuine possibility in itself and for God.

. Assuming now what has been said in (a) and (b), we may follow
two complementary ways in order to further our argument that
polygenism as an object of the divine action is impossible.

1. It is impossible that the same thing (specifically the same, such
that the *only* distinction would be that of a purely *negative* difference of
spatio-temporal location) should be able to have two categorically
different causes. Or putting it in another way, two causes which *as
such* are (specifically) different cannot cause the same thing (specifically). Now men arise through generation. Thus this is not one
specific mode but *the* specific of their genesis, i.e. another specifically
different mode of genesis is impossible for them.

It cannot be argued against this that the first man, and thus 'a' man
did not arise through generation. For obviously the transcendent
institution of the cause of an effect is categorically different in kind
from the institution of the effect by this cause. The institution of the
world and its original potencies by the world-transcending causality
of the Absolute and the institution of the terrestrial effects of these

[1] The Thomist may be reminded here of an example which shows how
easily man's quantitative imagination deceives him in such matters. Even in
the philosophy of mature scholasticism there were still countless people for
whom it was 'evident' that God could create two angels 'Gabriel'. This is
nonsensical for the Thomist.

[2] The case in which something is duplicated with identical local and
temporal characters is easily seen to be impossible by everyone. But it would
be false to assert that this is the only conceivable case. This is not a matter of
course for the simple reason that the real unity of place in general can bring
it about that something at one place makes 'the same thing' impossible at
another.

potencies are categorically different. But the institution of the firs
man (without injury to his individuality) is an institution of a prim
cause (*Ur-sache*), not the institution of an effect like that instituted b
this cause. For the first man is instituted precisely as capable o
generating; and he is instituted by God, not by a terrestrial cause. Bu
if the Absolute, without being obliged to achieve itself in the institutio
of the conditioned, does institute something conditioned, which ca
produce effects and whose capacity to produce effects belongs to it
nature; then the Absolute is not 'able' once again to produce and t
wish to produce that precisely for which it has created the cause dis
tinct from itself. Of course the Unconditioned 'can' do what tha
which was conditioned by it can do. But it cannot wish once again t
institute without the conditioned that of which the conditioned i
capable, once it has instituted the conditioned.

2. A *repeated* institution of the terrestrial cause by God[1] woul
make his own action, in so far as he is Creator, and thus meta-physica
condition of the possibility of the finite, into a *terrestrial* event. Th
question to arise here would not only be that of the meaningfulnes
of such a divine action. Why does he himself do what he has given t
the creature itself to do and to perform, or why does he giv
the creature a power from which he himself immediately removes th
field of activity by himself doing that for which in fact he created th
creature? Such activity would be contrary to the principle of economy
which is not only a methodological principle of cognition but a meta
physical principle too. God's action would become a terrestrial event
it would become a miracle. That divine activity, of a miraculous kind
is terrestrial which takes place at a fixed point in space and time withi
the whole of material reality; and there on the one hand is as suc
observable, and on the other can be recognized as the divine institutio
of novelty. But such action on the part of God is precisely his actio
in *saving* history, in which he wishes to reveal himself as someon

---

[1] We must always reflect on the fact that the humanity in question is *on
in kind, goal and living-space. The first single human pair is already sufficien
as a cause for that. Thus if several first human pairs had been created, th
cause would have been instituted more than once for the same end: for al
generated men, who are intended to form a unity of a more than conceptua
kind.

who conducts a personal dialogue with the spiritual person and in regard to him, and does not only maintain his sway as transcendent cause of the world itself. The fresh creation of a man in the realm of a man already in existence would thus be a terrestrial, miraculous activity on God's part, which therefore ought necessarily to belong to *saving* history and yet in itself would form a part of the purely natural history of creation. It is thus a contradiction. But in saving history and there alone the transcendent cause steps forth from behind the veil of space and time and conducts a dialogue with man. Otherwise it institutes the world and its individual, irreducibly separate origins, without putting itself as an agent *in* the world. Every occasion on which it does this immediately and necessarily has the character of personal dialogue addressed to man. But that is Revelation, not Creation.

A polygenistic account of man's coming into being may take one of two forms. It may either be a biological materialism, holding that no transcendent cause (i.e. one not capable of being localized as cause in space and time)[1] is needed for the genesis of man, nor any intervention of God from beyond space and time.[2] Or it may be a naive anthropomorphism, to which pious people are especially liable, imagining that God as Creator produces effects in the world (instead of the world itself), that transcendent miracles of creation can take place every day in the world (instead of saying that the days of the world, its course—not a link in its course—are instituted), that God fills out gaps in the world with his activity, why, he even continues to appear (as in our case) where he has not even left a gap, since he has already seen to the multiplication of men and their historical connexion by the institution of the one human pair capable of procreation.

Certainly it follows once again, when one considers more closely what has been said, though no further examination in detail will be undertaken here, that the first man must not only be thought of as just temporally and numerically the first. However true it may be that he

---

[1] The institution of space and time in general or of a determinate spatio-temporal order (such as that of a—metaphysical—species) is itself transcendent with respect to the corresponding spatio-temporal order because it institutes the latter; now that which conditions is not subject to that which is conditioned.

[2] An event which for this reason is inaccessible to us in its inner *now* is unquestionably metaphysical.

is an individual, he is also the transcendent humanity instituted by God; he is the origin, not just the beginning, the created source of humanity, not just the first drop from a source which lies behind humanity in God. There is no need of argument to show that a train of thought like this, which would need to be explained in more detail and defined more sharply in conceptual terms, is at least advisable from the viewpoint of a theology of original sin. We may enlarge the scope of the problem in the following general terms. Our somewhat medium-quality philosophy today knows only of the really isolated individual, the 'universal' as an abstract concept, and, as the real principle of unity beyond the real individuals of the material world, God alone, who merely by 'pushing from outside' orders together into a single world-machine the pluralities of the world in their reciprocal inter-action, which is something wholly subsequent to their ontological constitution. In reality there are cosmic, created, ontologically real principles of unity apart from God: the one first matter, the real unity of origin of all genuine metaphysical species, the angels as created origins ($\dot{\alpha}\rho\chi\alpha\acute{\iota}$) and principles of the unity of order of the material world. God is the supporting ground of these cosmic principles of unity, not a substitute for them. Where he is conceived of in this way, where for example the unity of the human race is seen merely in the one transcendent divine origin, God's transcendence is misconceived and he is made into a cosmic demiurge.

d. It would be false to argue that if what has been said is true, it would follow for the plant and animal kingdoms too that, supposing the theory of descent were maintained, the first appearance of a new species could only come about in a single exemplar. The objection may be answered as follows. Where a really new species appears for the first time in severally mutually independent exemplars and yet arising from a species which had been different up to that time, what is in question is not really a *metaphysically* new species, however true it may be that this 'species' must be assessed as new and independent from the viewpoint of a biological systematics orientated to the phenotype. A new 'entelechy' or 'form' of an essentially diverse species (which as a new 'Idea' not to be derived from elsewhere can only arise through a transcendent divine causality) does not arise in several mutually independent instances, or alternatively these 'in-stances' do not generate—like the angels. But in regard to the animal

ngdom man is a metaphysically new, essentially diverse species, not
erely in the biological sense of the phenotype, not only in name, but
that ultimate root of his psychosomatic nature, lying behind the
ace of outward appearance, in his spiritual form.

Thus while it is entirely conceivable that biological development in
e animal kingdom reached so advanced a stage of development in a
umber of exemplars that the transcendent miracle of 'becoming man'
uld take place in them, this miracle took place only once, because
established something metaphysically new, which, because it should
d could unfold itself by self-multiplication, did not come to pass
ore than once, if indeed genuine creation was not to become a cosmic
ectacle.

Nor consequently is it surprising that the animal world, which drew
ar in the course of its development to the metaphysical locus of this
iracle without being able to arrive at it by its own powers, developed
ay from this point again, after the miracle of 'becoming man' took
ace. We are told by an authority[1]:

> In the last $1\frac{1}{2}$ million years of the Tertiary epoch, shortly before
> the appearance of man, simian forms very close to man emerge.
> They lived on the steppe, walked upright, their hands were free and
> they had a human or nearly human set of teeth. Their instinctive
> activities must have gone far beyond those of our modern primates
> (gorillas, orang-outangs, chimpanzees). South-east Africa is
> where they have been discovered. The most recent fossil examples
> were approximately contemporary with the first man. But in com-
> parison to their predecessors they seem to have been already more
> simian, more specialized, than the earliest specimens of *Australo-
> pithecus*. This group of prehuman, animal forms died out at the
> time of the first man. Among their number may be reckoned the
> giants of East and South-east Asia, which likewise seem to have
> died out when the first man appeared.

hy did they die out? The simplest and surely the truest thing to say
uld be, 'Because they had fulfilled their purpose: to prepare the
y for man'. We need only ask once in return: Why do the primates,
sest systematically speaking to man, which once existed, no longer
ist? Why does the family tree of the primates develop away from

[1] Philipp Dessauer, in a manuscript not yet published.

man again in the modern geological period? Would it have been impossible for such manlike forms to exist today? The answer is simple: now that what was to be achieved is standing, the scaffolding which served the achievement is simply taken down again. But if the event of man could often take place as origin, these approximations to man would always be meaningful.

Nor can it be said that men would not have been able to continue if they had first appeared in a single pair. This cannot be proved. And conversely, even a greater number, which must in any case have been small one, is no assurance against becoming extinct. Entire groups from which man may have come under a certain aspect, have died out although they were more closely related to him than modern primates. Remaining alive or dying out are alternatives which must depend on other factors than that of the original number of ancestors.

It further follows from these considerations that a moderate theory of anthropological evolution, maintained simultaneously with monogenism, does not lead to a shameful compromise. On the contrary both arise in the same way from a single metaphysical principle of economy: the transcendent divine causality influences the terrestrial course of things in the most discreet and economic way, only, in fact where something essentially and irreducibly new is to appear for the first time as an origin. What the world can do by itself, it must do in the highest possible way; and that includes both the preparation of the biological substratum which was to 'become man' and the spreading abroad of the one stock.

9

CONCERNING THE RELATIONSHIP BETWEEN NATURE AND GRACE

THE questions which have recently been raised concerning the relationship between nature and grace are well-known. There is no need to provide an historical account of them. We assume here that the reader is familiar with what has been said on this subject by such theologians as de Lubac, Bouillard, Delaye, von Balthasar or Rondet (who are associated in the popular mind, not wholly without justification, with what is called 'la nouvelle Théologie'). We assume too the criticisms which have been offered in regard to these freshly formulated questions by other writers, such as de Blic, L. Malevez, C. Boyer, Garrigou-Lagrange, A. Michel, de Broglie or Philippe de la Trinité, in the way of considerations of principle, or such as Alfaro in the way of historical investigations. We assume that the point made by the encyclical 'Humani Generis' is generally accepted: 'Alii veram gratuitatem" ordinis supernaturalis corrumpunt, cum autument Deum entia intellectu praedita condere non posse, quin eadem ad beatificam visionem ordinet et vocet' (Denz 3018). There is no intention of dealing here with the whole complex of questions to do with the relationship between nature and grace; we shall attempt this neither historically nor systematically. All we have in mind is to set in motion a few considerations of principle without any idea of even touching upon everything of importance.[1]

---

[1] The original publication of these considerations (here merely expanded slightly) in *Orientierung* XIV (1950), pp. 141–5, met with more attention than I had expected, not only of an unfavourable kind (though missing the real point) as in the *Schweizer Kirchenzeitung* of 7 September 1950, pp. 441–4 (cf. also *Civitas* VI (1950–1), p. 84). It also met with a friendly reception and a large measure of agreement, for example from H. U. von Balthasar in *Karl Barth, Darstellung und Deutung seiner Theologie* (Cologne 1951), specially pp. 278–335, 'Der Naturbegriff in der katholischen Theologie', and, in a detailed examination, from L. Malevez, 'La Gratuité du surnaturel',

Nor shall we be concerned then to present the criticism offered by the 'nouvelle théologie' of the average textbook-conception of the relationship between nature and grace. Ultimately this amounts to the reproach of 'extrinsecism': grace appears there as a mere super-structure, very fine in itself certainly, which is imposed upon nature by God's free decree, and in such a way that the relationship between the two is no more intense than that of a freedom from contradiction (of a 'potentia oboedientialis' understood purely negatively); nature does indeed acknowledge the end and means of the supernatural order (glory and grace) as in themselves the highest goods, but it is not clear why it 'should have much time for' these highest goods. For more is required for this than the simple facts that the good is high (higher than another) and its attainment possible. A free being at least could always reject such a good without thereby having *inwardly* the experience of losing its end. And this is especially the case because in the average (if not unanimous) view grace in itself remains absolutely beyond consciousness.

It cannot be denied that an extrinsecism of this kind has been current in the average teaching on grace in the last few centuries. It has been usual to presuppose a sharply circumscribed human 'nature' with the help of a concept of nature one-sidedly orientated to the nature of less than human things. It has been felt that one knows quite clearly what *precisely* this human nature is and how far precisely it extends.[1] What is still more problematic, it is tacitly or explicitly pre-

---

NRT LXXV (1953), pp. 561–86; 673–89. The study by Malevez drew my attention to the fact that the theory of the 'supernatural existential', of which Malevez approves (apart from some small improvements which meet with my agreement), had already been put forward in substance by E. Brisbois, 'Le Désir de voir Dieu et la métaphysique du vouloir selon saint Thomas', NRT LXIII (1936), pp. 1103–5. I can only express my happiness at discovering this predecessor, for in questions like this there are no rights of priority for which one has to struggle. The citation from Blondel in Malevez (p. 679) may be compared here as pointing in the same direction. An account, as detailed as that by Malevez and equally in agreement, of the first publication of this study was also given by J. P. Kenny, 'Reflections on human nature and the supernatural', TS XIV (1953), pp. 280–7. (See also by K. Rahner, 'Natur und Gnade', in *Fragen der Theologie heute*, ed. Feiner, Trütsch and Böckle (Einsiedeln 1957).—Tr.)

[1] This is not intended to deny that something which is recognized to be present in consequence of a *transcendental* analysis of the human reality

supposed that whatever man comes to know by himself (independently
of Revelation) about himself or in himself belongs to his 'nature'
(because 'supernatural' and 'knowable by verbal Revelation alone' are
identified as a matter of course), and that so a sharply circumscribed
concept of man's nature can be produced out of the anthropology of
everyday experience and of metaphysics. Thus it is presupposed that
the concretely experienced (contingently factual) quiddity of man
squarely coincides with man's 'nature' as the concept opposed by
theology to the supernatural. Supernatural grace then can only be the
superstructure lying beyond the range of experience imposed upon a
human 'nature' which even in the present economy turns in its own
orbit (though with a relationship peculiar to itself to the God of
creation). Hence this nature is first of all merely 'disturbed' by the
purely external 'decree' of God commanding the acceptance of the
supernatural, a decree which continues to be a purely exterior divine
ordination so long as grace has not yet laid hold of this nature, justifying and divinizing it, and has in this way made the vocation to the
supernatural end into man's inner goal. If this external decree, which
obliges man to the supernatural purely from without, is not taken into
account, a man in the present economy without grace is equal on this
view to the man of 'pure nature'. Again, since this decree is known
only through verbal Revelation, it follows that man in his own
experience of himself experiences himself as this pure nature. And

belongs to human nature (even in the theological sense). To this extent one
does know *precisely* that this belongs to the nature, and to this extent I am
in agreement with Malevez (pp. 685 s.). But conversely Malevez will have
to grant that one cannot ascertain the *whole* of human nature by such a
transcendental method. Any moral philosopher (so far as he retains the *lex
naturalis*) would have to protest in the strongest terms if someone tried to
assert that that alone belonged to man's immutable nature which allowed of
being demonstrated to belong there by means of such a method. At any rate
I would not venture to maintain such a position. But once anthropology (in
the widest sense) is forced to make use of a non-transcendental (and in this
sense *a posteriori*) method in ascertaining man's nature, it begins at this
point to become unavoidably 'imprecise'. For there is no way of establishing
quite clearly in all cases from experience alone (at least without recourse to
theology) whether what experience shows about man belongs to his nature
as such (invariably and without exception) or to his historical nature, so far
as this displays features (invariably and without exception from the empirical
point of view, but conditioned by the fact of vocation to a supernatural end)
which it would not have had if this vocation had not existed.

because on this view original sin and its consequences only represen
a state of man which ought not to be, in so far as once again man ough
to be otherwise only in accordance with a divine decree binding from
without, man is not even disturbed in the immanent experience of hi
pure nature by original sin. In short, what by himself he experience
of himself here and now he could have on this view also experience
in an order of pure nature.

This average view is in fact open to serious objection. There is n
difficulty in seeing that it is problematic and dangerous from a religiou
point of view: if man, just so far as he experiences himself existentiall
by himself, is really nothing but pure nature, he is always in danger c
understanding himself merely as a nature and of behaving accordingl
And then he will find God's call to him out of this human plane merel
a disturbance, which is trying to force something upon him (howeve
elevated this may be in itself) for which he is not made (on this vie
he is only made and destined for it *after* he has received grace, an
then only in a way entirely abstracted from experience). This
particularly true since this offer of inwardly elevating grace remair
ex supposito outside or above his real experience, and only become
known in a faith which knows of its object *ex auditu* alone. A portray;
of the historical and spiritual consequences of this view may be foun
in de Lubac's *Surnaturel*. Even if it is a little on the gloomy side,
certainly provides food for thought. And even if the consequences a
in great part due to the influence of a whole spiritual and cultur
climate of opinion reflected in this particular view as well rather tha
consequences of just this theological theory, yet the portrayal of the
is not without importance for the assessment of the theory itself.

But the view is also problematic in regard to its tacit presuppositio
and its ontological conceptions. How am I to know that everything
in fact encounter in my existential experience of myself (the ultima
yearning, the most profound inner dispersion, the radical experien
of the universally human tragedy of concupiscence and death) does
fact fall within the realm of my 'nature', and would also exist, exist
just this form, if there were no vocation to supernatural communic
with God? There is no way of providing a justification for this tac
presupposition starting from man, nor is it really proved by any the
logical argument. And this for the simple reason that the possibility
experiencing grace and the possibility of experiencing grace *as* gra
are not the same thing. If this is not assumed beforehand or taken f

granted, is it so easy to say what belongs to human 'nature', and what is more not merely to the contingently factual nature of this concrete economy but to 'pure' nature, in such a way that if it were lacking man would cease to be man? How could one give this question a precise answer philosophically, without recourse to Revelation? It may with justice be said that man is an *animal rationale*. But do we know whether the subsistent object actually envisaged in terms of this formula would really be just such as we actually experience it, if this man were not called to eternal communion with the God of grace, were not exposed to the permanent dynamism of grace and were not to feel its loss a mortal wound on account of being continuously ordained to it in his inmost depths? One may have recourse to a transcendental deduction in order to ascertain the irreducible quiddity of man, i.e. take that for man's purely natural essence which is simultaneously posited in first asking the question about this essence at all. But even then one does not know whether one may not have introduced too little into this concept of man, or whether in the very act of asking the question, contingently but for us unavoidably, a supernatural element may not have been at work in the questioner which could never in actual fact be bracketed off, and so would prevent one from laying hold *purely* of man's natural essence in the concept.[1] A

[1] The *phantasma* of the 'conversio ad phantasma' which is necessary in order to grasp the most abstract concept of man's nature is the concrete experience, never to be absolutely and exhaustively analysed, which man has of himself. To this extent, like every concept, even the most highly purified metaphysical concept of man's nature remains 'historical', i.e. consisting in and apprehended only in a synthesis, already achieved beforehand and never wholly resolvable, of *a priori* conditioned 'concept' and 'intuition' (experience). But in this experience supernatural, grace-qualified factors are involved too in the present concrete economy (the contrary at least cannot be proved). And this in such a way that no process of elimination could ever be exhaustive, since the intuition which is necessary if we are to have the concept inevitably contains more elements than would be necessary for the concept, for its power to represent. In other words, we inevitably think the abstract nature of man with our eye upon a model of man offered us by experience. But right to the end of his history man will never be quite done with learning what in him is essence and what merely contingently factual model. The whole spiritual and cultural history of man testifies to this. For in this history he continually experiences new modes of the single process of the realization of his essence, which he would never have been able to infer from his essence *a priori*. And in each new mode he

precise delimitation of nature from grace (supposing it were possible at all) and so a really pure concept of pure nature could thus in every case only be pursued with the help of Revelation, which tells us what in us is grace and so provides us with the means of abstracting this grace from the body of our existential experience of man and thus of acquiring pure nature (in its *totality*) as a 'remainder'.

The ontological presuppositions of this extrincesism are equally problematic. One in particular is quite unintelligible, though it is tacitly assumed, to the effect that where grace has not yet laid hold of the man who has awakened to freedom by justifying him, his binding ordination to the supernatural end can only consist in a divine decree still external to the man. Even if this binding ordination is not counted among the constituent elements of human *nature* as such, who is going to prove that it could only be interior to man in the form of a grace already justifying, that an interior supernatural existential of the adult man could only consist in justifying grace already stirred into faith and love? On the contrary, *must* not what God decrees for man be *eo ipso* an interior ontological constituent of his concrete quiddity 'terminative', even if it is not a constituent of his 'nature'? [1] For an ontology which grasps the truth that man's concrete quiddity depends utterly on God, is not his binding disposition *eo ipso* not just a juridical decree of God but precisely what man *is*, hence not just an imperative proceeding from God but man's most inward depths? If God gives creation and man above all a supernatural end and this end is first 'in

---

learns anew by living it the difference between essence and its concrete historical realization, the synthesis of which he had held before to be more or less incapable of being dissolved.

[1] Malevez says with justice (p. 678): 'Toute volonté divine ad extra se définit par le terme, qu'elle pose; si donc le décret divin, qui a présidé à la création, a été un décret de destination des hommes au Royaume, cette destination a dû se traduire par un certain effet au plus profond de nous mêmes: au décret immanent à la volonté divine, a répondu en nous une certaine disposition, une ordination aux biens qui nous étaient promis.' *This* starting point for the considerations we shall be offering about the 'supernatural existential' should be noted. This existential is *not* postulated in order to simplify the problem of the 'potentia oboedientialis', to explain why nature has an affinity to grace. If this were the starting-point it could be said that the problem was merely shifted by introducing this term (cf. E. Gutwenger, ZKT LXXV (1953), p. 462). (For the term 'existential' see the Introduction.—Tr.)

ntentione', then man (and the world) *is* by that very fact always and
everywhere inwardly other in structure than he would be if he did not
have this end, and hence other as well before he has reached this end
partially (the grace which justifies) or wholly (the beatific vision).
And it is entirely legitimate to start from this point in an attempt to
outline the one concrete 'quiddity' of man (if not indeed his 'nature'
as opposed to grace). In short, we admit the basic contention that there
is widely prevalent in the average teaching on grace an extrinsecist
view which regards this as being merely a superstructure imposed
from without upon a nature in itself indifferent with regard to it. It
would seem to be a genuine concern of theology to put an end to the
extrinsecism. Nor is it wholly overcome by emphasizing (e.g. with
Malevez[1] against de Lubac) that the *potentia oboedientialis* of nature
includes nevertheless a kind of velleity, indeed a yearning (only a
conditional one of course) for the immediate possession of God in the
depths of the essence, and that a spiritual nature cannot really be
thought of without this *appetitus*, so that the *potentia oboedientialis* is
not simply an absence of contradiction in a purely negative way. For
so long as this yearning is really conceived of as conditional and,
contrary to this basic position, a half unhappiness is not made out of
the finite happiness which would be man's lot without the *visio* and a
proper capacity not made out of the *potentia oboedientialis* which is
identical with human nature, this *desiderium* remains so hypothetical
that nature can always become enclosed within its own plane.

But is this inner reference of man to grace a constituent of his
'nature' in such a way that the latter cannot be conceived without it,
i.e. as pure nature, and hence such that the concept of *natura pura*
becomes incapable of complete definition? It is at this point that we
are bound to declare our inability to accept the view which has been
attributed to the 'nouvelle théologie' and has met with so much
opposition.[2] It is here that 'Humani Generis', in the statement

[1] L. Malevez (in a review written *before* the article frequently cited here),
RT LXIX (1947), pp. 3–31.
[2] It is certainly defended by the anonymous writer D. in *Orientierung* XIV
(1950), pp. 138–41, 'Ein Weg zur Bestimmung des Verhältnisses von Natur
und Gnade'. D. belongs to the circle of those theologians who are usually
grouped together (though some of them protest against it) as the school of
'a nouvelle théologie'. We are not concerned to decide whether and how
far D.'s presentation really reproduces de Lubac's views accurately, which
D.'s intention.

quoted above, set out a teaching about which there can be no miscon ceptions.[1] The problem is this: is it still possible to conceive of grac as unexacted,[2] supposing that the existential consisting in the inne and unconditional reference to grace and beatific vision were a con stituent of man's 'nature' in the sense that man as such could not b thought without it? That grace is absolutely unexacted, that thi proposition is the unquestioned point of departure for all furthe reflexion, this was an indubitable axiom for the 'new' teaching too which it accepted as much as any other theology. The only questio then is whether this axiom is objectively consistent with the theoren of an unconditional reference to grace in virtue of *nature* as such. Thi reference to the beatific vision was regarded in this recent view as o the one hand an intrinsic, inamissible constituent of man's nature, an on the other so conceived that the withholding of the end of thi directedness was expounded as being incompatible with God's wisdor and goodness and in this sense unconditional (provided of course th the creature does not fall short of the end by its own fault). We hol that with these presuppositions grace and beatific vision can no long be said to be unexacted. The precise point at issue is to be noted. Eve D., who is perhaps the most explicit champion of the view in question

---

[1] The teaching has been heard in quarters which previously had show appreciation of de Lubac's basic orientation—and still may show it eve today. Cf. H. U. von Balthasar (further to his book on Barth) in ZKT LXX (1953), pp. 454 s.

[2] *Ungeschuldet.* This word, derived from *schulden* 'to owe', appears often in this study that I have decided to translate it conventionally b 'unexacted'. The disadvantage of this translation is that 'unexacted' negat obligation from the point of view of the 'creditor', while *ungeschulda* negates it from the point of view of the 'debtor'. This is perhaps not qui so important in the present context as it might otherwise seem; and in an case it seemed intolerable to have to repeat the form 'unowed' (or wors 'unowedness'), or resort to continual paraphrase. The reader may like compare the relation between 'right' and 'obligation', a right in A involvir an obligation in B.—Tr.

[3] We concern ourselves in what follows chiefly with D., because his essa is perhaps the clearest, and also the most extreme, exposition of the stand point here rejected. Apart from H. de Lubac's essay, 'Le Mystère surnaturel' in RSR XXXVI (1949), pp. 80–121, most of the essays fro this circle were primarily historical in character, and are consequently n easily to be interpreted as regards their theoretical and systematic intentior Thus H. Bouillard, *Conversion et grâce chez S. Thomas d'Aquin* (Paris 1944 H. de Lubac, *Surnaturel* (Paris 1946); H. Rondet, 'Le Problème de la natu

himself holds (as the conclusion of the article already cited shows) that grace is unexacted for the man *actually in existence*; unexacted, then, not simply for an imagined or hypothetical man who is not yet in existence and to whom consequently God does not owe being and all that he needs to be, but for the man already supposed to be in existence. This unexactedness is significant from a religious point of view: as God's real partner I must be able to receive his grace (otherwise than my existence) as an unexpected miracle of his love, not first of all think myself out of existence and then conceive of my own being as such as the miracle of his freedom. But it would appear that against his will D. goes no further than the unexactedness which is proper to creation, and that for him grace is distinguished from other created things only in respect of the greatness of the gift but not in respect of unexactedness itself; for these other created things may also be said in a certain sense to be 'unexacted', in so far as they arise out of God's freedom.

It is true that one may perhaps say too that the defenders of the unexactedness of grace, of the possibility thereby derived of a pure nature and of the impossibility of an unconditional striving of nature for the immediate vision of God by grace, make the defence of their position into far too easy a matter. For a *less* than personal entity unconditional reference to an end and the 'unexactedness' of this end are incompatible assumptions when they are applied to the same thing at the same time. This is especially the case when the matter is looked at from God's point of view, in that he himself constitutes the unconditional reference through his own act of creation. But is this equally simple and obvious where a personal being is in question? Could it not be said here with apparent justice that it is precisely the essence of the personal being (his paradox, without which he cannot be understood) that he is ordained to personal communion with God in love by nature) and must receive just this love as free gift? Is this not true of earthly love too? It is (as the act of the partner) something to which the man giving and receiving love knows himself uniquely ordained, so that he would seem lost and unhappy to himself if he did not receive this love, and yet he accepts this same love as the 'miracle' and the unexpected gift of free (and so unexacted) love. Someone might

ure et la théologie du XVIe siècle', RSR XXXV (1948), pp. 481–521; —, Gratia Christi. Essai d'histoire du dogme et de théologie dogmatique (Paris 1948).

ask: cannot the *essence* of a personal spirit lie just in this (in this and nowhere else!), that it must accept personal love as unexacted if it is not to lose its own meaning, and that hence its unconditional ordination to this love and the unexactedness of the love not only do not exclude each other but mutually condition each other? To the objection in this more precise form it must still be replied that it does not prove what it sets out to prove. The example, first of all, is lacking in cogency. For where is it proved that the ordination of the one loving person to the other, so far as it is really 'unconditional', precedes a free decision, which would be necessary if the example is to prove anything? But the decisive reply is this: can that person, who has *himself created* such an ordination to the personal and intimate communion of love between two persons (in our case man and God), once this has been presupposed still simultaneously refuse this communion without offending against the meaning of this creation and his very creative act itself? This question however is to be answered in the negative, no matter whether one might still be able to say that the person so created must and can regard this love as gift and grace if it is in fact bestowed upon his unconditional ordination to it. But if this negative answer is correct, it follows that on the supposition of such an ordination (*in sensu composito* with it) the actual granting of the end of this ordination can no longer be free and unexacted. Thus if the ordination cannot be detached from the nature, the fulfilment of the ordination from *God's* point of view precisely, is exacted. And, as all admit, just this is false, and so must the presupposition be.

i.e., redeemed nature?

The defenders of the theory here rejected attempt to indicate various facts (as may be seen in D.) which in their opinion are of a kind to show that the state of absolute ordination of man's *nature* as such to grace and the unexactedness (supernaturality) of grace do not exclude each other. It may perhaps be profitable to examine these indications a little more closely.

So far as the first counter-argument to be found in D. is concerned it seems to us to be lacking in force. The Council of Trent does indeed declare that blessedness is both grace and simultaneously merit (Denz. 809; 842); but there is no difficulty in seeing here that on the one hand the *pre*-suppositions of this merit (justifying grace) are pure grace and that on the other hand—this grace once presupposed—the further consequences of this state can be true merit: thus glory in its mediate presupposition is grace, in its immediate cause is merit (exacted). Thu the example does not prove that the same thing (grace) in respect of the same (natural dynamism towards grace) can be both exacted and unexacted at the same time; thus it does not prove that a reality can possess at the same time and in the same respect the character of being unexacted and the character of being something which God could not refuse. This is not of course to deny a generosity and wisdom in God which do not annul the unexactedness of a gift as far as the receiver is concerned, although these divine attributes 'owe' it to themselves, 'exact' it of themselves, to bestow this gift, when in fact the wise and generous God has promised such a gift. But this does not prove that a gift may still be regarded as unexacted in respect of its receiver when God's wise generosity has objectified itself in the world primarily by creating in the receiver, in his very nature, a disposition which under pain of losing its own meaning finds uniquely in this gift its unique end and its only possible fulfilment. In this case God's wisdom owes 'itself' the fulfilment of this disposition, because and in so far as it has created this *disposition* in such a way that the disposition itself exacts the fulfilment. The example of the beggar who is promised a meal fails at the decisive point: the beggar does not have a 'disposition' to be fed by just this determinate particular host, and the host has not got to take upon himself a responsibility for the beggar's hunger: thus what we have here is a gift bestowed in pure generosity. But where an unconditional disposition of nature has preceded the gift, such a gift can at most be a part or a partial end of nature, and hence can only be unexacted in the sense in which nature itself is (i.e. God need no more have created it than the whole of nature).

[margin note: God has disposed us to receive his grace]

An appeal to the *mysterium* of the paradox whereby grace is both unexacted and yet cannot be refused would only be appropriate once it had been satisfactorily demonstrated from positive theological sources that the impossibility of refusing a 'desiderium *naturale*' for grace was an assured theological datum and not itself a theological hypothesis. The proof of this has so far not been provided.

[margin note: ?]

Of course one can and should define the essence of supernatural grace in its own terms and not in terms of nature merely. It is correct to say that its essence is God's self-communication in love. One might with justice say that a gift of such a divine order and the communication of personal love are essentially unexacted. But all that follows from this is that a disposition cannot subsist on the human side which would inevitably draw this divine self-communication of personal love after it, or that if it did, the disposition must likewise be unexacted. But it does not follow that as a natural disposition it would allow the unexactedness of such a divine love to subsist. But if this disposition is conceived of as belonging to nature, grace would be unexacted merely as something given in just the same way as nature and *with* it; in fact it would represent the highest (because uncreated) gift within the formal framework of just *this* unexactedness, a gift essentially distinguished from other (created) unexacted gifts (though not under the formal aspect of unexactedness). In neither case does it cease to be impossible to say: grace is unexacted in respect of this nature. In other words, it follows from the innermost essence of grace that a disposition for grace belonging to man's nature is impossible, or it follows that such a disposition, in case it is needed, itself belongs to this supernatural order already; but it does not follow that as natural it would permit the unexactedness of grace to subsist.

It is certainly true that man's concrete end is the first object of God's will and that it is with this in view that he first devises the concrete quiddity of man. But it only follows from this that if God wills a supernatural and unexacted end and if he wills this (or must will it) in such a way that the created quiddity has for it a disposition of a positive and unconditional kind, then God must simultaneously give to this created thing the disposition to this end. But it does not follow that the disposition must itself belong to the nature of this thing. Otherwise God would be creating a creature which would as a whole, together with this natural disposition, be created freely and in this sense unexactedly, but not a creature in respect of which precisely once again grace would be unexacted. It might however be objected that it would ultimately be necessary to suppose yet again a 'disposition' to this supernatural disposition in the creature, and that this 'disposition' would then have to be conceived of as an essential constituent of man's nature. This may by all means be granted; but where has it been proved that this natural disposition cannot so be conceived of that while remaining simply identical with man's spiritual nature it still continues to have its meaning and significance even when it is not fulfilled by this inner, supernatural disposition for grace?

We may omit any consideration here of the question whether the condemnation of Baius has any relevance for or against the view here being discussed. Any attempt to answer it would drive us too deeply into the details of historical theology.[1] But there is no doubt that this condemnation must be interpreted very cautiously—something which is frequently forgotten in the average sort of theology. If for example it results from this condemnation that God could have created man, even without his having sinned, in the state in which he now finds himself (in actual fact because of original sin), it does not follow from this that the state of man now experienced is simply identical materially with that of a *natura pura*. For obviously God could not have created man without his guilt in the state of an unfulfilled and yet binding demand for the supernatural (that, for instance, is the obvious presupposition behind the condemnation of Baius' proposition in Denz 1055). But what the persistence of this ordination to the beatific vision signifies for the man without grace in respect of his nature, whether this ordination is ontologically intrinsic to his concrete quiddity or is only juridically external, and hence whether it makes itself perceptible in his experience of himself or not, all this is something concerning which the condemnation of Baius offers no decision.[2]

Whether or not the unbounded dynamism which is held on this view to belong to nature and yet to be meaningless without grace and the beatific vision, is capable of being fully known philosophically *quoad nos* and of being analysed in terms of its supernatural end, in D.'s view however it objectively includes the supernatural as the end intrinsically necessary to its essence. But this is immediately to threaten the supernaturality and unexactedness of the end, no matter whether independently of Revelation we should in actual fact have succeeded in sounding these *ex supposito* natural depths of our being so comprehensively that they themselves objectively and compellingly refer us to the beatific vision as possible and real.

The paradox of a natural desire for the supernatural as a link between nature and grace is conceivable and necessary if by 'desire' is understood an 'openness' to the supernatural, and it is taught in every type of Catholic theology, even if this often interprets the *potentia oboedientialis* in too purely formal and negative a way as a mere nonrepugnance. But a 'desire' which is natural and at the same time, even if only objectively, inevitably attracts grace to itself (the desire itself,

[1] Cf. e.g. L. Renwart, 'La "Nature pure" à la lumière de l'encyclique "Humani Generis"', NRT LXXIV (1952), pp. 337–54.

[2] See the study below, 'The Theological Concept of Concupiscentia', especially pp. 375–82.

not just God's wisdom and his promise but the latter through the former!), is a desire which 'demands' grace, demands precisely because it would otherwise be meaningless. But this is incompatible with the unexactedness of grace.

After this critique of an unconditional and yet natural ordination of man to the supernatural, we should like to try to suggest in a few brief words how we ourselves conceive of the relationship between man and grace. God wishes to communicate himself, to pour forth the love which he himself is. That is the first and the last of his real plans and hence of his real world too. Everything else exists so that this one thing might be: the eternal miracle of infinite Love. And so God makes a creature whom he can love: he creates man. He creates him in such a way that he *can* receive this Love which is God himself, and that he can and must [1] at the same time accept it for what it is: the ever astounding wonder, the unexpected, unexacted gift. And let us not forget here that ultimately we only know what 'unexacted' means when we know what personal love is, not *vice versa*: we don't understand what love is by knowing the meaning of 'unexacted'. Thus in this second respect God must so create man that love does not only

[1] Two things are meant by this 'can and must'. Firstly, merely the *fact*: God wishes so to communicate himself that his self-communication to the creaturely subject is unexacted. Hence he must create man just 'so' that he can receive this self-communication only as grace; thus he must not only give him an essence but also constitute him as a 'nature' (as opposed to an unexacted supernatural). But this formula is intended to convey a second point: the self-communication simply *cannot* be other than unexacted, i.e. the will to a 'purely' *unexacted* self-communication is not only a fact but a *necessity*: there is no essence of a creaturely kind which God could constitute for which this communication could be the normal, matter-of-course perfection to which it was compellingly disposed. This is indeed (against Ripalda) the general teaching of theology today: grace and glory are simply speaking supernatural. But then one would have to draw the consequence of this proposition, more clearly than is usually the case: this grace is only then conceived of in its true essence when it is recognized to be not just the *created* 'accidental' reality produced by God's efficient causality 'in' a (natural) substance, but includes 'uncreated grace' in its own concept in such a way that this may not be conceived of purely as a consequence of created grace. For it is difficult to see from an ontological point of view why it should not at least be *possible* for a created accident (however 'divinizing' it may be thought to be) to be ordered to a natural substance connatural with it, i.e. it is difficult to see how a purely created, accidental reality could be supernatural *simpliciter*.

pour forth free and unexacted, but also so that man as real partner, as one who can accept or reject it, can experience and accept it *as* the unexacted event and wonder not owed to *him*, the real man. As unexacted, not only because he does not deserve it as *sinner*, but further because he can also embrace it as unexacted when, already blessed in this love, he is allowed to forget that he was a sinner once. That is all we have to say on this matter 'kerygmatically'. It will appear that one need not discourse at such great length about nature and the supernatural in one's proclamation of the Gospel as one has been accustomed to do in this connexion.

Now if one quite rightly sets about transposing these simple propositions, which every Christian can in a true sense make his own, into 'theology', because this transposition is necessary for the theologian and the preacher if he is to be preserved from the danger of misinterpreting them or rendering them innocuous, the following points may be made.

1. Man should be *able* to receive this Love which is God himself; he must have a congeniality for it. He must be able to accept it (and hence grace, the beatific vision) as one who has room and scope, understanding and desire for it. Thus he must have a real 'potency' for it. He must have it *always*. He is indeed someone always addressed and claimed by this Love. For, as he now in fact is, he is created for it; he is thought and called into being so that Love might bestow itself. To this extent this 'potency' is what is inmost and most authentic in him, the centre and root of what he is absolutely.[1] He must have it

---

[1] H. U. von Balthasar holds (at least in his book on Barth, pp. 310 s.) that if one allows this determination to the acceptance of God's unexacted loving self-communication to be the 'inmost' thing in man, one can no longer disregard this inmost centre in favour of the possible concept of a pure nature; thus he holds that the position put forward here is an uneasy compromise between the views of Maréchal and de Lubac. This is not the place to discuss Balthasar's theology of the grace-nature relationship as a whole. The reader may be referred to the essay by L. Malevez cited above and Balthasar's own most recent explanations in ZKT LXXV (1953), pp. 452 s. All that needs to be established here is: 1. If one wishes positively to contest (and that ultimately is what we are doing here) the possibility of a pure spiritual nature 'for God' (Balthasar, p. 311), i.e. looked at from his point of view, one could no longer speak of admitting such a possibility 'from the standpoint of a creaturely theology' either. Thus this distinction 'for God'—'for us' (which is our own) does not help to reconcile the opposed positions. 2. When Balthasar asks how it should be possible to

always: for even one of the damned, who has turned away from this Love and made himself incapable of receiving this Love, must still be really able to experience this Love (which being scorned now burns like fire) as that to which he is ordained in the ground of his concrete being; he must consequently always remain what he was created as: the burning longing for God himself in the immediacy of his own threefold life. The capacity for the God of self-bestowing personal Love is the central and abiding existential of man as he really is.[1]

2. The real man as God's real partner should be able to receive this Love as what it necessarily is: as free gift. But that means that this

---

subtract 'the inmost' with a view to which all else is in concrete fact devised by God, without leaving behind a *meaningless* remainder, it is easy and in this case fair to reply by recalling the paradox of the most intimate divine Love, or, in more harmless terms, its mystery: precisely if it is bestowed freely (hence in concrete fact, hence not by essential necessity), it is the inmost, and that with a view to which everything else is willed concretely and freely. Here too it holds good that the *summum* is the *intimum*. And yet this Love, precisely because it is the highest and inmost, is the most unexacted. Does not Balthasar himself slip into a naturalistic concept of nature when he takes it for granted that the 'inmost', the 'most personal' is *eo ipso* the most inamissible, the ever-available? Is it not precisely the essence of man to receive the unexpected as the inmost, and to have the inmost as grace? But then the inmost love is not only the love of an aristocratic 'gratuitousness from above' but that of a 'gratuitousness from below' (p. 311), because precisely *man* himself, man as existential (hence very much 'from below') is meant to accept this love as unexacted by him, not owed to him. But then the concept of a possible 'pure nature' is no longer to be avoided. What has been said about this Love holds good then necessarily of an ordination to it, in so far as this 'ordination' is apprehended not merely as the natural *possibility* of the *potentia oboedientialis*, but as 'unconditional'.

[1] The theologian must seriously ask himself how it is possible to explain the *poena damni* without adopting such an abiding supernatural existential foreordained to grace. In fact it cannot otherwise be explained. For the loss of a good which is possible, but not the object of an ontological ordination prior to free endeavour ('voluntas ut res'), can only be felt as a painful evil when the loser wills it *freely* (but the damned have no use for this and do not do it). But the decisive argument for the existence of the supernatural existential is that already indicated above (p. 302 s.): even prior to grace man's binding, indissoluble ordination to the supernatural end is a real determination of man himself, and not merely a divine intention, a decree 'in God's will'. To make of this a purely 'juridical', purely 'moral' entity is nothing but a nominalism which has not taken cognisance of itself.

central, abiding existential, consisting in the ordination to the threefold God of grace and eternal life, is itself to be characterized as unexacted, as 'supernatural'. Not because man first of all—'obviously'—has a fixed, circumscribed nature in the sense that measured by it (as a fixed quantity known beforehand) grace, which is to say ultimately God himself, appears to be out of proportion and must therefore be called supernatural. But because the longing for, the ordination to, God's Love, this existential for supernatural grace, only allows grace to be unexacted grace when it is itself unexacted, and at the moment when, fulfilled by grace, it becomes conscious of itself *as* supernatural, i.e. shines forth as unexacted by the real man, not owed to him. Man is not to recognize himself merely as part of God's free creation; because he exists and although he exists already, he is to accept God's Love as gift and unexpected wonder. But if he were in a certain sense nothing but this existential, and were *this*—here there arises the *theological* word 'nature' for the first time—simply his nature, i.e. were it in absolutely no way capable of being dissociated from what he is otherwise and from what he could understand himself to be, then he could certainly as a free agent always continue to behave contrary to this nature in the despite of Love; but he could not accept this Love as bestowed gratuitously and without exaction upon him, God's really existent partner. Were he simply this existential, and were this his nature, then it would be unconditional in its essence, i.e. once it has been given, the Love which is God would 'have to' be offered by God.

3. Thus the man who receives this Love (in the Holy Spirit and thanks to the Word of the Gospel) will know this very existential for this Love as not owed to him, unexacted by him the real man. *This* knowledge is what allows him to distinguish and delimit what he always is (his concrete, indissoluble 'quiddity') into what is this unexacted real receptivity, the supernatural existential, and what is left over as remainder when this inmost centre is subtracted from the substance of his concrete quiddity, his 'nature'. 'Nature' in the theological sense (as opposed to nature as the substantial content of an entity always to be encountered in contingent fact), i.e. as the concept contraposed to the supernatural, is consequently a remainder concept (*Restbegriff*). By that is meant that starting as we have done, a reality

must be postulated in man which remains over when the supernatural existential as unexacted is subtracted, and must have a meaning and a possibility of existence even when the supernatural existential is thought of as lacking (for otherwise this existential would necessarily be demanded precisely by the postulated reality, and it could only be unexacted with respect to a purely possible man, as an element in creation in general). But this 'pure' nature is not for that reason an unambiguously delimitable, de-finable quantity; no neat horizontal (to use Philipp Dessauer's way of putting it) allows of being drawn between this nature and the supernatural (both existential and grace). We never have this postulated pure nature for itself alone, so as in all cases to be able to say *exactly* what in our existential experience is to be reckoned to its account, what to the account of the supernatural. Where life is a matter of concrete yearning for eternal Truth and pure and infinite Love, of the inescapability of a free decision before God, of the pangs of birth, of concupiscence, labour, toil and death (hence of man's real essence and its achievement), all this is unquestionably experienced by a man who (consciously or unconsciously) is subject to the influence of the supernatural existential (if not of grace). Thus there is no way of telling *exactly* how his nature for itself alone would react, what precisely it would be for itself alone. This is not to deny that in the light of experience and still more of Revelation it might not be possible in some determinate respect to use a transcendental method to delimit what this human nature contains. 'Animal rationale' may still in this respect be an apt description. Certainly the philosopher has his own well-grounded concept of the nature of man: the irreducible substance of human being, established by recourse to human experience independently of verbal revelation. This concept may largely coincide with the theological concept of man's nature, in so far as without Revelation the greater part of what goes beyond this theological 'nature' is not experienced, and at any rate is not recognized *as* supernatural without the help of Revelation to interpret it. But in principle the content of this philosophical concept of man need not simply coincide with the content of the theological concept of man's 'pure nature'. It can in concrete fact contain more (i.e. something already supernatural, though not as such). When therefore one undertakes to state with precision what exact content is intended by such a concept of a pure nature, in particular as regards God and his moral law, the difficulties, indeed the impossibility, of a neat horizontal once again become apparent for us, as the history of theology shows only too clearly. But these difficulties lie precisely in the nature of things: man can experiment with himself only in the region of God's supernatural loving will, he can never find the nature he wants in a 'chemically pure' state, separated from its supernatural existential. Nature in this sense continues to be a remainder concept, but a necessary and objectively justified one, if one wishes to achieve reflexive consciousness of that unexactedness of grace which goes together with man's inner, unconditional ordination to it. Then in fact this unconditional ordination must itself be grasped as unexacted and supernatural; man's concretely experienced quiddity differentiates itself into the supernatural existential as such and the 'remainder'—the pure nature.

4. Hence there is no longer any reason why speculative theology should avoid considering the relationship between the supernatural (including the supernatural existential) and nature in itself. It will be permissible to take hold with an easy conscience of the concept of *potentia oboedientialis* scorned by de Lubac. The spiritual nature will have to be such that it has an openness for this supernatural existential without thereby of itself demanding it unconditionally. This openness is not to be thought of merely as a non-repugnance, but as an inner ordination, provided only that it is not unconditional. It will be permissible at this point to point unhesitatingly at the unlimited dynamism of the spirit, which for D. is the natural existential immediately ordered to grace itself. All one must guard against is identifying this unlimited dynamism of the *spiritual nature* in a simply apodeictic way with that dynamism which we experience (or believe we experience) in the adventure of our concrete spiritual existence, because here the supernatural existential may already be at work—as subsequently emerges in the light of Revelation. And one will guard against asserting that this natural dynamism is an unconditional demand for grace. How should we know this, if we never experience it 'pure'? There is no reason why it could not retain its meaning and necessity even without grace, if on the one hand one can learn to see it as the indispensable transcendental condition of the possibility of a spiritual life at all; and on the other hand if this spiritual life, although in comparison with the beatific vision it remains eternally *in umbris et imaginibus,*

can at any rate be shown to be neither meaningless nor harsh but can always be seen as a positive, though finite, good which God could bestow even when he has not called man immediately before his face. Even according to D. the pure philosophy of man's nature (even his concrete nature) is not capable of discerning the possibility of a *visio beatifica*. Then D. too must hold that a spiritual life towards God as an end approached merely asymptotically is not to be dismissed as meaningless from the start. But as has already been said, we have no pure experience of this purely natural dynamism (or at any rate the contrary is not proved). Thus one who believes that he or humanity in the concrete is driven on the most sublime ways of its history, even apart from verbal revelation, by an impulse which would be meaningless if it did not lead to the immediate vision of God, need not on that account go on to assert anything which would be opposed to this view. All he would be bound not to assert (and his experience gives him no occasion for this either) is that this existentially (*existentiell*) real dynamism belongs to the substance of the nature of man in the theological sense.

Of course what has been said is far from providing an answer to all the questions which could be put concerning the relationship of nature and grace. It would be proper to speak with more precision of the *potentia oboedientialis* of nature as such. It would be necessary to examine more closely how the supernatural existential is related to grace itself, and in what sense it is distinct from it. All the questions and theses concerning the relationship of nature and grace would need to be wholly rethought in terms of an explicit recognition of the fact that grace is not just a 'neutral state' (however sublime), that it cannot be sufficiently described by purely formal ontological categories alone (created 'quality', accident, *habitus*, etc.), but that personal categories (love, personal intimacy, self-communication) can neither be avoided in the description of what grace is, nor, because they do not belong to the realm of formal ontology, are on that account inaccessible to a more precise philosophical or theological reflexion or stand in no need of it. In regard to the question of the nature-grace relationship it would be necessary to consider in more precise detail how a philosophical knowledge of a 'nature' really comes about. Scholastic philosophy and theology do indeed rightly insist (as 'Humani Generis' recently impressed upon us again too) that immutable 'essences' and concepts of essences are to be found

But too little thought is given to how in fact one arrives at such an individual concept of an essence and in particular that of the essence of man, meaning by that something more than the most general metaphysical propositions (about entities in general, the transcendentals and the most general metaphysical principles of identity, causality, finality, etc.). Even the distinction made above between a transcendental and an *a posteriori* empirical method in the investigation of the essence of man is not generally familiar. The view is too lightly taken as a starting-point that whatever has been empirically observed in man 'always and in all cases' also belongs *eo ipso* to the immutable substance of man's 'nature', which then supplies the foundation of the 'lex naturae'. But the question is not so simple. Can pure natures be produced? In atomic physics perhaps? Can and may man change his nature? Is the variable *eo ipso* something which lies outside the concept of nature as such? Even when this quantity once achieved (produced) was general and (relatively) stable? It might be asked whether the scholastic concept of 'nature' as applied to the 'nature' of man does not still owe too much to the model of what is less than human (in the train of archaic philosophy with its orientation towards 'physics'). What is signified by the 'definition', and hence the circumscription, of man's 'nature', if he is the essence of transcendence, and hence of the surpassing of limitation? Is it meaningful at all in such a perspective simply to assign to this 'nature' an end perfectly defined materially? Not as though the remotest doubt were being thrown here on the fact that man has a nature and that this in itself has an end assigned to it. But these must not and cannot be conceived in such simple terms as the mutual order of a pot and its lid or of a biological organism and its fixed environment. One has only to ask why a supernatural end can be set for man without annulling his nature, and why God cannot do this with the nature of something below man. Then it becomes apparent at once that however universally the formal ontology of nature, end, etc., may extend, these concepts can only be used in the particular matter of each individual grade of being in a highly analogical way. There are many more such questions, and they are not idle subtleties. For that nature should remain nature for the sake of grace and yet always be grasped by the Christian as an intrinsic element in the single object willed by God when he willed man as his beloved in his Son—to bring this about is a task of the Christian life, and so a serious question for theology.

SOME IMPLICATIONS OF THE SCHOLASTIC CONCEPT OF UNCREATED GRACE[1]

THIS brief essay has a very modest aim. Its only purpose is to inquire whether it might not be possible to use elements a - ready found *within* the conceptual equipment (*Begrifflichkeit*) of scholastic theology to define the essence of uncreated grace[2] more

[1] On its first appearance this study received a fairly detailed and very friendly treatment from J. Trütsch in his work *SS. Trinitatis inhabitatio apud theologos recentiores* (a printed dissertation for the Gregorian University of Rome, Trent 1949), esp. pp. 25, 107–16. Cf. the review by F. Lakner in ZKT LXXII (1950), p. 116. A survey may be found in Trütsch (pp. 21–5) of the most important literature of the last thirty years (Delaye, Gardeil, Garrigou-Lagrange, de la Taille, Galtier, Retailleau, Martinez-Gómez, Mersch, Beumer, Kuhaupt, Schauf), which will not be mentioned again here. Since the appearance of Trütsch's work have also appeared M. J. Donnelly, 'The Inhabitation of the Holy Spirit: A Solution according to de la Taille', TS VIII (1947), pp. 445–70; P. Galtier, *L'Habitation en nous des trois personnes* (éd. revue et augmentée, Rome 1950); S. I. Dockx, *Fils de Dieu par grâce* (Paris 1948; cf. ZKT LXXIII (1951), pp. 111 s.); R. Morency, *L'Union de grâce selon saint Thomas d'Aquin* (Montreal 1950); P. de Letter, 'Sanctifying Grace and our Union with the Holy Trinity', TS XIII (1952), pp. 33–58; M. J. Donnelly, 'Sanctifying Grace and our Union with the Holy Trinity: A Reply', TS XIII (1952), pp. 190–204; F. Bourassa, 'Adoptive Sonship: our Union with the divine Persons', TS XIII (1952), pp. 309–35. (Cf. also P. de Letter, 'Created Actuation by the Uncreated Act: Difficulties and Answers', TS XVIII (1957), pp. 60–92.—Tr.) There is no intention here of undertaking a detailed examination of these studies. While it is true that since the first appearance of our own study significant contributions have appeared, bearing both on the history and the objective substance of the question, which would have to be taken into account in any detailed presentation and solution of the whole topic (especially as bearing on the problem of proper or appropriated relations to the divine Persons), it still seems to us that this modest inquiry is not yet quite out of date. This all the more, since theologians as eminent as P. Galtier are still looking for a solution of the question by way of a combination of the theories of Vasquez and Suarez, so that the real starting-point of the theology of grace remains 'created grace'.

[2] This is not to imply that we propose to adopt any position with regard

sharply than has hitherto been the case. The inquiry is concerned neither to ask whether a more adequate understanding of the gracious communication and indwelling of God himself in the justified, attested by Revelation, may be better reached with the help of a conceptual equipment not so expressly a part of the substance of scholastic theology (in the terms, say, of a more personalist metaphysics)[1], nor does it propose more closely to establish and justify for themselves the conceptual elements called into service, independently of the application here in mind.

1. The Problem

a. *Grace in the primary sources of Revelation.*

All that is possible here under this heading, and all that is intended, is of course only a brief indication. As regards Pauline theology first of all, man's inner justification and renewal is primarily seen as a being endowed with the πνεῦμα ἅγιον, being dwelled in by it and led by it. The 'Spirit' is given to us, is (dwells) in us (Rom 5:5; 8:9.11.15.23; 1 Cor 2:12; 3:16; 6:19; 2 Cor 3:3; 5:5; Gal 3:2.5; 4:6; 1 Thess 4:8; 2 Tim 1:14; Tit 3:5; Heb 6:4), as in a temple (1 Cor 3:16 s.; 2 Cor 6:16). We are made to drink of the 'Spirit', anointed and sealed with it (1 Cor 12:13 (cf. Eph 5:18); 2 Cor 1:21 s.; Eph 1:13; 4:30). Like statements are made of Christ (Rom 8:10; Gal 2:20; Eph 3:17; Col 1:27). Now it is quite true that these statements do not exclude but on

---

to the much-discussed question whether the indwelling of the Holy Spirit in the justified is proper to the Spirit or merely appropriated. To this extent 'Spirit' and 'God' signify the same thing in this study. We shall return briefly to this question in our conclusion.

[1] Cf. e.g. J. Auer, 'Um den Begriff der Gnade. Grundsätzliches zur Frage nach der Methode, mit der Übernatur als Gnade im strengen Sinn bestimmt werden kann', ZKT LXX (1948), pp. 341–68; further his great historical work, *Die Entwicklung der Gnadenlehre in der Hochscholastik* I–II (Freiburg 1942–51), in which Auer sets out to test his threefold system of categories (the objective-metaphysical, the psychologico-moral, the personal-existential) on the historical data. See also A. Brunner, 'Gott schauen', ZKT LXXIII (1951), pp. 214–22; by the same author, *A New Creation. Toward a Theology of the Christian Life*, ET. Ruth Bethell (London 1955). Brunner seeks to describe the grace-relationship to God using the concepts of personalist philosophy.

the contrary include a created effect of the communication of the Spirit.[1] Being led by the Spirit (Rom 8:14), glowing with the Spirit (Rom 12:11), being sanctified and justified in the Spirit (1 Cor 2:15; 6:11), being made to drink of the Spirit, anointed and sealed by it, creation, renewal, rebirth, strengthening, illumination (by the Spirit, Christ, grace) (Eph 3:16; 1 Tim 1:12; 2 Tim 2:1; Eph 1:18; 5:14; Heb 6:4), etc., all these also essentially imply or embrace an inner transformation of the justified as such, hence an inner quality which inheres in him, hence what scholastic theology calls created grace. The same result may be derived from texts which speak in a partitive sense of the gift of the Spirit (Tit 3:5; Heb 6:4) or of the earnest and the first-fruits of the Spirit (2 Cor 1:22; 5:5; Rom 8:23), using expressions, that is to say, in which the genitive ('of the Spirit') can doubtless be understood as not merely epexegetic but at least in a partitive sense as well. We are not justified in saying that the $\pi\nu\epsilon\hat{\upsilon}\mu\alpha$ which appears in these texts as the principle of our sanctification and justification always refers to the personal Spirit of God. In many of these Pauline texts $\pi\nu\epsilon\hat{\upsilon}\mu\alpha$ may primarily and immediately signify a non-personal created quality of the sanctified man himself, especially when it is found without the article (Rom 5:5), or is opposed to the divine Spirit itself as 'our' $\pi\nu\epsilon\hat{\upsilon}\mu\alpha$ (Rom 8:16; cf. Rom 8:9: we are in the Spirit' because the Spirit of God dwells in us), and yet this spirit clearly means a supernatural principle and not our $\nuο\hat{\upsilon}s$ or our $\psi\upsilon\chi\acute{\eta}$ (1 Cor 14:14; Phil 4:23; 1 Thess 5:23). Yet it is *not* the case that $\pi\nu\epsilon\hat{\upsilon}\mu\alpha$ $\ddot{\alpha}\gamma\iota o\nu$ in St Paul (in its religious usage) refers primarily to a non-personal power communicated to man or a permanent quality of his sanctity, and then perhaps from time to time occurs secondarily as the name of the personal Spirit of God. Gaechter indeed has shown in a remarkable way[2] that the religious concept of $\pi\nu\epsilon\hat{\upsilon}\mu\alpha$ in St Paul

---

[1] Cf., e.g., W. Reinhard, *Das Wirken des Heiligen Geistes im Menschen nach den Briefen des Apostels Paulus* (Freiburg 1918); H. Bertrams, *Das Wesen des Geistes nach der Anschauung des Apostels Paulus* (Münster 1913); . Wobbe, *Der Charis-Gedanke bei Paulus* (Münster 1932); Bertrams in particular has shown that $\pi\nu\epsilon\hat{\upsilon}\mu\alpha$ in St Paul should not invariably be understood as referring immediately to the Third Person of the Trinity.

[2] P. Gaechter, 'Zum Pneumabegriff des hl. Paulus', ZKT LIII (1929), p. 345–408. Following in this R. Blüml, *Paulus und der dreieinige Gott* (Vienna 1929), Gaechter's study provides a certain corrective to Bertrams's conclusions concerning the concept of pneuma in St Paul.

is a unified whole in which the Trinitarian personal Spirit is the basic element from which all other modifications of the concept are to be derived. From this it follows that for St Paul man's inner sanctification is first and foremost a communication of the personal Spirit of God, that is to say, in scholastic terms, a *donum increatum*; and he sees every created grace, every way of being πνευματικός, as a consequence and a manifestation of the possession of this uncreated grace. Thus at least from the point of view of his concept of pneuma and its structure, we should say with St Paul that we possess our pneumatic being (our 'created sanctifying grace') because we have the personal Pneuma of God. The converse proposition, corresponding to the ordinary viewpoint of the scholastic teaching on grace ('God's Pneuma is present in us in a special way because we have created grace'), lacks the same measure of immediate and explicit support in St Paul. This is not to assert any absolute incompatibility of the two formulations; the question merely arises whether the scholastic theology of grace in the matter of the relationship between uncreated and created grace does sufficient justice to the first formulation. In the Johannine theology of grace the idea of inner sanctification does not rest so explicitly and exclusively on the conception of the communication of God's personal Pneuma, inasmuch as this communication, in the form of a possession of Life, a generation (being) *of* God, a being *in* God (Christ, Truth, Love, Light), a possession of God's seed, his unction, love, witness, takes its stand upon a created quality inhering in man. Nevertheless God's own indwelling is not forgotten here either; Christ is (abides) in us (Jn 6:56; 14:20; 15:5; 17:26; 1 Jn 3:24), the Father and the Son make their dwelling in us (Jn 14:23), God is in us (1 Jn 4:4; 4:12 s. 15), the Spirit is given to us and is in us (Jn 14:16 s.; 1 Jn 3:24; 4:13 —admittedly it is not clear in the two latter texts whether what is in question is an inner gift of grace and the personal Spirit of God (partitive expressions again!)). Nevertheless it may be said that nothing in St John is contrary to St Paul's way of looking at God's mercy to man. As for the teaching of the Fathers, it is still less possible to offer a detailed exposition in this merely preliminary discussion than for Scripture. However we hope that it will meet with no opposition from historians of dogma if we summarize the conception of the Fathers (especially the Greek Fathers) as regards our topic by saying that they see the created gifts of grace as a *consequence* of God's substantial communication to justified men. Gaechter has already established this for Irenaeus[1]: it is indeed true that for Irenaeus the personal Spirit of God and his gifts form a single, indissolubly linked principle of man's sanctification; but this result, which represents the intermediate position taken up by A. d'Alès[2] between the two extreme interpretations of his theology of grace proposed by R. Massuet and J. Körber, is not the whole of Irenaeus's conception: 'For anyone who reviews all the texts which speak of the Spirit will frequently discover that the gifts of the Spirit are *consequences* of his *conjunction with man*'.[3] That this remained the case in the later Greek tradition may be seen from Petavius[4] and de Régnon,[5] to whom it is still permissible to refer even now. For whatever the position may be as regards the soundness and theological tenability of the teaching they developed in connexion with this observation, that the conjunction of the Holy Spirit in particular with man is a proper and not merely an appropriated one, the soundness of the observation itself, with which

---

[1] P. Gaechter, 'Unsere Einheit mit Christus nach dem hl. Irenäus', ZKT LVIII (1934), pp. 503–32.

[2] A. d'Alès, 'La Doctrine de l'Esprit en saint Irenée', RSR XIV (1924), pp. 497–538, esp. 528–30.

[3] Gaechter, p. 531.

[4] Petavius, De Trinitate, lib. VIII, cap. 4–6.

[5] T. de Régnon, *Etudes sur la Trinité*, tom. IV, Etude 27, cap. 4 §7–8, pp. 553–8. Cf. also many of the texts adduced by Thomassinus, *Dogmata Theologica* III (Paris 1866), lib. 6, cap. 9–20, as well as those collected by J. C. Martinez-Gómez, 'Relación entre la inhabitación del Espíritu santo y los dones criados de la justificación', *Estudios Eclesiásticos* XIV (1935), pp. 22–50. It is demonstrated in the latter study with a wealth of texts from the Fathers and theologians—even if one may put a question-mark against some of the individual texts taken by themselves—that the idea persistently reappears in theology that a logical (not temporal) priority to created grace should be ascribed to uncreated grace (*as* given, not just as *to be* given or as *causing* grace). We refer to this article for confirmation from the theologians even for the later developments to which we proceed in this study. Martinez could have included Gregor von Holtum, 'Die heiligmachende Gnade in ihrer Beziehung zu der Einwohnung des Heiligen Geistes in der Seele', *Divus Thomas* IV (1917), pp. 435–63, esp. 448 s., among the theologians who defend such a priority of uncreated grace. Cf. also P. Dumont, 'Le Caractère divin de la grâce', *Revue des Sciences Religieuses* XIV (1934), p. 92: 'En optant pour l'antériorité de nature de l'inhabitation divine à l'égard des vertus surnaturelles, on aurait au moins l'avantage de se mieux conformer, semble-t-il, *à la manière habituelle dont les Pères se sont exprimés* en parlant de la grâce.'

we are concerned here, is not open to doubt. It is confirmed by a historian of dogma who is under no suspicion of favouring Petau's personal thesis; Galtier writes: 'Ex his omnibus (i.e. the texts cited from the Fathers) apparet gratiam creatam seu imaginem divinae substantiae efformatam melius iuxta Patres dici *logice consequi* quam antecedere ad praesentiam personarum in nobis'.[1] And he appeals to the Fathers for his own thesis: 'Praesentia divina *non* est *mera consequentia* seu merus effectus iustificationis, quae sit per solam gratiam.'[2]

b. *Grace in scholastic speculation.*

This is not the place to set out in detail the various scholastic theories about the relationship between created and uncreated grace. We wish to draw attention only to that common feature which concerns our present discussion, being clearly conscious of simplifying matters somewhat and leaving aside other approaches (which will be indicated later). However diverse they may be among themselves, it is true of all the scholastic theories that they see God's indwelling and his conjunction with the justified man as based exclusively upon created grace. In virtue of the fact that created grace is imparted to the soul God imparts himself to it and dwells in it. Thus what we call uncreated grace (i.e. God as bestowing himself upon man) is a function of created grace. It is not difficult to see the basis of this conception: 'uncreated grace' (God's communication of himself to man, the indwelling of the Spirit) implies a new *relation* of God to man. But this can only be conceived of as founded upon an absolute entitative modification of man himself, which modification is the real basis of the new real relation of man to God upon which rests the relation of God to man.[3] This absolute entitative modification and determination of man is created grace, which has in consequence a twofold aspect: it is ontologically the formal basis of the analogical supernatural participation in God's nature through entitative assimilation of man to God's spirituality and holiness (*consortium formale*), and it is the basis

[1] P. Galtier, *De SS. Trinitate in se et in nobis* (Paris 1933), n. 411, nota 2.
[2] *Ibid.*, n. 412.
[3] This is already suggested by St Bonaventure (*II Sent.* dist. 26, a. 1, q. 2 fund. 2) and later by St Thomas in *I Sent.* dist. 17, q. 1, a. 1 contra n. 3, (It is striking nevertheless that St Thomas no longer makes use of this argument to prove that grace (charity) is created in *De caritate* a. 1; Ia–IIae. 110.2 and IIa–IIae. 23.2.)

of a special relation (union, indwelling) between man and God himself (*consortium terminativum*). For our purpose it makes no difference how the various theories go on to explain the way in which created grace provides a basis for a new relation between man and the God of grace: whether for instance it is said that God's new efficient causality in respect of grace makes him present in a new way in the object of his activity (in virtue of the identity of being and operation in God and his immensity); or whether the view is put forward that the entitative elevation of man as regards his spiritual powers, which are thus orientated to the beatific vision as last end, gives him a new capacity (of an actual or potential kind) to take possession by knowledge and love of the God who is present in him by immensity; or whether one sees a perfect friendship with God established by grace, a friendship which provides a new and in itself sufficient basis for the presence of God in man (already there in fact). For in each case the indwelling of the Spirit in the justified man by grace is seen merely as a *consequence* of the bestowal of created grace, as the end-term of a (categorical) relationship of man to God given with created grace.

c. *The precise point at issue.*

Hence the question arises how the two ways of looking at things, that of Scripture and the Fathers on the one hand, and that of scholastic theology on the other, may be brought into harmony: there created grace as a *consequence* of God's communication of himself to the man whose sins have been forgiven, here created grace as the *basis* of this communication. There is not the slightest question of contesting the soundness of the positive aspect of the scholastic theory. Our only intention is to complete it by elaborating in more explicit terms a pattern of thought (already in principle to be found in scholastic theology) and applying it to our problem in such a way that the admissibility of the patristic formula should become clear too, and hence make available a more adequate appreciation of the nature of uncreated grace.

2. The Presuppositions of the solution offered

a. *The relation of the state of grace* (as a whole, not distinguishing between created and uncreated grace) *to the beatific vision of God.*

It is generally recognized in scholastic theology that the closest of

relations holds between grace (as a whole) and the ontological presuppositions of the beatific vision. The intrinsic supernaturality of
grace, for instance, is shown to follow from the supernaturality of the
beatific vision and is characterized in terms of it; since the latter is
supernatural simply speaking and in its inner nature, so must grace be,
for it is a commencement of the blessed life, homogeneous with the
ontological presuppositions of the vision (*inchoatio formalis*). The life
of grace, that is to say, and the life of future glory do not stand in a
purely moral and juridical relation to each other, such that the latter is
the reward of the former as merit; the life of glory is the definitive
flowering (the 'manifestation', the 'disclosure') of the life of divine
sonship already possessed and merely 'hidden' for the moment.
Hence grace, as the ontological basis of this supernatural life, is also
an inner entitative principle (at the least a partial principle) of the
vision of God. According to Scripture the possession of the Spirit is
the earnest and firstfruits of the definitive beatifying bestowal of God's
grace and mercy; thus it is not just its 'pledge' and legal title, but a
commencement of glory, still hidden, no doubt, only present to
consciousness in faith, but really and entitatively given already. Hence
the inner nature of grace as a whole in this life must allow of being
more closely determined in terms of the nature of the ontological
presuppositions of the immediate vision of God. We may formulate
this more cautiously in view of the obvious differences between grace
and glory: in accordance with what has been said, there is at least no
objection in principle to applying to an ontology of grace a set of
concepts which have proved themselves objectively valid in an ontology of the immediate vision of God, if such an application shows
itself to be feasible and unavoidable from a consideration of the essence
of grace itself.

b. *On the ontology of the visio beatifica.*

Clearly the answer to any question concerning the essence and the
presuppositions of the immediate vision of God must depend in
decisive fashion upon fundamental conceptions of the nature of knowledge in general. Even where terminological uniformity prevails with
regard to the interpretation of the presuppositions of the *visio beatifica*,
very far-reaching divergences of real meaning may prevail at the same
time, since the concepts applied bear an essentially different sense
according to the various metaphysical theories of knowledge they

presuppose. The metaphysics of knowledge presupposed here is that of St Thomas Aquinas, and with this as our starting-point we ask what is meant when St Thomas says that in the immediate vision of God God's essence itself takes the place of the *species* (*impressa*) in the created mind. Whether in some other metaphysics of knowledge (that of Suarez, say), even if it makes the very same statement here under discussion, the same thing is meant or not, is a question which may be left aside here. In order to understand what St Thomas means by *species* we must start from his basic conception of knowledge in general.[1] In the original and basic concept of knowledge (which alone provides a means of interpreting metaphysically all concrete modes of knowledge), knowledge is not an 'intentional' stretching out of the knower to an object, it is not 'objectivity' in the sense of the going forth of the knower out of himself to something other, not an externally orientated entering into contact with an object by means of the cognitive faculty; it is primarily the being-present-to-itself (*Beisichsein*) of an entity, the inner illuminatedness of an entity for itself on the basis of its determinate grade of being (immateriality), it is a being-reflected-upon-itself (*Insichreflektiertheit*). It is only from this point of departure that it becomes really possible to conceive what is meant by *species* as the ontological ground of any knowledge. The *species* must not unhesitatingly be conceived of as the 'intentional image' of an object, made present in the mind in a non-real 'mental' way as a copy of the object due to the object's impression upon it. Rather it is primarily (i.e. if we reflect upon the nature of the *connatural species* of a cognitive power) an ontological determination of the knower as an entity in his own reality, this determination consequently being logically prior to knowledge as consciousness, and, because it shares or bestows the knower's determinate grade of being, also participating in the consciousness (being-reflected-upon-itself, being-present-to-itself) of this entity thus 'in act'.[2] If and in so far as the *species* understood in this way is also the effect of an object distinct from the knower and so *entitatively* assimilates the knower to the

---

[1] Cf. K. Rahner, *Geist in Welt. Zur Metaphysik der endlichen Erkenntnis bei Thomas von Aquin* (Innsbruck 1939), esp. pp. 41 s. (I have not had access to the first edition, but this reference would seem to correspond to pp. 71 s. of the second edition (Munich 1957).—Tr.)

[2] Cf. e.g. J. Maréchal, *Le Point de départ de la métaphysique* V (Lyons 1926), pp. 60 s.

known, the being-present-to-its-own-self (*Beisichselbersein*) of the knower as an entity determined by the *species* becomes also the knowledge of the object itself (in a manner not further to be explained here). Thus *a posteriori* knowledge rests for St Thomas on an assimilation to the object entitatively determining the knower by means of the *species* as a reality of the knower's own being, through which the knower and the known are really 'the same thing'. The knower and the known do not become one through knowledge (as consciousness); but because they are entitatively one (whether this be immediately or by means of a real determination, representing the object, of the knower as an entity, i.e. by means of the *species*), the knower knows the object.[1] 'Species' is therefore primarily an ontological and only subsequently a gnoseological concept.

Thence arises the whole problematic (a necessary one, indeed) of St Thomas's proposition, that in the immediate vision of God, God's own essence takes the place of the *species*. As regards the *necessity* of this proposition: given this concept of the *species* there is no difficulty in seeing that an immediate, non-analogical vision of God cannot be based upon a *created species*, for this could only reveal its object, God's infinite Being, in the measure of its own entitative capacity as a finite determination of the knowing subject.

As regards the *problematic* of this proposition: when it is said that God's own Being appears in the place of a created *species* of the finite mind, this is to assert a real 'relation' (speaking with all due caution!) between creature and God which is not founded upon an accidental, real, absolute[2] modification of one of the related terms in itself and with regard to itself. For a modification like this is impossible in God on account of his utter transcendence and immutability. It is not to be asserted of the creaturely term of the relation in the present case, because as an accidental modification, from without, of the creature's being in itself and with regard to itself, it could not be the basis for a fundamentally and essentially new 'relationship' of God to the creature. For the only fresh feature such an accidental absolute modification of the creature could bring with it is that relation to God

---

[1] St Thomas, *De Veritate*, q. 1, a. 1 corp.: 'assimilatio ... est *causa* cognitionis'. For the rest cf. Rahner, *ibid.*

[2] 'Absolute' is used in this paragraph and occasionally later on to mean 'non-relative', of something merely inherent in the subject. 'Relation' translates *Beziehung* (*relatio*), 'relationship' *Verhältnis* (*habitudo*).—Tr.

which is a constituent of any creaturely being, namely the transcendental reference of absolute finite being to God as to its cause. But here it is a question precisely of a 'relation' which does not immediately imply an absolute created determination; for otherwise the *species* of the beatific vision would ultimately be yet again a created quality.

Such a new 'relationship' of God to the creature, which cannot be brought under the category of efficient causality but only of formal causality, is on the one hand a concept which transcribes a strictly supernatural mystery; and on the other hand its possibility must not be put in doubt in virtue of purely rational considerations. It transcribes in the mode of formal ontology the concept of supernatural being in its strictly mysterious character; for all the strictly supernatural realities with which we are acquainted (the hypostatic union, the *visio beatifica*[1] and—as we shall go on to show here—the supernatural bestowal of grace) have this in common, that in them there is expressed a relationship of God to a creature which is not one of efficient causality (a production *out* of the cause, 'ein Aus-der-Ursache-*Heraus*-stellen'), and which must consequently fall under the head of formal causality (a taking up *into* the ground [*forma*], 'ein In-den-Grund[forma]-*Hinein*nehmen'): the ontological principle of the subsistence of a finite nature in the one case, the ontological

---

[1] On the parallels between the *unio hypostatica* and the *unio gloriae* cf. e.g. St Thomas *Comp. Theol.* c. 201; Cajetan, *In IIIa.* 17.2; Contenson, *Theologia mentis et cordis* (Paris 1875) lib. I, diss. 5, cap. 1, spec. 1; Gotti, *Theologia scholastico-dogmatica* (Venice 1781), tom. I, tract. 3, q. 3, dub. 1 §3; E. Hugon, *Tractatus dogmatici*, vol. I (Paris 1933), p. 107; L. Billot, *De Verbo incarnato* (Rome 1927), p. 151. Billot offers the following excellent summary of the parallels: 'Unio hypostatica et unio gloriae inter se conveniunt: Primo quoad terminos, qui uniuntur. Utrobique enim creatura *immediate* unitur Deo, vel natura creata supposito increato, vel mens creata increato intelligibili. – Secundo quoad modum unionis. Utrobique enim Deus *actuat quasi formaliter*: vel scilicet naturam substantialem cui communicatione sui tribuit consistere, vel potentiam intellectivam cui communicatione sui tribuit adsistere obiecto in esse intellecto.—Tertio quoad *supernaturalitatem* unionis. Sicut enim natura creata non est in naturali potentia ad hoc quod trahatur ad esse divinum ut ad suum actum essendi: ita mens creata non est in naturali potentia ad hoc quod trahatur ad divinam essentiam ut ad suam speciem intelligibilem.—Quarto quoad *non repugnantiam* unionis. Eaedem enim rationes quae removent impossibilitatem circa unionem hypostaticam, similiter eam removent circa unionem beatitudinis. . . .'

principle of a finite knowledge in the other. And such a formal causality of God (a Trinitarian hypostasis, his Being) is not known to us in the realm of nature (i.e. in knowledge which proceeds from the creature and consequently attains God only as *efficient* cause), and so cannot be ascertained as regards its actual realization (and hence also as regards its possibility) without Revelation. Such a relationship of God's formal causality in regard to a creature must not be put in doubt by rational considerations so far as its *general* conceptual possibility is concerned. For firstly it is indubitably given for every Catholic theologian at least in the special case of the hypostatic union. And secondly, an in all respects analogous perplexity, capable of no further resolution, lies before us in the (admittedly distinct) field of God's efficient causality in respect of the world: for here too God stands in a certain connexion with something else and yet remains wholly transcendent to it, i.e. he is active and yet this fact in no way reacts upon him nor gives him a fresh determination; so that the concept, in itself finite, of efficient causality, once it is applied to God, has to be provided with a negation, in consequence of which the continued existence of a positive content in this concept becomes obscure. If such is the case in this field, it cannot be impossible in principle to allow an active formal causality (*eine formale Wirkursächlichkeit*) of God upon a creature without thereby implying that this reactively impresses a new determination upon God's Being in itself, one which would do away with his absolute transcendence and immutability. One may explicitly draw attention to this meta-categorical character of God's abidingly transcendent formal causality by a prefixed 'quasi', and in our case then be entitled to say that in the vision of God his Being exercises a *quasi-formal* causality. All this 'quasi' implies is that this 'forma', in spite of its formal causality, which must be taken really seriously, abides in its absolute transcendence (inviolateness, 'freedom'). But it does *not* imply that the statement, 'In the beatific vision God occupies the place of a *species* in virtue of a formal causality', is a mode of speech lacking all binding force; on the contrary, it is the *quasi* which must be prefixed to every application to God of a category in itself terrestrial.[1] The only reason why it is specially to be recommended in

---

[1] So it is a 'hesitation' founded in the nature of things when St Thomas once simply says that in the beatific vision God is the '*forma* intellectus ipsum cognoscentis' (*Comp. Theol.* cap. 105; similarly Ia. 12.5. corp.), and

ur case that the *quasi* should be explicitly added is that (as opposed
ɔ efficient causality) it provides an emphatic reminder of the ana-
ɔgical nature of our concepts in the matter of a relationship to the
vorld known only through Revelation; and above all because in this
natter of a formal, though ontological, causality of God the only
ausality in question is one which brings to its highest perfection the
uman mind as *knowing* (and in this respect only).

For the rest the ontological problematic of God's formal causality
a respect of a creature is treated of in scholastic theology in discussions
f the hypostatic union. What is there said about the compatibility (at
ast negatively demonstrable) of such a concept with God's immut-
bility, or about the category to which such an objective state of
ffairs must analogically be ascribed, etc., likewise holds good in our
ase *mutatis mutandis*. We need consequently not go into the matter

---

et also asserts emphatically: 'Non autem oportet quod ipsa divina essentia
at forma intellectus ipsius, sed quod *se habeat* ad ipsum *ut* forma' (*De Ver.*
. 8, a. 1 corp.; similarly *Suppl.* 92.1 ad 8, '*quasi* forma intellectus qua intel-
git'). It is usual today to distinguish two senses of 'forma' by speaking of
ctus *informans*' and 'actus *terminans*': thus 'forma' (the determination) in
ne first sense is that which in itself arrives at reality and perfection in virtue
f the act of determination; in the second sense it is that which in itself is
nd remains a perfect reality in spite of and prior to the act of determination.
: is indeed not to be denied that many theologians who continue to employ
ne *formula* of God as the *quasi-forma* of the beatified mind, in actual fact
ave it very little of its proper metaphysical sense. So for example Suarez
Vivès I, tract. 1, lib. 2, cap. 12–13), Pesch (*Prael. Dogm.* II n. 80) and
thers. Even Billot (*De Deo uno et trino*[4] (Rome 1902) p. 141) is not very
ear on this point when he speaks of the opposite of a *forma inhaerens* as
nformare non physice sed intentionaliter tantum'. If this is supposed to
iean that God is in fact an 'intentional' *known object*, the whole explanation
false, for it is a question here precisely of an ontological (hence 'physical')
resupposition of knowledge. Thus 'intentionaliter informare' can only mean
iat God's active formal causality does not interiorly determinate the 'form'
itself (as is the case with finite forms), or be attempting to express the fact
iat God's Being in spite of its relation as form to the finite mind does not
iake the divinity into an inner determination of this mind. An ontology,
eveloped in more detail than is here possible, of the formal causality of the
ivine Being in regard to finite being would doubtless be able to show (once
is concept had been presupposed) that something of the sort is basically
ɔssible, so long as the divine Being remains unaffected, only in two cases:
ther as *unio hypostatica*, or as the communication of this Being as the object
f immediate knowledge and love.

again here. Nor is this the place to specify this formal causality more sharply in view of the fact that the causality precisely under discussion here is one which determines the finite spirit in the direction of the object which it is to know and love (and in this way only!). It is sufficient here to hold firmly on to the fact that in the beatific vision there is present as its ontological presupposition a 'relation' between creature and God which is not a categorical one, resting upon an accidental absolute modification, but is a quasi-formal causality of God himself upon the created spirit; so that (corresponding to the general nature of the relationship of a 'forma' to its formal effect) the reality of the mind in the beatific vision, so far as such a reality in itself is due to a *species* as the means of knowledge, is the very Being of God.

Furthermore it goes without saying that this active formal causality of God on the human spirit must not be understood one-sidedly as engaging only the intellect. It is true that scholastic theology is concerned almost exclusively with the ontology of the immediate *knowledge* of God, but there is no doubt that God's immediate communication to the created spirit extends just as much to the 'will' (understood in the scholastic sense).[1]

There is still one question to be touched on briefly here: the relationship between God's formal causality on the spirit and the light of glory. We do not have to provide here a proof of the existence of the *lumen gloriae*; our only question is how, following St Thomas, we should conceive of its relationship to God's Being as the quasi-*species* of the spirit in terms of formal ontology. If one examines St Thomas' proofs for the *lumen gloriae* in themselves,[2] it becomes clear that he regards it as a *dispositio* of the spirit for the reception of the formal causality of God's intelligible Being upon it. Thus in respect of God's immediate conjunction with the spirit the *lumen gloriae* takes its place in the category of material causality, which does not exclude, but necessarily includes, the fact that this *dispositio*, as an entitative determination of the cognitive power, possesses the character of *formal* cause in regard to the human spirit. This *dispositio* needs however to be determined more sharply: it is (for reasons which may be

---

[1] Cf. B. Froget, *De l'habitation du Saint-Esprit dans les âmes justes*[2] (Paris 1900), pp. 148–154.

[2] *Summa contra Gentiles* III, 53, etc.

studied in St Thomas) a *dispositio ultima*.[1] Now according to St Thomas it is the case with a *dispositio ultima* (*dispositio quae est necessitas ad formam*) that on the one hand as *causa materialis* it logically precedes the *forma*, and yet on the other that it depends for its subsistence upon the formal causality of the *forma*,[2] so that to affirm its presence is simultaneously to affirm with inner necessity the presence of the formal causality of the *forma* and conversely.[3]

[1] *De Ver.* q. 8, a. 3 corp.

[2] Cf. e.g. *De Ver.* q. 28, a. 7 corp.; IIIa. 7. 13 ad 2, 9. 3 ad 2. Clearly it is of no importance in this connexion whether St Thomas's use of this *mutua causalitas* in the texts cited, which are concerned with other topics, is justified or not.

[3] Thus it becomes possible to say in what the strictly *supernatural* character of a created grace (here primarily the light of glory) consists: while in the created entity in general its relation to the divine cause does not belong to the inner distinguishing features of its *essence* (Ia 44. 1 ad 1), created grace, as *ultima dispositio* to an immediate communication of the divine Being itself in the mode of formal causality—a communication which can only exist in terms of this formal causality—involves a relation to God which belongs to its very essence.

And it is so and only so that a created grace can possess the quality of something absolutely supernatural. This is seen most clearly when one takes into consideration what sort of entity is capable of being an absolute mystery. It is necessary to provide an answer to this question if one bears in mind the Thomist doctrine of the relationship between knower and known, that a created thing purely as such can never be an absolute *mysterium*. For in principle it is always possible in virtue of the convertibility of being, knowing and intelligibility, to correlate with any finite grade of being a knower of the same or a higher level of being to which the former grade of being of a finite level is not in principle inaccessible. Accordingly Ripalda's view was in itself quite sound, when he held that created grace (the inner, essential connexion of which with uncreated grace he did not clearly perceive) can only be unexacted in concrete fact with respect to any really created substance, but not with respect to some still higher, conceivable and creatable substance (cf. H. Lange, *De Gratia*, Freiburg 1929, n. 260). Given a grace which on the one hand is ontologically an accidental reality and on the other remains as such purely in the created order, it is really impossible to show why to such an accident there should not correspond a created substance as possible, from which such an accident could proceed connaturally. Hence we may sum up our conclusions as follows: it is quite impossible for something purely created to be really absolutely supernatural and to present an absolute *mysterium*; but if there is something supernatural simply speaking which is absolutely mysterious, then God himself must belong to what constitutes it, i.e. God in so far as he is not merely the ever transcendent

3. The Proposed Solution

We are now in a position to offer a more exact answer to the question put above than is commonly the case, without really having to leave the traditional ways of scholastic thought.

a. *The statement of the solution.*

The possession of the Pneuma (and thus primarily uncreated grace) is conceived of in Scripture as the homogeneous germ and commencement of the beatific vision. And therefore we have the right to apply to uncreated grace in this life the concepts of formal ontology relating to the possession of God in the *visio beatifica*, at least in those cases in which the theological statements concerning this grace themselves suggest it. Now it has been seen that one fails to do justice to the essence of uncreated grace as this is declared in the sources of Revelation, if one sees it as exclusively founded upon a categorical relation to God of the man to whom grace has been shown, which relation rests merely (in some way or other) upon an accidental created modification of man's soul. This difficulty is resolved when we transfer to uncreated grace the concepts of formal ontology which appear in the *visio beatifica*: God communicates himself to the man to whom grace has been shown in the mode of *formal* causality, so that this communication is not then merely the consequence of an efficient causation of created grace. Thus it becomes clear that the proposition no longer holds good which maintains that man has uncreated grace because he possesses created grace; on the contrary, with Scripture and the Fathers the communication of uncreated grace can be conceived of under a certain respect as logically and really prior to created grace, in that mode namely in which a formal cause is prior to the ultimate material disposition.

In what more precisely the communication of God by way of formal causality to the creature consists—this almost purely formal ontological account says very little expressly about it—may be determined in terms of the *visio beatifica* only negatively. Just as grace in general as an entitative supernatural elevation of man can be described in more

---

Creator, the efficient cause of something finite which is distinct from him but in so far as he communicates himself to the finite entity in quasi-formal causality.

precise detail only in terms of its definitive unfolding, the *visio* (though this 'unfolding' and 'disclosure' are not *just* a 'growth' to a final stage arising out of an inner impulse but are also a new eschatological intervention of the God who is still in himself concealed), so too uncreated grace is only to be determined in terms of the *visio*: it is the homogeneous commencement, already given though still concealed and still to unfold, of that *communication* of the divine Being taking place *by way of formal causality* to the created spirit which is the *ontological presupposition* of the *visio*.[1]

Firstly, then, this union, so far as it takes place by way of formal causality, is not simply a consequence of created grace—indeed it precedes the created grace to the extent that this grace, as the ultimate disposition to the union, can only exist when God's formal causality is actually being exercized. Secondly, so far as it is the ontological *presupposition* of the beatific vision, this union is already posited independently of an actually exercised apprehension of the threefold God by man in knowledge and love, whether this should be through

---

[1] Cf. Leo XIII, 'Divinum illud munus' (ASS XXIX (1896), p. 653): 'Haec autem mira coniunctio, quae suo nomine inhabitatio dicitur, condicione tantum seu statu ab ea discrepans, qua caelites Deus beando complectitur . . .' As is well known, Pius XII in the encyclical 'Mystici Corporis' (AAS XXXV (1943), p. 231 s.; Denz 2290) has once more referred to this text as a starting-point for a consideration according to the *analogia fidei* so as to achieve a deeper understanding of the indwelling of the Spirit in the grace of justification. The Pope points out more clearly than before that the divine activity *ad extra* is common to the three Persons (Denz 428; 704) in the sense that this is to be understood of efficient causality (Denz 2290); and at the same time draws attention to the *visio beatifica* as the starting-point for a more profound theology of grace. In this way he clearly points to a theology of grace which seeks to make full use of that notion of God's formal causality with respect to the creature which is a traditional possession of the schools in the theology of the *visio beatifica* and is quite inescapable in the doctrine of the hypostatic union. The circumstance that Pius XII clearly seems to wish to leave open the question whether the relations to the three divine Persons of the man to whom grace has been shown are really only appropriated cannot be discussed here. There is hardly any need to establish the fact that the solution here proposed respects the Pope's warning against every kind of pantheism ('omnem nempe reiciendum esse mysticae huius coagmentationis modum, quo christifideles, quavis ratione, ita creatarum rerum ordinem praetergrediantur, atque in divina perperam invadant, ut vel una sempiterni Numinis attributio de iisdem tamquam propria praedicari queat'). Compare here Trütsch, *loc. cit.* pp. 112 s.

the supernatural acts of the theological virtues or through the beatifying vision and love of fulfilment. Thirdly, this ontological union is posited as a presupposition of the *visio*. By this is meant that this immediate, ontological union, in spite of or even because of its basis in formal causality, should not be conceived of vaguely as some sort of 'unity of nature', in which God and the created spirit are thought of as flowing into each other along arbitrarily adopted courses. This ontological unity arising out of the exercise of formal causality is nothing but the presupposition and the ontological aspect of the unity of the created spirit with God in the act of immediate loving contemplation, an act therefore which implies the highest degree of unity in the fullest distinction. And here our interpretation once again reaches a point at which it can either rejoin the traditional interpretation of God's indwelling in the line of St Thomas, Suarez, John of St Thomas or Gardeil,[1] or adopt the categories of a more personalist metaphysics of the relationship between God and the creature through grace. For in the last resort this interpretation of ours seeks nothing else than to focus more sharply for the human understanding the highest and most intimate union with God which is possible to a creature in the gaze of love, and to do so by grasping as precisely as possible the ontological presupposition of the union in the categories of formal ontology.

We need not attempt to decide here how we should interpret the distinction between the communication of the divine Being to man by way of formal causality in grace and in the *visio*: whether we should interpret it as a difference in the degree of this increasing communication *in itself*, or as a difference derived from the difference in the material *disposition* to this communication.[2] In other words, we

---

[1] At any rate, it is quite unjustified, on the basis of the fact that the created grace of the 'pilgrim' state (*status viatoris*) is distinct at least in degree from the light of glory, to conclude with B. Froget (*De l'habitation* ..., pp. 155 s.), M. Retailleau and others (cf. Trütsch, *passim*) that if the divine essence is already united immediately with the pilgrim's spirit as it is in the *visio*, he would have to possess the *visio* already. Such a conclusion presupposes that this immediate union is the unique cause of the vision. But if a *created* supernatural disposition (grace or the light of glory, which are capable of growth) is a necessary presupposition of the vision, the fact that it is deficient can explain why the *visio* is not posited, although an immediate informing communication of the divine Being to the created spirit has already been posited.

[2] Cf. Galtier, *De SS. Trinitate in se et in nobis* (Paris 1933), nn. 443 s.

do not intend to take up the question whether the growth from uncreated grace to the possession of God as the basis of the *visio beatifica* is an inner growth of this possession in itself or just the 'growth' (always understood with the restriction indicated above) of created grace into the light of glory—or whether this either-or is really not justified at all in a more precisely worked-out ontology of the relationship between *causa formalis* and *causa materialis*.

b. *Hints of this view in the theologians.*

If in order to confirm our view we refer here to a few texts of the great scholastic theologians (without any pretentions to completeness), we do so not in order to identify these theologians as defenders of our view but only so as to show *a posteriori* too how it is possible to find many examples of a preliminary movement in this direction in scholastic theology. As early as Alexander of Hales 'gratia increata' is not just the efficient cause of created grace but also the *perfectio complens* of the state of grace, as opposed to which *gratia creata* is only a *perfectio disponens*, a *medium*, a *dispositio in anima ad susceptionem gratiae increatae*. Indeed Alexander even teaches a priority of uncreated grace in a certain respect.[1] As regards St Bonaventure reference should at least be made to the fact that he regards the existence of uncreated grace as more certain theologically, and thus its existence is even objectively more basic for him than that of created grace.[2] There is to be found in this opinion not only a reflexion of the doctrinal situation which arose in the early scholastic period through the well-known teaching of Peter Lombard, but also an echo of Biblical and patristic theology: the Holy Spirit himself is the true gift—'et hoc a fide et Scriptura determinatur', as St Bonaventure says—while created grace (even if it is now no longer possible to say of it 'investigatur a doctoribus rationum probabilitate') is to be understood in terms of uncreated grace. Should there not be an ontological order corresponding to this logical order at least under one aspect? At any rate the approach almost exclusively adopted today, which grants to uncreated grace only a very modest little place in the tractate *de Gratia*, is very

[1] See the texts in E. J. Primeau, *Doctrina Summae theologicae Alexandri Halensis de Spiritus Sancti apud iustos inhabitatione* (Mundelein 1936), pp. 33 s.
[2] In *II Sent.* dist. 26, a. 1, q. 2 corp.

far removed from St Bonventure's point of departure.[1] In St Thomas too the idea is found that created grace stands to uncreated grace 'ex parte recipientis vel materiae', as 'dispositio'.[2] And even St Thomas once calls the Holy Spirit the *causa formalis inhaerens* of our adoptive sonship.[3] Nor again is created grace for St Thomas simply *causa materialis* for uncreated grace but also under a different aspect its *consequence*, as may be seen from IIIa. 7.13 corp.: 'gratia enim causatur in homine *ex praesentia* divinitatis, sicut lumen in aere ex praesentia solis'; nor is there any occasion to weaken the 'praesentia divinitatis' of the text to a merely natural divine omnipresence, since this omnipresence appears as an analogous case parallel to the hypostatic union. Besides we find him saying elsewhere: 'Personae divinae *sui sigillatione* in animabus nostris *relinquunt* quaedam dona quibus formaliter fruimur (Deo), scilicet amore et sapientia'.[4] Thus the sealing logically precedes the means by means of which man arrives at the fruition of the Godhead. Finally it is St Thomas who again and again on the one hand speaks of grace as *inchoatio gloriae*,[5] and on the other hand in the ontology of glory does not see this, as has already been shown, as based merely upon a created quality (and the relation to God posited with it). In the case of Lessius and Scheeben,[6] although their theory of the essence of grace and filiation is almost inextricably bound up with their theory—not under discussion here—of the union of the Holy Spirit with man as a property of the Third Person of the Trinity, yet their authority may be invoked here in so far as they both point to the parallels which, from an ontological point of view, hold between the

---

[1] Cf. the remarks of P. Dumont in *Revue des Sciences Religieuses* XIV (1934), pp. 62 s.

[2] In *I Sent.* dist. 14, q. 2, a. 1 sol. 2. Similarly in Ia. 43.3 ad 2: 'gratia gratum faciens *disponit* animam ad habendam divinam personam'.

[3] In *III Sent.* dist. 10, q. 2, a. 1 sol. 3. If to *Spirit* there is added here 'cui appropriatur caritas, secundum quam formaliter meremur', this must not straight away be translated as though it read 'cui appropriatur *productio* caritatis infusae'; for St Thomas has just before said simply (*loc. cit.*, qla. 3 obj. 4), 'sed caritas est Spiritus sanctus'.

[4] In *I Sent.* dist. 14, q. 2, a. 3 ad 2.

[5] Ia–IIae. 111.3 ad 2; IIa–IIae. 24.3 ad 2; *De Ver.* q. 8, a. 3 ad 10; q. 27, a. 5 ad 6; in *III Sent.* dist. 13, q. 1, a. 1 ad 5.

[6] Lessius, *De summo bono*, lib. II, cap. 1, n. 4; Scheeben, *Handbuch der Dogmatik*, II §169, nn. 851 s.; also in his controversy with Granderath, e.g. *Katholik* LXIV, 2 (1884) pp. 479 s.

unio hypostatica and the *gratia increata* even of the pilgrim state. Scheeben does indeed make much use of the concept of the *causa formalis*, but almost exclusively in the question whether and in what sense the indwelling of the Spirit is *causa formalis* precisely of the *adoptive sonship* of the justified; but the concept never or hardly ever appears in the only question which concerns us here, how in fact the indwelling *itself as such* ought to be conceived of. Franzelin[1] regards the *communicatio Dei ipsius per modum causae formalis* as the characteristic feature of a supernatural gift, and finds an example of it in the *unio hypostatica*, the *visio beatifica* and the grace of justification. In itself, we like to think, our view is in harmony with that of Galtier. As we have already said above, he recognizes as not merely historically accurate but also as theoretically valid today the principle, 'Praesentia divina non est mera consequentia seu merus effectus iustificationis quae sit per solam gratiam'.[2] When he goes on to explain how this principle can be maintained Galtier makes use of the concept of the 'actio proprie assimilativa ... (quae) praesentiam substantialem implicat *ratione sui*'.[3] This concept is clearly inspired by the Biblical and patristic image of the sealing of man with God's Spirit,[4] and renders it accurately. But the question then arises how precisely this sealing is to be conceived of, how, in other words, we are to understand Galtier when he writes: '(Personae divinae ...) animae ita se communicant et coniungunt, ut in eius essentia simul et potentiis imprimant suam ipsarum imaginem'.[5] Is the '*se* communicare' a pure consequence (*effectus formalis secundarius*) of the generation of the created image of God? In that case Vasquez' view is not finally disposed of,[6] or alternatively, recourse will have to be had once more to the Suarezian theory

---

[1] *De Deo uno*[3] (Rome 1883), pp. 340–2. Cf. also Scheeben's clarification of Franzelin's teaching on this point in *Katholik* LXIV, 2 (1884), pp. 480 s. C. Pesch (*Praelectiones Dogmaticae* II, nn. 681 s.) likewise conceives of the indwelling of the Spirit *ad modum formae assistentis et analogae*, but the formula is for him only another expression for the ordinary conception of uncreated grace.

[2] P. Galtier, *De SS. Trinitate* ..., n. 412.

[3] *Loc. cit.*, n. 456.

[4] *Loc. cit.*, n. 458.

[5] *Loc. cit.*, n. 456; cf. also n. 445.

[6] Accordingly Trütsch says of Galtier's theory too 'potest dici ulterior evolutio et modificatio explicationis Vasquesii' (p. 23). Nor has Galtier gone any further in developing his theory in the latest edition of his French book

of the indwelling, the point of departure adopted above being abandoned. But if the 'se communicare' precedes, at least under one aspect, the generation of created grace, or if at least it is not merely a consequence of it, then the question remains how precisely this communication of God himself to the creature is to be conceived of in its own right. Finally we may refer here to the two essays of P. Dumont and J. C. Martinez-Gómez[1] who declare themselves in favour of a priority of the communication of uncreated grace to created grace, without, it must be admitted, going more closely into the question how precisely the *donum increatum* is to be conceived of. We have already referred to the fact that the Encyclical 'Mystici Corporis' of Pius XII is favourable to the theory here proposed (and proposed before the appearance of the Encyclical) to the extent that it draws attention to two points of departure from which we have set out here: the admitted fact that in the relationship between God and man there evidently exists a categorical order which is not that of efficient causality; and the admitted fact that the doctrine of the *visio beatifica* should be drawn upon in order to determine the essence of grace. It has already been said that Trütsch 'awards the palm to the solution of de la Taille and Rahner'.[2] It would take us too far to examine the most recent literature, nor is it necessary, particularly as it is orientated more towards the question of whether the relations of the divine Persons to man in grace are appropriated or non-appropriated than to the question which concerns us here.

c. *Difficulties.*

There is no need here to discuss the *general* problematic of the concept of a communication of God to the creature. Consequently we

---

on this subject (see above, p. 319, n. 1). Cf. Lakner ZKT LXXII (1950), p. 116. Nevertheless Galtier's theory is worthy of note, since it recognizes the inadequacy of the classical solutions stemming from Vasquez and Suarez.

[1] Cf. above, p. 323, n. 5.

[2] So Lakner, in ZKT LXXII (1950), p. 116. It should be made clear in this connexion that the present investigation arose independently of de la Taille's work. This is not said in order to establish any rights of priority, which would certainly not be the case. On the contrary it is a deficiency of the present study (dating from 1939) that de la Taille's important essay, which had already appeared some ten years before, escaped my attention. But if two people reach the same conclusion independently of each other, there is a higher probability that they are not totally at fault, which is a comfort in this unfortunate accident.

have only to take up the questions which arise from the application of this concept precisely to the indwelling of God, to uncreated grace. Does not our view, with its emphasis on the relative independence of uncreated grace as regards created grace, endanger the significance of created grace for justification, adoption, etc., as Trent sees them? We need not here go into the familiar controversy conducted above all by Scheeben and Granderath as to the meaning of Chapter VII of the Sixth Session of the Council of Trent in the matter of the *unica causa formalis iustificationis*. In this question too we may surely have recourse to the concepts developed in scholastic theology in its treatment of the *visio beatifica*. Just as there the light of glory is seen as the *dispositio ultima quae est necessitas ad formam*, so here an analogous relationship may be assumed to hold between created and uncreated grace. In this regard created grace is seen as *causa materialis* (*dispositio ultima*) for the formal causality which God exercises by graciously communicating his own Being to the creature. In this way the material and formal causes possess a reciprocal priority: as *dispositio ultima* created grace is in such a way the presupposition of the formal cause that it can itself only exist by way of the actual realization of this formal causality. From this objective reciprocal priority there follows further the logical justification for inferring the presence of one reality from that of the other. Because created grace as *dispositio ultima* can only exist along with the actual formal causality of the form for which it is the *dispositio*, it is correct to say: If created grace is given, so too necessarily by that very fact uncreated grace, and hence the whole grace of justification, is communicated to man.

Thus on our view of the relationship between created and uncreated grace there does not exist even the beginning of a possibility of thinking of created grace apart from uncreated grace, and so of thinking of uncreated grace as a fresh gift arising out of a new and independent demonstration of God's grace. We must remember furthermore that created grace alone (as a finite determination of the subject) can be called *forma* in the strict (categorical) sense of the word (as opposed to the divine Being itself, which remains transcendent with respect to the creature in spite of its formal causality); and we must remember that the Council only wished to meet the imputation theory of the Reformers, Seripando and others, but did not wish to determine how created and uncreated (inner!) grace (of which latter it also says precisely 'signans et. ungens Spiritu promissionis Sancto . . .') are related to each other and together constitute the *single* grace of justification. In view of all this we may say that the Council's teaching on created grace as the *unica causa formalis* of justification does not exclude our conception of the relationship between created and uncreated grace. For in this conception too created grace remains the 'unique' formal cause of justification, in so far as it alone is the genuine (categorical) 'form' of the justified man, and once it is posited, justification as a whole is really posited with it already. In addition it must be said that Chapter VII of the Tridentine decree on justification only teaches explicitly that the *causa formalis* of justification is wholly *interior* (and thus not an *imputed* 'causa formalis extrinseca'), and that conversely therefore the *causa formalis* of justification is interior grace *alone*. It is true that the Council describes this interior grace in terms which in the theology of the schools hold good primarily of created grace, but it nowhere says that *interior* grace, as the unique formal cause of justification, must be understood *exclusively* of *created* grace.[1]

If on our view created grace is conceived of as the *dispositio* (*causa materialis*) for the *donum increatum*, this is in no way to deprive it of what is attributed to it by theology. In order that it can be a *dispositio* for uncreated grace at all, it does indeed have first of all the character of a *formal* entitative, supernatural determination of the human spirit; as such, however, on our view too all those *effectus formales* can be assigned to it ascribed to it by scholastic theology. Just in so far as and in virtue of the fact that it constitutes man as a subject fit to receive the substantial gift of the divine essence for a future *visio*, it assimilates man to God's nature considered as the principle of his possession of himself in Trinity; and thus it at once becomes the *causa formalis* of all the properties of man's supernatural elevation.[2]

---

[1] Cf. Galtier, *op. cit.*, n. 413: 'Propterea communior est in dies sententia, quae tenet specialem illam in anima habitationem, esse de ratione causae formalis justificationis. . . . Nec propterea ullatenus contradicitur concilio Tridentino.'

[2] In this sense our view is not in conflict with St Thomas's statement (Ia–IIae. 110. 1 ad 2; *De Ver.* q. 27, a. 1 ad 1) that created grace alone and not God himself is the 'causa formalis' in respect of supernatural 'life'. It is through created grace alone that man becomes a subject who is *capable* of knowing and loving God supernaturally, who has the *capacity* for it. But in order that such a supernatural 'life' should become actual there is need

It remains true, certainly, that the usual theological argument for the existence of created grace from the communication of uncreated grace must be formulated rather more cautiously in our interpretation than is usually the case. If there is someone who supposes, in accordance with the view of Cajetan or Suarez in respect of the manner in which the *unio hypostatica* is to be explained, that an active formal causality on God's part necessarily comprises a created modality, he will be able correspondingly to conclude to the presence of created grace from the premiss of uncreated grace. Someone who does not share these views of Cajetan and Suarez will use arguments to prove the existence of created grace[1] analogous to those used by St Thomas when he shows the necessity of the created light of glory in spite of and because of God's formal causality in the *visio*.

d. *A consequence of the proposed solution.*

The question is well-known and much discussed today whether God's indwelling in and conjunction with the justified man is only appropriated to the divine Persons or whether through grace a relationship to the man to whom grace has been shown arises which is peculiar to each divine Person. On the view according to which indwelling and so on is merely a relationship of God to man resting entirely upon created grace, this question can only be answered in the sense of a bare appropriation. For then we are required to apply the principle of theology recently emphasized once again by Pius XII: 'omnia esse habenda Sanctissimae Trinitati communia quatenus eadem Deum ut supremam *efficientem* causam respiciant' (Denz 2290). But if 'uncreated grace' is *not* ontologically speaking a pure consequence of created grace as a qualitative accident, if rather the view proposed here is correct, then the question which has just been put is by no means immediately answered yet; it can really be put for the first time as a question which is hence not obsolete but is still open. For it is above all at least conceivable then that the quasi-formal causality which we have attributed—simplifying the question for reasons of method—to

---

further of the self-communication of the object of this supernatural life, and this communication is not simply the mere *consequence* of the communication of the subjective potency of this life.

[1] For the diversity of the arguments brought forward in the great age of scholasticism, cf. Auer, *Die Entwicklung* ... I, pp. 97 s.; 111 s.

God and his essence, should also be proper, with regard to the recipient of grace, to the three divine Persons in their personal distinction. Of course one can at once raise the classical objection that this is inconceivable from the start. The argument here is that where one divine Person as such in distinction from the other two has a relation to a created reality which is proper to the given Person, this relation can only be a *hypostatic* unity (such as is given in Christ's case alone), since this union must on the one hand occur in respect of what is proper to the individual Persons, yet on the other hand proper, relative subsistence is the one thing which belongs to a divine Person in distinction from another (cf. Denz 703). We are not required here to go more closely into why this *a priori* objection, for all its apparent exactitude, need not for various reasons be taken as conclusive. H. Schauf, for instance, has treated of it at length.[1] Nor does it enter into the scope of this investigation to show the force of the arguments from Biblical theology and the Fathers in favour of the thesis that the relations of the divine Persons to the justified man are non-appropriated ones. Nor again is there any question of showing with the help of recent studies that, in spite of its justified opposition to Peter Lombard, medieval theology exhibited more nuances in its thought and sought to do more justice to the data of Scripture and Tradition than the simplified teaching of the schools of latter centuries might allow one to suppose.[2] We should like to draw attention here merely to one aspect of the question since it arises out of our previous considerations. If it is true that in the *visio beatifica* that alone can be grasped really immediately in its very self, without the mediation of some other known object, which communicates itself to the knowing mind in quasi-formal causality after the fashion of a 'species impressa', ontologically prior to knowledge as such, then this holds good equally of the three divine Persons each in its own personal property. In other words, they are either not beheld immediately as such in the *visio*

[1] H. Schauf, *Die Einwohnung des Heiligen Geistes. Die Lehre von der nicht-appropriierten Einwohnung des Heiligen Geistes als Beitrag zur Theologiegeschichte des 19. Jahrhunderts unter besonderer Berücksichtigung der beiden Theologen Carl Passaglia und Clemens Schrader* (Freiburg 1941), esp. pp. 224–49. See also M. Schmaus, *Katholische Dogmatik* I⁴ (Munich 1948), pp. 378 s.

[2] Cf. the writings cited above, p. 319, n. 1, especially the work by Dockx. See also C. Sträter, 'Het begrip "appropriatie" bij S. Thomas', *Bijdragen* IX (1948), pp. 1–41; 144–86.

beatifica; or, in logical priority to the *visio* as a conscious act, they have each *as* divine, mutually distinct Persons their own proper quasi-formal causality upon the created spirit, a causality which makes it possible for these divine Persons to be possessed 'consciously', and, what is more, immediately. Hence there also follows *one* aspect of the answer to the above-mentioned classical objection to the doctrine that the indwelling and communication of the three divine Persons are not appropriated but are proper to each. 'Communication of (in respect of) the proper hypostasis' can in fact mean two things. It can either mean: communication of (according to) the particular hypostasis in such a way that it exercises its hypostatic function in respect of that to which the communication is made. Or 'communication of (according to) the hypostasis' can mean that a true ontological communication of the hypostasis takes place, but to the end and only to the end that it can become in virtue of this quasi-formal causality the object of immediate knowledge and love. In the first sense we have such a communication only in the case of Christ, by reason of the relationship of the divine Word to the human nature assumed by him. We should have an instance of the second kind of communication in the 'uncreated grace' of the justified man. It would have to be proved in the strictest possible way that it was impossible for there to be this kind of communication of the divine Persons each in his own personal particularity and hence a non-appropriated relation to the three Persons. There is no way of producing such a proof. Consequently there can be absolutely no objection to maintaining on the basis of the positive data of Revelation that the attribution of determinate relations of the recipient of grace to the three divine Persons is not merely a matter of appropriation, but is intended to give expression to a proper relationship in each case. In Scripture it is the Father in the Trinity who is our Father, and not the threefold God.[1] The Spirit dwells in us in a particular and proper way.[2] These and like statements of Scripture

---

[1] See above, pp. 147–8.

[2] By this it is not of course meant that the Spirit alone makes his dwelling in us. Each Person communicates himself and dwells in us in a way proper to him. And because the indwelling ascribed to the Holy Spirit in Scripture (as a Power who sanctifies, consecrates, moves, etc.) corresponds precisely to the personal particularity of the Spirit and of his going forth from the Father and the Son, there is absolutely no objection to saying that in *this* way only the Spirit dwells in man.

and Tradition are first of all 'in possessione'. It would be necessary to prove that they may be merely appropriated, on the grounds that they can be understood merely as such and that the contrary is impossible; it cannot be presupposed. So long as this has not been achieved, we must take Scripture and the expressions it uses in as exact a sense as we possibly can. There is another point which should not be forgotten. In the history of Western piety an attenuation of the 'Trinity of the economy of salvation' into a kind of pre-Christian monotheism (and that is what the doctrine of bare appropriations in the theology of grace really amounts to) has not merely diminished the significance of the Holy Trinity in concrete religious life. In itself (i.e. logically, and if the contrary were not already defined) this attenuation could also endanger the 'interior Trinity' to the benefit of a rationalistic monotheism for which the three divine Names would only be for us three aspects under which to regard the one divine Essence. For in Scripture the interior Trinity and the Trinity of the economy of salvation are seen and spoken of in themselves with such simultaneity that there would be no justification in itself (logically) for taking the expressions literally and substantially in the first case and only in an 'appropriated' way in the second. We should like to think that here our proposed theory of uncreated grace in terms of the concepts of scholastic theology offers the possibility of determining man's relationship in grace as a non-appropriated relation to the three divine Persons, without doing injury to the principle of the unity of efficient causality in the creative action of the threefold God *ad extra*, and without making the indwelling conjunction of the three divine Persons into a hypostatic union.

II

THE THEOLOGICAL CONCEPT OF CONCUPISCENTIA[1]

T HE concept of concupiscentia as it is employed by theologians is undoubtedly one of the most difficult in dogmatic theology, not only because of its extraordinarily disturbed history from St Paul by way of St Augustine to Luther, Baius and Jansenius, but also because it must be regarded in Catholic theology from two points of view which are not easily reconciled. On the one hand concupiscentia must be seen as something which can be called sin in the sense of chapter VII of the Epistle to the Romans[2], i.e. sin at least in the

[1] The following reflexions were submitted to a detailed examination (based on their first publication in the *Zeitschrift für Katholische Theologie*) by J. P. Kenny in 'The Problem of Concupiscence: a recent theory of Professor Karl Rahner', *The Australasian Catholic Record* (Sidney) XXIX (1952), pp. 290–304; XXX (1953), pp. 23–32.

(I use 'concupiscentia' to translate *Konkupiszenz*, 'concupiscence' to translate *Begierlichkeit*. Both German words are to be regarded as technical terms, but *Konkupiszenz* is simply a Germanization of the Latin word adopted by Fr Rahner in order to have a neutral word at his disposal through which he can present his special view.—Tr.)

[2] As the Council of Trent allows (Denz 792). Certainly it is very doubtful whether it is really concupiscentia as such *alone* which St Paul calls ἁμαρτία. It is true that the Sin (ἡ ἁμαρτία) which appears in the world and affects all men in consequence of Adam's act is not regarded by St Paul as a purely static deprivation of the Spirit suffered by Adamite man; rather this primal and hereditary Sin contains a dynamic and active element which urgently seeks to reveal its own nature in the personal sins of the individual. Thus *the* Sin comes into the world like a ruler (Rom. 5:12), 'dwells' in man's flesh (Rom 7:20), subjects man to itself as its slave (Rom 6:6.17.20; 7:14), revives through the experience of the Law (Rom 7:8, 9), in this way becomes manifest in man's concrete life (Rom 7:13) by subjecting man to its law (Rom 7:23; 8:2) and using his 'members' as its weapons (Rom 6:13). This does indeed show that for St Paul '*the* Sin' (original sin) includes concupiscence as an element in its concrete concept. But this does not prove that he ever means by ἁμαρτία concupiscence precisely as such, inasmuch as he himself distinguishes it from the primal sin (Rom 7:8) and recognizes

sense that it arises out of transgression and can give occasion to fresh transgression as the Council of Trent explains (Denz 792); thus it must be possible to see it in a certain sense as a power weighing down upon man, with all the shattering impetus attested to by St Paul, St Augustine and Luther. On the other hand, according to Catholic teaching as it was laid down against the Reformers by the Council of Trent and above all against Baius by Pius V (Denz 792; 1026; 1078; 1516 s.), concupiscentia has to be conceived of in such a way that freedom from it represents even for unfallen man an unexacted, preternatural gift. If from the first point of view concupiscentia appears as a power oppressing man in his very depths and driving him on to moral transgression, from the second point of view it presents itself as something immediately given with human nature, and so really a matter of course, 'harmless', indeed almost necessary.

There is a further difficulty as well. Concupiscentia is a concept the content of which is on the one hand known to us from Revelation and yet on the other hand is available to our immediate human experience. Now from the point of view of this human experience of concupiscentia it is easy to see that the revealed theological concept of concupiscentia is always in danger of being interpreted subjectively according to man's understanding of himself, which is something to a large extent historically conditioned and to some extent variable. The various interpretations offered of the Pauline concept of σάρξ, for instance, show how hard it is not to shift the sense of a concept of Revelation without noticing it, in accordance with the unconscious *a priori* preconceptions of the interpreter's own anthropology or in accordance with that philosophical *a priori* by which he believes St Paul himself was influenced.[1]

---

it for something still remaining in the justified man (Rom 13:14; Gal 5:16; Eph 4:22; Col 3:5; 1 Thess 4:5; 1 Tim 6:9; 2 Tim 2:22; Tit 2:12) who is no longer under the κατάκριμα of sin (Rom 5:16; 8:1). It is correct to say that concupiscence is often included as a partial factor in the concept of ἁμαρτία and even stands in the foreground. But that it alone is ever called ἁμαρτία would still have to be proved. The fact that this view has been shared even by Catholics exegetes would seem to be the consequence of a long practice of applying, with St Augustine, chapter VII of the Epistle to the Romans to the justified man; for then of course the ἁμαρτία whose strength is there depicted can only be concupiscentia as such.

[1] Cf., e.g., W. Schauf, *Der Begriff 'Fleisch' beim Apostel Paulus unter besonderer Berücksichtigung seiner Erlösungslehre* (Munster 1924).

In what follows we shall attempt briefly to develop a conception of concupiscentia which will, as we believe, do justice to the real data of Revelation on the one hand, and at the same time avoid that disequilibrium which, so it seems to us, may still be encountered today in the usual theological conception of concupiscentia. For lack of space we deliberately and expressly renounce the task of supporting what we have to say with the apparatus of theological scholarship and of confronting it with the usual views in closer detail. The theologian who is familiar with scholastic teaching on concupiscentia will be able to make use of it to understand and assess this study. Our considerations proceed as follows: the conception of concupiscentia usual in modern Catholic theology will be briefly set out and submitted to criticism (I); and then an attempt will be made to offer a fresh formulation of this concept (II).

Naturally we do not suppose in the matter of this 'fresh' formulation that the elements for a 'fresh' determination of the concept are lacking in Tradition and the customary teaching of the theologians. On the contrary. In general we shall have recourse to doctrines and presuppositions of a quite self-explanatory kind (or at least also represented in scholasticism) which seem fitted to contribute to the understanding of the theological concept of concupiscentia and thus to make possible a clearer formulation of it. While it should not be necessary to discuss this point in detail, the theological *proof* for the proposed concept always consists in the fact that formulated in such a way it fits in with the assured theological data which we have about concupiscentia, and does so better than the previous concept. Once this is granted, it is unnecessary to be able to show that the conception proposed is itself clearly and explicitly to be found in Tradition, particularly as it may more easily be seen in detail that, as has been indicated, the sharper concept of concupiscentia actually found in certain Fathers and theologians is a product both of Revelation and of a philosophical anthropology.

One other preliminary remark is necessary if we are to avoid the danger that as a consequence of an insufficiently considered interpretation of human experience certain factors may be introduced into the theological concept of concupiscentia which do not belong to it, in such a way that this concept would be opposed to ours on the ground that it alone corresponded to experience. In the concrete experience of man's exposure to temptation, his moral weakness and sinfulness, elements are to be found which do *not* belong to the theological concept of concupiscentia. And this for the simple reason that we must necessarily presuppose their presence in Adam even before the Fall, because Adam too, in his preternatural state of integrity, could be tempted and could sin. Now it is only what was lacking in Adam in virtue of his gift of integrity that belongs to the theological concept of concupiscentia. Thus from the first two entirely distinct elements are given in our empirical 'concupiscentia': one an element which belongs essentially to every man so long as he forms a part of this cosmic epoch, and another which is a consequence of the loss of the integrity of Paradise due to the primordial sin. Hence it is not immediately easy to say what features of empirical 'concupiscentia' belong to *theological* concupiscentia—to that concupiscentia which Adam did not have originally. Nor is it any easier immediately to decide that theological concupiscentia is of more significance for moral decisions than those essential characteristics of man which independently of original sin and prior to it already provide the basis for his exposure to temptation and his power to sin.

I. A CRITICAL APPROACH TO THE CURRENT CONCEPTION OF CONCUPISCENTIA

Current expositions of dogmatic theology usually begin by distinguishing three concepts of concupiscentia. In the broadest sense concupiscence is for them any kind of conative potency (*Strebevermögen*) and its respective act; in a narrower and proper sense concupiscence is *sensitive* desire (*Begehren*)[1]; concupiscentia in the narrowest and strictly theological sense signifies for them the *sensitive* appetite (*Begehrungsvermögen*) and its act, in so far as this strives after its sensitive object *in opposition to* the law of the moral order independently of the higher, spiritual conative potency, and thus resists the spiritual free decision of man's will. For this reason this concupiscentia is also called evil, disordered, rebellious concupiscence, evil inclination. The gift of integrity is correspondingly defined today, generally speaking at least, as freedom from *evil* concupiscence.[2]

---

[1] Ia–IIae. 30.1.

[2] Cf., e.g., C. Mazella, *De Deo creante* (Woodstock 1877), n. 724; D. Palmieri, *Tractatus de Deo creante et elevante* (Rome 1878), thesis 44; M. J. Scheeben, *Handbuch der Kath. Dogmatik* II §155; J. B. Heinrich, *Dogma-*

Against this definition of concupiscence grave difficulties have been raised in two different directions. Franz Lakner has already drawn attention to the first of these difficulties as regards the concept of concupiscentia in more recent textbooks[1]; the reader may be referred to his discussion for further details. As Lakner justly says, the dogmatic and the ascetico-moral concepts of concupiscence are not distinguished in these treatments. A dogmatic consideration of concupiscentia ought not immediately to concern itself with the tendency of the sensitive appetite to what is morally *forbidden*, as the ascetico-moral consideration does—quite rightly; to the appetite there belongs in the first place the spontaneous character of a conative potency alone, on the basis of which conative acts anticipate and resist reflexion and free decision. This spontaneity is something which remains wholly *prior* to an ascetic qualification of concupiscentia as '*evil* inclination', so much so that in certain circumstances the spontaneous conative act may just as well be directed to a good of a morally positive value against man's bad free decision, as to a morally illicit good. By concupiscentia in the theological sense must be meant this character of spontaneity proper to the appetite, and correspondingly freedom from concupiscentia must be conceived of as total dominion over the appetite with respect to its character of spontaneity. Only then is it possible for an explanation of integrity to avoid the psychologically untenable view that the gift of integrity only comes into play when the appetite seeks for something morally *un*lawful; this would make the gift of integrity into a series of discontinuous new interventions of God in the psychological course of man's spiritual life. For this spontaneity (the exact nature of which we have still to discuss) and this tendency to resist found by nature in the appetite are either in themselves and of themselves suspended or they are not. In

---

tische Theologie VI (Mainz 1885), pp. 518 s.; C. Pesch, *Praelectiones dogmaticae* III, nn. 187 s.; H. Hurter, *Theologiae dogmaticae Compendium* II[8] (Innsbruck 1893), nn. 329–31; DTC III, col. 803–14; G. van Noort, *Tractatus de Deo creatore*[2] (Amsterdam 1912), n. 199; J. Pohle-M. Gierens, *Lehrbuch der Dogmatik* I[9] (Paderborn 1936), pp. 506 s.; F. Diekamp, *Katholische Dogmatik* II[9] (Munster 1939), pp. 126 s.; C. Boyer, *De Deo elevante* (Rome 1940), p. 276. This list could be considerably extended.

[1] ZKT LXI (1937), pp. 437–41. Cf. also L. Lercher, *Institutiones theol. dogm.* II[3] (Innsbruck 1940), nn. 608–10, where Lakner's exposition has already been put to excellent account.

the first case, this holds good then necessarily of *every one* of its acts, thus of those too which would be acts of resistance of the healthy nature to the morally *inferior* free decision of the person. For the concupiscentia itself cannot decide whether its object at any given time conforms to the moral norm or is opposed to it; such a decision rising from *spiritual* knowledge necessarily comes too late. A habitual inner binding of concupiscentia would thus have to extend uniformly to all its objects. In the second case, integrity could only be conceived of in an occasionalist way, as a continually renewed intervention by God from without, which suddenly puts a brake on concupiscentia just at the moment in which it is going to turn to a good opposed to the moral norm. But an idea like this would make the conscious life of man's soul into a chain of unmotivated accidents and surprises.

The second difficulty relates to the conception of concupiscentia, in the theological sense, as a purely sensitive power. Certainly in a metaphysical psychology we must distinguish between sensitive and spiritual appetites as between two really distinct powers of man. Yet this distinction must be conceived of with the utmost caution. For a human power must not be conceived of as a 'thing'; it is never more than that through which the one man acts. And a plurality of powers are and remain always powers of one and the same man, from whose substantial ground these powers, on St Thomas's view, arise, are supported by it and held together by it in a unity.[1] Consequently the objects of the sensitive and the spiritual appetites are present to the awareness of one and the same subject, related to one and the same subject. In a properly understood Thomist metaphysics of human knowledge, the relationship between the sensitive and the spiritual cognitive powers must be so conceived of as to fulfil two conditions. One the one hand the sensitive cognitive faculty will have to be seen as itself arising from the spiritual ground as a continuation of the information of matter by the spiritual soul and thus as completely mastered by the spirit right from the start. On the other hand the spiritual cognitive faculty, because it must allow sensibility to arise from itself as the presupposition of its own realization, will itself have

---

[1] On this point and on what follows see, e.g., Karl Rahner, *Geist in Welt. Zur Metaphysik der endlichen Erkenntnis bei Thomas von Aquin* (Innsbruck 1939), pp. 175 s. (2nd edn. 1957, pp. 243 s.—Tr.); W. Brugger, 'Die Verleiblichung des Wollens', *Scholastik* XXV (1950), pp. 248–53.

to be seen right from the start as a 'sensitized' spirituality. Thus in virtue of man's metaphysical structure it will be fundamentally impossible from the start for there ever to be an act of sensitive cognition which is not also *eo ipso* an act of spiritual cognition. And the converse holds good too.

It further follows from this that a sensible good is never pursued by man in virtue of his sensitive appetite alone. Every object (hence a sensible object too) is apprehended by man in a sensitive-spiritual way, and consequently pursued by him in the same way too. And conversely: a spiritual value is never apprehended in man's case in a purely spiritual way either. For neither is the purely spiritual object ever apprehended by pure intellect; it must also always be given sensibly in a certain way, on account of that reversion of man's spiritual knowledge to the senses (*conversio ad phantasma*) which is necessary for human cognition, and the same holds good for the spiritual conative power too. Every human cognitive and conative act is necessarily, in virtue of man's very nature, sensitive-spiritual or spiritual-sensitive. Now it follows from this that just as there exists a sensitive spontaneous act of desire, so too there exists at least as much an involuntary spiritual conative act prior to man's free personal decision. Thus where there exists a concupiscentia in the theological sense as an involuntary concupiscence anticipating free decision and resisting it, this is spiritual too. And it is quite impossible to see why this act of spiritual craving (*Begehrlichkeit*) should only be directed to sensible objects.[1] We may think for example of a persistent

---

[1] Thus it may be observed again and again in the literature on concupiscentia cited above, how the interpretation of concupiscentia as a *sensitive* impulse is found to be insufficient. Pesch, for example (*loc. cit.*, n. 188) finally recognizes an 'inordinatio motus in bona spiritualia . . . in quantum illa bona sub sensibili ratione apprehenduntur et facultatem sensibilem afficiunt'. But that is what all *bona spiritualia* necessarily do, when they are apprehended by a *man*! Palmieri does indeed exclude the 'indeliberatae affectiones . . . partis rationalis (motus superbiae, invidiae et huiusmodi)' from the concept of concupiscentia, but then goes on to explain (*loc. cit.*, p. 367): 'nihil modo refert, utrum hanc facultatem (sc. the concupiscent faculty) censeas esse potentiam formaliter sensibilem, an potius voluntatem ipsam, quae ferri potest in bonum delectabile sensui, apprehensum a sensu et proinde etiam ab intellectu'. Now if concupiscentia can be an attitude of the *spirit*, it is no longer clear why it can only be directed to sensible goods. At any rate for Palmieri it is something which characterizes man's sensibility and his spirituality in like manner. Hurter and van Noort also introduce into the concept of concupiscentia the conflict between the *ratio superior* and the

temptation against faith, or to despair. In such cases we are clearly faced with acts of the appetite which bear the typical marks of concupiscentia in the theological sense, namely the spontaneity of the act and its persistence in opposition to a free decision. And yet the act in question is plainly one which belongs specifically to the spiritual appetite.[1] Thus it is by no means clear why concupiscentia should be conceived of as a 'rebellion' precisely of the 'lower' man against the 'higher'. This always tends to suggest the idea that it is precisely the metaphysically (ontologically) lower in man which is also the more dangerous ethically and in this sense lower: as if the danger of turning away from God arises precisely from the ontologically lower spheres of man; as if the higher a being is entitatively, the less in danger it is in a moral way, while in reality there is just as much danger from the Luciferan heights of the spirit as from the dark depths of the purely sensitive. It is not that the ontically lower in man is intrinsically at variance with the higher, but that man is divided against himself. But we shall discuss this positive concept of concupiscentia in a monent.

If then no solid grounds can be offered why the front line of man's inner division against himself should exactly coincide with the metaphysical line which separates the ontologically higher and lower in man, it is at any rate clear what the historical basis of this conception is. It does not lie in Revelation itself. For the concepts of 'flesh', of the 'law of the members' and so on, with which St Paul tries to make vivid to our imagination man's inner division against himself on account of concupiscentia, are purely religious concepts, not the metaphysical concepts of an anthropology which ontologically stratifies man's essence. 'Flesh' for St Paul is not a part of man, but the whole man, in his spiritual dimensions too, in so far as for lack of the holy Pneuma and of grace he is subject to sin and to God's wrath.[2] Only an

---

ratio inferior, and so show in their own way that one cannot be content with the concept of a purely sensitive concupiscentia.

[1] The 'concupiscence of the flesh' in St Paul does not have the exclusive sense of 'sensitive desire' either. Cf. here Schauf, *op. cit.*, pp. 159–61.

[2] In offering a few remarks about St Paul's concept of *sarx*, what we have primarily in mind here is only *sarx* in St Paul so far as it is seen as the seat, the source and the revelation of sin. Thus from the start our only question is what σάρξ means in *these* texts. And once again the only question which concerns us here is whether the ontological quality of 'flesh' as the *sensitive* part of man over against natural 'spirit', man's intellectuality, is or is not for

interpretation which had not yet completely eliminated Gnostic or Neoplatonist tendencies with their *a priori* categories (and this is definitely the case with St Augustine) could have explained St Paul's

---

St Paul the exclusive or at least the preferred cause of sin. (If the first of these alternatives were true, we could go on to ask whether it was in its essential or merely in its historically evolved particularity that 'flesh' was with such exclusiveness the seat and source of sin.) Now it need not be denied that St Paul does see *one* of the sources of sin in 'flesh' as the sensitive and thus ontologically lower part of man. But it is not true that, when flesh is under discussion as *the* source and *the* seat of sin, what is referred to (and not merely *simultaneously* referred to) is exclusively man's sensibility and corporeality as meant by a metaphysical anthropology; nor does it become true by adding that the 'sarkic' quality of the lower part of man does not belong to it by metaphysical necessity but only because of the concrete particularity of history. The identification of the Pauline concept of *sarx* with the philosophical concept of human sensibility is excluded by the simple fact that for St Paul *sarx* is the contrary of *pneuma*. But *pneuma* for St Paul is not the 'spiritual' side of man; it is the divine spirit graciously bestowed from above which must cleanse and sanctify man's higher part too, so that it should not be—*sarx*. For in St Paul this *sarx* is the source of spiritual sin too, every graceless will to moral perfection is 'fleshly', the sarkic and the merely physical man are synonymous, etc.: all expressions which are incompatible with the identification of *sarx* and sensibility in the philosophical sense. For details see Schauf, *op. cit.* It is true that in a few places σάρξ is also seen in opposition to νοῦς. But this is far from implying that what is in question is an opposition of two 'parts' in man. The proper sense of these texts (Rom 7:23, 25) will be grasped if with St Paul one begins with the assumption that νοῦς is as a matter of course the locus of the knowledge of God and his law and of the reception of the *pneuma*; all this not because νοῦς is without further qualification ethically privileged, but because spirituality, as a morally quite neutral quality, is the ontologically necessary presupposition for all these things. Then there can be no difficulty in speaking *a parte potiori* of the *whole* man as flesh resisting the *pneuma*, and inclined to sin, and the *whole* man as νοῦς bound by God's law and requiring and receiving grace. This νοῦς for St Paul is not the part of man privileged in a moral respect on account of its purely ontological character, as may for example be seen from the fact that there also exists an ἀδόκιμος νοῦς (Rom 1:28), a νοῦς of the flesh (Col 2:18), a corrupted and defiled νοῦς (1 Tim 6:5; Tit 1:16), which like everything in man is in need of renewal (Rom 12:2; Eph 4:23). It remains true of him, as Catharinus once said (in Schauf, *op. cit.*, p. 157): 'Quodcumque enim non est a Spiritu Sancto, sed prodit ex homine, ex carne venit. Nam et ipse hominis spiritus in carne computatur; et totus homo caro dicitur in scripturis, in quo non est Spiritus Dei.'

purely religious concepts in the sense of a philosophy for which the ontologically less perfect is also *eo ipso* what is religiously further from God and the spirit is always something more divine[1], in such a way

---

[1] It would of course be possible to say a great deal more about this topic both from an historical and a systematic point of view. Just one further remark for the present: scholastic ontology will never forego its right to distinguish between 'higher' and 'lower', ontologically 'more perfect' and 'less perfect', within finite being. If this qualification, which establishes not just specific varieties but rather distinctions in density of being, in 'ontological level', between individual beings, is primarily a measurement of finite beings in regard to *each other*, nevertheless such a comparison between finite beings by grading them implies an absolute criterion, i.e. a knowledge of being in general (however little necessary it may be for this knowledge to be given with objective reflexivity). Yet a higher grading consequently always includes a judgment as to an ontologically more perfect 'participation' of this being in the Being of God. While it is true that for a Christian ontology the concept of creation (and thus of the distinguishing mark of the finite as something created from nothing) takes precedence before that of 'participation' in God's Being (and this originally unchristian concept must be subjected to radical transformation with the help of the concept of creation), yet it remains true that for a Christian doctrine of creation it is impossible to abandon the use of the statement that the creature is *like* the cause because it has been caused by God, and like it in varying degree: thus that the creature 'partakes' in God's perfection in the measure of its own ontological density of being. Otherwise any positive statement about God would be absolutely impossible from the start. In the end we should consequently have a *theologia negativa* identical with atheism. *But* where it is a question of justification, grace or salvation, as these occur in the present concrete order, these realities are incommensurable with the ontological criterion, because they are unexacted and beyond the reach of the creature by its own powers; for even the ontically 'most perfect' finite entity lacks any positive proximity to these saving goods in virtue of which these goods could fall within its reach or be demanded by it. But it is not only religiously and ethically that greater ontological perfection does not signify any greater proximity to God. It is not true for a scholastic *ontology* of grace either, that grace is simply a 'still higher' step in the ladder of entitative perfections, immediately below which ontologically comes, let us say, the spirit (as the highest natural level). Grace can only be bestowed where there is spirit, and to this extent spirit has something to do with grace in a way that would not be true of the purely material considered purely in itself. But grace, even looked at ontologically, as the communication of God so far as he is in himself precisely *distinct* from every merely participating creature, is precisely not just a 'higher' grade of being which remains in the finite order like the lower grades and would thus be strictly commensurable with them; it is (as 'uncreated grace') even ontologically the utterly incomparable,

that the opposition of the flesh to God and to the law of the holy pneuma (which is not just 'spirit' as meant by a philosophical anthropology) is transposed into an opposition of man's sensibility (in the metaphysical sense) to his intellectuality.

If these two elements (concupiscence precisely for what is evil, concupiscence as pure sensibility) are taken together, it is easy to see why such a concept of concupiscence, even against the will of those who so conceive it, tends to endanger the unexactness of the gift of integrity. For it is not clear why a rebellion of the lower part, which *exclusively* impels to evil, should be conceivable in a sinless human nature and could thus be part even of a state of pure nature. If concupiscentia in the theological sense is thought of exclusively as a quality of man's 'sensitive' part, and in such a way that this only impels to *evil* and has no other function, then just this quality is something immediately and exclusively *opposed* to the moral order as such, i.e. something opposed to the inner teleology of man as a whole, and nothing else. Such a quality, which is opposed in a merely negative way to the inner orientation of man as a whole (and to this totality even the individual parts must be subject), would from the first introduce an inner contradiction into man's ontological, stratified structure: the ontologically lower stratum of man would have the character merely of something burdensome and hindering, an encumbrance which works purely in *opposition* to the moral order.[1]

---

namely God himself. And for this reason the human spirit too, like everything else, is 'flesh', i.e. something even ontologically so distinct from God as God that in *this* respect it is impossible to think of a more or less in the degree of this distinction, inasmuch as the distinction of individual creatures *between themselves* is contained within their *common* infinite difference *(Differenz)* from God, and the former cannot be brought together with the latter over a common denominator.

[1] That the usual characterization of concupiscentia is only with difficulty to be reconciled with its 'naturalness' (taught by all Catholic theologians as a matter of course) and also with the unexactedness of freedom from it, may be seen for instance by reading what some of them say (consistently with their doctrine of concupiscentia): that even in the *status naturae purae* concupiscentia would have 'sufficed for our dishonour' (Heinrich, *op. cit.*, p. 527), that it is a 'convulsive and morbid excitability of the instinct' (Scheeben, *op. cit.*, n. 553), a 'rebellion' (Hurter, *loc. cit.*) of the lower against the higher, a 'disordered', 'evil', concupiscence (Pohle-Gierens, Diekamp), an 'evil inclination'. Of all these modes of expression Lakner says with justice

After these brief critical remarks on the current idea of concupiscentia we turn at once to the concept of concupiscentia which seems to us to be the correct one and which avoids the objections indicated above, in an attempt simply to develop it in a positive way from the nature of things and without further polemic. Some repetition of what has just been said will be unavoidable.

1. The Concept of Concupiscentia

a. *Desire* in the broadest sense is any witting (*bewusste*) reactive attitude adopted to a value or a good (both such an act and the permanent power of performing it) as opposed to a receptive act of awareness. Since we cannot here offer a phenomenology and metaphysics of the emotional and volitive side of man, those most general concepts with which scholastic anthropology describes human conation must be presupposed. We presuppose as familiar then what is involved in conation as a mere natural dynamism (*appetitus naturalis*) and as a witting conation (*appetitus elicitus*), what in sensitive and spiritual desire, in desire as potency and as act; the difference between a witting act which owes its existence to natural dynamism alone (*actus indeliberatus*) and one which owes its existence to its being freely posited by the person (*actus deliberatus*). Finally we also presuppose the scholastic concept of appetite, to the extent that this concept includes not only 'conation' or 'wanting' but also 'feeling' or 'emotion' (in the sense of modern descriptive psychology), not only the tending to a good not yet attained or to a value still to be realized but also the

---

(*loc. cit.*, p. 440): 'Ultimately all these expressions imply that concupiscentia is something which really does not belong to our nature, something which dishonours it, which ought not to be; but the consequence of this, even when the true definition of the concept is retained, is that what precisely forms the essential element in concupiscentia is denied.' The possibility of non-moral evil (death, sickness, etc.) cannot be adduced as an argument to the contrary. For evils of this kind are not in the same sense opposed without further qualification to the ultimate teleology of man as a whole (a religious and moral finality), as would be the case with concupiscentia if it were conceived from the first in a one-sided way as an inner impulsion purely towards the *morally* bad.

value-response to a possessed or present good; and finally we pre-suppose this concept so far as it includes both the positive tending to the good and the negative avoidance of the contrary disvalue and evil. The characteristic feature of this concept of concupiscentia as taken in its broadest sense is that it embraces both the free as well as the involuntary acts of human reaction to value.

b. Concupiscentia in the *narrower* sense is the act of the appetite in regard to a determinate good or a determinate value, in so far as this act takes shape spontaneously in the consciousness on the basis of man's natural dynamism, and as such forms the necessary presupposi-tion of man's personal free decision. We have already given reasons above for saying that as regards the theological concept of concupi-scence we make no distinction here between spiritual and sensitive desire. In the matter of this spontaneous act of desire we have to do with a sensitive-spiritual act, whether this act is directed to a (sensible) good immediately available to human experience or to an object which in its very being transcends immediate experience. In every case man's *whole* cognitive and appetitive powers take part, and this total sensitive-spiritual human conative act precedes man's free decision (*dictamen rationis*) and is its necessary precondition.

If we are later to mark off sharply the nature of concupiscentia in the narrowest (theological) sense from the concept of concupiscentia in the narrower sense, it is indispensable here to make still more clear the fact that the act of desire responding spontaneously to the object merely on the basis of natural dynamism is the *necessary* presupposi-tion of a free choice of attitude, and in what sense this is so. Every finite freedom, because of its finitude, implies, in the adoption of an attitude to an individual object given from without, a real transition from potency to act. Now such a transition implies that the power freely to adopt an attitude is not of itself invariably and from the first in possession of the object to which it is to adopt an attitude; thus it presupposes that the object is 'given' to the subject's appetitive power, 'given' to this power *itself* and not just to his cognitive power. In consequence of the active nature of desire (in contrast to the recep-tivity of knowledge) this givenness of an object for the conative power with a view to the free adoption of an attitude can only consist in a spontaneous activation of the conative power in regard to the object. For in view of the essentially active nature of the appetitive power, a purely passive givenness of the object for this power is excluded from the very beginning. Thus with the same metaphysical necessity with which a finite freedom (a spiritual power, that is to say!) must be given its object if it is to become active, there precedes the free operation a spontaneous (and spiritually spontaneous too!) act of the appetitive power; and this act ultimately is no other than the innate dynamic orientation of man to his goods, but on the conscious level so soon as an object is present cognitively. This alone is enough to show that freedom from concupiscentia in the theological sense cannot be a freedom from every kind of spontaneous act of the appetite really prior to the free decision; and consequently that man's dominion over this spontaneity of his appetitive power, if it neither can nor may be thought of as a simple lack of any such spontaneity, is fundamentally capable in itself of being realized in diverse ways, of which we shall have something to say later.

c. Concupiscentia in the *narrowest* (theological) sense.

We give first of all (ignoring the distinction between sensitive and spiritual desire) the usual description of concupiscentia in the narrowest sense (= concupiscence, *Begierlichkeit*). On this account concupiscence is man's spontaneous desire, in so far as it precedes his free decision *and resists it*.

If we are to understand this description of concupiscence aright, we must go rather further back. We ask: what can be meant by saying that concupiscence anticipates the free decision and resists it? With this in mind we begin first of all with a phenomenology (if we may so call it) of man's free decision. This free decision firstly is obviously a spiritual act. But this spirituality must not be conceived of as though it were a *purely* 'spiritual' act. For such an act does not exist in man. It is necessarily accompanied in man by a sensitive process, and therefore necessarily has its influence also on the sensitive sphere in man. The essential feature of the free decision is thus what is personal and free, as opposed to that spontaneous act of the appetite which, because of its non-free character is essentially pre-moral.

Now such a free decision in man permits of being more closely qualified in two ways. First of all it is an act through which man is explicitly or implicitly set before God, the absolute Good, and comes to a decision in his regard. This is true in so far as God is comprehended at least implicitly in every free decision in virtue of falling under the concept of the good simply speaking, for the individual finite good can only be freely assented to or rejected in the dynamism of a movement towards the good simply speaking. The spontaneous, involuntary act, on the other hand, is always referred to a finite (or finitely presented) good, for only such a good can be immediately set before man's cognitive and appetitive powers and thus call forth the spontaneous act.[1]

In the second place, man's free decision is an act by means of which he disposes of himself as a whole. For originally and ultimately moral freedom is not so much a decision with regard to an objectively presented individual value-object as a decision with regard to the freely operative subject himself. For in the last resort, on account of the first aspect of the moral act just mentioned, the morally free agent comes to a decision not so much with regard to his attitude to the finite good presented to his mind as to his relationship to God's absolute reality as value. Because man can only be free in regard to the finite good in virtue of his dynamic orientation to the infinite good, every free decision is a disposition made by man in respect of his situation before God, not only in virtue of a juridical or moral interpretation of this act but on the ground of its metaphysical structure. In this way the free decision tends of itself to dispose of man as a whole. For the spiritually knowing and willing subject necessarily brings to completion in every objective act of knowledge and decision a return upon itself as well (*reditio completa subiecti in seipsum*, *Summa contra Gentiles* IV, 11), and in this way is present to itself and itself acts as something so present to itself. In this way the free operation, as a

---

[1] This is not of course to deny but rather to affirm by implication that through the spontaneous, involuntary act (so far as it is a spiritual one), the unlimited horizon of spiritual aspiration is already opened up in a movement of transcendence towards being and the good in general, and that precisely by this means the necessity of having to decide freely in this way or that is for the first time disclosed. And conversely what has been said must not be taken to mean that the free spirit always comes to a decision before God (for or against him) in such a way that God himself is the express, objectively presented object of the free decision. Transcendence towards being and the good in general is disclosed as conscious (in receptive knowledge and spontaneous aspiration) through the finite object, which gives itself by being what it is; and in the free act the free spirit, through the finite object, adopts an attitude to the absolute good, which is simultaneously affirmed in voluntary transcendence.

genuine operation and not just a passive experience, arises from the inmost core of the subject and exercises a determining influence upon this subject. For otherwise the operative subject, in so far as it is identical with this personal centre, would merely undergo the free decision passively and not actively posit it. But that is in contradiction to the inmost essence of the free operation, inasmuch as the operative subject is really responsible for it. Now the operative subject itself can only be and remain responsible for the free decision if it posits this decision in such a way that the decision becomes a qualification of the operative subject itself. Thus the free decision is essentially a disposal of himself made by man, and one which proceeds from the inmost centre of his being. Now if man's free decision is the shaping (or in the terms of modern existential philosophy, the 'self-comprehension')[1] of his own being proceeding precisely from its *inmost* core —from that core, that is to say, from which man's whole metaphysical essence arises and is compacted—then the free decision also tends essentially to shape and modify this whole essence arising from the centre of the person. Thus the free decision tends to dispose of the operative subject as a whole before God.

The question now arises as to how far the freely operative subject when he makes his decision succeeds in actually extending this tendency totally to dispose of himself throughout the whole extent of his being. And here we simply lay it down *a posteriori*—the metaphysical justification of this fact will be briefly touched on later—that this tendency within man's ordinary free decision never completely succeeds in making its way. There always remains in the nature of things a tension between what man is as a kind of entity simply present before one (as 'nature') and what he wants to make of himself by his free decision (as 'person'): a tension between what he is simply passively and what he actively posits himself as and wishes to understand himself to be. The 'person' never wholly absorbs its 'nature'.[2]

---

[1] The reference here is to the notion, derived from Heidegger, that the personal existent (*Dasein*) contributes to its own being by a preforming comprehension of its own future realizations.—Tr.

[2] 'Nature' (objective presence, *Vorhandenheit*) and ' person' (existence, *Existenz*) are of course understood here in the context of modern metaphysics and the philosophy of existence. Man is a 'person' in so far as he freely disposes of himself by his decision, possesses his own definitive reality in the act of making a free decision about himself. By 'nature' is meant all that in man which must be given prior to this disposal of himself, as its

The metaphysical discussion of this fact can only be briefly indicated here. It presents special difficulty in that it is based upon two interdependent factors which not even a metaphysical anthropology has ever really succeeded in distinguishing in detail in a clear and concrete way.[1] Certainly in one essential respect the dualism of person and nature just indicated has its metaphysical root in the finitude of man; thus ultimately in the distinction between essence and existence, in virtue of which the essence, in its complete unfolding, always

---

object and the condition of its possibility, and in so far as this is the case. While these concepts must be distinguished from those which, for instance, are used in expositions of the Trinity and the hypostatic union by the scholastic theology usual in the Church, it must at the same time be emphasized that they cannot be avoided, and that they are not wholly alien to the scholastic tradition. They cannot be avoided, because a clear and handy distinction between that in man which is not open to question and that which he is in virtue of his capacity to dispose of himself, is of fundamental importance; otherwise the free operation is going to look like a sporadically occurring activity of the man in connexion with an object distinct from himself, and this transient operation will then leave the operative subject untouched and at most of significance for him by being imputed to him in a moral-juridical way. Apart from all else, this is already excluded by the ontological nature of the spiritual act: the spiritual act (the free decision, above all) is by its very nature reflexive, reflecting back upon the subject; the free act is not simply imputed to the subject, for the latter has from the first determined itself through this act. Further, the pair of concepts mentioned above have their roots in scholastic tradition. For instance, when a distinction is made between *peccatum naturae* and *peccatum personae*, the same distinction lies in the background: original sin is a *peccatum* of 'nature' because it is found prior to the free decision of the individual subject as an element in the space within which (the 'situation') man is first called to make his own 'personal' decision, and with regard to which he must take up a position by comprehending this situation in this way or that.

[1] The scholastic metaphysician knows only too well how heavily burdened the whole of scholastic metaphysics still is today by the question as to how far the concept of *materia* (in the strictly metaphysical sense of pure potentiality) may not in the last resort simply be the Greek counterpart of the concept of the real finitude of the finite in general, with this difference alone, that just this Greek pre-Christian philosophy had no knowledge of spirit as in itself finite and thus equated materiality and finitude. This does not mean that in our own view all we have here is a confusing duplication of concepts for the same thing. All we wish to point out is the reason why it would lead us much too far away if we set about the final clarification of the question: In what does the metaphysical root of the specifically human dualism of nature and (freely achieved) person consist?

remains an ideal capable of being attained only asymptotically by the concretely existent being, even as regards the freedom through which it makes itself what it is. But on the other hand it is equally a matter of course for an anthropology on the basis of Thomist metaphysics, that just as essential an element of the dualism of person and nature, of the resistance of the entity given prior to the free decision counter to the tendency of the free subject totally to dispose of its whole subsistent reality, arises from the materiality of the human being, from the real differentiation of matter and form, which prevents the form from bringing itself fully to manifestation in the 'other' of matter.

Here too is to be found the nucleus of truth in that otherwise too crude distinction between the spirit as the freely operative principle and the sensibility as the principle which resists this free decision. In reality of course the whole 'nature' given prior to freedom offers resistance to the 'person's' free and total disposition of himself, so that the boundary between 'person' and 'nature' stands as it were vertically in regard to the horizontal line which divides spirituality from sensibility in man.

The specifically *human* form of the distinction between person and nature (as distinguished, for example, from a like dualism which has to be supposed for the angels as well) is explained by the dualism of matter and form in man, regarded as each possessing its own consistency (*insichständig*); thus in the concrete experience of life this human dualism finds its sharpest expression—no one will contest this —in the resistance of the sensitive to the spiritual part of man.[1]

---

[1] This is seen most clearly in the connexion which holds between 'passio' (πάθος) as on the one hand a spontaneous act of nature, concupiscence, and on the other the influence of a cause from without, a being-determined from without, a 'suffering'. In other words, looked at from the point of view of the free person, 'passionateness' and 'passibility' (prior to the personal act) are *in themselves* the same thing: the accidental qualification of the person by circumstances which are not brought about by the person's own freedom. Both spring from the same metaphysical root, the materiality of the person, which is the condition which makes possible a 'passio' in both senses of the word: the condition which makes it possible for a person to be open to a finite, terrestrial cause which, although it has not instituted the 'patient' itself, can nevertheless act upon it, without the patient's necessarily having had to open itself freely to this action upon it in advance. The problem of Christ's freedom from concupiscence in spite of his passibility is not to be solved by denying or weakening the connexion between the two sorts of *pathos*; it may only be solved by understanding when and how *passio* as a

From what has been said it follows that the spontaneous act of desire (*actus indeliberatus*) belongs to the 'nature' in the sense indicated by our distinction above. For to the nature (as opposed to the person) belongs everything which must be given prior to the person's free decision, as a condition of its possibility. Now as we have just shown, the spontaneous act of desire, arising from the bare dynamism of nature and directed to a wittingly apprehended object, is one of the metaphysically necessary presuppositions of a concrete free decision made by a finite subject.

It is now possible to arrive by stages at a statement of what is meant by concupiscence in the theological sense. As we have said, the free decision tends to the end that man should dispose of himself as a whole before God, actively make himself into what he freely wishes to be. Thus the end to which the free decision is orientated is that everything which is in man (nature), hence the involuntary act as well, should be the revelation and the expression of what man as person wishes to be; thus that the free decision should comprehend, transfigure and transfuse the spontaneous act, so that its own reality too should no longer be purely natural but personal.

In connexion with this personal entry into and shaping of naturally spontaneous desire, we must not think straight away simply of those spontaneous acts which can be a hindrance to one of man's morally *good* decisions. Because a spontaneous act precedes every personal act of man, whether it be directed to good or evil, and because in every one of them the person never wholly absorbs and personally assumes what it is on the basis of its spontaneous acts and what is given prior to it, it follows that the dualism of nature and person in its specifically human form, which we call concupiscence, is something which is at work both in the case of a good decision of man's freedom against the spontaneous desire of nature for a morally negative good, and also in the case of a bad free decision against a natural inclination to something morally good.[1] Both the good and the bad moral decision encounter

---

suffering caused from without—which in itself (i.e. *in actu primo*) is always concupiscence as well, because it is an impulse to an action outside the person's free decision—may yet be taken possession of and transfigured by the free decision from within, and in this way does not become concupiscence (*in actu secundo*). But we shall have to speak of this in another context.

[1] For instance, a man wants to be brave and goes on trembling, although he would like to be so brave that he does not tremble. And this whole process

the resistance, the solidity and the impenetrability of nature. Concupiscence in the theological sense shows itself for instance just as much when a man blushes in the act of lying as when the 'flesh' refuses to follow the willingness of the 'spirit' for the good.

It must further be observed, as we have already indicated above, that the personal penetration of nature in the free decision can in itself be carried out in several ways, when the case in question is one where a decision has to be taken *against* a spontaneous inclination of nature. First of all it is absolutely speaking neither necessary nor possible that the spontaneous acts should precede the individual free decision in no sense whatever.[1] Such an absolute identity of nature and person, and so of suffered and freely-willed desire, is found only in the absolute freedom of the infinite Being. In the case of exhaustive, ideal dominion of the finite person over its nature, this exhaustiveness[2] can only con-

---

can be in the service of something good or bad, so that for instance the trembling can be an expression of the 'cowardly' nature (i.e. one whose resources of vital self-affirmation are nearer an end) or of the good nature (one which spontaneously reacts against baseness), and the bravery can be a hero's or a rogue's. Someone wants to be cordial to someone else (for good or bad motives), and only succeeds imperfectly (unfortunately or commendably). In a thousand ways like this, always in fact, a bit of the human material of free decision is left over without being refashioned, or (looked at in reverse) a bit of the inclination of the free decision remains without achieving anything, because it becomes stuck fast as it were in the sluggish mass of its natural material in man, in which it tries to realize itself. For this reason (if we confine ourselves to the empirical evidence) it makes no difference whether we say, 'The free principle is of itself too weak to achieve itself wholly in man's nature', or, 'The resistance of the material in which the decision tries to realize itself is too strong for the entire success of this intention.' And in accordance with the statement adopted, one can either say, 'The personal decision does not wholly make its own the potentialities of its material', or 'The free principle does not succeed in overcoming the resistance of its nature-material.'

[1] Most of the theologians cited above put the matter as if the man who is in possession of the gift of integrity only experiences acts of the sensitive appetite when he expressly commands them by a resolution of his spiritual will. This is an exaggeration, which would not only make the psychic life of a man in Paradise into something beyond our conception, but also comes up against the metaphysical principle that the object of a finite freedom must be given to it, while such a givenness is only to be found in virtue of an affection of the *conative* power, i.e. through its spontaneous act.

[2] This is an exhaustiveness which is and always must be essentially relative in the finite entity, because otherwise neither the phenomenon of

sist in the fact that the personal decision is wholly and securely achieved as regards the nature. Thus this permanent and (relatively) exhaustive dominion of the 'person' over its 'nature' by no means necessarily implies that no spontaneous act whatever can arise in the field of the nature so subject to personal dominion. All it implies is that no act can take shape in this nature which would be opposed to the personal engagement of the man so endowed. Now it is not the case that every kind of 'passivity' is necessarily a threat to man's actively free personal engagement. Where a graciously bestowed or freely acquired personal attitude of man really succeeds in shaping his *whole* natural being throughout, even the act passively endured from without must be subject to the inner law of this person in order to be able to arise at all. For wherever an activation encounters a 'patient' which already has its own structure and not an absolutely empty and undetermined potentiality, the effect of this activation is just as much an expression of the reality of the 'patient' as of the particular character of the impression from without. Thus where the person has a habitual dominion over the entire nature, even the spontaneous act of the appetite, excited from without and 'passively' undergone by the person, is from the first shaped throughout by the personal engagement of the person and so not an act of 'concupiscence' in spite of man's 'passivity' with respect to this act; thus it is unnecessary to suppose that this act should come about on the basis of a 'command' of the freely deciding will. Now it is possible *per se* to think of various ways in which this habitual dominion of the nature by the person, which becomes the *a priori* law of the spontaneous natural act itself, works itself out in detail in these acts. Firstly (and this is incorrectly what is alone

---

repentance nor that of the experience of its free decision as an inner distress and an inner condemnation would be metaphysically explicable. Looked at metaphysically, repentance is only possible where man's immoral free decision has not the power so exhaustively to impress evil upon his being that no starting-point for a new decision remains over from which a fresh redisposition of the elements of the human person could ensue. One's own morally wrong decision can only be experienced as inner distress and condemnation when it does not succeed in removing from one every resistance offered to it by what is given prior to freedom (by the 'nature'). Otherwise man could also be happy by making a heroic and radical profession of evil and by wholly delivering up his being to it (even though he may suffer 'physical' pain at the same time); only the evil man who is too cowardly and weak to be wholly evil would be the unhappy one.

thought of in the usual theological expositions of integrity) there is the way in which the free decision from the first excludes from man the spontaneous act of desire running in the contrary direction, and either prevents it from emerging at all or wholly suppresses it. But a second possibility is equally conceivable. Here the person does not annul the spontaneous natural act which in the last resort is only apparently contrary to its decision, either because this is impossible or not feasible for other reasons; it wholly assumes this act in a new way into the inner dynamism of its personal attitude, in such a way that finally the act is no longer resistant to the person, an undissolved remainder of nature, but becomes an intrinsic factor in the process which makes available the depths and the dominating force of the personal decision. We may consider, for example, Christ's fear and trembling on the Mount of Olives, which could be endured and experienced (in a truly human, passive way) in spite of the gift of integrity he continued to possess: this fear did not persist in Christ as a remainder, not yet in his power, of a resistance to his personal willingness to suffer and hence as a threat to this personal attitude; it was there in Christ as an intrinsic, necessary factor, wholly within his power, of this personal decision itself.[1] It depends on the particular nature of the spontaneous act of desire to be mastered in each individual case which of these two kinds of integrity is the appropriate one: whether it is one jointly given from the first, or whether it is one achieved only approximately in the course of moral struggle. We cannot go further into this question here.

It is now possible to see what is the essence of desire in the narrowest (theological) sense, the essence of concupiscence. In the concrete man of the present order free personal decision and self-determination are not capable of perfectly and exhaustively determining the operative

---

[1] Bravery 'in spite of' trembling and bravery 'in' trembling, strength against weakness and strength which can be and wants to be victorious precisely *in* weakness, are not the same thing. This remains true even when it may not be possible to decide in a given case which of the two is present. Weakness is really experienced and endured even in the second case. In the last resort it will be a secret of the God who is Judge whether in a concrete case the continuing weakness of the flesh was yet an intrinsic factor of the decision, integrated into this very decision, or whether this good decision, while undoubtedly present, did not succeed in so comprehending the sluggishness of the weak flesh without simply eliminating it that the sluggishness itself might become part of the victory of the willingness of the spirit.

subject throughout the whole extent of his real being. The free act does indeed dispose of the whole subject, in so far as it is as free act an act of man's personal centre, and so, by the root as it were, draws the whole subject in sympathy with it. And yet man's concrete being is not throughout its whole extent and according to all its powers and their actualization the pure expression and the unambiguous revelation of the personal active centre which is its own master. In the course of its self-determination, the person undergoes the resistance of the nature given prior to freedom, and never wholly succeeds in making all that man is into the reality and the expression of all that he comprehends himself to be in the core of his person. There is much in man which always remains in concrete fact somehow impersonal; impenetrable and unilluminated for his existential decision; merely endured and not freely acted out. It is this dualism between person and nature, in so far as it arises from the dualism of matter and spirit and not from man's finitude, the dualism of essence and existence and the real distinction of his powers given with it, that we call concupiscence in the theological sense. While it does indeed find its concrete experiential expression in a dualism of spirituality and sensibility, it is not identical with the latter. Thus concupiscence does not consist in any conceivable givenness of the spontaneous act prior to the free one[1]; nor does it in every case necessarily consist in a capacity of the spontaneous act to be despotically expunged by freedom nor precisely in the fact that the spontaneous act drives towards what is morally impermissible contrary to the direction of the free decision. Concupiscence consists essentially in the fact that man in this regime does not overcome even by his free decision the dualism between what he is as nature prior to his existential decision and what he becomes as person by this decision, not even in the measure in which it would absolutely speaking be conceivable for a finite spirit to overcome it. Man never becomes wholly absorbed either in good or in evil.

2. The Significance of Concupiscence

a. Concupiscence and moral action.

It is clear from what has been said that concupiscence as such in the theological sense is not open to moral qualification in the strict sense.

---

[1] Otherwise free human operation would be purely action and not reaction, and man himself would be pure 'existence'.

Even in the strict theological sense, therefore, one should not speak of 'evil' or 'disorderly' concupiscence. One may speak in this way with some justification from an ascetico-moral point of view; but then one is regarding concupiscence in the theological sense onesidedly in so far as the resistance of nature to the personal decision does admittedly in certain circumstances work precisely contrary to the morally good free decision. But according to what has been said this is only *one* aspect of concupiscence; regarded in its full theological sense, concupiscence is just as much capable of working in a positive sense as a resistance of nature to the bad moral decision, by making this less absolute. (Even for a theological anthropology, it may be noted in passing, this is why a merely venial sin[1] is possible in a being at once sensitive and spiritual, and only in it: the resistance of the nature considered as orientated to the good prevents the free decision from reaching that intensity and personal centrality which would be required for a grave sin). Thus in so far as concupiscence (in the theological sense) precedes the free decision, which is alone capable of producing a formally moral quality, and in this theological sense is bivalent in so far as it is capable of taking on a tendency to good as well as to evil, it cannot be characterized as morally evil, let alone as sin, even regarded in itself in this full (*adäquat*) theological sense. Yet it can of course be called 'evil' in so far as it is only present in man in its concrete existential form in virtue of the Fall of the first man (something which is admittedly beyond experience), and in so far as, on account of its tendency, bivalent in itself, to offer resistance, it can

---

[1] Primarily, at least, venial sin 'ex imperfectione actus'. As free, an act always 'originates' from the personal centre: but it is precisely never as simply originating but as having reached completion in the materiality of nature, as originated, that the act is itself. Were this not the case, such an act would be precisely not free or not a merely venial sin (because it is free). A further question (which we shall not pursue here) would be whether in the last resort venial sins 'ex parvitate materiae' may also be reduced to the first type and why this should be so; for unless it has a definite kind of content, the act cannot have even in its formal freedom that intensity which it must have as originated. We shall only note further in passing how surprising it is that this ontology of free acts is only touched on in theology (if it is mentioned at all) when bad acts, sin, are under discussion. Yet the ontological and existential distinction between venial and grave sins must also exist where morally good acts are concerned. There does not even exist a terminology for this situation yet.

on occasion also drive towards what is morally impermissible contrary to man's free decision and thus lead to sin (Denz 792).[1] What follows or does not follow from these conclusions for the question of the *experience* of concupiscentia (as 'something which ought not to be'), must be left for later discussion, since it is impossible to offer a satisfactory answer without first bringing certain other aspects to view which cannot be taken up yet.

b. In this way we gain some insight into the naturalness of concupiscentia and so into the unexactedness of the gift of integrity. Precisely because concupiscentia in the theological sense is something absolutely bivalent from the ethical point of view, because it can act as a retarding factor both as regards good and as regards evil and because it results from man's metaphysical nature as a material essence, the absence of it in men cannot be conceived of as intrinsically possible in purely natural terms, and still less can one assert a claim to this absence as something owed to man. Any idea of this kind becomes empty the moment it is seen that the absence of concupiscentia considered as an impulse to evil would also mean *eo ipso* the cessation of a retarding factor contrary to man's free decision to choose evil; in other words, it would make man into a kind of being concerning whose intrinsic possibility it is impossible to make any assertion in natural terms.

c. If we are to gain a better understanding of the nature of concupiscentia a few remarks on the gift of integrity will be in place here. From what has been said it appears that the gift of integrity, as it is ascribed to the first man before the Fall by the sources of Revelation, cannot lie in the absence of desire in the broad or in the narrower sense, but only in a freedom from desire in the narrowest and theological

[1] In so far as concupiscentia is to be subsumed under the 'deterioration in body and soul' due to original sin (Denz 788), this must be measured, as is quite generally taught today, by man's state in Paradise, and not by the state of some pure 'nature' possible in itself and what this nature 'ought' to be. But since this real term of comparison is not a datum of our experience, this 'deterioration', this 'corruption' is not an object of experience either, of the experience, that is, which man can test empirically for himself, purely by reference to his *nature* (in the theological sense). We shall have to discuss in its own right the question whether this excludes the *experience* of *every* kind of way in which concupiscentia is 'something which ought not to be'.

sense, a freedom from concupiscence. But it also follows at once from our analyses of the nature of concupiscence that the 'freedom' in question here is not so much a freedom *from* something as a freedom *for* something. A man who possesses the gift of integrity is no less 'sensitive', he is no more 'spiritual' in a Neoplatonic rather than a Christian sense, involving the lack of an intense vitality.[1] Rather he is free really to dispose of himself through a personal decision in so sovereign a way that within the area of his being there is no longer anything to resist this sovereign self-determination by a sort of passive sluggishness. If we conceive of concupiscentia as a bivalent property of man, it also follows that integrity was not bestowed on the first man purely and primarily to facilitate his decision as head of humanity for or against God, by removing dangers and impulses to evil; rather it was given to him in the first place in order that his free decision, even when it went out to the good, could acquire the exhaustive existential impetus of a self-determination which a man could never have without the gift of integrity. For even where the case is not precisely one of the *resistance* of a spontaneous act to a morally *good* decision, the essence of concupiscentia as we conceive it is such that it prevents man's personal decision from achieving total and definitive mastery over his nature on account of the inertia of the nature contrary to that decision. Hence integrity was given to Adam not so much for the sake of avoiding a greater danger of sin, as for making possible an exhaustive engagement of his being in a personal decision directed to the good. Indeed it might be said that Adam's state in Paradise was in a certain sense 'more dangerous' than our present state. For the gift of integrity, which was intended to make him capable of overcoming the dualism of nature and person (so far as this is possible at all in a finite entity) in the direction of a good decision, also implied for the morally bad decision which Adam in fact made, an existential impetus of which we in our present order of things are not normally capable with regard to evil either. In fact, though we shall not attempt it here, if one were

---

[1] This is already emphasized for instance by St Bonaventure (in *II Sent.*, dist. 9, a. 3, q. 1) and St Thomas (Ia: 98:2 ad 3). But for true vitality it is also required that involuntary impressions from without can be genuinely 'experienced' and 'undergone'. As has already been said above, this shows that statements like that of Pesch (*loc. cit.*, n. 190), 'nullos potuisse in iis oriri motus appetitus sensibilis independenter ab imperio voluntatis', are false and do not follow from the essence of integrity.

to try to explain in the terms of a theological and metaphysical anthropology the possibility of repentance for Adam (as opposed to the absence of such a possibility in the free decision of the angels), in the last resort one would only be able to do this by insisting that integrity was for Adam a preternatural gift, and that its loss[1] as a consequence of the loss of sanctifying grace in general, was only possible for *this* reason. But this loss of integrity once more releases the nature in respect of the personal decision, so that it is not wholly assumed by this decision and in this way repentance (purely as a psychological and personal phenomenon) is once more made possible. This is not to deny that concupiscentia produces a specifically new possibility of sin, namely that of sins of weakness in the strict sense, which are to be found where man finally gives way to the persistent inclination of his nature against a freely adopted attitude which had originally been a better one, and in a subsequent free modification of his attitude sets the centre of his being as it were in that region of it which is actualized in the spontaneous impulse of his nature at that moment. Such a modification of a freely adopted attitude by yielding to a dynamism of nature which is precisely there already and actively persists, cannot of course be found in a man who possesses the gift of integrity.

It has already been said that every free human decision tends of itself to dispose totally of the subject as a whole. If this is true it also follows that in spite of its unexactedness the gift of integrity perfects human nature in a direction in which man as a personal being is already turned. For integrity is in fact what makes possible the exhaustive realization of the tendency associated with every free decision: the tendency of the person totally to dispose of himself before God. Without the gift of integrity this tendency, which is undoubtedly proper to every free decision, will find expression in greater or less degree according to the circumstances. To this extent it is the goal of all moral growth that

[1] This loss is insufficiently explained in terms of sin as such, for the angel who has sinned retains the metaphysical essence of his integrity (the relative identity of 'nature' and 'person') even after his sin. Thus he is 'impenitent' precisely because he was in a position exhaustively to shape his entire nature through his personal decision; hence too no remainder is left over in him, either psychologically or ontologically, which might have escaped this personal decision and from which the reshaping of the person could begin.

man should increasingly bring the whole of himself into play in a morally good decision, in Biblical terms increasingly love God from his *whole* heart and with *all* his strength. The gift of integrity, we may say, made it possible for man from the first really to do from his whole heart and with all his strength what he wished to do, and none of his powers could refuse to follow this will, wholly or in part. Thus it also becomes clear that in a certain respect the goal of Christian moral maturity consists in a return to Adam's state in Paradise, not certainly in the sense of a return to some possibility still prior to moral decision, but as to a goal which is itself already the fruit and prize of moral concern. In this sense it may be allowed that the ascetic strives for the blessed ἀπάθεια possessed by Adam in Paradise, as the Greek Fathers often say. But the perfect Christian possesses it otherwise than Adam did. In Adam the person's freedom to dispose of the nature made it possible for him exhaustively to engage his nature both in a good and in an evil direction. The blessed freedom of disposal possessed by the perfect Christian, the saint, is the freedom of a man who has succeeded in surrendering his whole being and his whole life to God totally.

German mysticism often named as its ideal the man 'of the heart' (*innig*), the 'collected' (*gesammelt*) man, the man, that is, whose whole activity is an exhaustive expression of his innermost centre and his innermost vital decision, and who therefore remains 'collected' in this innermost centre without being dispersed in anything alien to this decision. The fact that man never wholly possesses this collected heartfelt inwardness of his whole life in the ultimate deed of his inmost being is what is really meant by concupiscentia in the theological sense, the index of his finitude and his terrestriality (his sensitive and spiritual essence). This inner division of man is often indeed the occasion of his ruin, but—who knows—perhaps still more often the occasion of his salvation, because it also prevents him from being utterly evil.

3. Concupiscence in the present order of Salvation

But we have not yet exhausted our subject. The whole movement of thought in what has so far been said, has been directed towards determining the character of concupiscentia in its relationship to *nature* as such. If we say 'nature' here, the word is no longer meant in the sense in which we have frequently used it in the course of this study, as something opposed to *person* (and *vice versa*). 'Nature' here is intended, in the usual theological sense, in distinction to the 'supernatural', that is to say as that essential content of an entity both spiritual and sensitive called man, which inamissibly persists through sin and righteousness, grace and alienation from God, and in regard to which the possession of the Holy Spirit, adoptive sonship, justification, etc., are to be characterized as an unexacted gift, as 'supernatural' grace, even prior to any question of the forgiveness of sin. What we have so far said in regard to this 'nature' is that concupiscentia is the inertia and impenetrability, in itself *bivalent*, of that 'nature' (in the earlier sense) which precedes the person's free decision, which inertia does not permit the person as freedom totally to integrate this 'nature' into his deeds. This impossibility, we have said, is *bivalent*, i.e. we have here a retarding factor in respect of both good and evil free actions in like manner, and hence may not simply be qualified without further consideration as 'evil', 'disordered' concupiscentia; it may therefore very well be conceived of conversely as a property arising from the nature of the spiritual-material and finite creature; thus further it cannot be experienced *on that account* as 'something which ought not to be', as 'shameful', as something which could only arise from a primordial moral catastrophe: on the contrary, this should be the starting-point of an attempt to elucidate the preternatural unexactedness of integrity.

But have we not thus 'taken the sting out of' concupiscentia? Can we, starting from this position, go on to gain some understanding of the Pauline experience, 'Unhappy man that I am, who will deliver me from this body of death?' Can we still do justice to Augustine, whose view of man, derived from his daily experience of concupiscentia and death precisely, was such that for him man could only be the creature either of a Manichean primordial principle of evil or of original sin, his primal constitution being perverted in its very depths by the sin of the first man? Is the opinion of the Reformers or of a Pascal (leaving aside the doctrine of the great scholastics for the moment) simply false in every respect when they held that man, driven as he is by his passions, could not have proceeded 'like this' from the hand of his Creator? Is not the teaching of Pius V, that concupiscentia (and death) can be found even in a sinless 'pure nature' (a teaching which our whole concern so far has served to justify), unchristian and naive as well in view of these testimonies to the meaning of Christian existence? On the other hand we may attempt to explain this concrete experience of concupiscentia in two different ways. We may ask whether it is not already exactly rendered by saying that even in our interpretation it precisely constitutes a threat to moral equilibrium, a danger of sin, however true it may be that it results naturally from man's essence. Or we may say that this lived awareness of concupiscentia as such is confused with the experience of real—but precisely personal—sinfulness,[1] and that this confusion is the cause of the doctrine of 'evil' cupidity and of a sinfulness which already adheres to man on its account alone.

If we want a clearer view of this question we must start from a position which has been established on a somewhat firmer basis elsewhere in these studies.[2] Even the man who has not been justified and inwardly sanctified by God's grace is *not*, in the present order, in such a way identical with a man in the 'status naturae purae' that he differs from him only in virtue of an *external* decree of God, in accordance with which he *ought* to have grace. The ordination which obliges him to a supernatural end consists (even when he is not 'in a state of grace') not just in a purely juridical obligation; as 'ens iuridicum' this would rest in reality on the reality of the divine will alone, and hence could *only* enter into awareness or experience in virtue of a communication by God in the *word*, since purely moral or juridical entities cannot present themselves to consciousness in virtue of their own reality. It is far preferable to think of the ordination to a supernatural end, which is binding on all men in the present order of reality and salvation, as a real ontological existential of man, which qualifies him really and intrinsically. Further, in the present order man is subject to the dynamism of God's saving grace, at least at those 'moments' at

---

[1] As a matter of fact the theological interpretation of the experience of concupiscentia would have to give more consideration than it usually does to the fact that in the concrete, man can never have a reflexive experience, which can be theologically interpreted purely as *reflexive*, of his essence as given prior to freedom and of pure concupiscentia *in isolation*. For in every reflexive act he already becomes aware of himself as someone who has freely chosen, which means that he is capable neither of assessing with absolute precision this 'option fondamentale' which he has already taken, nor of separating it with complete purity from his nature and from pure concupiscentia in those properties they possess prior to the free decision.

[2] Cf. pp. 302 s., above.

experience of concupiscentia as something which ought not to be (*von dem erfahrbaren Nichtseinsollen von Konkupiszenz*) rests by our own admission on a series of presuppositions, which may indeed be conceivable, but have not been proved, i.e. on the existence and givenness in consciousness of the supernatural existentials of which we have spoken. To this we answer first of all that it by no means follows from the fact that we have not proved these presuppositions *here*, that they cannot be demonstrated in themselves. They are only introduced by way of hypothesis here because to justify them here would mean going far beyond the limits of the present discussion of concupiscentia. But the following considerations seem to us decisive. In the order of realities our presuppositions really are—presuppositions. The reverse may be the case in the order of knowledge. That is to say: the experience of humanity, the analytics which considers it in the course of its history with respect to its own condition, finds no difficulty in showing that in concrete fact man does not conceive of concupi-scentia as something self-explanatory, but as something which ought not to be, which causes perplexity and which forces one to ask how it can be explained, if man is the work of a God who cannot create anything contradictory. It is irrelevant here whether each and every man finds his way to this experience for himself or whether it first reaches clear consciousness at the summits of human self-comprehension in the history of the spirit. It has always been the case that man only learns slowly and arduously to know who he is and all that is in him. When and where man is present to himself with the utmost clarity (and it is a rationalistic, unhistorical superstition, not a postu-late of a rational metaphysical anthropology, to suppose that he must be capable of this at any moment he chooses), he may not know why and how he finds himself to be like this; but he can notice the *fact* that he does not feel in order. And if an Augustine[1] and later the great scholastics too[2] were thoroughly convinced that the present

---

[1] Cf., e.g., *Contra Julianum* VI, 21 s. (PL XLIV, 863 s.); further DTC XII, col. 374, 377, 390 s.; C. Boyer, 'Dieu pouvait-il créer l'homme dans l'état d'ignorance et de difficulté?', *Gregorianum* XI (1930), pp. 32–57; J. de Montcheuil, 'L'hypothèse de l'état d'ignorance et de difficulté d'après le De libero arbitrio de s. Augustin', RSR XXIII (1933), pp. 197–221.

[2] Cf. for Anselm, DTC XII, col. 435; for Alexander of Hales, DTC XII, col. 459; for Bonaventure, DTC XII, col. 463 s.; for Aquinas, *Summa contra Gentiles* IV, c. 52.

constitution of man with his concupiscentia and subjection to death could not be intelligibly interpreted except on the presupposition of a primordial Fall, i.e if they felt that concupiscentia and death were very 'unnatural' and needed explanation (and this is the presupposition of the first affirmation); then it is possible that they were in the right, even if not every simple soul can verify this at every moment. It is also irrelevant what degree of certainty—greater or less—individual thinkers have allotted to this conclusion regarding a primordial fall (which is not the same thing as a conclusion to an hereditary sin), and also how they attempted to justify in more detail this 'unnaturalness' of concupiscentia and elucidate it rationally. The *fact* that they felt it to be unnatural is sufficient here. If today we possess in a still clearer form than even medieval theology a concept of pure nature and of the naturalness of concupiscentia, then we today are bound to explain the experience of the contradictoriness of concupiscentia in a somewhat different way and at any rate with more theological nuance; but nothing compels us to abandon this experience itself as false or exaggerated. It is not only the experience of something which objectively ought not to be, in so far as its object arises in objective fact from the primordial transgression; just this character, that it ought not to be, as such, is itself—however obscure and enigmatic it may still be—an element in the object of the experience as such.

Concupiscentia, and death too, is not just the manifestation of sin, in Christ's order it is not just what is left over in the justified, something to be overcome eschatologically because it is in contradiction with human nature in this concrete order; it is also the form *in* which the Christian experiences Christ's sufferings and suffers them himself to the end. But of this we shall say no more here.

nomic (T. of Revelation and entitative T.) 27, 28 n.1, 147 *sq.;* immanent and formal doctrine of T. 27, 28 n.1; graeco-biblical and latin-scholastic doctrine of T. 125-148

Unio Hypostatica (cf. Christology, Humanity of Christ): Hypostatic Union in its ontological, metaphysical and ethical aspects 28; U.H. as in quality highest case of a relation between Creator and creature 162 *sq.;* U.H. a real ontological determination of human nature, datum of human self-consciousness of Christ 168 *sqq.,* 170 n.3; necessity for fresh concept of unity of substantial, hypostatic kind 180 *sqq.,* 182 n.1; U.H. as foundation of satisfaction theory 194; parallels between U.H. and *unio gloriae* 329 n.1

Visio beatifica (cf. Grace): 183 *sq.,* 187; terminology of V.b. and *visio immediata* 170 n.2; ontology of V.b. 326 *sqq.;* God's essence takes place of *species impressa* in V.b. 327 *sqq.*

INDEX OF PERSONS